Global Capitalism at Bay?

John H. Dunning

London and New York

First published 2001
by Routledge
2 Park Square, Milton Park, Abingdon, Oxon, OX14 4RN

Simultaneously published in the USA and Canada
by Routledge
270 Madison Ave, New York NY 10016

Routledge is an imprint of the Taylor & Francis Group

Transferred to Digital Printing 2007

© 2001 John H. Dunning

Typeset in Baskerville by Wearset, Boldon, Tyne and Wear

British Library Cataloguing in Publication Data
A catalogue record for this book is available from the British Library

Library of Congress Cataloging in Publication Data
Dunning, John H.
    Global capitalism at bay? / John H. Dunning.
        p.   cm.
    Includes bibliographical references and index.
    1. Capitalism. 2. Globalization. 3. Competition, International.
    4. International finance. 5. Economic history—1990– I. Title.

HB501.D827 2000
330.12'2—dc21   00-059190

ISBN10: 0–415–23863–3 (hbk)
ISBN10: 0–415–43964–7 (pbk)

ISBN13: 978–0–415–23863–2 (hbk)
ISBN13: 978–0–415–43964–0 (pbk)

Publisher's Note
The publisher has gone to great lengths to ensure the quality of this reprint but
points out that some imperfections in the original may be apparent

Printed and bound by CPI Antony Rowe, Eastbourne

Contents

List of tables

Appendix to Chapter 5

List of figures

Preface and acknowledgments

In 1971, Raymond Vernon published a monograph entitled *Sovereignty at Bay*[1] in which he envisaged a growing tension between the spread of multinational enterprises (MNEs) and the economic and political sovereignty of the countries (and particularly host developing countries) in which they operated. Over a quarter of a century later, in the last book he was to write, he reiterated and extended his concerns about the future relations between MNEs and national governments. In an aptly titled *In the Hurricane's Eye*,[2] Vernon persuasively argues that the kind of alliances between MNEs and governments which has emerged over the last two decades or so – and which, in *Sovereignty at Bay* he had not articulated – are best regarded, not as a permanent feature of the global landscape, but rather as the eerie calm typified by the eye of hurricane, on either side of which there is the turmoil and devastation of terrific storms. So Vernon believed that the early years of the new millennium would witness a new confrontation between governments and MNEs, which, in many respects, could be more destructive of the global economic and social fabric than everything he wrote about in the early 1970s.

The title of this volume is shamelessly borrowed from Ray's first book. I hope he will forgive me for doing this! The title is deliberately chosen because I believe that the implications of contemporary global economic events are even wider and, potentially, more significant – for good or bad (or a mixture of the two!), than Ray's recent thoughts suggest. I would suggest that it is nothing less than our contemporary capitalist system – characterized by the ever closer economic interdependence between sovereign nation states, fuelled by a series of dramatic innovations, and by a variety of market friendly government policies – which is "at bay." Though currently creating more wealth and prosperity than the world has ever known, there are rising concerns about some of the downside of global capitalism, which, if left to fester and burgeon could lead to an even more dramatic confrontation than that to which Ray alludes in his 1998 book.

However, although the MNE which is one of the main agents for wealth creation, and its geographical allocation – it is economic globalization *per se* which I believe is the main focus of the concern of many institutions and people throughout the world. This, then, is the justification of the title of this volume of essays, although the critical issues surrounding the title are dealt with mainly (though not exclusively) in Part I of this volume.

An earlier version of many of the essays in this volume were originally published elsewhere, and I am grateful to several publishers of books and journals (later named) for permitting me to republish my contributions first written for them. Chapter 1, for example, was first published as an article under the same name in *Global Economy Quarterly*, Vol. 1, No. 1, 2000, pp. 3–48; Chapter 2 has not been previously published. In Part II of the volume, Chapter 3 was first published in *International Business Review*, Vol. 9, No. 1, 2000 pp. 163–190 and Chapter 4 in *Journal of International Business Studies*, Vol. 29, No. 1, 1998, pp. 45–66. Chapter 5, which is jointly written with John Dilyard of Rutgers University, first appeared in *Transnational Corporations*, Vol. 8, No. 1, 1999, pp. 1–52. I am indebted to John for agreeing to have our joint paper reproduced in this volume.

In Part III, Chapter 6 was recently published as a chapter in *Regions, Globalization and the Knowledge Based Economy* (Oxford University Press, 2000, p. 8 to p. 41); while Chapter 7 is an updated revision of a paper which originally appeared in *Oxford Development Studies*, Vol. 26, No. 1, 1998, pp. 47–69. Chapter 8 is a revised and extended version of a paper first presented at an international conference on Challenges for European Corporations and the Asian Globalizing Economy, sponsored by the Macau Institute of European Studies and held in Macau in April 1998. Chapter 9 is based on two papers of mine first published in the *Journal of Common Market Studies*, Vol. 35, 1997, No. 1, pp. 1–30 and No. 2, pp. 189–223. Chapter 10 was first published as a chapter in a volume edited by Gavin Boyd entitled *The Struggle for World Markets*, Edward Elgar, 1998, pp. 1–11.

In Part IV, Chapter 11 is a revised and upgraded version of the 24th Geary Lecture that I presented in Dublin, Ireland in 1993, which was later published as a booklet (in 1994) by the Economic and Social Research Institute.

Finally I wish to express my thanks to Mr Yong Pak and Mrs Phyllis Miller of Rutgers University and to Mrs Jill Turner of Reading University for helping me to revise and edit these various essays, and to prepare them for publication.

NOTES

1 New York, Basic Books (1971).
2 Cambridge, Mass., Harvard University Press (1998).

Introduction and overview

The changing face and determinants of international business activity – 1970–2000

This is the seventh volume of my writings which Routledge (and its predecessors) have published. The first, *Studies in International Investment* dates back to 1971. In the intervening years, my thoughts on this subject, and of the role of multinational enterprises (MNEs) in the world economy have evolved through a number of stages – some of which were described in the introductory chapter of my last book of essays, *Alliance Capitalism and Global Business* (1997a).

A comparison between the contents of this volume and that of *Studies . . .* is, I think, very illuminating. In 1970, comparatively little attention was given to the institutional framework underpinning the post-war upsurge in foreign direct investment (FDI) – although this was to change in the following decade. Even less attention was given to the merits and demerits of linking different capitalist societies through the operations of MNEs and cross-border alliances. Over four-fifths of FDI at that time was from the US and the UK (Dunning 1993). Much of the European Continent was only just starting to export capital again; Japanese and third world MNE activity was negligible. And, only some parts of the world were fully receptive to FDI – unlike before World War I, when capital flowed across most national borders quite freely (Wilkins 1999; Jones 1999).

In 1970, although trade barriers were starting to fall and European integration was well under way, the obstacles to trade and FDI were still very considerable. Most MNE activity was of a resource seeking or market seeking kind, the latter being largely prompted to protect – rather than augment – the home based competitive advantages of the investing firm.[1] The electronics age and the biotechnology revolution were still in their infancy; the Internet was unknown; and the greater part of FDI was geared towards adding value to existing home based competitive assets from a foreign location, rather than to creating or acquiring new income generating assets.

The situation is totally different today as many of the chapters of this volume show. Over the last decade, in particular, there has been marked reorientation in the content of scholarly research and writing on FDI and MNE activity. The reason for this reorientation is the juxtaposition of two systemic structural changes in the global economy. The first of these has been the renaissance of the market economy which, *inter alia*, has drawn many economies previously closed to or reluctant to accept FDI into the global economy. In 1990, for example, India, China and Russia, which accounted for 30 percent of the world's population drew in only 1 percent of the world's FDI stock. The corresponding figures for 1997 were 32 percent and 13.4 percent.

The second systemic change has been the maturation of the knowledge based economy, and the emergence of the Internet as a dominant technological force. Various indices may be adduced to illustrate the extent and form of this change, ranging from an increase in intellectual capital and other kinds of intangible assets to the number of Internet subscribers which have risen 50-fold between 1990 and 1997. It has now been predicted that at least 75 percent of all commercial transactions will be downloaded on the Internet by 2010.

These systemic changes have, in turn, generated other changes, which were given little attention in the 1970s. These include the spectacular rise in a wide variety of non-equity financed factor movements – notably portfolio investment and transfers of technology – by way of inter-firm transactions of one kind or another. At the same time, in the last decade, there has been a spectacular rise of cross-border mergers and acquisitions, which, relative to greenfield or start-up ventures, have been the main modality of new MNE activity.[2]

These events have affected our understanding of international business activity in three main ways. First, they have altered the nature and content of the competitive advantages of enterprises. Some of the contemporary core competencies of firms are set out in Chapters 4 and 5, but essentially they reduce to two. The first is the capability to generate new internally created assets, and to combine these with those of other firms across the globe in a way to maximize net value added. The second is the capability to continually reconfigure the content and form of the value-added chain – both at home and abroad – in such a way as to maximize long-term revenue and/or minimize production and transaction costs. It is here, particularly, that advances in electronic commerce and the economies of scale in innovatory and production activities are playing a critical role.

Second, the systemic changes and their geographical significance have fundamentally altered the parameters affecting the locational preferences of firms, and the actions which have to be taken by national and subnational governments if they are to attract and retain the intangible assets – and particularly intellectual capital – of mobile investors. Chapter 4 in this volume addresses this issue. In particular, it stresses the role of both private and public created location bound assets – notably, supportive educational and technological infrastructure and market facilitating government policies, in affecting the siting of value-added activities in the 1990s. These variables, although present in the 1970s, were thought to be much less significant by MNEs, relative to the more traditional locational variables of labor, material and transport costs, and the size and prosperity of the local market.

Third, the ways in which businesses organize their foreign activities – the I component of the eclectic paradigm – has undergone some profound restructuring since the 1970s – and it is likely this restructuring will continue well into the twenty-first century. In this connection we would emphasize two major points. First, the systemic changes described earlier have considerably aided the cross-border mobility of most kinds of products and assets – and particularly those of finance capital and services. Second, the modality of such transactions has not only changed but is much more complex than it used to be. Chapter 5, for example, demonstrates the spectacular growth of foreign portfolio investment (FPI) since the early 1980s. Over the 1992–1995 period it accounted for 70.2 percent of the combined FPI and FDI flows compared with 49.7 percent in the 1980–1983 period. At the same time, Chapter 5 suggests that, far from being alternative modalities to the transfer of assets across national boundaries, as they once were, these flows are becoming increasingly complementary to each other.

But, of no less – indeed, perhaps, of even greater importance – for the mode of cross-border transactions has been the emergence and fast burgeoning of electronic commerce. This is having two major affects. First, in some cases, e.g. written material, films, music, etc., it is changing – or has the potential to change the very nature of the product which consumers are buying. Magazines, mail, CD disks, video cassettes and tapes – physical products – are being replaced by downloading the services of such products on the Internet, and/or through the television screen. Second, it is offering both buyers and sellers more and less costly information about a large range of products than once they had. Third, it is changing the way in which goods and services, right through the value chain – from the supply of raw materials to the retailing of the final product are being purchased and delivered. This it is doing, primarily, by affecting the transaction costs of buying and selling. In some cases, by reducing the costs of externalized cross-border transactions it is lessening the need for FDI. In others, because the Internet facilitates the networking of diverse kinds of value-added activity, it is leading to more cross-border mergers and acquisitions (M&As) and/or strategic alliances between firms.

The jury is still out on whether E-commerce will lead to more or less, or a different kind of, MNE activity. It is, however, certain that it will both reconfigure and change the extent and quality of information about the products supplied by the majority of enterprises; and the organizational structure of their supply chains. Much, we suspect, will depend on the types of goods, services and assets being considered. The more standardized, i.e. the less idiosyncratic nature of the products supplied, and the less face to face contact among producers or between consumers and producers, is needed, then the more cross-border transactions will be externalized. The more uncertain the outcome of interdependent transactions and the more an end product comprises customized inputs which are complementary to each other, or can benefit from being jointly supplied with other products, the more FDI or alliance formation seems likely to be a principle modality of cross-border commerce. In such cases, Internet transactions may increase *intra*-firm, compared with *inter*-firm transactions.

So far, there has been relatively little scholarly work on the impact of electronic commerce on the activities of MNEs. No doubt, however, this deficiency will be rectified in the years to come – perhaps in time for inclusion in another volume in this series in the first decade of the twenty-first century.

The contents of the volume

This volume is divided into four main parts. Part I consists of two essays. The first – and it is the longest – contribution in the volume identifies necessary conditions which need to be in place if global capitalism is to succeed. After describing the unique features of contemporary capitalism, it addresses reasons why it is not currently living up to its expectations, and what must be done if it is to survive and prosper in the twenty-first century. In particular, it focuses on some of the basic dilemmas facing all capitalist systems in the global economy; and identifies measures which its main constituent institutions, viz. markets, non-profit organizations, governments and supranational entities, must take both to upgrade their efficiency, and to better relate their goals and aspirations to those of democratic societies.

The second essay takes up some of the issues identified by the first, but views these from the lens of a Christian apologist. However, it is quick to point out that many of the moral imperatives which need to be heeded if the global marketplace is to be the servant and not the master of those individuals and institutions it seeks to serve, are common to all the major religions, and, indeed, to all men of goodwill. In identifying these moral imperatives, the analysis steers a middle course between moral relativism and moral imperialism. More particularly, it asserts that in any civilized society worthy of its name, there are certain absolute and universal virtues such as truth, the advance of human dignity and human rights, and the support of institutions which promote these, i.e. good citizenship rights (Donaldson 1996). There remains ample room for differences in the prioritization of these values and to the identification and interpretation of secondary or alternative values, e.g. social justice, environmental protection, sustained development, etc., in what Donaldson and Dunfee (1994) refer to as "moral free space."

Part II of this volume contains three essays, each of which is concerned with the development of new theoretical insights into the determinants of international production (i.e. production financed by FDI and undertaken by MNEs). Chapter 3 presents our latest thoughts on the status of the eclectic paradigm. In it, we assert that while the paradigm continues to offer a robust framework within which several complementary (operational) economic and businesses can be contained, these theories, themselves, need to be constantly modified to take account both of the changing motives for MNE activity, and particularly their need to access intellectual capital from throughout the world, and of new technological developments, e.g. the Internet.

This theme is taken up in more detail in Chapter 4, which focuses on the location (L) component of the OLI paradigm. In doing so, it suggests that not only have the critical parameters making up the locational advantages of countries undergone a marked change – as a result of the liberalization of many markets and advent of the knowledge economy – but that the increasing ease at which many kinds of intellectual capital cross national borders, the emergence of asset seeking FDI, and the dramatic growth of cross-border mergers and acquisitions (M&As), have considerably affected the priority of the locational attractions sought by firms.

Chapter 5 seeks to do two things. First, it examines the extent to which it is possible to embrace FPI within the rubric of the eclectic paradigm of FDI. The answer is "yes," but only up to a point. This conditional affirmative is based on the proposition that there is a growing complementarity between FDI and FPI – at least at a macro-level and viewed from a developmental perspective. The second task of Chapter 5 is to review – from an historical and contemporary perspective – the nature and form of this complementarity, and to suggest reasons why we believe scholars should give more attention to this phenomena than they have so far done.

The contributions in Part III of this volume are also devoted to the spatial dimension of the global economy. Chapter 6 examines some apparent contradictions between the trend towards the globalization (or regionalization) of markets and production, and the tendency for particular types of value added activities to be concentrated within a limited geographical area.[3] It concludes that increased spatial specialization is entirely consistent with the widening geographical scope of markets – and, indeed, is another illustration of George Stigler's classic dictum that division of labor is limited by the extent of the market (Stigler 1941).

While Chapter 6 concentrates most of its attention on the location of MNE activity at a sub-national level, Chapter 7 examines the changing inter-country geography of FDI over the past two decades. It uses the eclectic paradigm to explain the growing number of source countries engaging in FDI and the changing profile of the leading recipient countries. Giving empirical verification to several of the locational issues raised in Chapter 4, it documents the widening spatial distribution of FDI, and, particularly, the growing attractions of transitional economies, notably China, India and Central and Eastern Europe, as host countries. Truly, at the beginning of the twenty-first century, MNEs and their affiliates are spanning the world to a greater extent than at any time since the First World War.[4] At the same time, most cross-border M&As – currently the dominant modality of FDI – are undertaken by firms within the triad (UNCTAD (1999)); and the production of knowledge or information intensive goods and services remains strongly embedded in the US, Western Europe and Japan. The growing multinationalization of the leading foreign direct investors is also described and analyzed in Chapter 7.

Chapters 8 and 9 turn to consider the growth, structure and impact of MNE activity in two of the major regions of the world, viz. Asia and Western Europe. Chapter 8 traces and explains the recent trends of foreign direct investment into three groups of Asian developing countries, which are classified by their size and levels of development. *Inter alia*, it shows that the impact of globalization has been very uneven, although the Asian developing countries now attracting an increasing share of FDI are those which have most recently embraced the benefits of economic interdependence. The chapter also touches on the Asian crises of 1997–1998, and suggests that most evidence interprets this as a pause in the inflow of FDI – particularly extra-Asian FDI. On the other hand, outward FDI may take longer to reach its 1997 peak, as economic circumstances, including a devaluation of exchange rates by many Asian countries, are tending to resuscitate exports from these countries, and the formation of cross-border alliances by Asian firms as modes for serving foreign markets and accessing new knowledge.

Chapter 9 tries to assess the effect of completion of the Internal Market in Europe – a point which was initiated by the European Commission in 1985, but did not come fully come on stream until January 1, 1993 – has so far had on the flow of both intra-European and extra-European FDI. After comparing the locational pattern and industrial structure of FDI flows since 1985 with those prior to that date, it reviews several attempts by scholars (including the present author) to isolate the impact of this latest phase in European integration on the activities of MNEs, in the European Union, compared with that of other economic and political variables. It concludes that the impact has been more marked for intra-EC FDI than extra-EC FDI; and also that, while the Internal Market has led to some decentralization of low to medium value activities to lower income countries – notably Spain – higher value activities, both in the goods and service sectors, continue to be clustered in the wealthier and larger countries, especially Germany and the UK. The chapter also offers some quantitative estimates of the effect of the Internal Market on the outflow of FDI from two EC countries, viz. the UK and Germany.

Chapter 10 focuses on trans-Atlantic economic relationships and shows how and why these have evolved over the past century or more. It identifies some quite fundamental differences between US and European style capitalism, but, nonetheless, asserts a closer and more collaborative economic relationship between the two major players in the triad is essential for global economic prosperity. The chapter concludes by an examination of a relatively new initiative for forcing up trade and FDI between Europe and the US via the Trans-Atlantic Economic Dialogue.

Part IV of the monograph contains only one chapter. In my previous volume in this series, *Alliance Capitalism and Global Business* (1997a) and in an edited volume for Oxford University Press, *Governments, Globalization and International Business* (1997b), I explored various aspects of changes in the interface between MNEs and national governments arising from the convergence of the global, knowledge based economy. Chapter 1 in this volume also touches upon the demands made on national governments of global capitalism is to prosper. It emphasizes that while the globalization is eroding some of the macro-economic functions of governments, the content and efficiency of their micro-management policies (especially their education and innovation policies) is becoming a more critical determinant on the location of (mobile) MNE activity, and of national competitiveness.

This being so, this volume contains only one chapter on the implications of globalization for national economic regimes. It was originally written in 1993, but I believe most of its contents remain relevant at the turn of the millennium. I have updated some of the earlier analysis in the light of new writings and events of the later 1990s. However, the challenge of the next two decades or more will be to reconcile the economic and social priorities of national and sub-national governments with those of supra-national entities in a way which is acceptable to each, and to the demands of social justice. The survival of global capitalism is very much dependent on the extent to which such a reconciliation is both wished for, and successfully pursued.

It is hoped that the reader will find these essays interesting and useful to his (or her) understanding of some of the features and implications of global capitalism (or, as Chapter 1 suggests, as a more appropriate nomenclature, multi-domestic capitalism). Clearly, while each of the constituents of capitalism has an important role to play, that of MNEs and national governments are likely to be the most pervasive and critical. Both influence and are influenced by a series of systemic changes arising out of technological advances and the institutional environment which conditions their actions. Both, too, need to address the challenges posed by techno-scientific forces which, on the whole, are drawing the nations of the world together; and very different social and ethical value systems – particularly in respect of safety nets in society – which are tending to drive them apart. I believe that opportunities for a fruitful alliance between the private and public sector in the creation, harnessing and allocation of the world's natural resources and created assets are greater than ever before. But, even greater, I fear, are the costs of a combative interaction between the main wealth creators, facilitators and beneficiaries, not just to global capitalism, but to the economic and social welfare of all people – both rich and poor.

NOTES

1 Exceptions include some FDI in some service sectors, as documented by Jones (1999).
2 Details of these developments are set out in the annual publications of the World Investment Report of UNCTAD. See, for example, UNCTAD (1999).
3 What Ann Markusen (1996) has referred to as the paradox of sticky places within slippery space.
4 For a recent examination of the "ebb" and "flow" of MNE activity in the world economy since the late 1920s, see Jones (1999).

REFERENCES

Donaldson, T. (1996), "Values in tension: ethics away from home," *Harvard Business Review 74* (5), September/October, pp. 48–56.

Donaldson, T. and Dunfee, T. W. (1994), "Toward a unified conception of business ethics: integrative social contracts theory," *Academy of Management Review 19* (2), April, pp. 252–84.

Dunning, J. H. (1993), *Multinational Enterprises and the Global Economy*, Wokingham, England and Reading, Mass.: Addison Wesley.

Dunning, J. H. (1970), *Studies in International Investment*, London and Boston: Allen & Unwin.

Dunning, J. H. (1997a), *Alliance Capitalism and Global Business*, London and New York: Routledge.

Dunning, J. H. (ed.) (1997b), *Governments, Globalization and International Business*, Oxford: Oxford University Press.

Jones, G. (1999), "The historical development of multinationals from the 1930s to the 1980s," paper presented at a conference on *Mapping the Multinationals* at the Pontantico Conference Center of the Rockefeller Brothers Fund, New York, and organized by the Global History Initiative of Massachusetts Institute of Technology, October 1999.

Markusen, A. (1996), "Sticky places in slippery space: a typology of industrial districts," *Economic Geography 72* (3), pp. 293–313.

Stigler, G. (1951), "The division of labor is limited by the extent of the market," *Journal of Political Economy LIX*, pp. 185–93.

UNCTAD (1999), *World Investment Report 1993, Transnational Corporations and Economic Development*, New York and Geneva: UN.

Wilkins, M. (1999), "The historical development of multinationals to the 1930s," paper presented at a conference on *Mapping the Multinationals* at the Pontantico Conference Center of the Rockefeller Brothers Fund, New York, and organized by the Global History Initiative of Massachusetts Institute of Technology, October 1999.

World Bank (1998), *World Development Report 1999: Knowledge for Development*, Oxford: Oxford University Press.

Part I

Global capitalism at bay?

1 Whither global capitalism?

Introduction

The subject of this chapter has already intrigued scholars, business practitioners and politicians and various interest groups; and, no doubt, will continue to do so well into the twenty-first century. Yet, within the last decade or so, attitudes towards economic globalization, and predictions about its future, have undergone a profound transformation. From the euphoria which followed the fall of the Berlin Wall, and the liberalization of many goods, services and money markets, we are currently experiencing a kind of backlash – not dissimilar to that which followed the first positive reactions to the industrial revolution of the late eighteenth and nineteenth centuries (Kennedy 1996, Searle 1998).

For now, as then, a different set of winners and losers are being created, and new social and political concerns are emerging. Titles of books published in the last couple of years – such as: *The Global Trap* (Martin and Schumann 1997); *The Manic Logic of Global Capitalism* (Greider 1997); *Has Globalization Gone Too Far?* (Rodrik 1997); *False Dawn* (Gray 1998); *Global Capitalism in Crisis* (Soros 1998); *Turbo-Capitalism* (Luttwak 1999); *The Lexus and the Olive Tree* (Friedman 1999) all emphasize some of the (perceived) downsides of globalization, which need to be set against its benefits emphasized by most economists and business strategists. *Globaphobia* (Bartlett and Lawrence 1998), indeed, may not be an exaggerated word to describe the current and growing disquiet about the future of global capitalism.

Where next then, one might ask? Will the current round of concerns and anxieties – so dramatically displayed at Seattle in December 1999 at the time of the World Trade Organization (WTO) meetings – escalate and force a back-tracking from the path now being pursued by so many countries; or will the more optimistic view of the future prevail – albeit with a greater emphasis on what Claude Smadja, at the 1999 World Economic Forum in Davos referred to as "responsible globality"?

Let me declare my hand straight away as a "conditional" optimist. What does this mean? Well, it is my belief that global capitalism *can* succeed, but *only* if certain conditions, which are not being currently met, are met. And it is the "identification" of these conditions, and of how these might be advanced, on which this article focuses.

Two underlying paradoxes

I start by offering two paradoxes of global capitalism, then go on to look at its objectives, describe some of its unique features, and examine some of its costs and benefits. I then proceed to discuss on what (I believe) needs to be done if it is to continue as the dominant form of economic organization well into the twenty-first century.

The first paradox is this: The success of global capitalism rests largely on the efficient operation of unfettered cross-border markets. *However, it is a feature of many of these markets – notably knowledge and financial markets – that they incur substantial transaction costs of one kind or another, such as those associated with structural discontinuities, volatility and information asymmetries.* Hence, it follows that the role of both internal and external market governance in helping to reduce these costs, and in setting rules and standards within which transactions take place is becoming more, rather than less, important than once it was.

The second paradox – or perhaps dilemma would be a better word – is *how best to reconcile the inevitably uneven distributional effects of the global marketplace with the imperatives of social justice, and to do so in the context of a reduced leverage of national governments to compensate those who, through no fault of their own, find themselves especially disadvantaged by globalization.*

The objectives and nature of global capitalism

But, first, what is global capitalism; and what are its distinctive characteristics? Let me distinguish between "ideal" and "actual" global capitalism. By "ideal" global capitalism I mean the optimal cross-border interaction between, or integration of, the different forms or brands of national or regional capitalism,[1] each of which is designed to meet the specific economic social and cultural demands of its citizens. By "actual" capitalism I mean the existing state of the economic and social interconnections between regions and nation states, each of which is committed, in principle at least, to the market system of organizing economic transactions, but each of which embeds, and in some cases influences, the character of the system by its own institutional structures, ideologies, and social and cultural mores.

Let me next rehearse some of the conditions necessary to sustain "actual" global capitalism, and move it closer to "ideal" global capitalism. First, it should be concerned with the creation of both tangible *and* intangible wealth;[2] with both the quantity and the quality of assets, goods and services; and with the output of both private and collective (i.e. public) goods and services. Second, global capitalism needs to incorporate a set of appropriate ethical mores, which will fashion the behavior of the participants in the marketplace. Third, it is important that these mores should acknowledge, and, where appropriate, influence, the *unique* characteristics of both global capitalism and its constituent national institutions. Fourth, sustainable global capitalism must rest on the acceptance and promotion of such transcendent moral virtues as social justice, human dignity, respect for basic rights, and the absence of racial and religious discrimination. Its scope and content must also be embedded in democratic regimes.[3]

Let me pause at this point to give a working definition of economic globalization. According to the International Monetary Fund (1997):

> Globalization refers to the growing interdependencies of countries worldwide through the increasing volume and variety of cross-border transactions in goods and services, and of international capital flows; and also through the rapid and widespread diffusion of all kinds of technology.[4]

I might add that this definition takes as axiomatic that these tasks will best be achieved through the workings of the free markets – aided, abetted, and suitably modified by the actions and policies of extra-market institutions.

The unique features of global capitalism

What, then, is unique and special about global capitalism? Let me highlight just five features; and it is the combination of these which, I believe, sets apart the global economy from the international economy of the last century or more.[5]

1 Cross-border transactions are deeper, more extensive and more interconnected than they have ever been.
2 Resources, capabilities, goods and services are more spatially mobile than they have ever been.
3 Multinational enterprises (MNEs) play a more significant role as creators and disseminators of wealth, than they have ever done before; and they originate from, and produce in, more countries than ever before.
4 There is more real and financial volatility in cross-border markets – and particularly in capital and exchange markets – than there has ever been.
5 The advent of the digital environment and electronic commerce is completely changing the character and locational profile of cross-border transactions – particularly of all kinds of services.

Widening our analysis out a little, we might identify four distinctive features of the present stage of capitalism – of which the spatial dimension is only one. These are set out in Table 1.1. Let us consider each of these. First, in contrast to the earlier stages of capitalism, the main source of contemporary wealth creation is knowledge or intellectual capital of all kinds – be it embodied in human or physical resources, or in tangible or intangible assets. Second, although the production of many enterprises, particularly MNEs, span the planet, there is a greater spatial concentration of some kinds of economic activity – both between and within countries – than there has ever been.[6] (This is the paradox of "sticky places" within "slippery space" (Markusen 1996).) Third, the world is entering a phase of capitalism in which all forms of alliances and cooperative ventures (e.g. within and between enterprises, between enterprises and non-market institutions and between governments) are playing a more important role. Fourth, I believe that the kind of social and moral virtues which twenty-first century capitalism especially needs to nourish if it is to properly fulfil its functions, are somewhat different from those demanded by industrial, merchant or land-based capitalism.

But, let me make three other points about the nature of global capitalism. First, to reiterate an earlier observation, there are currently many varieties of capitalism in the world economy. That of Japan and Germany is very different from that of the US or Canada; that of Taiwan and Thailand is not the same as that of Korea; that of Chile is totally different from that of China. One of the tasks of "ideal" global capitalism is then to integrate the rich mosaic of these species of capitalism in a way which acknowledges and respects their unique cultural heritages and institutional frameworks, but internalizes and builds upon their common goods. Second, to some scholars (of which I am one) global capitalism is best regarded as a process; to others it is an accomplished fact. Third, to some commentators, regionalization is part of globalization; to others it is a substitute for it; and, indeed, may impede its progress.[7]

How does one measure the extent of economic globalization?

How does one measure the extent and depth of global capitalism? The data set out in Appendix Tables A.1.1 and A.1.2 speak for themselves. Although some of these are a little dated, they all portray a similar picture. In particular we would point to the growing importance of FDI, and all forms of cross-border financial transactions over the last 30 years or so; to the more gradual dispersion of innovatory capacity, at least among the medium- and high-income industrial countries; and to the increased significance of trade, and especially intra-FDI trade as a percent of world GNP.

But do these figures over-play the uniqueness of globalization? Perhaps

Table 1.1 Features of three stages of market-based capitalism (a Western model)

	Seventeenth–Early nineteenth century	Nineteenth century–Later twentieth century	Late twentieth century onwards
Primary source of wealth and form of activity	Land based: agriculture and forestry. Some local and international merchant commerce	Machine/finance based: manufacturing	Finance/knowledge based: producer and consumer services
Spatial dimension	Local/regional	Regional/national	Regional/global: but with some national or sub-national clusters
Principal organizational form	Traditional economy: mixture of feudal and entrepreneurial: nation state only in its infancy	Managerial/hierarchical: generally adversarial economic relationships: elements of a command economy	More market-oriented: alliance/heterarchical: more cooperative economic relationships
Moral virtues	Obedience, externally imposed discipline and enforced trust. Some familial and community spirit of cooperation	Hard work, civic responsibility, social justice, entrepreneurship, individualism	Personal responsibility, creativity, spontaneous sociability, trust, reciprocity and compassion

Table 1.2 Some indices of globalization

- *Foreign direct investment*: As a proportion of world gross product the combined stock of outward and inward investment rose from 7.8% in 1967 to 14.0% in 1988 and to 23.6% in 1997. The average value of cross-border M&A sales rose from $25 billion in 1980 to $160 billion in 1990 to $544 billion in 1998.
- *Foreign portfolio investment*: As a proportion of world gross product, the flow of outward and inward foreign portfolio investment rose over 14 times between 1970 and 1996 – from 0.33% in 1970 to 1.94% in 1985 and 4.70% in 1996.
- *The international banking market*: The sales of international banking firms as a percentage of world gross output rose from 1.2% in 1964 to 1995, to close on 50% in 1997.
- *Foreign exchange transactions*: By 1997, the turnover in the foreign exchange markets has risen to over $1.5 trillion each day, 12 times that of its level in 1979 and over 50 times that of world trade.
- *Innovation*: As more countries engage in innovatory activities, the proportion of R&D activities undertaken by the foreign subsidiaries of MNEs is rising, although it is still only one-half that of their sales and assets (in 1994–1995 it was 22% in the case of the world's leading industrial corporations, compared to 10% in 1980).
- *Foreign trade*: The annual average percentage growth of world trade in goods and services rose from 4.0% between 1853 and 1913, to 6.0% between 1950 and 1985 (after declining in the interwar years) to 7.0% between 1985 and 1997. In 1960, less than 10% of trade conducted by MNEs was intra-firm; in 1997 it was between 35 and 40%.

Sources: A variety of official publications, notably the UN, World Bank and IMF.

they do. A lot depends on the perspective one takes. Certainly, it has only been in the last 25 years that the significance of trade and FDI as a percentage of GNP of the major industrialized countries has exceeded that of 1913 (Kleinknecht and ter Wengel 1998). Certainly, too, not all industries, firms, or activities of firms are as globalized as others. Moreover, the majority of wealth in most countries – particularly in large countries such as China, India and the US – continues to be internally generated.

But, perhaps most significantly, virtually all national governments still strongly influence the character and content of innovation and corporate governance systems, education and training policies, institutional infrastructures and the entrepreneurial ethos of both institutions and individuals within their sphere of jurisdiction (Doremus, Keller, Pauly and Reich 1998). In the last resort, too, it is national governments which are the main socializers of the risks of globalization; and it is they – or their representatives at the international negotiating tables – who will determine both the extent and pattern of globalization (or regionalization); and of how many of its costs and benefits are distributed between countries and interest groups.[8]

The causes of global capitalism

In Table 1.3, I set out some of the main driving forces making for contemporary – and particularly – global capitalism. These may be identified as *attracting, enabling* and *threatening* forces. Table 1.3 gives examples of each of these. Each, in its various ways, has led to a more *knowledge-based* economy; *more alliance-based organizational* patterns, *more global or regional production and marketing strategies* by firms, and a shift in the *significance or prioritization of particular moral or ethical norms.*

The costs and benefits of global capitalism

I shall confine my attention to identifying just some of the more important of these. The benefits are primarily – though not entirely – economic. They encompass gains from the specialization of economic activity, and those from market-oriented trade and FDI; speedier rates of innovation and the diffusion of intellectual capital across national boundaries; more inter-firm competition; a revival of entrepreneurship particularly in the small firm sector; the convergence of growth and income levels – at least, among the more open industrial and advanced industrializing economies (Sachs and Warner 1995);[9] more devolution or subsidiarity in economic decision taking (at least in some cases); and the dissemination of welfare enhancing social, cultural and behavioral mores.

What about the downsides, or – no less importantly – the perceived downsides of global capitalism? These are both economic and non-economic. The former are frequently endemic, and are a consequence of rapid technological and social change. They include a variety of cross-border market and institutional failures, and the increased prevalence of economic shocks, discontinuities and uncertainties. The latter include a continuing spatial unevenness (both between and within countries) of the distribution of higher value-added activities (particularly between the most and least prosperous nations); the costs of structural adjustment; an increase in some kinds of long-term unemployment; widening income

Table 1.3 Causes of global capitalism

Attracting	E.g. the renaissance of the market economy, and the liberalization of many markets, several new emerging economies, increasing geographical dispersion of created assets
Enabling	E.g. technological advances, lower barriers to cross-border transactions, decreased cost and improved quality of transport and communication facilities, global capital markets
Threatening	E.g. more intensive global competition, volatility of exchange and financial markets, accelerating rates of technological obsolescence

Source: *Investment Canada* (1990).

gaps (e.g. between skilled and unskilled workers, and between the very rich and very poor); and the challenge to social cohesion and national insurance schemes. Of no less concern is the fact that the growing porosity of national borders is facilitating the cross-border movement of *disbenefits* like drugs, unsafe products, environmental pollution, crime, and terrorism. Finally, in some cases, globalization is eroding the political sovereignty and weakening the economic autonomy of nation states.

The obvious trick then – which will determine the form and sustainability of global capitalism – is then to minimize its costs while maximizing its benefits. Or, in the words of a communiqué issued by the Group of 7 in Lyon three years ago:

> In an increasingly interdependent world, we must all recognize that we have an interest in spreading the benefits of economic growth as widely as possible, and diminishing the risk either of excluding individuals or groups in our own economies or of excluding certain countries or regions from the benefits of globalization.
>
> (Quoted in Rodrik 1997)

The institutions of global capitalism

Let us now consider how this objective might be achieved – or at least take the debate a step further. At the moment, three future scenarios are "on the table." These are set out in Table 1.4. Although I would like to think option 3 will prevail, I think it more likely that option 2 will win the day – although there is a danger that if one backs away from option 3, option 1 could be forced upon us.

To implement option 3 with any chance of success, and to move towards a more acceptable global capitalism, I believe that a more systemic approach to the organization and governance of international economic activity is needed. It is the purpose of the rest of this chapter to set out the main agenda of such an approach. In so doing, I shall focus on the four key institutions of global capitalism, viz. markets, intermediate associations (IAs), governments and supra-national entities. These are presented in Figure 1.1 as points on a diamond. Outside the diamond, but affecting the

Table 1.4 Three possible future scenarios of global capitalism

1	The "creative" destruction of global capitalism. (NB: Several economists in the past, e.g. Karl Marx, Alfred Marshall and Joseph Schumpeter, expressed considerable doubts on the sustainability of capitalism as it existed in their day and age.)
2	The "muddling through" or "Band-Aid" solution; marginal adjustments to the *status quo* of existing markets, extra-market institutions (including governments), social mores and behavioral patterns
3	Proactive measures to recognize the unique characteristics and imperatives of global capitalism, and to minimize its costs and maximize its benefits

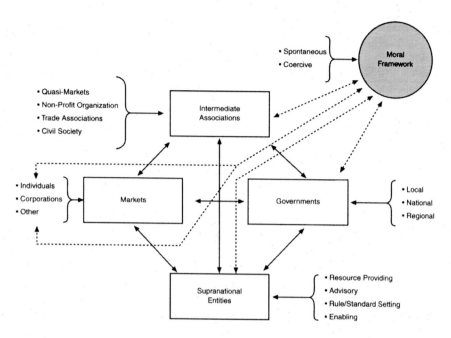

Figure 1.1 The institutions of global capitalism (the G.C. diamond)

conduct and performance of these institutions is the social and moral order. It is my contention that the role and functions of each of these needs to be reappraised in the light of the unique features and imperatives of contemporary capitalism earlier described.

This task, I believe, should be primarily accomplished by reconstituting and strengthening the governance of the G.C. diamond. If achieved successfully, this could be the main – unique – public or collective good of global capitalism (Prakash 1999). Table 1.5 distinguishes between two main forms of governance. The first is *spontaneous* and internal to the institutions in question, and/or represents a voluntary response to the advisory or non-coercive actions taken by higher order institutions. The second is *coercive*. Freedom can only work within the protection of a rules-based system, and the same holds good for each of the institutions of global capitalism. Strong and effective laws, regulations and enforcing agencies are frequently required both to counteract market distortions and the unacceptable behavior of some non-governmental activist groups; and to promote social justice and civil stability. Democratically elected governments and supra-national entities are the main rule-setters and enforcers – although they, may (and sometimes do), behave in a sub-optimal way. The respective roles of each of these forms of governance is likely to vary between societies, between functions and according to established cultural and ethical mores.

Table 1.5 The governance of global capitalism

- **The markets**
  Comprising: individuals, groups of individuals, corporations, groups of
  corporations and, sometimes, intermediate associations and governments
  (Types of governance: Self-imposed – spontaneous on part of participants;
  decreed by agreement with intermediate associations; coercive action and/or
  macro-economic and organizational policies initiated by governments and/or
  supra-national entities.)
- **Intermediate associations**
  Comprising: civil society, clubs, non-profit organizations, interest groups and
  trade associations
  (Types of governance: Self-imposed and/or market driven;
  incentives/penalties and/or coercive action initiated by governments or supra-
  national entities.)
- **Governments**
  Ranging from sub-national to supra-national governments (e.g. EU)
  (Types of governance: policy formation; initiators of incentives/penalties and
  of regulatory and legal framework for market-related activities.)
- **Supra-national**
  May be government or independently financed entities
  (Types of governance: Advice and guidance to national governments and to
  market participants, action taken on behalf of national governments;
  recommendations for actions to be taken by regional and national
  governments. Initiators of regulatory frameworks on behalf of market
  participants and extra-market institutions.)

The market

Consider, first, the market as an institution. Figure 1.2 identifies three
main market participants, the different types of markets, why markets
might fail, and what might be the possible responses to market failure.
Some points worth emphasizing are:

1   In the context of contemporary capitalism, the market should not be
    regarded as the sole determinant of how scarce resources are utilized,
    but rather as an institution embedded in a web of interrelated institu-
    tions, which, taken as a whole, characterize a society. *It is within this
    broader context that the performance of markets should be judged.*
2   Markets succeed when they promote the efficient allocation of
    human, physical and financial resources by maximizing the net bene-
    fits of innovation, production and exchange. They fail when they fall
    short of achieving this objective.
3   The market system, *qua* system, comprises a network of many thou-
    sands of individual markets. The fastest growing markets in global
    capitalism are those involving the production and exchange of intan-
    gible assets, goods and services – and particularly all forms of informa-
    tion and intellectual capital.

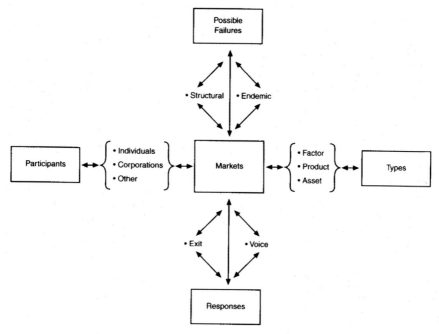

Figure 1.2 Markets and the G.C. diamond

4   Market imperfections are of two kinds. The first are *structural* imperfections. These arise from the actions of one or other participants of the markets, e.g. natural resource monopolists, or of extra-market institutions such as governments, which inhibit the efficient workings of markets. The second are endemic market failures, which usually reflect the intrinsic characteristics of the assets, goods and services being exchanged, and the uncertainties and externalities attached to them. Such failures may affect individual markets differently and the same markets differently over a period of time.

What, then, is the specific impact of global capitalism on markets? We would make three observations.

1   The relative importance of different markets is changing; and those which are growing the fastest are demonstrating the most significant endemic market failure.
2   In one way or another, an increasing proportion of economic transactions are being undertaken across, rather than within, national borders.
3   Goods and services which, at one time, were non-tradable, are now tradable across the exchanges. The arrival of electronic markets is

likely to substantially add to this tradability – particularly in the case of retailing, financial and professional services.

How do these features – together with the advent of alliance capitalism – affect the likely success of markets? As one might expect, the answer is a mixed one. Those characteristics likely to exacerbate market failure include: more unpredictability and volatility in financial markets, the rising costs of structural adjustment associated with rapid technological change, an increase in the output of collective or public goods, including those designed to reduce the "bads" of economic activity, new information asymmetries – particularly in the exchange of technologically complex goods – externalities (i.e. the costs and benefits of transactions incurred by non-market participants), new kinds of moral hazard and opportunities arising from the extension of the boundaries of corporations to unfamiliar cultures and political regimes, and, perhaps most important of all, the growing perception that the market mechanism, by itself, cannot ensure the production of those goods and services whose value cannot easily be measured in monetary terms (Sacks 1999).[10]

At the same time, other features of economic globalization are helping to promote the efficiency of cross-border transactions. These include many technological advances, such as electronic markets and improved cross-border communication facilities, the liberalization and deregulation of many financial and other service markets, more intensive competition among firms, a better appreciation by national governments of the benefits of the market system, the increased flexibility of many labor markets, and an improved capability of market supporting institutions.

How, then, might national or cross-border markets be made more efficient. Using the terminology first introduced by Hirschman (1970), we might identify two kinds of reaction, viz. *"voice"* and *"exit."* Exit reactions include the by-passing of markets by hierarchies, e.g. MNEs or by the direct intervention of governments.[11] Voice reactions are those designed to actively reduce the imperfections to markets without exiting from them. These reactions may be *spontaneous* or *coercive.* Spontaneous reactions fall into three main groups.

1   Voluntary learning experiences, informal social norms, and self-regulation.
2   The creation of new markets, the specific purpose of which is to lower the transaction costs of existing markets.
3   The facilitation of efficient markets by actions of extra-market institutions, notably by governments providing information, setting standards, upgrading the legal and commercial and financial infrastructure, aiding structural adjustment, and so on.

The type of coercive voice strategies, which might be aimed at reducing market failure include formal sanctions, mainly imposed by national governments against the structurally distorting behavior of market participants (particularly corporations), and actions taken to reduce, or cushion the effects of, the volatility associated with some markets.

In brief, for market-based global capitalism to meet the demands expected of it, more effort needs to be directed to increasing the efficiency of those markets which are inherently the most imperfect. These include knowledge-related, alliance-related and distance-related markets; and those transactions which, because of the uncertainty of their outcome, or the information asymmetries between the parties to the exchange, are the most volatile.

Intermediate associations

Next let us turn to examine the role of extra-market institutions in affecting both "actual" and "ideal" global capitalism. The first of these are intermediate associations (IAs) which I believe are destined to play a more important economic and social role in the future. In Figure 1.3 we identify the main kinds of IAs, their distinctive functions and of how they can play a more effective role.

First, what are they? IAs are sometimes called the "third" sector and comprise the civil society of a democratic capitalist economy. They are by no means a new phenomenon. They are intermediate in the sense they display some of the characteristics of markets and some of those of governments.

IAs are of two main kinds. The first are non-profit organizations (NPOs). These include a variety of clubs and associations, which supply goods and services for a price (sometimes a zero price) to their members and/or customers. The second are institutions, usually referred to as non-government organizations (NGOs). For the most part, these act as pressure groups to attain certain economic, political or social objectives on behalf of the interests they represent. In this chapter, I chiefly concern myself with the first kind of IAs. But I do want to make a brief comment on the increasing role of NGOs in the global economy.

NGOs are an extremely heterogeneous collection of institutions – they number many tens of thousands across the globe, of which by 1990 upwards of 2,000 were international in scope.[12] Each of these has its own distinctive agenda. These include some NPOs, but for the most part, NGOs are policy-oriented advocacy groups whose main purpose is either to affect, by whatever means they deem appropriate, the goals of individuals, interest groups, enterprises and governments, or to influence the ways in which – through the normal course of economic activity – these goals are achieved. Of course, many NGOs, most of which are single-minded in their objectives, have little or nothing to do with global capitalism. But directly or indirectly, many others, e.g. the green or environmental lobby, human rights activists, and those speaking for the poorest sections of the global community

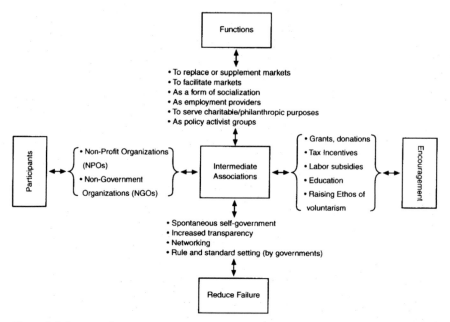

Figure 1.3 Intermediate associations and the G.C. diamond

certainly do; and their recent influence on the deliberations of the North American Free Trade Agreement (NAFTA), the Rio Earth Summit in 1994, the (aborted) Multilateral Agreement on Investment (MAI), and the WTO in 1999 has been considerable and pervasive.[13]

At their best, NGOs can and do play an important part in the democratic process. In the past, they, rather than markets or governments, have spearheaded important changes in the social attitudes and values of individuals and communities. At the same time, NGOs, because they tend to focus their interests to a specific part of a wider problem, because they ascribe to globalization consequences which though associated with it are not caused by it; because they frequently fail to examine the counterfactual position to that which they are seeking to change; and because they sometimes use anti-social methods to highlight their concerns can reduce rather than increase economic and/or social welfare. Indeed they are capable of behaving in a thoroughly undemocratic way, in the sense that they are not accountable to the general public for what they do in the way in which both governments and markets are.

To the best of my knowledge, there has been no systematic study on the ways in which NGOs may affect the wealth creating and welfare enhancing process in a democratic capitalist economy;[14] nor on the rules of the game or standards of behavior which should underpin their conduct. Such a study is long overdue and is now needed more than ever as NGOs are increasingly organizing themselves across national boundaries; and through the Internet, and other means, are forming a powerful coalition of a variety of interest groups, each of which has its own particular anti-globalization agenda.

Let us now turn to consider NPOs. These are mostly of three types. The first comprise collections of individuals and/or corporations whose main purpose is to gather information, conduct research, provide advice, set standards and monitor the conduct of their members. By and large these act to reduce search and negotiating costs, and to protect the property rights and upgrade the intellectual capital of their members.

The second type of NPOs are quasi-market institutions, which normally supply goods and services at below the full market price. They do not seek to make a profit, and are often subsidized by individuals, corporations, or governments, contributing either money or labor. Examples include museums, art galleries, some educational services, and many recreational activities. The third type of NPO consists of a variety of charitable and philanthropic organizations, and organizations designed to reduce economic and social "bads," e.g. crime detection and law enforcement agencies. Globalization is requiring these latter organizations to extend their activities beyond their national boundaries, and to engage in cross-border collaborative ventures (e.g. Interpol).

Some other features of NPOs worthy of note are: first, they tend to supply non-tradable services rather than tradable goods; second, they largely engage in labor-intensive activities, and third, their output is primarily geared to meeting the needs of individuals and families, and is largely supplied by small and medium-size enterprises.

There are no comprehensive data on the numbers, value added or employment of NPOs. But, to give just one example, in the US – perhaps the most market oriented economy in the world – their numbers run into many thousands, and it is reckoned that the assets of the independent sector – and these may include those of some NGOs – are about one-half of those of the federal government; and that this sector accounts for about 10 percent of total national employment. Moreover, these percentages are growing (Van Til 1998, Ben-Ner and Gui 1993, Rifkin 1995, Salamon and Anheier 1997).

Why then should we concern ourselves with NPOs? Primarily because we believe they offer a wide range of economic and social benefits, not to mention values, which, if nurtured, can help to cushion some of the adverse consequences of global capitalism, and foster communitarism at a national or local level. Let me cite just a few examples of these benefits. First, socialization and voluntarism are worthwhile acts in themselves, and can foster the bonding and communitarism of all groups in society. Second, they can act as useful adjuncts to efficient markets, e.g. by providing information and setting standards to consumers and to small and medium-size enterprises. Third, they help provide quality-of-life enhancing goods and services, which otherwise might not have been supplied or supplied as economically. Fourth, they can create jobs, the quality of which is frequently rewarding to the providers of the services. Fifth, since much of the output of NPOs is not tradable, employment is likely to be less volatile than that in the tradable goods sector. And finally, NPOs may provide a useful "safety net" of employment for those who either wish to withdraw from the mainstream labor market, or are forced out by technological change, or by other causes.

How might IAs be made more effective and encouraged? They can be made more effective by upgrading the quality of their governance structures, increasing their transparency and accountability, and by better networking. In the case of NGOs, there is a strong case for governments and/or supra-national agencies to move clearly the acceptable limits of activist behavior; and where appropriate encourage more dialogue between the NGOs and other institutions. In the case of NPOs their activities might be fostered in three main ways:

1 By tax and related fiscal incentives offered by local or national governments.
2 By direct grants or subsidies, and by appropriate government supported training schemes.
3 By moral suasion, improving the "image" of NPOs, and by publicizing and fostering the virtues of social responsibility and voluntarism.

In short, I believe that IAs can and should play an important part in the kind of institutional reform and reconfiguration which is needed if some of the current and likely future economic costs and social disharmonies of global capitalism are to be avoided or minimized. Whether they will, or whether the activities of NGOs will "kill the capitalistic goose that lays the wealth creating golden egg" remains to be seen.

The role of national and sub-national governments

What next of the role of national and sub-national governments? Consider Figure 1.4, which identifies the various levels of governance, the functions of governments, the actions of governments and how governments can perform their duties more effectively.

The unique economic tasks of democratic governments are well known.[15] We do, however, sometimes need to remind ourselves of these – particularly when we are tempted to think that the best contribution governments can make to promoting "ideal" global capitalism is an "opting out" one – viz. *not* to interfere with the workings of the free market.

What, then, are these functions? First, governments bear the primary responsibility for designing and implementing a variety of macro-

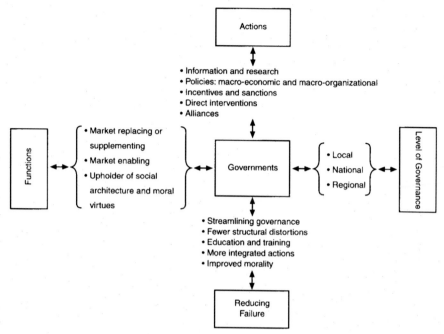

Figure 1.4 National and sub-national governments or the G.C. diamond

economic and macro-organizational policies, each of which are essential to the pursuance of economic goals of the constituents they represent. Second, they are (or should be) enablers of efficient factor, asset and product markets, and as upholders of the legal and commercial institutions underpinning these markets. This task includes – as we have already seen – rule and standard setting, which over-arch market transactions. Third, they are the main providers of most kinds of social capital and public goods. Fourth, it is their duty to ensure that structural distortions and/or an abuse of economic power by market participants (e.g. firms, labor unions, special interest groups, including NGOs), are minimized. Fifth, they are the main initiators of a range of laws, regulations and policies intended to promote a range of non-economic goals, e.g. notably those to do with social justice, environmental protection, health and safety standards, etc. Sixth, they are the primary vehicle for protecting and promoting national economic interests at the international negotiating table (e.g. at the WTO and IMF). Seventh, they bear the responsibility for minimizing the social disruptions of structural change. And lastly, they are, at the last resort, creators and sustainers of a social architecture and upholders of a set of moral values consistent with, and supportive of, democratic capitalism. These, I think you will agree, are no mean tasks.

What is likely to be the impact of economic globalization on national governments? First and foremost, it is *not* to reduce their role, as several commentators have suggested, but rather to redefine and transform it. For most of the present century, the main micro-management task of governments has been to minimize the (perceived) socially unacceptable effects of market transactions. Today it is to provide the most propitious economic environment for knowledge generation, and for upgrading the productivity of indigenous resources and capabilities; and to equip its citizens with the skills, expertise and motivation they need to face the demands of the global marketplace (Smadja 1999). But, no less important is the increasing need for national governments to address the social consequences of contemporary economic events, and to find ways of dealing with their uneven, destabilizing or unjust consequences. The penalty for failing in this task is, at least, social unrest and political instability; and, at most, the overthrow of democratic capitalism.

What actions, then, might governments take? Let me offer the following points.

1 Governments need to upgrade their information and statistical data providing services. This is particularly important for small and medium-size enterprises struggling to compete in a globalizing, knowledge-based economy.
2 They need to invoke codes of conduct and/or offer incentives for their constituents to engage in market friendly but socially responsible courses of action; and to reconfigure their institutional structures and behavioral norms to best promote these actions.
3 They need to reconsider the allocation of decision-taking among different levels of governance, and to delegate, where appropriate, responsibility to IAs, sub-national authorities and specialized investment agencies for matters specific to their constituents.
4 By various policy measures, they need to increase the benefits and reduce the costs of dynamic structural adjustment.
5 They need to enact legislation to ensure that the behavior of participants in markets works in the public interest. Some of this legislation, e.g. with respect to restrictive practices, transfer pricing, safety and working conditions, etc., may need to be modified in the light of the growth of cross-border FDI and strategic alliances.
6 They need to give more attention to identifying and providing the location bound resources and capabilities sought by foreign investors; and, as far as possible, carve out a set of unique (and non-imitatible) competitive advantages, which might encourage the firms and assets they desire to become more embedded within their boundaries.
7 They need to pay more attention to the social and economic contributions IAs might make to promoting social capital (Etzioni 1996), and to counteracting some of the less desirable affects of globalization and

technological change. On the other hand, while working together with IAs to better achieve these goals, they need to take firmer measures against NGOs that use undemocratic means to pursue their objectives.

8 In a variety of ways, they should foster an ethos and set of moral virtues conducive to the advance of "ideal" global capitalism, and to ensure that its institutions meet and, where appropriate, enhance, their social obligations.

9 They need to actively participate in the decisions of supra-national entities. They need to be better informed and more effective in their bargaining and/or mediatory skills at the international negotiating table.

10 They need to give more attention to encouraging entrepreneurship and the innovatory *et al.* contributions of small and medium-size enterprises.

11 They need to reconfigure their modes of governance to better respond to the premium placed by the new globality on such qualities as speed, flexibility, versatility and ability to deal with change and insecurity. In the words of Claude Smadja, "Managing the trade-off between unpredictability associated with flexibility and the desire for security will increasingly present *governments* a challenge" (Smadja 1999) (my italics).

12 Most of all, they need to avoid engaging in "beggar my neighbor" micro-management policies aimed at steering economic activity to their own territories. In the contemporary globalizing economy, both national and sub-national governments may be tempted to offer quite substantial fiscal *et al.* incentives to attract inbound foreign investment. Yet, all too frequently, these result in a series of locational tournaments from which no-one benefits except, of course, the investing firms and/or governments (UN 1998).

Table 1.6 summarizes some of my views about the likely consequences of global capitalism for the role of national and sub-national governments in policy formation. It will be seen that while I believe that, for the most part, the macro-organizational and ethos forming role of national governments is tending to increase or remain about the same; at the same time, at least, some of these functions are being taken over by sub-national administrations. By contrast, the leeway of national governments to pursue independent *macro-economic* policies is being diminished by the increasing cross-border mobility of both financial and real capital.

Supra-national entities

Let me now turn to consider Figure 1.5. It is generally accepted that economic globalization will increase the role of supra-national entities. Such

Table 1.6 The impact of global capitalism on the role of national and sub-national governments

Actions	The dimensions of global capitalism					Level of governance	
	Knowledge	Alliance	Spatial	MIR	MF	National	Sub-national
1 Macro-economic policies	0	0	?	–	+	–	0
2 Macro-organizational policies							
Trade	0	0	–	–	+	–	0
Innovation	+	+	0	0	+	+	+
Education	+	+	0	+	+	+	+
FDI	0	+	?	–	+	–	+
Transport and communication	+	+	+	+	+	+	+
Industrial	+	0	–	–	+	–	0
Regional	+	0	0	–	+	+	+
Competition	0	+	–	–	–	–	0
Fiscal	0	0	?	0	+	–	+
Labor	+	0	+	+	+	+	+
Environment	0	0	–	–	+	+	0
3 Ethos forming/encouragement	+	+	+	–	+	+	0

Source: Author's perception.

key: + = Increased role
0 = No change in role
– = Reduced role
? = Uncertain
MIR = Market intervening/replacing
MF = Market facilitating

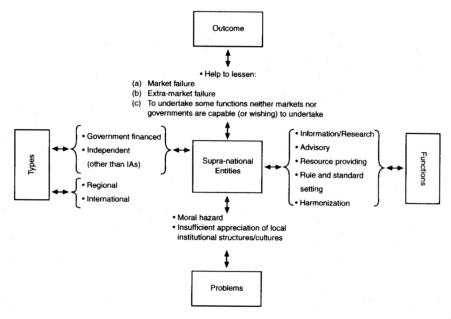

Figure 1.5 Supra-national institutions or the G.C. diamond

entities embrace a wide organizational spectrum, e.g. from formally con-
stituted regional bodies (e.g. EU) to purely advisory institutions, e.g.
UNCTAD. Why is this so? Why, in fact, do we need supra-national entities?
I would suggest there are three main reasons:

1   Because national or sub-national governmental regimes are unable, or
     unwilling, to deal with various types of market or extra-market failures
     in cross-border transactions, particularly those which are associated
     with the activities of MNEs, and/or those of international NGOs.
2   Because national or sub-national governments may themselves behave
     in a way which: (i) structurally distorts market or extra-market transac-
     tions; and/or (ii) creates or exacerbates endemic market failure;
     and/or (iii) initiates a range of non-economic policies which may
     have adverse consequences on the efficient operation of markets.
3   Because national or sub-national governments, on their own, may not
     have the leverage to implement the appropriate social policies to
     cushion some of the more damaging effects of the global marketplace
     on the wellbeing of their constituents.

To what extent, then, are supra-national entities equipped to meet the
demands of an either actual or "ideal" global capitalism? Can such entities

adopt more regionally or globally integrated strategies? Should they? Consider the role of two spatial levels of supra-national entities, viz. the regional and the international.[16]

First, regional entities. There are a plethora of these, which vary considerably in their scope and modes of governance. Much has been written on the costs and benefits of regional economic integration;[17] and I will not repeat them here. I would, however, make three points:

1   Essentially any form of regional integration suggests sacrifice of *some* degree of national autonomy in decision taking. This sacrifice is presumably though a worthwhile price to pay by the participating nations to gain the (perceived) economic and social benefits from the liberalization of intra-regional markets.
2   The costs and benefits of economic globalization I earlier identified no less apply at a regional level. However, the scale, content and distribution of these costs and benefits may be different. So, too, may the form of the governance of regional authorities, and the ease or difficulty with which participating nations can reach agreement on critical issues.
3   Regional integration may be seen either as part of, or a stepping stone towards, global capitalism,[18] or as an alternative to it. Much will depend on the policies pursued by the regional authority in respect of its transactions with the rest of the world. If, taking an extreme case, regional integration leads to the abolition of all intra-regional trade and FDI barriers, but the retention or increase in such barriers against other nations or regions, then, while regionalization may have been advanced, globalization will not have been. (This, incidentally is the scenario which scholars such as Alan Rugman fear will happen in the next decade or so (Rugman 2000).) If, by contrast, regional economic integration also leads to a reduction in *inter*-regional trade and FDI barriers, then regionalization and globalization may be regarded as complements to each other. In any case, supra-regional authorities may need to treat the actions of regional authorities in exactly the same way as they do with national or sub-national authorities.[19]

Next, then, we examine the likely impact of global capitalism on the role of supra-national entities. Here it may be helpful to distinguish between four groups of entities.

1   Those which are primarily *resource providers* and are currently *multi-domestic* in their outlook and policies. Examples include the IMF and the World Bank. Recent experience (e.g. the Asian economic crisis) has demonstrated that these entities would do well to take better account of (a) the distinctive characteristics of national or regional capitalist systems, and (b) the extent to which and the ways in which

these systems are converging, or are not converging. To do this, such entities almost certainly need additional resources, which only national governments can provide.

2   Those which are primarily *rule or standard setters*, and which tend to view their functions from a *more global perspective*. But, as yet, only a few such entities exist. The leading example is that of WTO, whose brief may, in due course, be extended to some non-trade areas, e.g. foreign direct investment, intellectual property rights, the environment and competition policy.[20] Is the attention of existing entities likely to be increasingly directed to resolving conflicts of interest between macro regions, as it is between nation states? Does the extension of rules of the game demanded by global capitalism require new entities? In the finance field the answer is probably "yes."[21] More generally, is a new umbrella entity, e.g. a World Economic Organization, needed? Is it possible? Is it desirable? Certainly the idea of globalizing the concept of *public* goods (and bads) by encouraging inter-government cooperation, and the setting up of new institutions charged with the task of ensuring that such goods are provided with minimum market and/or institutional failure, is favoured by several economists notably Amartya Sen, Joseph Stiglitz and Jeffrey Sachs (Karl, Grunberg and Stern 1999).

3   Those which are primarily *coordinators of action* pursued by national or regional extra-market institutions. These tend to be issue oriented entities, e.g. those concerned with the environment, intellectual, law and order, health, air traffic control and so on. Here there is some evidence that more globally coordinated strategies are being pursued.

4   Those which act as a *focal point for information gathering, research, dialogue and an exchange of views* among the national participants; and on occasions to take supra-national action which affects the global or regional allocation of economic activity. Examples include the UN (and its various agencies) and the OECD, whose role is currently being redefined in the light of contemporary events.

I would assert that each of the four kinds of supra-national entities needs to better recognize that those kinds of market or institutional failure, which are unique to global capitalism, cannot fully be resolved either by spontaneously generated action on the part of the market participants or by more formal norms and rules set down by national governments or regional authorities. This is particularly the case with capital flows which are both huge and subject to extreme volatility. Only by appropriate international macro-stabilization policies, and by the encouragement of national policies designed to reduce short-term speculative capital movements, and to combat the moral hazards inherent in some transactions, can this be achieved. At the same time, there is pressure from many quarters for a greater transparency and accountability (not to mention democratization) of some supra-national entities – and particularly those which are re-evaluating their roles in the light of globalization. Finally, as David Henderson (1999) has observed à propos the MAI negotiations, there needs to be much more commitment on the part of national governments to effect the gains of multilateral arrangements; not to mention abiding by the existing rules of the multilateral trading system, e.g. by self-imposed codes of good behavior introduced by multinational enterprises (MNEs).

The moral imperatives

Yet, when all is said and done – and even if the main institutions of global capitalism are technically capable of performing efficiently, there remains the issue of social acceptability of the system and its underpinning moral framework. Among others, Ralf Dahrendorf, Hans Küng and Claude Smadja have consistently argued that unrestrained globalization might well tax the social integration mechanisms of societies and lead to the exclusion of a considerable number of people from its benefits. This, in turn, could lead to mounting conflicts between "the haves" and the "have nots," and endanger the very social cohesion which proponents of globalization assert that it advances. This, indeed, as I have already pointed out is one of the – and perhaps *the* – critical challenges of globalization, which not only requires some recognition of existing institutions, but the revitalization and reconstruction of the existing moral order. So let me, finally, turn to Figure 1.6, which shows how I believe the moral dimension can shape the working of the capitalistic system, and the attitude of individuals and institutions to improving it.

In particular, I suggest that the framework should consist of three building blocks, each of which represent the presence or absence of three sets of virtues which are especially germane to global capitalism, viz. *creativity* (essential for the upgrading of intellectual capital), *cooperation* (without which alliance capitalism cannot succeed) and *compassion* (an integral part of the globalization of social justice, and of the stability and cohesiveness of societies). Further details are set out in Table 1.7. It is the extent to which these virtues can be translated into the ideologies and actions of the four main institutions of global capitalism, which will ultimately determine its success or failure.[22] The reasoning behind this statement is set out in the following three propositions:

1   Over the long haul, in democratic societies, global capitalism can only work at the suffrage of their electorates. If, however, the majority of the electorate perceive they, or others for whom they feel responsible, do not benefit from global capitalism, in the way they believe they should, they can vote for – or take other action to promote – some alternative social order.

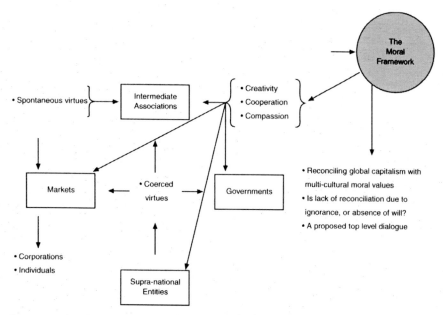

Figure 1.6 The moral underpinnings of the G.C. diamond

Table 1.7 What are the particular moral virtues which a knowledge- and alliance-based globalizing economy demands?

(a) *Intellectual capital* (Creativity)
Imagination, individual initiative, an entrepreneurial spirit, perseverance, a willingness to learn and upgrade one's intellectual assets, self-discipline, self-confidence and self-respect.
(b) *Alliance capitalism* (Cooperation)
Trust, spontaneous social responsibility, forbearance, probity, reciprocity, an ability to compromise, adaptability, group loyalty, an appreciation of the common good, and a respect for the goals, opinions and judgements of others.
(c) *Global geography* (Compassion)
A sense of fairness and justice, an awareness of, and respect for, the needs and rights of others – particularly those in least developed countries – brotherly love, stewardship, neighborliness, generosity of spirit.

2 It then follows that perceived economic inclusiveness and social justice must be an integral part of the objectives of global capitalism if it is to flourish.
3 But these goals can only be achieved if there is a strong and sympathetic moral ethos pervading all institutions and governance structures.

What is the justification for these propositions? Consider the following points:

- Throughout history, most, if not all, successful economies have been initiated and girded by a strong moral ethos, albeit the contents of which have been country or time specific. And frequently, these same economies collapsed when this moral foundation was undermined.[23]
- In the past, new social orders or new trajectories in economic progress have frequently been preceded by a reconfiguration of a renewed attention on existing moral cultures, as, for example, was the case in Biblical times and in nineteenth-century western Europe. However, as we enter the new millennium it would seem that the (appropriate) order of the social capital of many societies is lagging behind that of scientific, technological and organizational developments.

How might moral virtues – and particularly those germane to the three "C"s – be promoted? Although I would like to think this could be achieved by spontaneous, i.e. voluntary, action on the part of individuals, families and institutions, I am sufficiently a realist to accept that externally imposed codes, rules, laws and sanctions by governments and supra-national entities must also play a critical part.[24]

But exactly *who* should be responsible for initiating and practicing moral virtues? Consider two approaches to answering this question: (i) the "top-down" approach; and (ii) the "bottom-up" approach. The top-down approach suggests that the responsibility to promote the three "C"s and their ingredients rests primarily with supra-national entities and national governments. This approach embraces the direct or indirect promotion of such virtues, and implementation of penalties and sanctions against individuals and institutions behaving in an unvirtuous way. The points in favor of it are that governments and, at least some supra-national entities, have the authority, and can acquire the necessary resources to put ethically justifiable social *et al.* programs into action.

But there are also drawbacks to this approach. One is that coercive action is always second best. Another is that incentive and social welfare schemes may encourage moral hazard among their beneficiaries. It may lead to an abrogation of personal responsibility and self-discipline; and, in some cases, lead to libertarianism. It opens up distance, i.e. reduces connectivity, between those who define the moral virtues and those expected to abide by them.[25]

By contrast, a bottom-up approach is based on the presumption that, to be effective, the adoption of moral virtues must be the spontaneous and voluntary decision of individuals, families and institutions. Indeed, some commentators would argue that the market is, itself, a highly moral institution depending as it does on its participants practicing such virtues as honoring promises, respecting property and taking responsibility for one's actions (Barry 1999). Others, e.g. Soras (1998), Sacks (1999) disagree, and contend that without some form of extra-market rules, norms and values, the integrity of a transactional market economy cannot be preserved.[26] These principles stem from various sources, including the teaching and moral suasion of religious and educational leaders, the printed word, familiar structures, corporate values[27] and by the behavioral mores of society as a whole.[28] The main advantage of such an approach is that, in democratic capitalism, voluntarism is normally to be preferred to the imposition of sanctions; while there are few of the cons attributable to the top-down approach.

On the other hand, only so many welfare enhancing goals can be accomplished by voluntarism; there is the "free rider" problem; and finally, if it is to flourish, individual liberty must be linked to some form of communitarism (Etzioni 1996). But when all is said and done, does not global capitalism need a global ethic (Kung 1998)? Is, indeed, such an ethic feasible? Are there fundamental or core values that cross national boundaries and which are acceptable to both Western, and non-Western cultural and religious traditions. Tom Donaldson (1996) is certainly one who believes that there are, and that such values should provide a moral compass for business practices (I would add that governments, supra-national entities, IAs, consumers, and other market participants, no less need such a compass).

As things stand at the moment, the epicenter of global capitalism is the triad of North America, Western Europe and Japan. But they are not the epicenter of the planet's social norms or moral codes. Two issues of related interest then arise. First, to what extent is the integration of multi-domestic capitalism likely to be constrained by differing interpretations of the content and significance of moral free space.[29] Will global capitalism adapt to multiple ethical conventions; or will the latter become more harmonized? And, if so, in what direction?

Second, there is the question as to whether "ideal" global capitalism can accommodate substantially different religious or ethnic mores (Huntington 1996). Is it possible to design an overarching global ethic – but one which can accommodate and respect different non-core cultural *et al.* values? For if, instead of uniting nations by a common pursuit of democratically acceptable wealth creation and distribution, it divides nations with different ethical mores, then it is possible such capitalism will be rejected at the global ballot box (or by less democratic means). However, it may well be that insensitive attitudes towards cross-cultural differences arise from ignorance. If this is so, a top level dialogue between the upholders and practitioners of different religious traditions and moral values may have some merit. The purpose of the dialogue would be to see if it were possible to identify and give operational substance to a universal code of moral virtues; and to examine and perhaps map the contours of moral free space. Moreover, such a dialogue should be a continuing one as the interpretation of the context absolute and contextual moral values and the boundaries between them is constantly changing. After all, since it is human beings – rather than physical assets – are the main instruments by which new wealth is created, organized and distributed, it is critical to nurture the intellectual, social and spiritual qualities which determine their willingness and ability to best achieve this goal.[30]

Conclusions

Let me now briefly summarize the main thrust of my thoughts. Figure 1.7 links together the kinds of inadequacies of contemporary markets and institutions, and the moral behavior underlying these, which, in our opinion, need to be tackled if global capitalism is to succeed and be continually upgraded. I believe the contents of this figure are self-explanatory. Table 1.8 further illustrates these points by looking at some of the failures which were brought to light by the recent Asian crisis and which still beset Russia. As can be seen, there is no one single reason why "actual" capitalism of the late 1990s is not delivering the kinds of benefits expected of it. Rather, there are a multiplicity of interconnected deficiencies in the various ingredients of capitalism, each of which needs to be

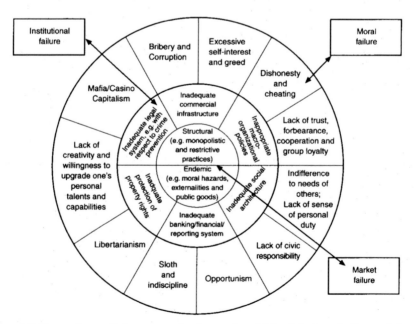

Figure 1.7 Illustrations of three perceived ways in which global capitalism might fail

Table 1.8 Illustrations of four "failures" of global capitalism as revealed in the case of recent economic events in seven countries

	Japan	Korea	Indonesia	Thailand	Hong Kong	Malaysia	Russia
Managerial failure							
• Imprudent risk management*	X	X	X	X	X	X	X
• Misjudgement of economic conditions/trends	X	X	X	X	X	X	X
Market failure							
• Moral hazard*		X	X	X	X	X	
• Inappropriate macro-economic policies*	X	X	X	X	X		X
• Excessive speculation (land and stock market)	X						
• Overvalued currency/tied exchange rates*				X	X		
• Bad timing of short-term debt*		X		X			
• A presence of a strong black market			X				X
• Contagion affect					X	X	
Institutional failure							
• Inappropriate regulatory/supervisory system	X	X	X	X	X	X	X
• Inadequate banking system	X	X		X			X
• Inadequate legal (et al.) infrastructure	X		X	X		X	X
• Inappropriate financial system*	X	X	X	X		X	
• Inadequate protection of property rights		X	X				
• Lack of transparency/inadequate accounting standards	X	X	X	X		X	X
Moral failure							
• Crony/mafia capitalism*	X		X		X	X	X
• Bribery and corruption	X	X	X	X			X
• Lack of trust/social responsibility*		X	X			X	X
• Excessive greed of investors/institutions*		X			X	X	X

* At an international level as well as a domestic level

addressed – and addressed as holistically as possible – if anything approaching optimal, or "ideal," capitalism is to be reached.

It is, then, my contention that the answer to "Whither global capitalism?" – or perhaps, more appropriately, "What must be done if global capitalism is to survive and prosper?" – rests on a number of conditions being fulfilled. First is recognition of the fact that since human beings – rather than physical assets – are the main instruments by which new wealth is created, organized and distributed, it is critical to nurture the intellectual, social and spiritual qualities which determine their willingness and ability to best achieve this goal. Second is that means are found, by both private and public institutions, of overcoming the more deleterious economic and social consequences of global volatility and change.

The third condition is that national governments need to promote the appropriate macro-economic and macro-organizational policies which are consistent with the promotion of efficient and socially acceptable global capitalism. Fourth, suitable adjustments require to be made to the structure and content of institutions – especially financial institutions – which might (i) improve risk management, (ii) foster more efficient, accountable and transparent transactions in the global marketplace, (iii) and reduce moral hazard. Fifth, supra-national entities should be given sufficient authority or persuasive powers to encourage, and where appropriate enforce, a minimum standard of institutional infrastructure across nations, and the adoption of "best practice" macro-economic and management policies on the part of national governments.

Sixth, while applauding the rich mosaic of different capitalist modes throughout the world, such pluralism needs to be directed to ensuring the benefits of the global capitalism are greater than the sum of its parts. And seventh, it is necessary for individual and social moral virtues to be strengthened and reconfigured in a way which is both consistent with a knowledge-intensive, alliance-based, multi-cultural society, and which will best enable markets and extra-market institutions to work together to promote efficient growth and social justice. Only then will the global marketplace be an acceptable servant of individuals and society, and not an unacceptable master.

So, "Whither global capitalism?" *Is* global capitalism at bay? Is it likely to be? Perhaps the most one can realistically hope for is a step beyond both euphoria and globaphobia; and a real appreciation of the social and moral imperatives which need to be addressed and resolved if what is, perhaps, the most promising form of wealth creation the world has ever known is not to sew the seeds of its own destruction.

APPENDIX

Table A.1.1 Indicators of extent to which a country is globally involved: FDI[1] to GDP ratio

Order	Country	1980	1990	1995	1996	1996/1980 (1980 = 100)
1	Singapore	7.1	51.1	52.9	56.2	791.5
2	Hong Kong	3.4	18.6	55.8	43.8	1288.2
3	Netherlands	18.3	33.6	35.0	39.8	217.5
4	Belg/Lux	5.2	23.6	27.1	38.6	742.3
5	Switzerland	18.1	22.0	32.9	33.6	185.6
6	New Zealand	8.2	13.2	28.0	33.2	404.9
7	Malaysia	13.5	19.2	32.4	31.7	234.8
8	UK	13.6	23.0	28.0	25.6	188.2
9	Canada	14.4	16.7	20.0	21.7	150.7
10	Sweden	3.6	13.5	23.6	21.0	583.3
11	Australia	4.9	18.1	21.4	20.7	422.4
12	Chile	1.7	16.9	13.6	16.4	964.7
13	Norway	1.2	10.1	14.4	15.5	1291.7
14	Ireland	9.8	8.5	13.4	14.1	143.9
15	Denmark	4.7	6.4	12.3	13.2	280.9
16	Indonesia	7.1	18.3	12.8	12.9	181.7
17	Spain	2.8	8.3	11.8	12.4	442.9
18	France	3.2	8.2	10.7	11.6	362.5
19	Mexico	2.2	6.7	13.4	11.5	522.7
20	Finland	1.2	6.1	9.5	10.7	891.7
21	Taiwan	3.0	7.1	9.3	9.7	323.3
22	USA	5.8	7.6	8.8	9.4	162.1
23	Germany	5.5	8.8	8.4	9.2	167.3
24	Venezuela	1.3	5.3	6.7	9.1	700.0
25	Italy	1.8	5.2	7.2	9.0	500.0
26	South Africa	13.4	7.6	7.7	8.8	65.7
27	Greece	5.7	9.0	8.5	8.7	152.6
28	Brazil	3.6	4.5	9.5	7.6	211.1
29	Austria	2.6	4.9	6.8	7.2	276.9
30	Thailand	1.5	4.9	5.9	6.8	453.3
31	Portugal	2.5	4.2	5.4	4.9	196.0
32	Japan	1.1	3.7	2.5	3.2	290.9
33	Korea	1.0	1.6	2.2	2.7	270.0
34	Hungary	N/A	3.2	16.4	17.2	N/A
35	China	N/A	2.1	10.3	13.7	N/A
36	Czech Rep.	N/A	0.5	4.6	7.2	N/A
	World	9.7	15.9	20.0	21.4	220.6

Source: UN, various editions of *World Investment Report* (an annual publication).

N/A – Not available

1 Inward + outward investment as a percentage of GDP

Table A.1.2 Indicators of extent to which a country is globally involved: trade[1] to GDP ratio

Order	Country	1980	1990	1995	1996	1996/1980 (1980 = 100)
1	Hong Kong	104.1	129.0	151.7	142.3	136.7
2	Singapore	206.9	151.0	142.0	136.3	65.9
3	Malaysia	44.9	81.8	97.4	91.5	203.8
4	Ireland	55.2	57.1	72.8	74.2	134.4
5	Belg/Lux	58.0	67.0	65.0	66.1	114.0
6	Netherlands	44.9	51.9	50.0	50.9	113.4
7	Philippines	26.0	30.4	40.3	46.9	180.4
8	Taiwan	53.1	33.1	46.4	46.4	87.4
9	Thailand	23.5	37.9	44.9	42.2	179.6
10	Austria	27.3	88.1	38.8	41.1	150.5
11	Hungary	40.2	29.8	35.5	39.7	98.8
12	Canada	24.2	25.4	36.3	37.2	153.7
13	Sweden	26.2	29.7	37.7	36.6	139.7
14	Norway	30.9	37.4	35.1	36.3	117.5
15	Korea	34.2	30.0	33.6	34.4	100.6
16	Finland	29.8	23.8	33.5	34.0	114.1
17	Switzerland	32.5	36.0	33.1	34.0	104.6
18	Denmark	27.0	33.3	33.3	33.0	122.2
19	Portugal	32.0	34.5	31.5	31.8	99.4
20	Mexico	10.4	19.2	29.1	31.4	301.9
21	UK	22.5	25.5	28.7	29.6	131.6
22	Chile	24.9	33.0	29.6	29.2	117.3
23	Venezuela	25.5	29.8	24.0	29.0	113.7
24	New Zealand	23.3	27.3	29.1	28.3	121.5
25	South Africa	30.1	22.6	25.1	26.9	89.4
26	Poland	29.7	25.1	24.8	26.2	88.2
27	Indonesia	23.4	26.2	27.0	26.1	111.5
28	Spain	13.8	18.8	23.9	25.1	181.9
29	Germany	23.2	30.8	22.5	23.3	100.4
30	France	18.9	22.6	22.3	22.8	120.6
31	Australia	14.3	17.1	20.1	19.8	138.5
32	Greece	22.0	22.4	20.0	19.4	88.2
33	China	6.3	15.1	19.5	17.4	276.2
34	USA	9.1	10.3	11.9	12.0	131.9
35	India	8.3	8.3	7.5	9.8	118.1
36	Japan	12.7	10.3	8.7	9.7	76.4

Source: UN, various editions of *Statistical Yearbook*.

1 Exports + imports as a percentage of GDP

NOTES

I am most grateful for the comments and constructive suggestions made by H. Peter Gray, Robert Heilbroner, Steve Kobrin and David Robertson on an earlier draft of this chapter.

1 For a discussion of the differences between various capitalist systems – and particularly the way in which extra-market institutions exercise control, or

adjust to the imperatives of the market system, see Chandler (1990), Lazonick (1991), McCraw (1997), and Groenewegen (1997). Chandler, for example, refers to the US style of capitalism as "competitive managerial," to the UK style as "personal" and to the German style as "cooperative managerial." Various adjectives have been used to portray Japanese style capitalism. These include "competitive communitarism," "human capitalism," and "relational capitalism." Taiwan's capitalism has been referred to as "familial," Korea's as "statist" and France's as "Colbertian" or "hierarchical," and China's as "socialist"!

2   Intangible wealth includes such products as protection of the environment, the provision of social services, and the reduction of crime. It will be noted that this is a much broader definition of economic welfare than that contained in gross domestic or gross national product (GDP or GNP). Indeed, I suspect that much of the future debate about the merits or demerits of global capitalism will centre on the goals one is seeking to achieve, rather than the best means by which any particular set of goals may be advanced. In other words, any evaluation of the costs and benefits of globalization will increasingly reflect the cultural and ideological perspectives of the evaluators! For some examples, see Levy (1999).

3   Each of these conditions, it will be noted, were emphasized, e.g. by Adam Smith and others, as being necessary for the successful pursuit of market-based (national) capitalism of the late eighteenth and nineteenth centuries.

4   For other, but similar, definitions see, e.g. Kilminster (1997), Kobrin (1997) and Gundlach and Nunnenkamp (1998).

5   For a more skeptical view on the distinctiveness of economic globalization, see Hirst and Thompson (1996) and Kleinknecht and ter Wengel (1998).

6   As set out by several authors in Dunning (2000).

7   In cases where regional trading and investment bloc are formed, and which encourage intra-regional economic transactions but impose tariff or non-tariff barriers on inter-regional transactions, such regionalization is (we would argue) best described as regionalism. For a recent discussion on the trend toward regionalism, see Rugman (2000).

8   As is clearly seen in such regional associations such as the European Union and OECD, and in such international institutions such as the WTO and various UN agencies. Witness, for example, the recent failure of the Multilateral Agreement on Investment (MAI) and the breakdown of the WTO discussions in Seattle.

9   Using data from the World Development Report (1997) it can be shown that those countries classified as *upper middle income* in 1980 increased their GNPs per head at a faster rate than those classified as *high income* countries in that year.

10   In his own words "markets are the best way we know of structuring exchanges – goods to be bought and sold. They are far from the best way of ordering relationships or preserving goods whose value is not identical with their price" (Sacks, 1999, p. 53).

11   By way of "command" strategies or by intervention in the workings of the market (e.g. by regulatory and other means).

12   Sylvia Ostry (2000) for example writes about international non-governmental organizations or INGOs.

13   See, e.g. Scholte, Obrien and Williams (1999).

14   For example, one useful exercise might be to examine the affect of NGOs on the flows of FDI following the breakdown of the MAI agreement; at the same time this would best wait until the repercussions of the breakdown of the MAI talks are fully known.

15   For a recent examination of these tasks see various chapters in Dunning (1997).

16 Strictly speaking, one also ought to address the various kinds of bilateral eco-
    nomic arrangements which countries might conclude with each other.
    However, space precludes us from doing this. Data on the extent and composi-
    tion of bilateral investment treaties are, for example, given in the annual *World
    Investment Reports* published by the UN. See, for example, UN (1998).
17 For a comprehensive examination of these, see Jovanovic (1997).
18 For example, as part of their globalization programs, MNEs frequently pursue
    regional production strategies (Rugman 2000).
19 Thus it is quite possible (indeed, from recent history, this appears all too
    likely) that the WTO will be faced with as many dispute cases between the EU
    and (say) the US and Japan, as it will between the member states of the EU
    and those countries.
20 Here especially, thorny issues arise. For example, to what extent may the
    harmonization of environmental standards be perceived to impose a non-tariff
    barrier to exports from developing countries who may be forced to incur costs
    in meeting these standards? For an examination on the role of the WTO in
    helping to promote multilateral investment liberalization, see Brewer and
    Young (1999). For a discussion of the reasons why the WTO failed to come to
    an accord on a multilateral investment agreement, see Kobrin (1998).
21 See for example, IMF (1997), Soros (1998), Lloyd (1999) and Messner (1999).
22 It will be observed that different varieties of capitalism possess these virtues to
    a greater or lesser extent. Thus US style capitalism is relatively strong on crea-
    tivity, but relatively weak on compassion; European capitalism is relatively
    stronger on cooperation and compassion; Japanese and Korean capitalism is
    particularly strong on cooperation but less strong on creativity; Chinese
    capitalism is also relatively strong on cooperation, but relatively weak on both
    creativity and compassion, and so on. At the same time, there are suggestions
    that economic globalization is leading to a convergence of at least some
    aspects of capitalism practiced by different countries (Jacoby 1998).
23 For a full analysis of this and related theses see, e.g. Landes (1998).
24 The intrusive use of mobile (cellular) telephones is one!
25 Such a criticism is less directed to sub-national governments and to many IAs.
26 As presupposed by Emile Durkheim many years ago (Durkheim 1938) and
    later by Friedrich von Hayek (1988).
27 Hirschman (1970) – referred to earlier – regarded loyalty as an important
    determinant of success of any voice strategy of firms and states to market
    failure. We would regard it as an important element of a successful voice
    response to moral failure.
28 These virtues make up what Francis Fukuyama in his latest book (Fukuyama
    1999) terms, social capital. He defines social capital as "a set of informal values
    or norms shared among members of a group which permits cooperation
    among them" (p. 16). Much of his treatise, which I only came across after com-
    pleting this chapter, is devoted to explaining how social capital needs to be
    upgraded and reconstituted if it is to meet the needs, and indeed influence
    the course, of contemporary economic, political and social events.
29 Another way of thinking of moral free space is that of situational ethical behav-
    ior. The real problem, however, is to identify the boundaries between core
    values, e.g. human dignity, respect for human rights, etc., and those which
    defy absolute prescriptions for behavior.
30 I am, of course, aware that many other institutions, notably the UN Commis-
    sion on Human Rights are actively engaged in pursuing many of these issues,
    but the idea of setting up a group of 7 or 8 (or whatever number) of religious
    et al. leaders is I think worth exploring.

REFERENCES

Barry, N. (1999), "The Market Still Adequate?" in Sacks J. *Morals and Markets*. London IEA. Occasional Paper No. 9, pp. 27–34.

Bartlett, G. and Lawrence, B. Z. (1998), *Globaphobia: Confronting Fears about Open Trade*, Washington: The Brookings Institution.

Ben-Ner, A. and Gui, B. (eds) (1993), *The Non-Profit Sector in the Mixed Economy*, Ann Arbor: University of Michigan Press.

Brewer, T. and Young S. (1999), "The World Trade Organization: Global Rule-maker," in Hood, N. and Young, S. (eds) *The Globalization of Multinational Enterprise Activity and Economic Development*, Basingstoke: Macmillan Press.

Chandler, A. D. Jr. (1990), *Scale and Scope: The Dynamics of Industrial Capitalism*, Cambridge, MA: Harvard University Press.

Donaldson, T. (1996), "Values in tension: ethics away from home," *Harvard Business Review*, Sept.–Oct., pp. 48–62.

Donaldson, T. and Dunfee, T. W. (1994), "Towards a United Conception of Business Ethics: integrative social contracts theory," *Academy of Management Review*, April.

Doremus, P. N., Keller, W. W., Pauly, L. W. and Reich, S. (1998), *The Myth of the Global Corporation*, Princeton, NJ: Princeton University Press.

Dunning, J. H. (ed.) (1997), *Governments, Globalization and International Business*, Oxford: Oxford University Press.

Dunning, J. H. (ed.) (2000), *Regions, Globalization and the Knowledge Based Economy*, Oxford: Oxford University Press.

Durkheim, E. (1938), *The Rules of Sociological Method*, Glencoe, Illinois: Free Press.

Etzioni, A. (1996), *The New Golden Rule*, New York: Basic Books.

Friedman, T. L. (1999), *The Lexus and the Olive Tree*, New York: Farrar, Straus and Giroux.

Fukuyama, F. (1999), *The Great Disruption*, London: Profile Books.

Gray, J. (1998), *False Dawn*, New York: The New Press.

Greider, W. (1997), *One World or Not: Ready or Not: The Manic Logic and Global Capitalism*, New York: Simon and Schuster.

Groenewegen, J. (1997), "Institutions of Capitalism: American, European and Japanese Systems Compared," *Journal of Economic Issues 31* (2), pp. 333–47.

Gunlach, E. and NunnenKamp, P. (1998), "Some consequences of globalization for developing countries," in Dunning, J. H. (ed.), *Globalization, Trade and Foreign Direct Investment*, Amsterdam: Elsevier, pp. 153–74.

Handy, C. (1997), *The Hungry Spirit*, London: Avon Books.

Hayek, F. A. (1988), *The Fatal Conceit: The Errors of Socialism*, Chicago: University of Chicago Press.

Heilbroner, R. L. (1992), *Twenty-first Century Capitalism*, London: UCL Press.

Henderson, D. (1999), *The MAI Affair: A Story and its Lessons*, Melbourne: Melbourne Business School, Felham Paper No. 5.

Himmelfarb, G. (1995), *The De-moralization of Society*, London: IEA Health and Welfare Unit Choice in Welfare No. 22.

Hirschman, A. (1970), *Exit, Voice and Loyalty: International Differences in Work-Related Values*, Cambridge, MA: Harvard University Press.

Hirst, P. and Thompson, G. (1996), *Globalization in Question*, Cambridge: Polity Press.

Huntington, S. P. (1996), *The Clash of Civilizations*, New York: Simon and Schuster.

IMF (1997), *World Economic Outlook: Globalization, Opportunities and Challenges*, Washington: International Monetary Fund, May.

Investment Canada (1990), *The Business Implications of Globalization*, Ottawa: Investment Canada Working Paper No. V.

Jacoby, S. M. (1998), *Welfare Capitalism in Japan and the United States*, Los Angeles, UCLA CIBER Working Papers 98–125.

Jovanovic, M. N. (1997), *International Economic Integration*, London and New York: Routledge, Critical Perspectives on the World Economy (4 volumes).

Kaul, I., Grunberg, I. and Stern, M. A. (1999), *Global Public Goods*, Oxford: Oxford University Press.

Kennedy, P. (1996), *Globalization and its Discontents. The 1996 Analysis Lecture*, London: BBC.

Kilminster, R. (1997), "Globalization as an emerging concept," in Scott, A. (ed.), *The Limits of Globalization. Cases and Arguments*, London and New York: Routledge, pp. 257–83.

Kleinknecht, A. and ter Wengel, J. (1998), "The myth of economic globalization," *Cambridge Journal of Economics 22*, pp. 637–47.

Kobrin, S. (1998), "The MAI and the clash of globalization," *Foreign Policy*.

Kobrin, S. (1997), "The architecture of globalization: State sovereignty in a networked global economy," in Dunning, J. H., *Governments, Globalization and International Business*, OUP, pp. 146–71.

Kung, H. (1998), *A Global Ethic for Global Politics*, New York and Oxford: Oxford University Press.

Landes, D. (1988), *The Wealth and Poverty of Nations*, London: Little, Brown and Co.

Lazonick, W. (1991), *Business Organization and the Myth of the Market Economy*, Cambridge: Cambridge University Press.

Levy, B. (1999), *Global Good Governance in the Age of Globalization and Issues and Policy Implications*, Ottawa Faculty of Administration Working Paper, 99-30, September.

Lloyd P. J. (1999), Economic dynamics and the new millennium: the architecture of the multinational organizations, *Journal of Asian Economies 10*, pp. 211–36.

Luttwak, E. (1999), *Turbo-Capitalism*, New York: Harper-Collins.

Markusen, A. (1996), "Sticky places in slippery space: a typology of industrial districts," *Economic Geography 72* (3), pp. 293–313.

Martin, H. P. and Schumann, H. (1997), *The Global Trap*, London and New York: Zed Books.

McCraw, T. K. (1997), *Creating Modern Capitalism*, Cambridge: Harvard University Press.

Messner, D. (1999), "Towards a new Bretton Woods," *Development and Cooperation 1*, 4–5, 19.

Osborne, D. and Gaebler, T. (1992), *Reinventing Government: How the Entrepreneurial Spirit is Transforming the Public Sector*, Reading, Mass.: Addison Wesley.

Ostry, S. (2000), "Convergence and sovereignty: policy scope for compromise," in Prakash, A. and Hart, J. A. (eds), *Coping with Globalization*, pp. 52–76. London and New York: Routledge.

Prakash, A. (1999), *Governance and Economic Globalization: Continuities and Discontinuities*, Washington D. C.: Washington University, School of Business and Public Management.

Rifkin, J. (1995), *The End of Work*, New York: G. P. Putman's Sons.

Rodrik, D. (1997), *Has Globalization Gone too Far?*, Washington: Institute for International Economics.

Rugman, A. (2000), "Multinational enterprises and the end of global strategy," in Dunning, J. H. and Mucchielli, J. L. (eds), *Multinational Firms' Strategies and the New Global Competition*, Reading: Harwood Academic Publishers, (forthcoming).

Sachs, J. and Warner, A. (1995), *Economic Convergence and Economic Policies*, Cambridge, MA: NBER Working Paper No. 5039.

Sacks, J. (1999), "Morals and Markets," London: IEA Occasional Paper, No. 109.

Salamon, L. M. and Anheier, H. K. (1997), *Defining the Non-Profit Sector*, Manchester (UK): Manchester University Press.

Scholte, J. A., Obrien, R. and Williams, M. (1999), "The WTO and Civil Society," *Journal of World Trade 33* (1), pp. 107–23.

Searle, G. R. (1998), *Morality and the Market in Victorian Britain*, Oxford: The Clarendon Press.

Smadja, C. (1999), "Living dangerously," *Time*, February 22, 1999.

Smart, T. (1998), "Globalization: a dream or a deadly fantasy?," *International Herald Tribune*, November 10.

Soros, G. (1998), *The Crisis of Global Capitalism*, London: Little Brown and Company.

UN (1998), *World Investment Report 1998: Trends and Determinants*, Geneva and New York: UN.

Van Til, J. (1998), *Mapping the Third Sector – Voluntarism in a Changing Social Economy*, Washington DC: Foundation Center.

Vernon, R. (1998), *In the Hurricane's Eye: The Troubled Prospects of Multinational Enterprises*, Cambridge, Mass.: Harvard University Press.

World Bank (1997), World Development Report 1997, Oxford: Oxford University Press.

2 The Christian response to global capitalism

Introduction

It is, I believe, entirely appropriate that in this holy city of Jerusalem – the crucible and meeting place of three of the world's great religions – that we should reflect for a little while on the attitudes and responses of the Christian, Jewish and Moslem communities to the emergence of global capitalism; and of the opinions and actions which religious leaders (as contrasted with economists and politicians) might take, or prescribe might be taken, to ensure that the ideologies, values and institutions which they cherish, are nourished, rather than eroded, by contemporary economic events.

Before proceeding further, I would like to make four introductory points. First, there is a great deal of common ground between the ethical and behavioral norms of the three mono-religious traditions represented here today; and, indeed, between those of other religions, whatever their beliefs may be. In each and every case, there is a ready acceptance that, if the global capitalism is to operate as intended, it must be buttressed by a strong moral code guiding both personal and institutional behavior. Second, while I fully recognize that such a code and patterns of behavior are fashioned by particular religious dogmas and teachings, I do not intend to get involved in a theological debate; it is not necessary for the points I wish to make. Nor, for the most part, will I seek to distinguish between the teachings of various branches of the Christian Church.

Third, I shall be concerned less with the Christian response to market-based capitalism *per se*, and more with the unique aspects of *global* capitalism, and the particular opportunities and challenges it offers. Fourth, in my consideration of the nature and content of global markets, I shall concentrate on those features germane to the attitudes and behavior of individuals, firms, governments and civil interest groups as they affect, and are affected by, these markets. This being so, I shall not deal with macro-economic issues (critical as they may be) but rather with the micro-management of wealth creation, and the distribution of the benefits arising from it.

My remarks will be divided into three sections. The first will describe the main characteristics of three phases of market-based capitalism as they have evolved in Western economies over the last three or more centuries; and how these characteristics have fashioned, and been fashioned by, not only by the market system *per se*, but by the political, legal and commercial institutions underpinning it; and by the ethical norms driving human behavior. Secondly, I will outline the Christian response to the advent of global capitalism and, as you might expect, I shall assess these primarily from the criteria of a number of virtues stressed in the Bible – especially in the New Testament – and, most notably, those of creativity, personal responsibility, respect for both people and the environment, social justice and empathy for the poor and underprivileged. I shall identify several options open to Christians and Christian leaders to influence the contemporary moral climate, and to best ensure that global capitalism advances economic welfare and social harmony. However, I shall also argue that in our multicultural societies, it is only by the combined wisdom of the leaders of the main religious traditions, and the acceptance and practice, by ordinary men and women, of a common set of virtues that this goal be can be achieved. Section 4 will summarize my conclusions.

The three phases of capitalism

In this section, I shall identify four of the critical ingredients of market-based capitalism, and will show how the content and form of these ingredients has evolved over the past three centuries, and especially with the advent of the globalizing economy. I shall also describe the main changes which have taken place in the moral milieu over this time. The three phases of Western capitalism, which were earlier set out in Table 1.1, (p. 15), are: (i) the pre-modern era of land-based and merchant capitalism (up to the end of the eighteenth century); (ii) industrial and finance capitalism (nineteenth to mid-twentieth century); and (iii) the contemporary phase of global capitalism.

The four characteristics of these phases of capitalism, also set out in Table 1.1, are:

1   the dominant (but not exclusive) form of wealth creation;
2   the main organizational and institutional modes by which wealth is created, utilized and distributed;
3   the spatial, or geographical, dimension of economic activity; and
4   the moral virtues which have tended to underpin each stage of capitalism.

Stage 1

As can be seen, in the first phase, the dominant source of commercial wealth[1] was the land and mercantile commerce. Upwards of 80 percent of the output generated in Europe and the US in medieval times came directly or indirectly from the land, agricultural labor and colonizing and trading activities. The main organizational mode of wealth creation and utilization was feudalism, set within a macro-economic framework of mercantilism; although there were some relatively free markets for simple manufactured goods, and for locally produced crafts. While there was some cross-border trade in minerals, precious metals and agricultural products, the spatial focus of economic activity was primarily local or national. This was an era in which street markets, domestic fairs and bazaars flourished on the basis of inter-personal knowledge and trust (North 1981, 1993). The moral foundations for such capitalism were the values of obedience, loyalty, discipline and self-sacrifice.

Stage 2

The industrial revolution heralded the first major watershed in Western capitalism. During the nineteenth and for much of the twentieth century, the basis of wealth shifted from the land to tangible *created* assets, namely machines, buildings and financial capital; and increasingly to a more educated and better trained workforce, and to innovatory activities. By the mid-twentieth century, the agricultural sector of most advanced economies was accounting for less than 10 percent of their gross domestic pro-ducts (GDPs). At the same time, the organization of economic activity moved out of the hands of individual entrepreneurs to private corporations and to public bodies. In so doing, hierarchical forms of governance and impersonal contacts, superseded those of inter-personal transactions and master–servant relationships. This, together with advances in transport and communications technologies, widened the geographical boundaries of economic activity to embrace cross-border buyers and sellers.

Stage 3

While in some economies – particularly emerging developing economies – the characteristics of these two stages of capitalism still persist, for most of the industrial world, the last two decades has seen the emergence of a new phase in capitalism, which, as I shall seek to show, is having a profound affect on Christian attitude towards wealth creation and distribution. By the late 1990s, intellectual capital of all kinds had replaced machine power and finance as the primary vehicle for increasing both tangible and intangible assets. Services had replaced goods as the main output of economic activity. Hierarchical forms of organization were being supplemented by non-hierarchical inter-firm alliances, and more heterarchical modes of governance. Since the late 1980s, the liberalization of markets, falling transport and communication costs, and the advent of electronic commerce have truncated geographical distance, and led to both a widening and deepening of cross-border transactions of all kinds. The nature and content of work is also undergoing a profound transition (Rifkin 1995).

Contemporary capitalism is then becoming increasingly knowledge and alliance based, and recognizes few spatial boundaries. Economically successful corporations and nations are those which can harness and effectively deploy natural and created assets from throughout the world, and continually upgrade their indigenous resources and capabilities. Capital, goods, services and people all move more freely than ever before across national borders; while, to be competitive, firms frequently need to access, and learn from the experiences and competencies of other firms. Finally, corporate hierarchies are embracing at least some of the features of heterarchies, as horizontal and vertical exchanges of information, ideas, entrepreneurship and learning experiences, are flattening pyramidal structures of decision taking and control.

The scenario just presented demands a very different response by Christian apologists than those which it supplants; but more of this later. For the moment, let us consider how the main features of democratic capitalism have changed;[2] and what are the unique demands the global economy (our shorthand expression to cover the characteristics just described) are making on the political, institutional and ethical foundations of the capitalist system if it is to operate in a socially acceptable way.

I would make the following broad observations:

1   Over the past three centuries – particularly over the last two or three decades, most markets – and especially those for created assets and intermediate products – have become more complex and interdependent of each other. This has led to more endemic market failures, such as those to do with information asymmetries, moral hazard, opportunism and bounded rationality; and, in spite of the growing sophistication of contracts, has placed a greater emphasis on trust, mutual commitment and forbearance as ingredients of fair and efficient exchange mechanisms. Partly the reason for this greater complexity and uncertainty is that an increasing proportion of market transactions are cross-border, and involve buyers and sellers from different cultures, political systems, ideologies and institutional regimes.[3]

2   At the same time, some technological advances, e.g. the advent of the Internet, have, by lowering the costs of acquiring and utilizing information and codifiable knowledge, reduced the extent and degree of market failure. *Inter alia*, this has led to the renaissance of some markets, e.g. some kinds of franchising and technical service

agreements, and also the revival of value-added activity by small and medium-size firms.

3   The geography of markets has also undergone a number of significant changes (Dunning 1998). On the one hand, the reduction of transport costs, and the removal of many artificial barriers to trade, has enabled many kinds of production to be more widely dispersed. On the other, new and more efficient communication technologies, and the growing importance of idiosyncratic and tacit knowledge, have made for a greater geographical concentration of some of these same activities in order to minimize the transaction costs of spatial distance. This is the paradox of "sticky places within slippery space" (Markusen 1996).

4   The role of legal, commercial and social institutions affecting the institutional foundation of markets, and the motives and behavior of the participants in the market, has fluctuated as economic development has proceeded. In *land-based* and *merchant capitalism*, the personal bond between the parties involved in any exchange was based partly on obedience, partly on kinship and ethnic solidarity, and partly on common ethical and moral values (North 1981, 1993). In *industrial and finance capitalism*, as markets became impersonal, and managerial hierarchies more powerful, the nation state gradually assumed the role as the main initiator, protector and enforcer of property rights and the interests of non-market participants. In *knowledge-based alliance capitalism*, where the source of wealth is often embodied in human capabilities and experiences, the spotlight is once again on interpersonal relationships. Notwithstanding the growing importance of formal contracts or agreements, it is frequently the quality of the face-to-face interaction between the parties to any economic transaction which is the deciding factor on its success or failure.

The moral response

Throughout history, the moral response to markets has been closely linked to the perception – both by individuals and institutions – of the purpose of economic activity, and the respective roles of enterprises, governments and the individuals in the process of wealth creation and distribution. Let us now give some attention to how this response has changed as capitalism has evolved.

Pre-industrial capitalism

At the time of *land-based* and *merchant* capitalism, religious and commercial values were closely intertwined. Indeed, as R. H. Tawney has described in some detail, up to the period of Enlightenment (in the seventeenth century), the Christian Church not only dominated and fashioned the values of ordinary people towards wealth creation and social justice; but, within the framework of feudalism, it also set the ground rules for such markets as existed at the time (Tawney 1929). The medieval age was one in which social theology was rooted in the concept of an unchanging and stable world. Given that concept, man's economic role was perceived to be the efficient husbandry of the existing – and mainly natural – resources within his domain. Not only was little attention given to the value of innovation as an instrument of growth; but usury as a means of encouraging savings was disfavored. This, too, was a period of strong social hierarchies; and one in which, for the most part, equity issues played a secondary role, and when individual initiative was downplayed.[4]

The Reformation of the sixteenth century introduced a new set of values and behavioral mores into pre-industrial capitalism. In the religious sphere, the emergence of Protestantism, as proclaimed by John Calvin and Martin Luther, directly led to the upgrading of the role of the individual (cf. the collective discipline of the Church) in matters of faith and behavior, and helped foster a new kind of business ethic. In the secular realm, John Locke was one of the first scholars to argue the case for liberty, religious tolerance and the separation of private and public morality; while Thomas Hobbes proclaimed the interests and rights of the self-seeking individual. The age of enlightenment followed and, with it, a new attitude towards wealth-creating activities. Colonialism and mercantilism brought an uneasy alliance between the Church and commercial interests, while, at the grass roots level, a new spirit of adventure and entrepreneurship emerged. With the advent of a number of critical inventions, such as the printing press, gunpowder and clocks, a new view of man's purpose in creation began to surface. There was also some criticism by Churchmen and others of monopolies and unacceptable business practices.[5]

Industrial capitalism

The initial moral reactions to the emergence of *industrial capitalism* were voiced by clergymen with an interest in political economy. Notably among these were Thomas Malthus, Richard Whateley and Joseph Tucker. During the nineteenth century, two contrasting moral perspectives dominated thinking; and, indeed, the tension between them has continued to this day. The first – *the liberal view* – espoused the social benefits of free markets, and gave a pre-eminent role to the individual (as opposed to groups of individuals or to society in general) in fashioning his own economic destiny. This perception was strongly held by scholars such as Adam Smith and statesmen such as Thomas Jefferson.

Although the economics of this view were amoral, it is important to emphasize that the free market protagonists believed that, alongside and, indeed conditioning, personal *freedom* was personal *responsibility*. Adam

Smith, for example, passionately espoused that, if market forces were to achieve their objectives, not only did buyers and sellers need to behave in a morally and socially responsible way, but the state had to assume the ultimate responsibility for ensuring that the legal and institutional underpinnings of the market were adequate to correct any social inequities arising from it.

The view that the social good was best promoted by individuals pursuing their own self-interest held sway for much of the nineteenth and early twentieth century as the moral – even the theological – justification for industrial capitalism. It was markedly different from that of the previous era, where the individual's interests were assumed to be subservient to the social or religious group of which he (or she) was part. It was also a reaction to the Mercantilist philosophy which assigned a pivotal role to the nation state in promoting or protecting the economic interests of its constituents. It was, too, partly shaped by a more dynamic, or evolutionary, view of the material world, and by the belief that, by investment, innovation, education and training, *new* wealth could be created, living standards improved, and poverty and disease reduced, and economic justice advanced. A new and less static social theology was being called for; and one which took account of the opportunities and challenges of change and progress.

At the same time, other commentators took a less liberal view of the effects of industrial capitalism. The uneven distribution of income, the concentration of capital, unacceptable working conditions in mines and factories (the "dark satanic mills" of William Blake), the exploitation and erosion of human dignity – particularly of women and children – the continuation of slave, or near-slave, labor (e.g. in the US), the declining moral standards of the early nineteenth century, the growing cult of acquisitiveness – all these combined to lead religious leaders and others to denounce industrial capitalism and the market system; and to demand that the state, civic groups and individuals – by regulatory or spontaneous action – should eradicate or minimize these disbenefits. In various Papal announcements of the time, the Roman Catholic Church was severely critical of the adverse affects of advertising on consumer preferences, the lust for economic power, the corruption of affluence and the envy, which the market system was perceived to foster. Even as recently as 1971, the eminent theologian Paul Tillich portrayed democratic capitalism as "demonic" (Tillich 1971). In doing so, he was re-echoing the sentiments of a long line of critics throughout the previous century, which included F. D. Maurice, Max Weber, Karl Marx, R. H. Tawney and William Temple to name just a few.

Contrasting the ethics of the creation of wealth, then, was the ethics of the distribution of wealth, and/or of the income arising from that wealth; and of the consequences of the free markets for human relationships and social justice. The growth of socialism from the mid-nineteenth century onwards was essentially a response to the (perceived) unacceptable face of industrial capitalism and unbridled individualism. Although politically oriented, the majority of Christian leaders and writers strongly supported the principles of socialism and its emphasis on communitarism, egalitarism and human dignity. This they considered to be more in accord with Christ's teaching – particularly as enunciated in the Sermon on the Mount – than that of a *laissez faire* philosophy, which was perceived to cater to, and, indeed, promote, the worst, rather than the best, in human values.

At the same time, and partly in response to the downsides of industrial capitalism, there emerged in the mid to late nineteenth century, in both Europe and the US, a wide range of voluntary charitable associations which came to play a vital part in fostering a sense of collective solidarity and a new culture of social concern. The philosophy of Victorian England also came to reflect the belief of Edmund Burke, that civil liberty could only prosper if individuals "put moral chains on their appetites"; and that this could only be achieved if society placed a high premium on such virtues as self-restraint, duty, benevolence, encouragement, example and the development of character. In any event, the second half of the nineteenth century saw a dramatic fall in some of the social disbenefits, e.g. crime, prostitution and intemperance, which industrial capitalism had earlier seemed to spawn (Searle 1998).

The knowledge-based economy

The emergence of knowledge-based capitalism at the end of the twentieth century is prompting a further reappraisal of the Christian attitude towards wealth creation and distribution, and to the scope and ingredients of social justice. It is also bringing into even sharper focus some of the economic and social dilemmas which have perplexed the Christian apologist throughout the ages. Four of these, which we have identified in Table 2.1, are of especial importance. In Table 2.2, we have set out how

Table 2.1 Some paradoxes of Christian moral virtues

1. Individualism [Self-interest	vs. cf.	Community Social responsibility]
2. Efficiency [Productivity	vs. cf.	Equity Social justice]
3. Preservation [Man's responsibility to preserve natural resources: a state concept]	vs. cf.	Creation [Man as "partner" with God]
4. Spontaneous moral values [Internally and voluntarily covenanted moral values, judgments and values, e.g. by persons, families, civic groups]	vs. cf.	Externally coerced values [Moral judgments and values largely imposed by external authorities; these vary from codes of conduct to contractual agreements and legislation]

Table 2.2. The changing balance of moral virtues at three stages of market-based capitalism

	1	2	3	4	Key moral virtues underpinning successful capitalism
Stage 1: Merchant land-based capitalism					
(a) Pre-Reformation	Mixed	Community	Preservation	Largely external	Obedience, good husbandry, group loyalty, duty → a more enterprising and adventurous spirit
(b) Post-Reformation	Mixed → Efficiency	Community → Individualism	Preservation → Creation	External → Spont. (particularly in US)	
Stage 2: Machine-based capitalism					
(a) eighteenth → nineteenth century	Efficiency → Equity	Individualism → Community	Mixed	Mixed	Entrepreneurship, reliability, diligence, conformity, prudence →social justice, civic responsibility →self-expression and self-reliance
(b) nineteenth → twentieth century	Mixed → Efficiency	Mixed	Mixed → Creation	Mixed → External	
Stage 3: Knowledge-based capitalism					
	Mixed (Equity now viewed from perspective of productive justice)	Mixed	Creation, yet within sustainable development	Mixed → Spont.	Creativity, responsible individualism, spontaneous sociability, trust and forbearance, neighborliness, compassion, ability to compromise and adapt to change

Key:
1–4 = Paradoxes of virtues
1 = Efficiency cf. Equity
2 = Individualism cf. Community (includes both collectivism and voluntary association)
3 = Preservation cf. Creation
4 = "Spontaneous" moral virtues cf. "Externally imposed" moral virtues (external)
→ = moving towards

the balance between these (apparently) conflicting virtues seems to have fluctuated as capitalism has progressed to its present stage.

I shall make no further comment on these paradoxes at this point in the chapter, other than to observe that it is no wonder that the "yo-yo" nature of both scholarly thinking and practical politics towards capitalism and the market system over the last three centuries or more has led to confused and often contradictory pronouncements by Christian leaders on economic and social issues. While being in broad agreement about Christ's teachings on how one should welcome wealth creation and social justice, the appropriate mechanisms to achieve such goals were – and still are – hotly debated. Particularly in studying alternative socio-economic systems, conflict arises between intentions and abilities to achieve intentions. Sometimes the focus of the debate is about the role and priorities of individuals, and those of groups of individuals, or society as a whole. Sometimes, it revolves around how a liberal society can also be a responsible society; or how an efficient society can be a caring society, without the State playing a major regulatory role.

Certainly, the trade-off between conflicting goals and/or priorities has fluctuated with the development of new technologies and institutional structures; as economic systems have come and gone; and as the cultural composition and customs of society, and the values, beliefs and behavior of individuals have changed. To my mind, the principal lesson to be learned from the rejection of communism is not that its objectives were wrong in themselves (although some people may think they were), but that the attitudes and behavior of its institutions and individuals failed to live up to the expectations of its advocates. Moreover, the pressures on contemporary economies to continually innovate new goods and services, and to upgrade their human resources and organizational capabilities, is leading Christians (and adherents of other religious faiths) to reinterpret their views on capitalism and the role of our market. If nothing else, the early twenty-first century world is characterized by rapid technological progress, change, uncertainty and volatility – features which were much less prevalent in the earlier phases of capitalism – and which demand a new kind of social theology and a reprioritization of moral virtues.

The Christian response to globalization

Let me now come to the kernel of my argument. It is that the ingredients of global capitalism – which, while in a state of constant flux, I believe, are largely irreversible – are sufficiently different than those of industrial and machine-based capitalism, as to require some modification, both of Christian social theology and of the actions which Christians might take, or persuade others to take, to ensure that the market, and its legal, political and moral underpinnings, work to advance, rather than inhibit, Christian values. For at no time has the dictum that the "market is a good servant to mankind but a bad master" been more apposite; and, perhaps, at no time, is the success of the democratic capitalism more dependent on its being grounded in a strong and generally acceptable moral foundation.

Let me first offer an optimistic – and perhaps a controversial – perspective. It is that the three attributes of global capitalism, which currently shape both the nature and composition of global markets, and their underlying institutions, and are all – potentially at least – more in accord with Christian social teaching than those which preceded it.

This is certainly the view of Pope John Paul II. The following statements are taken from various Papal pronouncements.[6]

> "The free market is the most efficient instrument for utilizing resources and effectively responding to needs." "The right to private property . . . is fundamental to the autonomy and development of the person." "The modern business economy has (as) its basis human freedom exercised in the economic field." "[We] acknowledge the legitimate role of profit as an indication that a business is functioning well. When a firm makes a profit, this means that productive factors have been properly employed and corresponding human needs have been duly satisfied." "Economic activity, especially the activity of the market economy, cannot be conducted in an institutional, juridical or political vacuum. On the contrary it presupposes sure guarantees of individual freedom and private property, as well as a stable currency and efficient public services. Hence the principal task of the State is to guarantee this security, so that those who work and produce can enjoy the fruits of their labours and thus feel encouraged to work efficiently and honestly."

Let me now explain why, subject to certain conditions being fulfilled, which I shall describe later, I believe that global capitalism should be welcomed by the Christian apologist.

Knowledge as a source of wealth

This suggests (to me at any rate) that man – rather than any inanimate asset – is back in charge of his economic destiny. But, in contrast to earlier phases of capitalism, the *relative* (I stress relative) contribution of the intellectual, cf. the physical attributes, of man, in preserving and increasing economic wellbeing is enormously greater. In the Bible, man is viewed as a partner with (although subject to the commands of) God, the ultimate and all encompassing Creator. Yet, for most of history, the task of man has been perceived of as a harnesser of the fruits of the earth, and as a preserver of all natural assets.[7] In pre-industrial society, for example, God is not praised for social and technological change (Preston 1993).

Today, however, the focus is more on the enhancing value of assets of the earth and those of man's abilities and wellbeing. This, after all, is what sustainable development is all about.

Here the concept of man's partnership with God – the ultimate Creator – takes on a new and exciting connotation. This is for two reasons. First, there is still a huge amount of genuine poverty on the planet, with 90 percent of its inhabitants living at below the poverty line identified by the World Bank. So, to suggest that wealth creation, by encouraging acquisitiveness, greed, selfishness and related "sins" is, *of itself*, not a Christian virtue, seems to me entirely wrong, even though *de facto* it may lead to unvirtuous actions on the part of its main beneficiaries. The Bible, for example, never condemns wealth as such, but rather certain attitudes and behavior of human beings towards it, or of some of the consequences of possessing it.[8] In particular, the advancement in man's physical and intellectual capabilities should be welcomed by Christians, because, more than anything else, they offer the wherewithal to alleviate poverty and to advance human dignity and social justice.

Second, the development of man's intellectual capital – viz. his knowledge, skills, organizational talents and learning experiences, is a worthy objective in its own right, as is the fostering of individual enterprise, personal responsibility and job satisfaction. These attributes and virtues all help man to better utilize his God-given capabilities and talents; and to engage in more creative, worthwhile and congenial work. In his 1981 *Centesimus Annus*, the Pope acknowledged that, in the contemporary global economy that "besides the earth, man's principle resource is man himself"; while throughout his pontificate, he has frequently emphasized the creative possibilities of humanity in the belief that, "to be creative, is the essential human vocation" (Novak 1993, p. 13).

So, I believe the Christian should respond positively to the first ingredient of global capitalism. This is not to deny that it may bring its own problems, tensions and challenges – and, in particular, those arising from the unequal distribution of intellectual capital among human beings, and the social disbenefits of technological *et al.* change. But, more of this later in this presentation.

The advent of alliance capitalism

While the Christian faith is intensely personal or individualistic, Christian teaching also avers that the individual can only be completely self-fulfilled if he (or she) is a responsible and an active participant in the wider community – be it a family, a Church, a social group, a business or a nation. This, of course, implies that the community is fashioned spontaneously, and sustained by men and women of goodwill, who have similar aspirations, and, who, by co-operating with each other, seek to serve the interests of the group – and, indirectly, themselves. At its best, communitarism works to enhance individualism; at its worst – as Communism has all too clearly shown – it can swallow it up altogether.

In a market economy, from the earliest of time, individuals have needed to work together to create and utilize wealth. For Adam Smith, natural man was also social man (Smith 1776). That, after all, is what the division of labor is about. To be effective, most economic activities involve some degree of coordination and interdependence among the participants. In the first century A.D., St Paul was at pains to stress the spiritual benefits which stemmed from the specialization of tasks within the Christian Church. Chapter 12 of Corinthians 1 is, indeed, a beautifully constructed narrative of the potential benefits of a spiritual division of labor among the members of the church at Corinth.

However, the concept and nature of community, and its relation to individualism, has changed over the years. In *land-based* capitalism, community was coerced by a series of master–servant relations and a political regime, which above everything, was geared towards the maintenance of the existing social and economic order (Novak 1982). Citizens were rarely free to make their own decisions; and they worked primarily to promote the interests of their rulers, or that of their communities of which they were part, rather than vice versa.

In *industrial* capitalism, although the invisible hand of markets brought widespread economic benefits, most division of labor in the workplace was directed to promoting the interests of public or private hierarchies. This it did, not by any genuine partnership between managers and workers, but by a rigidly enforced chain of command in which the lower tiers largely carried out the instructions of the upper echelons, e.g. with respect to the allocation of work. Although many aspects of hierarchical capitalism still remain today, increasingly the creation and utilization of wealth is resting on the voluntary but artifactual co-operation between the participating parties. Such alliance capitalism, as I have described elsewhere (Dunning 1997a), may be of various kinds, e.g. between different groups of workers in the same firm, between different departments of a firm, between suppliers and customers, between competitors, between firms and governments, between different interest groups, and between governments. Co-operation as part of the competitive process of global capitalism is the order of the day. Governments work together to better advance their own long-term interests. Firms form attachments with other firms to reduce costs, speed up innovations and tap into new knowledge and markets. Individuals join together to enhance their personal aspirations, needs and capabilities, and to promote the well-being of others. Nowhere is the social value of such interpersonal co-operation better seen than in the growth of all kinds of voluntary and non-profit organizations.[9]

Consider again the words of Pope John Paul II – who welcomes alliance capitalism as a vehicle both for fostering Christian virtues and for adding to man's creative possibilities.

It is (man's) disciplined work in close collaboration with others that makes possible the creation of ever more extensive working communities which can be relied upon to transform man's natural and human environments. Important virtues are involved in this process such as diligence, industriousness, prudence in undertaking reasonable risks, reliability and fidelity in interpersonal relationships, as well as courage in carrying out decisions which are difficult and painful, both for the overall working of a business and in meeting possible setbacks.

(*Centesimus Annus*, quoted in Novak (1993, p. 17))

At the same time, the Pope's words also identify the essential ingredients of "successful" co-operation – ingredients which, it should be noted, may have little or nothing to do with the technical characteristics of whatever is being produced or sold, but rather reflect the moral commitment of the individuals or institutions involved.

To the extent, then, that global capitalism encourages communitarism, the object of which is to advance the interests of a particular communities of people; and to the extent that such communitarism helps provide the kind of social and institutional support which individuals need to make better use of their own capabilities, it should be perceived as Christian friendly. It also lays to rest the notion that individualism and communitarism are contradictory to each other. Far from it; each complements – and should complement – the other. What is unique about contemporary alliance capitalism is that it offers a moral antidote to both the excesses of communitarism and of individualism (or as Jonathan Sacks would have it, libertarianism (Sacks 1997)). Our contemporary era offers the opportunity for a fruitful balance between the benefits of liberalism and community – which, if nurtured and used wisely, can advance, rather than detract from, the economic and social merits of global capitalism.

Towards a global village

But, perhaps, the unique feature of *global* capitalism is its spatial dimension; and it is here, perhaps, where the greatest challenge to Christian behavioral norms presents itself. In principle, the tenets of Christian teaching, with respect to such variables as wealth creation, working conditions, the distribution of income and social justice, should know no spatial boundaries. The parable of the Good Samaritan,[10] when originally told by Jesus, involved two people of different races. Though, when it is short supply, it may be appropriate for "charity to begin at home," modern communications, particularly the TV and electronic commerce, by increasing our awareness of the needs and aspirations of our more distant neighbors, are forcing us to reappraise our social priorities and responsibilities.

Much of the business literature on globalization stresses its benefits.[11] But, recently, more attention has been given to its downsides and how these can be overcome or mitigated.[12] Comparisons are being made with the structurally disruptive and often socially divisive affects associated with (note I said associated with, not caused by) the industrial revolution in the UK two centuries ago. The major difference between now and then is that now there are a different set of winners and losers (Luttwak 1999); and these are spread across national jurisdictions. Whereas, for example, in the mid to late nineteenth century the UK government was able to mitigate the worst aspects of industrial capitalism as they affected its domestic constituents, by a variety of regulatory measures and social welfare instruments, there is currently no such supra-national mechanism to protect the well-being of those most rudely treated by the global market economy.

There is, in addition, the thorny issue of how much moral right any government, or a supra-national agency, has to impose its own working, safety or environmental standards (to give just three examples) on the government of another country – particularly a very poor country – whose economic and social well-being, and opportunity to upgrade their indigenous resources and capabilities may have been even more dire in the absence of globalization. There can be no doubt that gross disparities of privileged wealth and income, particularly when accompanied by abject poverty and a degradation of the human spirit, are an anathema to the Christian's concept of compassion and social justice. Neither is there much disagreement among economic commentators that, in the short run at least, however much it may raise the living standards of a great many people in the world;[13] globalization will, almost certainly, widen the average *absolute* income differences between and within countries.

However, I believe the challenge this poses the Christian church should not be primarily directed to the act, or form, of globalization *per se,* neither to one of its main instruments – the transnational corporations (always a favorite scapegoat for attack by national governments who will not (or cannot) put their own economic houses in order), but to the way in which all of us – both individually and collectively – respond to our heightened awareness of the plight of the poor and disadvantaged in distant lands – a plight incidentally, which was around long before globalization.

But, I also believe that for this response to be translated into meaningful action and on the scale which is required, there needs to be a wholesale recasting of the legal, political and moral infrastructure of the global economic system so that wealth can be created and distributed in a way which is in accord with "productive" social justice. Productive social justice, while accepting the moral imperative of wealthier individuals and nations to help improve the lot of their poorer counterparts also asserts that these latter individuals and nations have no less a responsibility to make the best use of their resources and capabilities, and to promote an

economics of respect towards a wider community, towards future genera-
tions, and towards the environment of which they are part.[14] More about
this later.

At the same time, the advent of the global village is bringing with it
other daunting challenges, which are affecting people in all walks of life,
and societies at all levels of prosperity. These are primarily the economic
and social disbenefits of the cross-border traffic in such "bads" as drugs,
unsafe products, terrorism, arms, environmental pollution and crime,
associated with the increasing ease at which people, assets goods and services can move across the globe (including, in some cases, through the
Internet). Clearly, while improved detection measures, tighter border controls, and a tougher stance to the perpetrators of these disbenefits can
reduce such trade, more attention needs to be given to demotivating
those responsible for this kind of economic activity. And that is a moral
issue, which all of us have a part to play in helping to resolve.

Reforming the market and its moral framework

I have so far argued that the critical elements of global capitalism should
be welcomed by Christians inasmuch as they give opportunities for
mankind to upgrade his intellectual assets and creative spirit by his own
initiative and by interpersonal co-operation. But global capitalism also
brings with it huge challenges, most notably of how to ensure that its
various attributes can add to the well-being of the maximum number of
individuals and to the common good; and of how the growing awareness
of the huge disparities of income, and the (inevitably) disruptive effects of
change and uncertainty can be sympathetically tackled without eroding
individual initiative, the distinctiveness of national cultures and behavioral
mores, and the sovereignty of national governments.

Let me now briefly consider how, I believe, globalization is affecting the
functions, efficiency and social justice of the market system, and of its
institutional and moral foundations.

The market

As yet, in an imperfect world, inhabited by sinful human beings, I would
aver that no-one has yet devised an economic system, directed to the creation and utilization of wealth (but not necessarily its distribution) better
than the market, *when it performs at its best.* In principle, then, I would
argue that economic liberalization, by removing barriers to the cross-
border movement of assets, goods and services should lead to an increase
in market efficiency; and that this should be applauded by all.

On the other hand, the growing number of those constituents which
do not engage in market transactions – which currently exceed those that
do[15] – the increasing volatility and unpredictability of markets, the

continued concentration of economic power in the hands of a relatively few companies and countries (and this factor is rarely given proper acknowledgement), the growing importance of societal assets[16] (and the public goods and services flowing from these assets), all suggest that a social market system does not come naturally or without its costs. Extra-market intervention, e.g. by governments and supra-national entities, may well be needed for two reasons. The first is to eradicate, or reduce, the less desirable consequences of free markets (e.g. the supply of social "bads," undesirable business behavior or labor practices. The second is to intervene in a variety of ways wherever the operation of markets leads to a conflict between private and social costs and benefits. Such a conflict may arise where there are information asymmetries, uncertainties (e.g. with respect to the output of research and development) and where private interests might exploit common non-renewable resources at too speedy a rate.

On all these issues, there is little conflict between the views of (most) economists and Christian apologists. (I am not suggesting there are no Christian economists!) However, up to now, neither economists or apologists appear to have had much influence on the responses of national administrations towards global capitalism. Indeed, apart from acknowledging its more obvious costs and benefits, most governments have yet to recognize that major changes in their existing actions (i.e. pre-globalization) are required. In any case, it may be argued that, while Christians have a right to express views on the morality of the market system (as it is), they are on less secure ground when they try to offer (what might be construed as) professional or technical advice of how this might be improved.

The institutional dimension

Let me now turn to offer some thoughts about the implications of global capitalism for the institutional underpinnings of the market system.

Whatever particular brand of democratic capitalism one is considering,[17] consider again the first three of the four main features of globalization set out in Table 2.1. I shall deal with the moral dimension in the next part of the chapter. First, the emergence of intellectual capital as the main engine for wealth creation has huge implications, both for the measurement of wealth and the protection of property rights associated with it. Only quite recently have economists, national statisticians, corporate accountants and lawyers begun to try to calculate the "hidden" or intangible ingredients of a company's or nation's assets, and, indeed, the return on such assets. How, indeed, can one measure the productivity of investment in human capital, in strategic alliances, in organizational capability, or in creating market networks? An OECD Conference in 1987 (OECD 1998) identified some of these issues, a satisfactory resolution of which is critical to the long-term success of the post-industrial market economy.

No less urgent is the need to ensure the judicious protection (sic) of intellectual capital once created, so that firms may be encouraged to innovate new intangible assets (or upgrade their existing assets), and to gain a fair return on them. For the last century, we have had the patent system, which works reasonably well for the protection of "codifiable" intellectual capital. But what about non-codifiable or tacit assets, e.g. organizational competence, experience and wisdom, information "banks," management capability, and so on? Governments have long since recognized the need to protect property rights.[18] Since it is, in fact, the case that "property" is increasingly taking on the form of intangible assets, should not the responsibility of governments be extended to devise and sustain the necessary legal framework and complementary institutions to offer these assets the same kind of protection?

Second, what of the legal and institutional implications of alliance capitalism? Partly, these relate to the extension and/or modification of various aspects of corporate law and anti-trust legislation to embrace hybrid forms of business organization, notably strategic alliances, inter-firm networks, research and development (R&D), consortia and so on. Partly, too, the growth of cross-border alliances and inter-firm networks poses its own unique challenges to national administrations. How far, for example, should foreign owned firms be allowed to participate in national R&D consortia, e.g. in the semi-conductor or aircraft industry, where issues of national security are involved? Alliance capitalism opens up a whole new set of issues related to competition, trade, the environmental *et al.* policies, to innovatory and educational systems. These, unless efficiently and equitably resolved, can undermine the beneficial effects of both intra-national and international market transactions.

Third, and most unique to global capitalism, the erosion of economic boundaries – as evidenced by the huge explosion of all kinds of international transactions – but especially cross-border financial flows, foreign direct investment, and strategic partnering[19] – is forcing national governments to redefine the extent and form of their roles. The growth of macro-regional entities, e.g. the European Union, NAFTA, etc. and a gamut of international agencies, WTO, UNCTAD, OECD, ASEAN, etc., with various degrees of authority and influence; and the widening scope of their activities (e.g. ere long the WTO is likely to embrace FDI, competition, environmental and labor standard issues within its terms of reference), will inevitably reduce the economic leverage of national authorities in the management of their domestic economic affairs. Such supra-national intervention in the global marketplace is as necessary to prevent market distorting behavior on the part of national governments as it is on the part of business corporations.[20]

At the same time, for a variety of reasons, national governments are being compelled to decentralize or devolve various aspects of economic decision taking to sub-national authorities, and particularly to those which have jurisdiction over economic activities which are internationally oriented (Ohmae 1995). In the US – to give just one example – the individual States have much more influence on the intra-US location of inbound direct investment than does the federal government;[21] and to a large extent, the same is true of the regional authorities in Europe.[22] Increasingly, it seems there is a reconfiguration of the level and geography of extra-market governance – as well as its extent and form – which needs to be taken account of in any evaluation of the efficacy of the emerging global market system.

The moral challenge of global capitalism

Let me now turn more specifically to the moral challenges posed by global capitalism. It is here I believe the Christian – and, indeed, any other observer interested in behavioral issues – can make a useful contribution to the debate on the kind of ethical framework which needs to be in place if the market system, together with the actions of extra-market institutions described in the previous paragraphs, are to fulfil their proper function. Here a number of challenging philosophical and practical issues – not to say dilemmas – arise.

The first is to ascertain what *is* the "appropriate" moral foundation for global capitalism;[23] and in what ways this is likely to be different from that demanded by earlier phases of capitalism. The second is to identify the costs and benefits (both tangible and intangible) of achieving that foundation, or coming near to achieving it. The third is what should the Christian response be if the preferred moral framework is unfavorable *in principle* to a wider community? e.g. as might be the case in a multi-cultural community, or unacceptable *in practice*, e.g. because of the unwillingness of individuals and institutions to change their behavioral patterns in the desired way. The fourth is, given the dilemma posed by the third question, is the appropriate response to change the market system to fit in with the values and behavioral patterns of the community (which I suspect would be the favored course of action by the Islamic faith) or to change the values and behavior of the community to help make the market work better (which I suspect would be more in accord with Jewish thought) – or a mixture of the two alternatives (which I suspect would be the Christian reaction)?

In considering each of these questions, the Christian apologist first turns to the teachings of Christ in the New Testament, as interpreted by his disciples and by scholars and religious leaders from St Paul onwards. Here, while, for the most part, the teachings of the Bible and Church are clear, there are sufficient nuances and ambiguities to allow much debate over particular courses of moral actions, and of orders of priority when one set of guidelines (e.g. good husbandry) may conflict – or seem to conflict – with that of another (e.g. the interests of the poor).

What implications does global capitalism have for the moral framework debate? The first is that its various attributes so far described pose a host of new moral challenges or dilemmas. The second arise from the increasing intermingling of different religious cultures, which may affect (for good or bad) the resolution of these challenges and dilemmas. On the face of it, Islam, Judaism, Hinduism and Buddhism each have their different behavioral and cultural norms, and the pursuance of a "lower common denominator" moral framework might not be sufficient to achieve the goals desired of it.

In fact, I don't know whether this is the case or not. I would like to think there *is* enough in common among the major religions of the world to produce a meaningful and workable code of conduct in the global marketplace, which both discourages some of the adverse characteristics frequently attributed to it, e.g. excessive acquisitiveness, envy, materialism, inappropriate advertising, the production of "bads," etc. while applauding its more worthy virtues, e.g. those to do with entrepreneurship, initiative, personal responsibility, trust and forbearance and the promotion of a division of labor which benefits all.

De facto, the moral underpinnings of the market system have varied over time, and vary today between countries. In *land-based* capitalism, as I have already described, the framework was based on a strong moral order, and a rigid social order. Political, religious and civil society were one and the same thing, as the Church set the ground rules for most commercial transactions. In *industrial-based* Western style capitalism, a new moral code, fashioned both by the ideas of the Reformation,[24] and later the philosophy of John Locke and John Stuart Mill which heralded the emergence of liberalism, held sway for much of the nineteenth and first half of the twentieth century. Liberalism separated the moral life of the community from its sources of authority; the political from the civil society; and Church from State (Sacks 1997). It introduced a more open and tolerant society. It emphasized the role of the individual and the values of self-reliance, personal initiative, honesty, trustworthiness, reliability and social responsibility. It separated the practices of government from the pursuit of faith (Sacks 1997). It was these virtues – most clearly expressed in mid-Victorian England and the US in the early 1830s[25] – that provided the moral underpinnings for the economic writings of Adam Smith and the later maturation of market-based capitalism (Himmelfarb 1995).

Since around the mid-twentieth century, the respective roles of the State, Church and civil society have changed once more. Today, in Western societies at least, many of the moral underpinnings of classical liberalism have all but disappeared. Since the emergence of the welfare state, the social responsibilities of individuals have been increasingly assumed by governments. There are few absolute standards of belief or behavior; moral relativism reigns supreme. Many of the virtues of liberalism, such as loyalty, self-sacrifice and civility, have been downgraded or replaced by others, such as self-fulfillment and freedom of expression. Increasingly, liberalism has given way to libertarianism. which, in the view of Jonathan Sacks,[26] currently dominates the ethical foundation of the market system in Western cultures today. A Catholic apologist, Michael Novak (1982, 1993, 1997) goes further. He claims it is weakening the very authority of democratic capitalism – and could ultimately destroy it. In the Islamic critique of Western capitalism, it is, I suspect, the relaxing of moral standards which is the main target, not the market system *per se.* And, in that sentiment, I would aver they have much in common with the Jewish and Christian observers.

Consider, for example, the moral underpinnings of three attributes of global capitalism: First, the emphasis on *knowledge* as a source of wealth. Above all, this suggests that society needs to give the highest priority to education – at all levels. But education does not come easily or cheaply. It requires a reprioritization of spending values. It requires, among other virtues, those of making the best use of one's talents, dedication, sacrifice and self-discipline. It requires parents who will put their children's education at the forefront of their goals, and to give them the encouragement and support they need to develop their latent skills and capabilities to the full.

Second, what of the implications of *alliance*-related modes of organizational behavior? Here, only if there is a strong moral framework which exhorts trust, forbearance, flexibility, honesty, mutual understanding, teamwork, and a readiness to link one's own interests to that of the group or community of which one is part, are such modes likely to fulfil their objectives. Indeed, the history of successful joint ventures and strategic alliances – particularly those involving Japanese firms – provides ample support for this viewpoint.[27]

Third, the unique *spatial dimensions* of global capitalism also emphasizes these same values – and especially the need for mutual understanding and respect of different social priorities, cultural perspectives and business customs. Rigid ethnocentric and xenophobic attitudes by individuals and firms from one country and a lack of respect for the ideologies and conventions of other societies are particularly destructive to the efficiency of cross-border markets. It is, for example, difficult for such markets to be optimally efficient where sellers come from countries with libertarian moral values and buyers come from an Islamic, Hindu or Confucian business culture. This, indeed, is one of the greatest challenges to the future of global capitalism, but one which has little to do with the technical efficiency of free markets.

In a different context, Samuel Huntingdon (1993) has written about the coming clash of civilizations – a clash based not on economic and political ideologies and regimes, but on religious and ethnic cultures. Whether one accepts Huntingdon's prognosis or not, I would aver that, unless there is some consensus among the peoples of the world about the critical moral foundations of everyday economic and social life, then global capitalism is being built on shifting sands, rather than on hard rock.

But what, indeed, should be the content of this consensus and how real and effective might it be? This, indeed, is the $64,000 question! One suggestion which I made in a presentation to an UNCTAD conference four years ago (Dunning 1994) is that an international forum of religious leaders – rather like the G8 in the economic arena – should be convened whose initial brief would be to examine the possibility of devising a common moral code, or set of ground rules, governing the values and behavior of their followers. *Inter alia,* such a code should acknowledge, first, the different historical profiles, political and business systems, social priorities and institutional structures of particular countries and regions; and second, the ways in which the global capitalism may foster a harmonious integration of the "best" attributes of these value systems.[28]

Is such a vision a naïve or impracticable one? Perhaps. Would the deliberations and recommendations of such a forum – which, to be effective, would need to meet regularly and be supported by a secretariat – have any influence on the actions of business, governments and people throughout the world? Possibly not. Certainly what I am proposing is an act of faith. At the same time, it is prompted by a very real concern that unless there is some consensus of spiritual values among people from widely different cultures, any gains in material welfare which global capitalism may bring could so easily be destroyed by a clash of civilizations, the like of which is too terrible even to contemplate.[29]

Consistent with Christian theology, but going well beyond it, I would further aver that the libertarian attitude to moral issues, and the relationship between the individual and social responsibility, which has been the prevailing attitude since the 1960s – is particularly inappropriate to the needs of global capitalism. To be effective – and to do its job as efficiently and responsibly – global capitalism needs a secure ethical foundation, which contains all the virtues of the classical liberal society, but with particular emphasis on those specific to this day and age. Furthermore, while the acknowledged practice of each of these virtues is the ultimate responsibility of the individual, these need to be embedded in a strong civil society. In the words of Jonathan Sacks again,

> Civil society rests on moral relationships. They are covenant rather than contractual. They are brought about not by governments but by us as husbands and wives, parents, friends and citizens, and by the knowledge of what we do and what we are makes a difference to those around us. That is why morality is prior to politics. Renewing society's resources of moral energy is the program, urgent but achievable, of a new politics of hope.

(Sacks 1997, p. 269)

To conclude this section, let me reiterate and enlarge upon some of the virtues which I think need to be nurtured, if socially responsible and sustainable global capitalism is to be achieved. These were earlier set out in Table 1.7 (p. 35). I call them the three "C"s.

(i) Creativity

Individual responsibility to personal self-betterment and the prudent investment of time and talents to help create additional global wealth and to utilize it more efficiently. To the Christian, this means a renewed recognition of the responsibility of man as a partner with God in the continued acts of both preservation[30] and creation. *Creativity* is, perhaps, the key virtue underpinning knowledge-based capitalism. It also means that the new freedom offered by the global marketplace has to be used wisely. More than ever before the virtue of self-control is required; more than ever before, man will need to limit his greed and acquisitiveness, and his desire for power.

(ii) Co-operation

A greater willingness of individuals *to work together as economic and social groups*, not only to create wealth, but to add to the personal fulfillment of each member of the group by being part of it.[31] To do this, and achieve the fruits of interpersonal socialization and empathetic communitarism, a new emphasis is needed on the values of mutual trust, forbearance, tolerance and understanding – particularly among people of different cultures, ethnic and religious groups. *Co-operation* is, therefore, the critical virtue underpinning alliance capitalism. To the Christian, the analogy of St Paul's reference to Christian's being part of one body (the Church) as applied to the economic sphere is especially apt.

(iii) Compassion

A broadening of the concept of *social justice* (who is my neighbor?) beyond national boundaries. Here, as I have already described, we are in particularly difficult territory. Partly, this is because of the huge scale of the problem (what can we as individuals do?). Partly, it is because of the (legitimate and understandable) "charity begins at home" syndrome. Partly, it is because the interpretation of social justice differs so much between cultures; and this being so, any attempt to impose one individual's, or nation's, concept of social justice – which includes the notion of "sufficiency" referred to earlier – on another may be construed as unwarranted extra territoriality. Moreover, one man's interpretation of sufficiency may be another man's interpretation of luxury. Is it possible, one may ask, to identify and foster a minimum standard of living which different religions may regard as man's due, not because of what he initiates towards society, but because of *what he is?* (General Assembly of the Presbyterian Church 1984).

It is the consideration of such moral issues as raised by the three "C"s of global capitalism – and particularly the dilemmas posed by the third C – which I believe should comprise an important part of the brief of any new supra-national advisory body – such as the Group of 8 (or whatever number) of religious leaders referred to earlier – which might be established. To be effective and to avoid unnecessary duplication of effort, such a body would need to work closely with other institutions designed to promote efficient and socially responsible global capitalism.

Conclusions

In this chapter, I have suggested that the world is entering into a new phase of market-based capitalism and that the characteristics of this phase – which I have dubbed global capitalism – are demanding a reconfiguration of the content and structure of the market system as it has evolved over the years – and of its institutional and ethical underpinnings.

In considering these issues, I have offered a Christian perspective, though I readily recognize that much of this perspective is shared by many of the other great religions and, indeed, by men of goodwill the world over.

My main conclusion is that if global capitalism is to be socially acceptable and sustainable, several groups of people have a critical role to play. First, it is necessary for national policy makers to ensure that those structural distortions and endemic market failures peculiar to global capitalism are minimized, or compensated by appropriate action on the part of extra-market institutions. Second, it is incumbent on the same group of people, and on international statesmen and supra-national agencies to reappraise the efficiency of the existing institutional underpinnings and rule-based mechanisms of both domestic and cross-border markets, so that market forces can be a good servant to societal values rather than a demanding master of them. Thirdly, it is incumbent on religious leaders and all men of goodwill to look more carefully and deeply into ways in which the particular moral virtues we have suggested are necessary prerequisites of socially acceptable global capitalism are best fostered.

On this latter issue – to which I have given especial attention in my presentation – I have argued that the unique characteristics of global capitalism are demanding a new kind of liberalism – which cultivates the virtues of individual responsibility and self-betterment on the one hand, and those of interpersonal socialization and a geographically broadened concept of social justice on the other. I have further asserted my belief that such virtues are acknowledged and nurtured, the intermingling of cultures – which is an integral feature of globalization – far from promoting global economic welfare, may not only inhibit it, but plunge the planet into a new round of destructive protectionism. I have also suggested that consideration be given to the setting up of a new supra-national institution, consisting primarily of religious leaders, to give advice on some of the moral issues and dilemmas specific to global capitalism; and of how these may be resolved in an environment in which, for the foreseeable future at least, there will be substantial cross-border differences in the interpretation of social justice and economic sufficiency, and in the prioritization of different components of virtuous behavior.

At any rate, I rest my case! I believe that the Christian Gospel *is* relevant to meeting the opportunities and challenges of global capitalism; and that the Christian apologist *does* have a role to play in ensuring that such capitalism advances the social good in a morally virtuous way. Only then do we believe that the question posed by the title of this book can be answered in the negative.

APPENDIX

DEMOCRATIC CAPITALISM AND DEMOCRATIC SOCIALISM

A SUMMARY BY SOME ADVOCATES AND BY SOME CRITICS

Democratic capitalism (DC)

Definition

DC is a socio-economic system in which:

1 The means of production (land, factories, machines, etc.) are privately owned (but not necessarily by single individuals).
2 Goods and services are sold in a free and competitive market, according to the law of supply and demand. Human need is given consideration but it is not first in priority.
3 Private ownership of the means of production and reliance on the market are recognized as morally legitimate.

Some advocates of democratic capitalism say:

1 *Economic*: DC is the most productive social system history has known, improving the standard of living for millions and offering the best hope for those still in poverty. It provides opportunity, rewards individual initiative, has enabled and encourages "upward mobility."
2 *Political*: DC is the natural ally of democracy and shares its concern for the protection of individual rights.
3 *Moral*: DC promotes the realization of human values, especially the value of individual freedom.

4   *Realism*: DC is realistic in that it relies on enlightened self-interest, the exercise of which – as by an "individual hand" – enriches the community.

Some critics of democratic capitalism say:

1   *Economic*: Although DC is productive, it is inherently irrational (unplanned), and the drive to maximize profits has had serious social consequences: instability, unemployment, dehumanization, materialism, social inequities.
2   *Political*: DC, with its intrinsic movement toward concentration of economic power, leads to the domination of society by huge corporations.
3   *Moral*: Private ownership of the means of production is inherently unjust: workers produce the goods, but owners receive the profits.
4   *Realism*: In the guise of realism about human nature, DC fosters privatism, selfishness, ruthlessness and greed.

Democratic socialism (DS)

Definition

DS is a socio-economic system in which:

1   The means of production are socially owned (but not necessarily by the state).
2   The production of goods and services is planned in light of society's goals. Human need is given consideration, but is not first in priority.
3   The social ownership of the means of production and the use of social planning are recognized as morally legitimate.

Some advocates of democratic socialism say:

1   *Economic*: Every business looks ahead and plans; it simply makes sense for society (through elected representative to plan the economy so as to meet human needs and realize social goals).
2   *Political*: DS is committed to political democracy and simply seeks to extend democracy into the economic realm so that we will have an economy "of the people, by the people, for the people."
3   *Moral*: We are all members of the human community, and in concern for the equal worth of each, we must provide for the needs of all and promote equality of well-being.
4   *Realism*: Nothing is more real than a great idea whose time has come. It is time now to create a society in which people are recognized as having equal worth, basic needs are met, and all participate in the

decisions that shape their lives. We need not remain resigned to the way things are now with all its misery.

Some critics of democratic socialism say:

1 *Economic*: DS is not nearly as productive as DC because no group of planners can successfully anticipate needs, demands and available supplies.
2 *Political*: DS dangerously combines political and economic power in the same hands and thus is constantly tempted to tyranny.
3 *Moral*: DS focuses on the "community" at the expense of the individual, and is ever tempted to deny individual rights for the sake of what is regarded as "the common good."
4 *Realism*: DS unrealistically calls for a "new humanity" and ignores the reality of self-interest and the persistence of sin. DS makes great promises, but it cannot deliver them.

DC as a point-of-view and way of life:

1 *View of social system*: DC views economic activity as a separate part of a complex 3-in-1 social system in which political democracy and moral-cultural pluralism are the other two parts, and insists that economic life should not be dominated by the state.
2 *View of the person*: DC sees the person primarily as an individual who is responsible for his or her own welfare. But individual self-interest is always defined in awareness of a larger community.
3 *Primary value*: DC holds that it gives primary value to freedom (interpreted as freedom from interference) and encourages risks, openness, creativity.
4 *Equality*: DC calls for equality of opportunity; assumes the opportunity of upward mobility; rejects as tyrannical and economically foolish all efforts to realize equality of results, e.g. income for all.
5 *Greatest fear*: DC fears political tyranny most, and guards against it by private ownership of the means of production and limits on the role of government.

DS as a point-of-view and way of life:

1 *View of social system*: DS sees the political economy holistically. Because the political, economic and moral-cultural dimensions of social life are inseparable, we should recognize this and rationally plan for the common good.
2 *View of the person*: DS sees the person primarily as a social being, bound inseparably with others. Thus, the welfare of the individual is a social problem calling for social response.

3   *Primary value*: DS holds that it gives primary value to equality and encourages compassion, mutuality, community.
4   *Equality*: DS holds that the equal worth of each person calls for a strong tilt toward equality of result and puts a heavy burden of proof on any effort to justify inequality.
5   *Greatest fear*: DS fears most of the concentration of power of any kind of the hands of a few, and guards against economic domination by the social ownership of the means of production and democratic decision-making in economic affairs.

Source: General Assembly of the Presbyterian Church (1984).

NOTES

This chapter is based upon an address which the author gave to a conference of the European Academy of International Business in Jerusalem in 1998. Similar talks were given by Jewish and Moslem scholars.

1   We say commercial wealth, yet much social capital was contributed by the civil society, which often involved the work of skilled craftsmen, e.g. the building of cathedrals.
2   Throughout this chapter, we shall confine our attention to a discussion of the merits and challenges of democratic capitalism (and also, where appropriate, democratic socialism); although we recognize both socio-economic systems may be operated by undemocratic states. For an excellent summary of the main features of democratic capitalism and democratic socialism, as seen by its advocates and critics, see Appendix 1 of this chapter and General Assembly of the Presbyterian Church (1984).
3   We accept Douglass North's view of institutions as "an existing framework of moral and behavioral norms that influence the way the values are and the costs of compliance" (North 1981, 1993).
4   Exceptions to these sentiments were the writings of the scholastic economists who saw moral merit in economic liberty and market-based institutions.
5   For an extended examination of these issues, see Tawney (1929), Preston (1979 and 1993), Weber (1930) and Sacks (1997).
6   As quoted by various authors, notably Novak (1982, 1993).
7   Except, perhaps, in terms of increases in the population. "Be fruitful and multiply . . ." Genesis 1 (28) 9 (1).
8   See especially St Mark's Gospel, Chapter 10, verses 23/25.
9   The contribution of these "intermediate" organizations to the global economy is explored in more detail in Dunning (1999).
10 As recounted in St Luke's Gospel, Chapter 10, verses 29/37.
11 See, for example, Ohmae (1995) and OECD (1997).
12 See, for example, Rodik (1997), Gray (1998), Luttwak (1999) and Dunning (1999).
13 As well as conferring many social *et al.* benefits, e.g. a reduction in infant mortality and a range of diseases, lower illiteracy, the upgrading of educational programs and institutional infrastructure.
14 There is a great temptation of Christian scholars to concentrate on distributive, rather than the wealth creating aspects of social justice as a means of

reducing income inequities. This is most understandable as the gospel of Jesus Christ pays particular attention to the responsibilities of individuals and communities, to the most disadvantaged members of society. Hence the doctrine of "sufficiency" for all, irrespective of merit. How one measures sufficiency, which embraces the basic necessities of life, in a global economy in which there are huge differences in living standards, between the rich and the poor nations (and also within those nations) is a real challenge, both to Christian apologists and politicians. However, one thing is certain. At the end of the day, only a limited amount can be accomplished by any redistribution of income. The only lasting way to alleviate physical suffering and economic poverty is by increasing wealth in the "have-not" countries. And if this can only be accomplished by increasing wealth in the "have" countries in a socially beneficial way – so be it!

15 For example, in 1997, the world's labor force was 47.2 percent of its population (World Bank 1998).

16 Such as roads, railroads, and airports, the natural environment, a country's cultural heritage and legal and social institutions designed to protect the rights and properties of individuals.

17 And there are many; for example, that of Korea and Japan are very different from that of the US and the UK; that of Singapore and Hong Kong very different from that of Columbia and Ghana; and that of Germany very different from that of Australia. Many adjectives have been used to describe different types of democratic capitalism. These include managerial, familial, statist, relational, consensus, competitive communitarism, consumer and producer, each of which both affects and responds to the workings of the global marketplace differently. For a more detailed analysis, see, for example, McCraw (1997) and Luttwak (1999).

18 Indeed, without such protection, the modern market system could never have developed in the way it has.

19 For further detail see UNCTAD (1998).

20 For a recent examination of these and other issues, see various chapters in Dunning (1997b).

21 See, for example, Donahue (1997) and Wallace (1998).

22 For example, see Donahue (1997), European Policies Research Center (1997) and Oman(2000).

23 Once again, we accept that global capitalism may take various forms, and what is perceived as "optimal" global capitalism by one country, or sectoral interest, or individual, may not be by another country, sectoral interest or individual. Certainly, there is a great deal of inefficiency in contemporary global capitalism.

24 Note, especially, the contrast in the role of the individual and the Church in Calvinist and Catholic teachings. See Weber (1985).

25 By, for example, Alexis de Tocqueville (1981).

26 The Chief Rabbi of the United Hebrew Congregations of the Commonwealth.

27 For a recent compendium of the most renowned contribution on the subject see Beamish (1998).

28 We do not accept that any one system of democratic capitalism is inherently superior to any other; although given societal goals and the competencies (and constraints) to achieve these goals, it is possible to suggest an optimal, or first best, allocation of resources and capabilities and a distribution of the benefits arising from these. On the other hand, the incorporation of the various components of a common moral code (based, for example, on the three "C"s shortly to be identified) may be more easily achieved in some capitalist systems than in others. Thus, any emphasis on the virtues of individu-

alism and creativity is likely to be comfortably embraced by US style capitalism; while communitarism and the social responsibilities of the state strike a sympathetic cord among European style capitalism. The virtues of self-sacrifice, interpersonal bonding, trust and commitment are important attributes of Japanese style capitalism; while in Chinese and Jewish communities those of familial loyalty, a strong sense of duty, and a culture of self-betterment are especially valued.

29 This view is shared, *inter alia*, by Michael Novak in a thoughtful, albeit provocative, view of the future of capitalism (Novak 1997).

30 For example, any erosion of the natural environment may be considered as negative creation.

31 It is noteworthy how, in spite of the cult of libertarianism, there has been a dramatic increase in the number and range of voluntary associations and special interest groups ranging from amateur dramatics through gardening clubs and railroad enthusiasts to age concern and welfare support agencies. For further details see Dunning (1999).

REFERENCES

Beamish, P. (ed.) (1998), *Joint Ventures and Strategic Alliances*, London: Edward Elgar.

Bell, D. (1993), *The Cultural Contradictions of Capitalism*, London: Heinemann.

Ben-Ner, A. and Gui, B. (eds) (1993), *The Non-Profit Sector in the Mixed Economy*, Ann Arbor: University of Michigan Press.

Centesimus Annus (1991), Rome: The Vatican, pp. 32–42.

Commission on Global Governance (1995), *Our Global Neighborhood*, Oxford and New York: Oxford University Press.

Demond, V. A. (1952), *Religion and the Decline of Capitalism*, Excelsior, Minnesota: Melvin McLosh Bookseller.

De Tocqueville (1981), *Democracy in America* (abbreviated with an introduction by Thomas Bender), New York: The Modern Library.

Donahue, J. D. (1997), *Disunited States*, New York: Basic Books.

Dunning, J. H. (1994), *Globalization, Economic Restructuring and Development*, Raul Prebisch Lecture, Geneva: UNCTAD.

Dunning, J. H. (1997a), *Alliance Capitalism and Global Business*, London and New York: Routledge.

Dunning, J. H. (ed.) (1997b), *Governments, Globalization and International Business*, Oxford: Oxford University Press.

Dunning, J. H. (1997c), "Technology and the changing boundaries of firms and governments," in OECD (ed.), *Industrial Competitiveness and the Global Economy*, Paris: OECD, pp. 53–68.

Dunning, J. H. (1998), "Globalization and the new geography of foreign direct investment," *Oxford Development Studies* 26 (1), pp. 47–69.

European Policies Research Centre (1997), *Policy Competition and Foreign Direct Investment in Europe*, Glasgow: Strathclyde University, EPRC, October.

Fukuyama, F. (1995), *Trust: The Social Virtues and the Creation of Prosperity*, London: Hamish Hamilton.

General Assembly of the Presbyterian Church (1984), *Christian Faith and Economic Justice*, New York: Office of General Assembly (OGA).

Gray, J. (1992), *The Moral Foundations of Market-Institutions*, London: IEA Health and Welfare Unit, Choice in Welfare No. 10.

Gray, J. (1998), *False Dawn*, New York: The New Press.

Green, D. G. (1993), *Reinventing Civil Society*, London: IEA Health and Welfare Unit, Choice in Welfare Series No. 17.

Hayek, von F. A. (1990), *The Fatal Conceit: The Errors of Socialism*, London: Routledge.

Heilbroner, R. L. (1992), *Twenty-first Century Capitalism*, London: UCL Press.

Himmelfarb, G. (1995), *The De-moralization of Society*, London: IEA Health and Welfare Unit, Choice in Welfare No. 22.

Huntingdon, S. (1993), "The clash of civilizations," *Foreign Affairs 72*, Summer, pp. 22–49.

Kennedy, P. M. (1993), *Preparing for the Twenty-first Century*, New York: Vantage Books.

Landes, D. (1998), *The Wealth and Poverty of Nations*, London: Little, Brown and Company.

Lipsey, R. G. (1997), "Globalization and national government policies: an economist's view," Dunning, J. H. (ed.), *Governments, Globalization and International Business*, Oxford University Press.

Luttwak, E. (1999), *Turbo-Capitalism*, New York: Harper-Collins.

Markusen, A. (1996), "Sticky places in slippery space: a typology of industrial districts," *Economic Geography 72* (3), pp. 293–313.

McCraw, T. K. (1997), *Creating Modern Capitalism*, Cambridge: Harvard University Press.

Moltmann, J. (1975), *The Experiment Hope*, translated by M. Douglas Meeks Meeting, Philadelphia: Fortress Press.

North, D. (1981), *Structure and Change in Economic History*, New York: Norton.

North, D. (1993), *Institutions, Transaction Costs and Productivity in the Long Run*, Paper presented to Eighth World Productivity Congress, Stockholm, May.

Novak, M. (1982), *The Spirit of Democratic Capitalism*, New York: Madison Books (new edition 1991).

Novak, M. (1993), Eight arguments about the morality of the marketplace, in Davies, J. (ed.), *God and the Marketplace*, London: IEA Health and Welfare Unit, Choice in Welfare No. 14.

Novak, M. (1997), *Awakening from Nihilism: In Preparation for the 21st Century: Four Lessons from the 20th Century*, London: IEA Health and Welfare Unit.

OECD (1997), *Industrial Competitiveness in the Knowledge Based Economy: The New Role of Government*, Paris: OECD.

Ohmae, K. (1995), *The End of the Nation State: The Rise of Regional Economies*, London: Harper.

Oman, C. P. (2000) *Policy Competition for Foreign Direct Investment*, Paris: OECD Development Centre.

Preston, R. H. (1979), *Religion and the Persistence of Capitalism*, Philadelphia: Trinity Press International.

Preston, R. H. (1993), *Religion and the Ambiguities of Capitalism*, Cleveland, Ohio: The Pilgrim Press.

Putman, R. D. (1995), "Bowling alone: America's declining social capital," *Journal of Democracy 6*, pp. 65–78.

Rifkin, J. (1995), *The End of Work*, New York: G. P. Putman's Sons.

Roberts, R. H. (1993), *Religion and the Resurgence of Capitalism*, London: Routledge.

Rodik, D. (1997), *Has Globalization Gone Too Far?*, Washington: Institute for International Economics.

Sacks, J. (1997), *The Politics of Hope*, London: Jonathan Cape.

Sandel, J. (1996), *Democracy's Discontent: American in Search of a Public Philosophy*, Cambridge, MA: Harvard University Press.

Searle, G. R. (1998), *Morality and the Market in Victorian Britain*, Oxford: Oxford University Press.

Sirico, R. A. (1994), *A Moral Basis for Liberty*, London: IEA Health and Welfare Unit, Religion and Liberty Series No. 2.

Smith, A. (1776) *An Inquiry into the Nature and Causes of the Wealth of Nations*, 1937 edition edited by Edwin Cannon, New York: Modern Library.

Tawney, R. H. (1929), *Religion and the Rise of Capitalism*, New York: Harcourt Brace and Co.

Tillich, P. (1971), *Political Expectations*, in Adams, J. L. (ed.), New York: Harper and Row, p. 51.

UNCTAD (1998), *World Investment Report 1998*, Geneva and New York: United Nations.

Wallace, L. (1998), *Foreign Direct Investment in New Jersey*, Newark, NJ: Rutgers University Ph.D. dissertation.

Walzer, M. (ed.) (1995), *Towards a Global Civil Society*, Oxford: Berghan Books.

Weber, M. (1930), *The Protestant Ethic and the Spirit of Capitalism*, London: Allen and Unwin.

World Bank (1998), *World Development Report 1998/99: Knowledge for Development*, Oxford: Oxford University Press.

Part II
Theoretical perspectives

3 The eclectic paradigm as an envelope for economic and business theories of MNE activity

Introduction: the contents of the eclectic paradigm

For more than two decades, the eclectic (or OLI[1]) paradigm has remained the dominant analytical framework for accommodating a variety of operationally testable economic theories of the determinants of foreign direct investment (FDI) and the foreign activities of multinational enterprises (MNEs).[2]

The eclectic paradigm is a simple, yet profound, construct. It avers that the extent, geography and industrial composition of foreign production undertaken by MNEs is determined by the interaction of three sets of interdependent variables, which themselves comprise the components of three sub-paradigms. The first is the competitive advantages of the enterprises seeking to engage in FDI (or increase their existing FDI), which are specific to the ownership of the investing enterprises, i.e. their ownership (O) specific advantages. This sub-paradigm asserts that, *ceteris paribus*, the greater the competitive advantages of the investing firms, *relative to those of other firms* – and particularly those domiciled in the country in which they are seeking to make their investments – the more they are likely to be able to engage in, or increase, their foreign production.

The second is the locational attractions (L) of alternative countries or regions, for undertaking the value adding activities of MNEs. This sub-paradigm avers that the more the immobile, natural or created endowments, which firms need to use jointly with their own competitive advantages, favor a presence in a foreign, rather than a domestic, location, the more firms will choose to augment or exploit their O specific advantages by engaging in FDI.

The third sub-paradigm of the OLI tripod offers a framework for evaluating alternative ways in which firms may organize the creation and exploitation of their core competencies, given the locational attractions of different countries or regions. Such modalities range from buying and selling goods and services in the open market, through a variety of interfirm non-equity agreements, to the integration of intermediate product markets, and an outright purchase of a foreign corporation. The eclectic paradigm, like its near relative, internalization theory,[3] avows that the greater the net benefits of internalizing cross-border intermediate product markets, the more likely a firm will prefer to engage in foreign production itself, rather than license the right to use the intangible assets transferred, e.g. by a technical service or franchise agreement, to a foreign firm.

The eclectic paradigm further asserts that the precise configuration of the OLI parameters facing any particular firm, and the response of the firm to that configuration, is strongly contextual. In particular, it will reflect the economic and political features of the country or region of the investing firms, and of the country or region in which they are seeking to invest; the industry and the nature of the value-added activity in which the firms are engaged; the characteristics of the individual investing firms, including their objectives and strategies in pursuing these objectives; and the *raison d'être* for the FDI.

Regarding this last contextual variable, scholars have identified four main types of foreign-based MNE activity:[4]

1   That designed to satisfy a particular foreign market, or set of foreign markets, viz. *market seeking*, or demand oriented, FDI.
2   That designed to gain access to natural resources, e.g. minerals, agricultural products, unskilled labor, viz. *resource seeking*, or supply oriented FDI.
3   That designed to promote a more efficient division of labor or specialization of an existing portfolio of foreign and domestic assets by MNEs, i.e. *rationalized or efficiency seeking* FDI. This type of FDI, though related to the first or second kind, is usually sequential to it.
4   That designed to protect or augment the existing O specific advantages of the investing firms and/or to reduce those of their competitors, i.e. *strategic asset seeking* FDI.

Combining our knowledge of the individual parameters of the OLI paradigm with that of the economic and other characteristics of home and host countries, and of the investing, or potentially investing, firms, it is possible to derive a wide range of fairly specific and operationally testable *theories*. Thus, it may be hypothesized that some sectors, e.g. the oil and pharmaceutical sectors, are likely to generate more FDI than others, e.g. the iron and steel or aircraft sectors, because the characteristics of the former generate more unique O advantages, and/or because their locational needs favor production outside their home countries, and/or because the net benefits of internalizing cross-border intermediate product markets are greater.

Similarly, it is possible to predict that the significance of outward FDI will be greater for some countries, e.g. Switzerland and the Netherlands, than for others, e.g. Russia and India, simply by knowing about their economic histories, the core competencies of their indigenous firms, the size of their home markets, their experience in foreign markets, and the locational attractions of their immobile resources and capabilities, relative to those of other countries. Finally, some firms, even of the same nationality and from the same industry, are more likely to engage in FDI than others. Sometimes, this might reflect their size – on the whole, large firms tend to be more multinational than small firms; sometimes their attitude to risk – particularly those associated with foreign ventures and of foreign partnerships with foreign firms; and sometimes their innovating product, marketing, locational, or FDI strategies.

The extent and pattern of foreign owned production will depend on the challenges and opportunities offered by different kinds of value-added activity. Thus the growth of existing, and the emergence of new markets, e.g. in China, over recent years, has led to a considerable expansion of various kinds of market seeking FDI – particularly in fast growing industries, e.g. telecommunications. By contrast, the rate of expansion of several natural resource sectors has been less impressive, as many products have become less resource intensive, due, for example, to the innovation of new alloys, improved recycling techniques, the miniaturization of components, and the replacement of natural by synthetic materials. The reduction of both transport costs and artificial barriers to most forms of trade has led to more efficiency seeking FDI – both among developed countries and between developed and developing countries.[5] While as some kinds of technology have become more standardized and/or more codifiable, licensing agreements and management contracts have replaced FDI, e.g. in the hotel and fast foods sectors, in the more knowledge and trade intensive industries, e.g. pharmaceuticals, industrial electronics and management consultancy, the economies of global integration have made for a dramatic increase in merger and acquisition (M&A) activity (UN 1998).[6] Moreover, the advent of call centres and electronic commerce is not only heralding the end of the geography of some financial and information markets, but is revolutionizing the organization of intra-firm production and trade.[7]

The content and predictions of the eclectic paradigm are firmly embedded in a number of different economic and business theories. Although *taken separately*, none of these offer a comprehensive explanation of the growth and decline of MNE business activity,[8] *taken together*, i.e. as a group, they do so. Most of the theories, too, are complementary, rather than substitutable, to each other. Some tend to focus on particular kinds of FDI, but not others. Others are designed to explain different aspects of international production, e.g. its ownership, structure, its locational profile or its organizational form Thus, location theory forms the basis of the "where" of MNE activity; industrial organization and resource based theories of the firm offer some reasons "why" foreign owned affiliates may have a competitive edge over their indigenous competitors; while the concept of the firm as a "nexus of treaties" (Williamson 1990) is critical to an understanding of the existence of MNEs, and of why firms prefer to engage in FDI rather than sell their O specific assets, or the rights to use them, to independent foreign producers.

Much of this chapter will, in fact, seek to demonstrate how, and in what ways, these approaches are complementary to each other; and of how the eclectic paradigm offers both an envelope of these theories, and a common analytical framework within which each can be accommodated and fully enriched in their application.[9]

Finally, the relevance of the individual components of the eclectic paradigm, and the system of which they are part, will depend on whether one is seeking to explain the static or dynamic determinants of MNE activity. For example, one of the earliest theories of FDI, viz. the product cycle theory, put forward by Raymond Vernon (1966), was concerned not only with explaining the *process* by which firms deepened and widened their markets,[10] but also how their locational needs might change as they moved from the innovatory to the standardized stage of production. By contrast, much of extant location theory and internalization theory seeks to identify and explain the optimum spatial and organizational dimensions of the existing resources and capabilities of firms and nations. Knickerbocker's "follow my leader," and Graham's "tit for tat" thesis (Knickerbocker 1973, Graham 1975) also contain a longitudinal dimension, which, for the most part, is absent in most variants of industrial organization theory, for example as originally propounded by Hymer (1960) and Caves (1973). Initially, too, the eclectic paradigm primarily addressed static and efficiency related issues (Dunning 1977), but more recently has given attention to the dynamic competitiveness and locational strategy of firms, and particularly the path dependency of the upgrading of their core competencies (Dunning 1995, 1998, 1999).

The kernel of this paper is directed to examining the changes in the boundaries, constraints and structure of the eclectic paradigm over the past 20 years;[11] and those now being demanded of it by contemporary world events and scholarly thinking. In doing so, it will pay especial attention to the emergence of alliance capitalism[12] and the growth of asset augmenting FDI (Wesson 1993 and 1997, Makino 1998 and Kuemmerle 1999). In particular, it will set its analysis in the context of four significant happenings of the 1980s and 1990s, viz.:

a   the maturation of the knowledge-based economy,[13]
b   the deepening integration of international economic and financial activity, including that fostered by electronic networks (Kobrin 1999),
c   the liberalization of cross-border markets, and the flotation of the world's major currencies, and
d   the emergence of several new countries as important new players on the global economic stage.

The next three sections will examine how the main intellectual thrust in explaining each of the OLI triumvirate of variables has evolved over this time. In particular, it will argue that, as the dynamic composition of these variables has assumed more significance, so the value of the eclectic paradigm has increased relative to the sum of its parts, with the contribution of each becoming increasingly interdependent of each other. Finally, the chapter will give especial attention to the contribution of strategic cum managerial approaches to understanding the growth and composition of MNE activity, while averring that the relevance and richness of these is enhanced if set within the overarching construct of the eclectic paradigm.

The ownership sub-paradigm

In explaining the growth of international production, several strands of economic and business theory assert that this is dependent on the investing firms possessing some kind of unique and sustainable competitive advantage (or set of advantages), relative to that (or those) possessed by their foreign competitors. Indeed, some would argue that in traditional neoclassical theory, in which the firm is a "black box," no FDI is possible – as all firms have equal access to the same resources and capabilities *within* their own countries, while there is complete immobility of resources and capabilities *between* countries.

When the eclectic paradigm was first put forward (in 1977),[14] it was assumed that such competitive or O specific advantages largely reflected the resources and capabilities of the home countries of the investing firms; and that FDI would only occur when the benefits of exploiting, i.e. adding value to, these advantages from a foreign location outweighed the opportunity costs of so doing.

Since the 1960s, the extant literature has come to identify three main kinds of firm or O specific competitive advantages.

1   Those relating to the possession and exploitation of monopoly power, as initially identified by Bain (1956) and Hymer (1960) – and the industrial organization (IO) scholars (e.g. Caves 1971, 1980, Porter 1980, 1985). These advantages are presumed to stem from, or create, some kind of barrier to entry to final product markets by firms not possessing them.
2   Those relating to the possession of a bundle of scarce, unique and sustainable resources and capabilities, which essentially reflect the superior technical efficiency of a particular firm relative to those of its competitors.[15] These advantages are presumed to stem from, or create, some kind of barrier to entry to factor, or intermediate, product markets by firms not possessing them. Their identification and evaluation has been one of the main contributions of the resource-based and evolutionary theories of the firm.[16]

3   Those relating to the competencies of the *managers* of firms to identify, evaluate and harness resources and capabilities from throughout the world, and to co-ordinate these with the existing resources and capabilities under their jurisdiction in a way which best advances the long-term interests of the firm.[17] These advantages, which are closely related to those set out in (2) are especially stressed by organizational scholars, such as Prahalad and Doz (1987), Doz Asakawa, Santos and Williamson (1997) and Bartlett and Ghoshal (1989, 1993). They tend to be *management*, rather than *firm*, specific in the sense that, even within the same corporation, the intellectual *et al.* competencies of the main decision-takers may vary widely.

The *relative* significance of these three kinds of O specific advantages has changed over the past two decades, as markets have become more liberalized, and as wealth creating activities have become more knowledge intensive. In the 1970s, the unique competitive advantages of firms primarily reflected their ability to internally produce and organize proprietary assets, and match these to existing market needs. At the turn of the millennium, the emphasis is more on their capabilities to access and organize knowledge intensive assets from throughout the world; and to integrate these, not only with their existing competitive advantages, but with those of other firms engaging in complementary value-added activities. Hence, the emergence of alliance capitalism, and the need of firms to undertake FDI to protect, or augment, as well as to exploit, their existing O specific advantages (Dunning 1995). Hence, too, the growing importance of multinationality, *per se*, as an intangible asset in its own right.

The question at issue, then, is whether the changing character and boundaries of the O specific advantages of firms can be satisfactorily incorporated into the eclectic paradigm, as it was first put forward. We would argue that as long as they do not undermine the basic tenets of the paradigm, and are not mutually inconsistent, they can be, although most certainly, they do require some modification to existing subparadigms and theories.

In Table 3.1, we set out some of the models and hypotheses which have been sought to explain the origin, nature and extent of O specific advantages. We divide these into two categories, viz. those which view such advantages as the income generating resources and capabilities possessed by a firm, at a given moment of time, i.e. *static* O advantages; and those which treat such advantages as the ability of a firm to sustain and *increase* its income generating assets over time, i.e. *dynamic* O advantages. Both kinds of advantages tend to be context specific, e.g. with respect to industry or country; and related to the kinds of competitive advantages (as identified earlier) which firms seek to attain or sustain. While over the past two decades, changes in the world economic scenario and knowledge about MNE activity have led to a *relative* decline in market-seeking (MS) and resource-seeking (RS) FDI – both of which tend to be based on the static O advantages of the investing firms – they still help to explain a major part of first-time FDI, particularly in developing countries (Dunning 1999).

However, one of the key characteristics of the last two decades has been the increasing significance of FDI based on the possession of, or need to acquire, dynamic O advantages. Thus, rationalized or efficiency-seeking (ES) FDI is only viable if: (a) the investing firm is already producing in at least one foreign country; and (b) both intermediate and final product, trade is relatively unimpeded by natural or artificial cross-border barriers. Strategic asset-seeking (SAS) FDI is dependent on intellectual capital being located in more than one country, and the proposition that it is economically preferable for firms to acquire or create these assets outside, rather than within, their home countries.

To successfully explain dynamic and alliance related O specific advantages, each of the particular theories of FDI identified in Table 3.1 requires some modification. Thus, the *resource-based* theory needs to reexamine the content and significance of existing resources and capabilities of the firm in terms of:

i   their ability to sustain and/or upgrade these advantages;
ii their ability to harness and influence the quality and price of complementary assets, and to efficiently coordinate these with their own innovating competencies; and
iii their ability to locate their value-added activities in countries and regions which offer the optimum portfolio of immobile assets, both for creating or acquiring new O specific advantages, and for exploiting their existing advantages. *Inter alia*, such immobile assets may reflect the bargaining and negotiating skills of MNEs in their dealings with foreign governments (Rugman and Verbeke 1998).

While accepting much of the content of *resource-based* theory, the *evolutionary* theory of the firm pays more attention to the *process* or *path* by which the specific O advantages of firms evolve and are accumulated over time. In contrast (or in addition) to internalization theory, it tends to regard the firm as an innovator of created assets, rather than a "nexus of treaties." It is, by its nature, a dynamic theory, which, like the resource-based theory, accepts the diversity of competencies between firms; however, unlike the latter, it focuses on the firm's long-term strategy towards asset accumulation and learning capabilities, and its implications both for established routines and the development of new ones (Nelson and Winter 1982, Nelson 1991, Foss, Knudsen and Montgomery 1995, Teece, Pisano and Shuen 1997).

Zeroing down to management as the unit of analysis, contemporary organizational scholars, such as Prahalad and Doz (1987), Doz, Asakawa,

Table 3.1 Theories explaining O specific advantages of firms

A: Group 1 Explaining static O advantages	(1) MS	(2) RS	(3) ES	(4) SAS
Product cycle theory Vernon (1966, 1974, 1979)	• Country (largely US) specific resources and capabilities of firms • All asset exploiting FDI • Further hypothesizes that competitive advantages of firms are likely to change as product moves through its cycle		• Oa advantages based on efficiency of investing firms also described in various empirical studies from Dunning (1958) and Safarian (1966) onwards.	
Industrial organization theories Hymer (1960, 1976), Caves (1971, 1974, 1996), Dunning (1958, 1993), Teece (1981, 1984)		• Largely Oa advantages initiated, or protected, by entry and/or mobility barriers to product markets. These include patent protection and marketing, production and financial scale economies. • All asset exploiting FDI. • Little attention paid to asset augmenting FDI.		
Multinationality, organizational and risk diversification theories Vernon (1973, 1983), Rugman (1979), Kogut (1983, 1985), Kogut and Kulatilaka (1994), Doz *et al.* (1997), Rangan (1998)		• Mainly Ot advantages, but also some Oa advantages arising from presence of investing firms in countries with different economic political, cultural circumstances. Ot advantages include ability to access, harness and integrate differences in distribution of natural and created assets and of organizational and managerial experience related to these. • FDI primarily asset exploiting, but also some asset augmenting. (Potentially could be extended to include why markets for sustaining or increasing O specific advantages are best internalized.)		

Internalization theory
Buckley and Casson (1976, 1985, 1998a, b), Hennart (1982, 1989), Rugman (1982, 1996)

- Entirely confined to Oa and Ot advantages arising from internalization of intermediate product markets.
- All asset exploiting FDI.
- Largely, though not exclusively, a static theory, though some acknowledgement that relative transaction costs of markets and hierarchies may vary as firms seek to exploit dynamic market imperfections

Capital imperfections theory
Aliber (1971)

- Largely independent of type of FDI. The theory argues that firms from countries with strong exchange rates or which discount capital at higher rates of interest will be tempted to invest, often by M&As, in countries which are economically weaker. The theory, as initially put forward, has no time (t) dimension; and, in essence, is a financial variant of internalization theory.

Follow my leader, tit for tat theory
Knickerbocker (1973), Graham (1975, 1990, 1998), Flowers (1976)

- Mainly concerned with explaining FDI as a space related strategy among competing oligopolists. The main hypothesis is that FDI will be bunched in particular regions or countries over time; and that there is likely to be an inter-penetration of the territories occupied by the oligopolists. Though originally applied to explain asset-exploiting FDI, it is now also being used to explain some asset augmenting FDI.

Resource-based theory
Wernerfelt (1984, 1995), Conner (1991), Helleloid (1992), Montgomery (1995), Conner and Prahalad (1996)

- As initially formulated, mainly concerned with identifying and evaluating variables influencing sustainability of competitive advantages of firms. Less attention given to traditional barriers to entry and more to such variables as specificity, rareness and non-imitability of resources, and the capabilities of firms to create and utilize them. Mainly concerned with asset exploiting FDI and only limited recognition of O_t advantages.

- FDI designed to augment domestic-based resources and capabilities (Wesson 1993, 1997, Makino 1997, Dunning 1996, Chen and Chen 1999, Kuemmerle 1999)

Table 3.1 continued

	(1) MS	*(2) RS*	*(3) ES*	*(4) SAS*

B: Group 2
Explaining dynamic O advantages

Evolutionary theory
Nelson and Winter (1982), Cantwell (1991), Cantwell (1989, 1994), Cantwell, Dosi, Freeman, Nelson, Silverberg and Soete (1988), Saviotti and Metcalfe (1991), Teece, Pisano and Shuen (1997)

- A holistic and time-related approach, mainly directed to identifying and evaluating dynamic Oa advantages of firms. Basic proposition relates to the path dependency of accumulated competitive advantages, and that the more efficient firms are in managing these advantages, the more likely they will have the capability to engage in asset exploiting and asset augmenting FDI.

Organizational (management-related) theories
Prahalad and Doz (1987), Bartlett and Ghoshal (1989, 1993), Porter (1991), Doz and Santos (1997), Doz, Asakawa, Santos and Williamson (1997)

- Essentially explain O advantages in terms of ability of managers to devise appropriate organizational structures and techniques to effectively access, coordinate and deploy resources and capabilities across the globe. These theories, in recent years, have especially focused on the cross-border sourcing of intellectual assets and the coordination of these assets with those purchased within the MNE.

Oa = ownership advantage based on the possession or privileged access to a specific asset:

Ot = ownership advantages based on capabilities to organize assets, both internal and external to the investing firm, in the most efficient way.

(1) Market seeking   (2) Resource seeking   (3) Efficiency seeking   (4) Strategic asset seeking

Santos and Williamson (1997), and Bartlett and Ghoshal (1989, 1993) are paying increasing attention to the harnessing, leveraging, processing and deployment of knowledge-based assets as a core competence. While the subject of interest is similar to that of the resource and evolutionary theories, the emphasis of this kind of approach is on the capabilities of management to orchestrate and integrate the resources it can internally upgrade or innovate, or externally acquire, rather than on the resources themselves. But, as with the resource-based and evolutionary theories, the objective of the decision-taker is assumed to be as much directed to explaining the growth of firm specific assets, as to optimizing the income stream from a given set of assets.

The question now arises. To what extent are the theories relating to the origin and content of O specific advantages, as set out in Table 3.1 – and particularly their contemporary versions – consistent with, or antagonistic to, each other? Our reading is that, when the eclectic paradigm was first propounded, they were largely aimed at explaining different phenomena, or offered complementary, rather than alternative, explanations for the same phenomena. It is true the unit of analysis was frequently different; and that the underlying philosophy and some of the assumptions of industrial organization theory were different than those of resource-based theories (Pauwells and Matthysenns 1997). But, in general, within their specified analytical framework, the predictions of the various theories were consistent with those of a general "envelope" paradigm, and also the more specific predictions of the O sub-paradigm about the kind of competitive advantages likely to be possessed by MNEs, and the industrial sectors and countries in which their affiliates were likely to record superior levels of performance relative to those of their indigenous competitors (Dunning 1993, Caves 1996).

The locational sub-paradigm of countries (and regions)

For the most part, until recently, neither the economics nor the business literature gave much attention as to how the emergence and growth of the cross-border activities of firms might be explained by the kind of location-related theories which were initially designed to explain the siting of production *within* a nation state; nor, indeed, of how the spatial dimension of FDI might affect the competitiveness of the investing entities. In the last decade or so, however, there has been a renaissance of interest by economists (e.g. Audretsch 1998, Krugman 1991, 1993, 1998 and Venables 1998), and industrial geographers (e.g. Scott 1996, Storper 1995 and Storper and Scott 1995) in the spatial concentration and clustering of some kinds of economic activity; by economists in the role of exchange rates in affecting the extent, geography and timing of FDI (Cushman 1985, Froot and Stein 1991, Rangan 1998); and by business scholars (Porter 1994, 1996 and Enright 1991, 1998, 1999) in the idea that an optimum locational portfolio of assets is a competitive advantage in its own right.

The eclectic paradigm has always recognized the importance of the locational advantages of countries as a key determinant of the foreign production of MNEs (Dunning 1998).[18] Moreover, since the 1930s, at least, there have been numerous context-specific theories of the geographical distribution of FDI and the siting of particular value-added activities of firms.[19] Some of these "partial" theories are set out in Table 3.2. They include the locational component of Vernon's product cycle theory (Vernon 1966), and that of Knickerbocker's "follow my leader" theory (Knickerbocker 1973) which was one of the earliest attempts to explain the geographical clustering of FDI; and Rugman's risk diversification theory, which suggested that MNEs normally prefer a geographical spread of their foreign investments to having "all their eggs in the same (locational) basket" (Rugman 1979).[20]

However, for the most part, the question of *where* to locate a particular FDI, given the configuration of the O and I variables, was not thought to raise new issues of interest to students of the MNE. At the same time, throughout the last three decades, there have been many *empirical* studies on the determinants of both the export v. FDI choice of corporations, and the spatial distribution of MNE activity.[21]

Once again, in conformity with our earlier analysis, and as Table 3.2 shows, these explanatory variables are seen to differ according to the motives for FDI, its sectoral composition, the home and host countries of the investing firms, and a variety of firm specific considerations. But, in the main, scholarly research has extended, rather than replaced, standard theories of location to encompass cross-border value-added activities. In particular, it has embraced new locational variables, e.g. exchange rate and political risks, the regulations and policies of supra-national entities,[22] inter-country cultural differences; and has placed a different value of other variables common both to domestic and international locational choices.[23] However, these add-on or re-valued variables could be easily accommodated within the extant analytical structures.[24] This marked off most pre-1990 explanations of the location (L) specific advantage of nations from those of the O specific advantages of firms.

The emergence of the knowledge-based globalizing economy and asset augmenting FDI is compelling scholars to take a more dynamic approach to both the logistics of the siting of corporate activities, and to the competitive advantages of nations and/or regions. In the former case, firms need to take account not only of the presence and cost of traditional factor endowments, of transport costs, of current demand levels and patterns, and of Marshallian type agglomerative economies (Marshall 1920); but also of distance related transaction costs (Storper and Scott 1995), of dynamic externalities, knowledge accumulation, and interactive learning (Enright 1991, 1998, 1999, Florida 1995, Malmberg, Sölvell and Zander

Table 3.2 Theories explaining L specific advantages of countries

	(1) MS	(2) RS	(3) ES	(4) SAS
1 Traditional location theories Hoover (1948), Hotelling (1929), Isard (1956), Losch (1954), Lloyd and Dicken (1990), Weber (1928)	• Demand related variables, e.g. size, character and potential growth of local and adjacent markets. • Presence of competitors	• Supply oriented variables, e.g. availability, quality and price of natural resources, transportation costs, artificial barriers to trade.	• Supply oriented variables, especially those related to comparative advantages of immobile assets, e.g. labor, land and infrastructure.	• Location and price of created assets, including those owned by firms likely to be acquired. • Exchange rates.
2 Theories related to the process of internationalization Anderson and Gatignon (1986), Buckley and Cavusgil (1980), Daniels (1971), Forsgren (1989), Hirsch (1976), Johanson & Vahlne (1977, 1990), Luostarinen (1979), Vernon (1996), Welch and Luostarinen (1988)	• Mainly MS and RS, using traditional locational variables, but also several firm specific variables and transaction costs. • Emphasis on role of psychic distance, particularly in exploiting knowledge-based O advantages (Daniels 1971, Johanson and Vahlne 1977, 1990).			• Some attention given to FDI as a learning activity.
3 Theories related to agglomeration of economic activity Audretsch (1998), Enright (1991, 1998, 1999), Forsgren (1989), Krugman (1991, 1993, 1998), Malmberg, Sölvell and Luostarinen (1988)	• Some clustering of products for convenience of consumers, including industrial consumers. • Economies of scale and scope.	• Supply related clusters, based on static external economies, e.g. pooled labor markets. • Economies of scale and scope.		• Supply related clusters based on asset augmenting activities, local accumulation of knowledge, and exchange of information and learning experiences.

Table 3.2 continued

	(1) MS	(2) RS	(3) ES	(4) SAS
Zander (1996), Porter (1994, 1996), Storper (1995), Cantwell and Piscitello (1997)				
4 Theories related to spatially specific transaction costs Florida (1995), Scott (1996), Storper and Scott (1995)	• Given production and transport costs, external ties and scale economies, spatially related transaction costs are hypothesized to lead to a clustering of related activities. (a) to reduce overall costs and (b) to maximize benefits of inter-related innovating and learning activities.			• As for MS, RS and ES, but directed to asset augmenting activities, and strategic networking.
5 Theories related to complementary assets Teece (1992), Teece, Pisano and Shuen (1997), Chen and Chen (1998, 1999)	• The presence of related activities which help lower transport costs and promote joint economies in innovation, production and marketing.			• Mainly incentives to promote innovation-driven alliances, and the upgrading of existing O advantages of investing firms.
6 Theories related to government induced incentives Loree and Guisinger (1995), UNCTAD (1996a)	• Especially fiscal and other incentives leading to increase in demand for products of MNEs.	• Supply related incentives, concessionary rights for exploitation of natural resource-based sectors; intellectual property rights, tax advantages for RS and ES.		
7 Theories related to oligopolistic behavior and product cycle Graham (1978, 1998), Knickerbocker (1973), Vernon (1974)	• Follow my leader and other forms of oligopolistic behavior may apply to all four forms of international production, although incentives and pressures for such behavior are likely to be context specific.			

8 Theories of risk diversification Agmon and Lessard (1977), Rugman (1979)	Types of location specific risk vary with kind of FDI, but theory suggests that firm will diversify their portfolios to minimize their risk exposures, which include exchange, political and economic risks.	• Risks of SAS FDI also relate to inappropriate timing (especially for M&As) and insufficient knowledge about the assets being acquired.
9 Exchange rate theories Aliber (1971), Cushman (1985), Froot and Stein (1991), Blonigen (1997), Rangan (1997)	Theories which assume exchange rates or changes in exchange rates, suitably discounted for risk, capture most of the differences in cross-border locational costs, and also expectations of investors about the future course of exchange rates. These embrace all kinds of FDI, but particularly that of the timing of M&As.	
10 Knowledge enhancing (dynamic) theories of location Dunning (1997), Kogut and Zander (1994), Kuemmerle (1996), Porter (1994, 1998), Chen and Chen (1998, 1999)	See also SAS column, for 1–7 above. More specifically, dynamic theories are directed to explaining locational strategy in terms of sustaining and promoting location specific advantages in a world of uncertainty, learning and continuous innovation and upgrading of products. Applies especially to research and development activity of all kinds of FDI. The need to exploit dynamic locational advantage especially pronounced in high technology sectors.	• Theory is that firms will invest in those countries which offer the greatest opportunity for upgrading their existing core competencies and that such a locational strategy is path dependent.

1996), of spatially related innovation and technological standards (Antonelli 1998, Sölvell and Zander 1998), of the increasing dispersion of created assets, and of the need to conclude cross-border asset augmenting and/or asset exploiting alliances (Dunning 1995, 1998).

Contemporary economic events are suggesting that the nature and composition of a country or region's comparative advantage, which has been traditionally based on its possession of a unique set of immobile *natural* resources and capabilities, is now more geared to its ability to offer a distinctive and non-imitatible set of location bound *created* assets, including the presence of indigenous firms with which foreign MNEs might form alliances to complement their own core competencies. Recent research not only reveals that some nation states are not only becoming increasingly dependent on the cross-border activities of their own and foreign-based corporations for their economic prosperity (Dunning 1996, UNCTAD 1998);[25] but that the competitiveness of these corporations is becoming increasingly fashioned by the institutional framework within which they operate (Oliver 1997, Doremus, Keller, Pauly and Reich 1998). In particular, both nation states and sub-national authorities are becoming more aware of the need to provide the appropriate economic and social infrastructure, both for their own firms to generate the O specific assets consistent with the demands of world markets, and for foreign investors to engage in the kind of value-adding activities which advances the dynamic comparative advantage of the immobile assets within their jurisdiction (Porter 1994, Peck 1996, Dunning 1998).

As yet, business strategists, organizational, and marketing scholars have paid little attention to how their own explanations of the timing and geographical profile of international business activity need modifying in the light of the new forms of FDI and of alliance capitalism. There is, for example, little treatment of spatially related factors in either the resource-based or the evolutionary theories of the firm; although the role of spatially related agglomerative economies is being increasingly recognized as an important source of learning and innovating capabilities. Indeed, Michael Porter has gone as far as to say that, in the modern global economy, "anything that can be moved or sourced from a distance is no longer a competitive advantage" (Porter 1998, p. 29), and that "the true advantages today are things that are sticky, that is not easily movable" (ibid. p. 29). If this is correct, it may be inferred that as the dynamic gains from spatial clustering and network linkages become more pronounced,[26] so will the locational choice of firms become a more critical strategic variable. It also follows that national and regional authorities should pay more attention to the fostering of immobile complementary assets and cluster related public goods as part of their policies to attract and retain mobile investment.

As in the case of O specific advantages, scholarly research on the kind of L advantages most likely to explain the "where" of international production has taken on a new trajectory over the past decade. More particularly, the dramatic increase in cross-border mergers and acquisitions,[27] has reflected the availability and price of assets that firms wish to acquire or tap into to protect or augment their competitive advantages. While the exchange rate might certainly affect a timing of the FDI, the extent to which the acquired assets – together with the business environment of which they are part – advances the competitiveness and strategic trajectories of the investing firms, are the critical locational determinants.

Finally, we would observe that, although several strands of intellectual thought contribute towards our understanding of the locational dynamics of MNE activity, these offer complementary, rather than alternative, explanations. This is not to deny that there are differences of emphasis or methodology among scholars,[28] but we believe that they are not substantive enough to preclude their incorporation into any revised paradigm of international production.

The internalization sub-paradigm

Given that a firm has a set of competitive or O specific advantages, and the immobile assets of a foreign country are such as to warrant locating value-adding or asset augmenting activities there, what determines whether such activities are undertaken by the firms possessing the advantages, or by indigenous producers buying the advantage, or the right to its use, in the open market, or acquiring them by some other means?[29] Orthodox internalization theory offers a fairly straight-forward answer, viz. as long as the transaction and coordination costs of using external arm's length markets in the exchange of intermediate products, information, technology, marketing techniques, etc. exceed those incurred by internal hierarchies, then it will pay a firm to engage in FDI, rather than conclude a licensing or another market related agreement with a foreign producer. In general, the transaction costs of using external markets tend to be positively correlated with the imperfections of those markets. Over the last two decades, an extensive literature has identified a whole range of market failures, such as those associated with bounded rationality, and the provision of public and jointly supplied products and common intangible assets, and which permit opportunism, information asymmetries, uncertainty, economies of scale, and externalities of one kind or another.[30]

In explaining why firms choose to engage in FDI rather than buy or sell intermediate products in some other way (the third question which any international business theorist must answer) internalization theory has provided the dominant explanation over the past two decades. Yet it has not gone unchallenged. The major criticisms have been of three kinds. The first is that it is an incomplete theory in that it ignores other functions which a firm may perform, other than those which are transaction related; and other reasons, apart from short-run profit maximization, why firms may wish to engage in value-added activities outside their national boundaries. For example, firms have abilities of learning, memory adaptation and the capabilities to produce – tasks which markets cannot emulate. Many cross-border M&As are undertaken to gain new resources and/or to access to new capabilities, markets, or to lower the unit costs of production, or to gain market power, or to forestall or thwart the behavior of competitors.

Such objectives fit less comfortably with the conception of a firm as a "nexus of treaties," and more with that of a firm as a "collection or bundle of resources" (Barney 1991), or as a "repository of knowledge and capabilities" (Kogut and Zander 1994, Madhok 1996). This does not destroy the validity of internalization theory *per se*. It does, however, suggest that its contents should be widened to incorporate *all* costs and benefits associated with corporate activities; and not only those which are transaction related![31] Contemporary writings, both by resource-based and evolutionary scholars have refocused attention on the *unique* characteristics of the firm,[32] *vis à vis* those of other institutions; viz. as a unit of production, whose function is to efficiently convert a given set of resources into economically rewarding products.

The second criticism of orthodox internalization theory is that it is a static theory, and gives little guidance as to how best a firm may organize its activities to create future assets, rather than optimize the use of its existing assets. The increasing role of innovation in the contemporary global economy, and the need of firms to tap into, and exploit, resources and capabilities outside their home countries, is requiring a reappraisal of the rationale for, and economics of, extending the boundaries of a firm. It is also requiring scholars to judge the success of managerial strategy less on the criteria of short-run profitability, and more on that of long-run asset appreciation. To be relevant in a dynamic context, extant internalization theory needs to explain why firm-specific transaction costs are likely to be less than market-specific transaction costs in the *creation*, as well as in the *use*, of resources and capabilities.

Third, the growth of a range of inter-firm coalitions is resulting in *de facto* internalization, but without equity ownership. This is most evident in two cases. The first is where the competitive advantage of a firm is based on its ownership of a set of proprietary rights, the use of which it can effectively control and monitor through a contractual agreement. The second is that where firms engage in collaborative agreements for a very specific purpose, which is usually time limited, e.g. a research and development project or a joint marketing arrangement in a particular country or region. Here, full internalization, which, in essence, addresses ownership issues, is not a realistic option for the participating firms. At the same time, most strategic partnerships now being formed cannot be construed as arm's length transactions as the participants have a continuing knowledge sharing relationship with each other (Dunning 1995, UN 1998).

The advent of alliance capitalism, which may be perceived as a variant of hierarchical capitalism, offers opportunities for new inter-firm organizational modalities, the rationale for which internalization theory can only partly explain.

In Table 3.3, we set out some of the mainstream theories which have attempted to explain why, given a set of O and L specific advantages, firms prefer to own their foreign value-added or creating activities, rather than lease the right to use their O advantages to independently owned foreign firms. It is our contention that changing world economic events, the growing multinationality of many foreign investors, and the need for firms to engage in highly specific cross-border alliances and in asset augmenting FDI, is necessitating both a reappraisal of static organizational theories, and an integration between "production based," "innovation based" and "transaction based" theories of the firm.

Again, we do not think these approaches to internalization are mutually exclusive. At the end of the day, managers will take decisions, which in any particular context (including those of competitor firms) will come closest to meeting an amalgam of short-term and long-term objectives. Yet, to be effective, these decisions need to take account of, and resolve in a holistic way, conflicts between very specific objectives. It is extremely unlikely, for example, that any one firm will be successful, at one and the same time, in minimizing short-run transaction costs, maximizing short-run and long-run productive efficiency, accessing new markets, optimizing the net benefits of asset creation and asset augmenting activities, and pursuing a variety of cost-effective strategies to improve its competitive position, *vis à vis* that of its main rivals – all within a macro-economic environment of uncertainty and volatility.

This, then suggests that any comprehensive explanation of the existence and the growth of the contemporary MNE must almost inevitably be "judiciously pluralistic" (Foss 1996), unless the context in which the explanation is being made is very narrowly delineated. And, it is a fact that most new explanations of the territorial expansion of firms tend to be incremental to extant theories, rather than a replacement of them. Any conflict between alternative theories or models is, as likely as not, to be about the relevance of, or emphasis placed on, these theories or models, rather than about their logical construction.

We would make one other point. In discussing alternative interpretations of the I component of the OLI triumvirate, organizational scholars such as Chris Bartlett, Sumantra Ghoshal, Yves Doz and C. K. Prahalad, focus on the individual manager – rather than on the firm – as their main unit of analysis. This results in a somewhat different analytical perspective towards the rationale for existence of hierarchies and the internalization of markets, than that offered by Oliver Williamson (1985, 1986, 1990), notwithstanding the fact that, in his various writings, he incorporates the concept of managerial discretion as an explanation for the behavior of

Table 3.3 Theories explaining why firms choose to own foreign value-added facilities

	(1) MS	(2) RS	(3) ES	(4) SAS
1 Orthodox internalization theory **(i) Resource or productivity enhancing** Caves (1996), Dunning (1993) **(ii) Cost reduction** Anderson and Gatignon (1986), Aoki, Gustafson and Williamson (1990), Buckley and Casson (1976, 1985, 1998a,b), Hennart (1982, 1989), Rugman (1982, 1996) **(iii) Risk reduction** Vernon (1993)	• To capture coordinating and transactional benefits of common governance of related activities; to benefit (mainly through M&As), from innovating, production or marketing scale/scope economies. • To reduce transaction and coordinating costs of arm's length markets and/or non-equity contractual relations. Such costs include opportunism and shirking, and those designed to protect the reputation of the contractor. Most empirical work relates to entry modes. See, for example, Anderson & Gatignon (1986). • To reduce organizational and related risks implicit in (ii) above.			
2 Dynamic internalization theory Ghoshal, Hahn and Moran (1997), Buckley and Casson (1998a)				• To tap into learning and experience related assets and to speed up the innovation process. To capture the advantages of Schumpeterian integration and the common governance of R&D related activities

3 Agency theory
Eisenhardt (1989), Jensen and Meckling (1976), Strong and Waterson (1987)

- As with internalization theory, but primarily to reduce risks of external agents behaving against the interests of the principals.
- To reduce moral hazard and adverse selection.

4 Market power theories
Hymer (1960, 1976), Cowling and Sugden (1987)

- Growth by M&As intended to increase market power, rather than to upgrade efficiency.

5 Efficiency related theories
Caves (1982, 1996), Teece (1981, 1984)

- To capture scale related production economies. To raise dynamic technical efficiency through shared knowledge, learning experiences and management expertise.

6 Knowledge acquisition and sharing theories
Antonelli (1998), Kogut and Zander (1994), Makino (1998), Wesson (1993, 1997), Teece, Pisano and Shuen (1997)

- To augment existing intellectual assets, thereby increasing competitive prowess
- To capture synergies of knowledge creation and augmenting activities

firms. Moreover, for the most part, Williamson's analysis tends to be concerned with the efficiency of asset exploitation, rather than that of asset augmentation. Because of this, his focus is more on the optimal mode of coordinating the use of existing resources and capabilities, rather than on that of upgrading such resources and capabilities, by innovating and other means.

Conclusions: the eclectic paradigm as an envelope for complementary theories of MNE activity

In the three previous sections of this chapter, we have suggested that, for the most part, the many and varied explanations of the extent and structure of FDI and MNE activity are complementary, rather than substitutable for, each other, and are strongly context specific. We have further observed that, as the international production by MNEs has grown and taken on new patterns, as the world economic scenario has changed, and as scholars have better understood the *raison d'être* for FDI, so new explanations of the phenomena have been put forward, and existing explanations have been modified and, occasionally, replaced.

According to Kuhn (1962) and Foss (1996, 1997), an existing paradigm can accommodate several contrasting theoretical models as long as these are not addressing exactly the same questions or addressing these in the same context.[33] At the same time, a paradigm that leaves no issues unresolved is of dubious value as a guide to further theorizing (Loasby 1971). By contrast, a paradigm shift may be required when new phenomena arise which cannot be addressed within the existing paradigm, or where there are serious and irreconcilable conflicts among the theories contained in the paradigm.

However, we believe that the criteria for a successful paradigm are more demanding. More specifically, we would mention three of these. The first is that the sum of the value of the constituent theories must be greater than the whole. This suggests that there are intellectual interdependencies or externalities to each of the theories, which a paradigm can "internalize" through its integrated approach. It follows then that the more any general paradigm of international production can advance understanding about the determinants of its constituent parts, the more successful it may be judged. Viewed in this way, we would aver that dynamizing the eclectic paradigm, and recognizing the interdependence of the OLI components not only adds value to its original conception, but helps point the way to improving a variety of the individual theories it embraces.

Second, we would assert that the strength of a paradigm also depends on the extent to which it can offer some generic hypotheses, or, indeed, predictions about the phenomena being studied. In the case of the earlier versions of the eclectic paradigm, we offered some general hypotheses about the nature of the relationship between the O, L and I variables and FDI (Dunning 1977, 1980). However, we did not think it appropriate to put forward specific hypotheses about the relationship between particular OLI variables and particular kinds of FDI – as the paradigm itself was not context specific.

In the case of the contemporary version of the paradigm, which embraces alliance related and asset augmenting MNE activity, even generic hypotheses are harder to make without knowing whether a firm is contemplating a FDI to exploit a competitive strength or to overcome, or counteract, a competitive weakness. Only by treating the search for, and acquisition of, competitive advantages as part of the dynamic and cumulative process of sustaining and advancing O specific advantages (rather than a discrete and once-and-for-all transaction) can this conundrum be resolved. This, then, suggests that the eclectic paradigm might better address itself to explaining the *process* of international production, than to its level and composition at a particular moment of time.

Third, a paradigm may be judged to be robust if it continues to address relevant problems and offers a satisfying conceptual structure for resolving them (Loasby 1971); and if there are no serious contenders to it. Here, it would be foolish to deny there are not other paradigms which seek to offer general explanations of the internationalization process of firms and/or their international management strategies. But, for the most part, we would not consider these to be competing paradigms.

Managerial related paradigms, for example, are interested in explaining the behavior of managers in harnessing and utilizing scarce resources, not the overall level and pattern of FDI or MNE activity. Moreover, unlike FDI theories, they tend to be process oriented, unlike most FDI theories (Buckley 1996). Organizational paradigms are directed to evaluating the costs and benefits of alternative institutional mechanisms for organizing a given set of resources and capabilities, independently of the location of these assets. Paradigms offered by marketing scholars usually focus on the process and/or form of international market entry and/or growth (Johanson and Vahlne 1977, Luostarinen 1979, Welch and Luostarinen 1988, Anderson and Gatignon 1986). Technologically related paradigms of international production (Cantwell 1989, 1994, Kogut and Zander 1994) come nearest to our own approach, but cannot comfortably explain FDI in developing countries and in some service sectors. With a few exceptions (notably Gray 1999, Markusen 1995), modern paradigms of international trade ignore or downplay the significance of firm specific advantages. Finance related paradigms can offer only limited insights into the growth of corporate networks and cross-border strategic alliances.

We conclude, then, that an add-on dynamic component to the eclectic paradigm, and an extension of its constituent parts to embrace both asset augmenting and alliance related cross-border ventures can do much to uphold its position as the dominant analytical framework for examining the determinants of international production. We believe that recent economic events, and the emergence of new explanations of MNE activity have added to, rather than subtracted from, the robustness of the paradigm. While accepting that, in spite of its eclecticism (sic), there may be some kinds of foreign owned value-added activities which do not fit comfortably into its construction, we do believe that it continues to meet most of the criteria of a good paradigm; and that it is not yet approaching its own "creative destruction" (Foss 1996).[34]

NOTES

I am grateful to Jean Boddewyn, John Daniels, Mira Wilkins, Stephen Young and two anonymous referees for their helpful comments on an earlier draft of this chapter.

1 Ownership, Location and Internalization.
2 As described, for example, in Caves (1982, 1996) and Dunning (1993). For the purposes of this article we use FDI and international production, viz. production financed by FDI, as interchangeable terms.
3 As, for example, set out in Buckley and Casson (1976, 1985 and 1998a,b), Hennart (1982, 1989) and Rugman (1982, 1996).
4 For an elaboration of these and other kinds of FDI (e.g. escape, support, and passive investments), see Dunning (1993), chapter 3, pp. 61–3.
5 The former mainly in the form of the growth of horizontal, i.e. product specialization and the latter in the growth of vertical, i.e. process specialization.
6 Such activity is estimated to have accounted for between 55 percent and 60 percent of all new FDI flows over the period 1985 to 1997 (UN 1998).
7 As witnessed, by the growth of intra-firm trade both of intermediate and of final products, documented, for example, by UN (1996b).
8 The explanation of foreign direct *divestment* by MNEs is exactly the reverse of that of foreign direct investment. It may be brought about by a decline in their O specific advantages and/or the L advantages of foreign countries, and/or a reduced motive by firms to internalize the cross-border market for buying or selling intermediate products (Boddewyn 1985, Dunning 1988).
9 Throughout our analysis, we shall proceed on the assumption that paradigmatic and model building theoretic structures to understanding international business activity are complementary rather than alternative scientific methodologies (Buckley and Casson 1998b). While accepting the need for rigorous theorizing and the empirical treating of specific hypotheses, we also believe that encompassing related hypotheses into an open-ended and comprehensive conceptual framework, which not only identifies and evaluates the interaction between the theories, but makes its own generic predictions, provides a useful, and in many cases, an essential, foundation to these theories. We, therefore, view the eclectic paradigm as a systemic framework which provides a set of general assumptions and boundary criteria in which operationally testable theories, germane to FDI and MNE theory, can be comfortably accommodated. It is, perhaps, the most expressive of the research tradition in international business which has evolved over the past two decades (Weisfelder 1998). For an elaboration of the concept of a research tradition, see Laudan (1977).
10 See also the writings of the Scandinavian school on the internalization process

(e.g. Johanson and Vahlne (1977), Luostarinen (1979) and Welch and Luostarinen (1988)).

11 For a longer term perspective, and particularly for an appreciation of the evolution of the O advantages of firms, and their changing locational patterns and organizational modalities, see two classic studies by Mira Wilkins (Wilkins 1970 and 1974).

12 A generic term which suggests that the wealth of firms and countries is increasingly dependent on the kind and quality of alliances they form with other firms and countries. This concept is explored in more detail in Dunning (1995).

13 Which elsewhere (Dunning 1997), we suggest represents a new stage in the development of market-based capitalism, the previous two stages being land-based and machine-based capitalism.

14 The origins of the paradigm date back to 1958, when the distinction between the O advantages of firms and the L advantages of countries was first made, in a study by the present author, of American investment in British manufacturing industry (Dunning 1958, revised 1998). The I component was not explicitly added until 1977, although some of the reasons why firms prefer to engage in FDI rather than cross-border licensing *et al.* agreements were acknowledged by the author and other scholars in the early 1970s. (See the 1998 revised edition of Dunning 1958, Chapter 11.)

15 Implicitly or explicitly, this assumes some immobility of factors of production, including created assets, and that factor markets are not fully contestable. Much earlier, several kinds of competitive advantages specific to *foreign* owned and *domestic* firms were identified by such scholars as Dunning (1958), Brash (1965) and Safarian (1966).

16 For a full bibliography, see Barney (1991), Conner (1991), Conner and Prahalad (1996), Cantwell (1994), Dosi, Freeman, Nelson, Silverberg and Soete (1988), Foss, Knudsen and Montgomery (1995) and Saviotti and Metcalfe (1991). See also the writings of David Teece (1981, 1994 and 1992) and of Teece, Pisano and Shuen (1997).

17 Which includes minimizing the transaction costs and of maximizing the benefits of innovation, learning and accumulated knowledge.

18 Unlike with internalization theory; where the locational decision is normally taken to be independent of the modality of resource transference.

19 One of the first of these studies was that of Frank Southard in 1931 on the locational determinants of US FDI in Europe (Southard 1931).

20 Earlier, Agmon and Lessard (1977) had suggested that US MNEs commanded a higher price than their uninational counterparts because individual investors looked on the former as a means of internationally diversifying their investment portfolios.

21 For a survey of these studies, see, for example, Dunning (1993) and Caves (1996).

22 See particularly the impact of WTO agreements and dispute settlements on the locational decisions of MNEs, as documented by Brewer and Young (1999).

23 Notably, wage levels, demand patterns, policy related variables, supply capabilities and infrastructure.

24 As set out in textbooks on location theory, e.g. Lloyd and Dicken (1977) and Dicken (1998).

25 Especially small states like Switzerland, Belgium and Sweden.

26 Chen and Chen (1998, 1999) have argued that the access to foreign located networks would both augment the O specific advantages of the investing firms,

and enable firms which otherwise do not engage in FDI, so to do. The authors back up their assertion that FDI might act as a conduit for strategic linkages by drawing upon the experiences of Taiwanese firms.

27 Which, within the triad of countries, are estimated to have accounted for around three-fifths of all new FDI between 1985 and 1995 (UNCTAD 1997).

28 For example, there are several socio-economic and geographical theories of the rationale for industrial clustering; see, for example, Storper (1995).

29 E.g. by a subcontracting, or turn-key, agreement.

30 For two recent explanations of the various kinds of market failure and the response of firms and governments to these, see Lipsey (1997) and Meyer (1998).

31 I am grateful for one reviewer of this paper who pointed out that orthodox internalization theory addresses a single question, viz. "where are the boundaries of the firm drawn?" I agree. But, up to now, this particular question has been approached mainly from a transaction cost perspective, which, I would argue, cannot cope with all the issues raised by it.

32 As compared with markets.

33 Thus, for example, although the transaction cost and resource-based theories of the firm offer alternative predictions of the behavior of firms, they, in fact, are addressing different aspects of that behavior, e.g. the former is concerned with defining the boundaries of a firm's activities and the latter with the origins of its competitive advantages.

34 For a somewhat different, and highly refreshing, approach to some of the concepts dealt with in this paper, see a recently published article by Boddewyn and Iyer (1999).

REFERENCES

Agmon, T. and Lessard, D. R. (1977), "Investor recognition of corporate international diversification," *Journal of Finance 32*, September, pp. 1049–55.

Aliber, R. Z. (1971), "The multinational enterprise in a multiple currency world," in Dunning, J. H. (ed.), *The Multinational Enterprise*, London: Allen & Unwin, pp. 49–56.

Anderson, E. and Gatignon, H. (1986), "Modes of foreign entry: transaction costs and propositions," *Journal of International Business Studies 17*, pp. 1–26.

Antonelli, C. (1998), "Localized technological change and the evolution of standards as economic institutions," in Chandler, A. D. Jr., Hagström, P. and Sölvell, O. (eds), *The Dynamic Firm*, Oxford: Oxford University Press.

Aoki, M., Gustafson, B. and Williamson, O. E. (eds) (1990), *The Firm as a Nexus of Treaties*, London and Newbury Park, CA: Sage Publications.

Audretsch, D. B. (1998), "Agglomeration and the location of economic activity," *Oxford Review of Economic Policy 14* (2), pp. 18–29.

Bain, J. S. (1956), *Barriers to New Competition*, Cambridge, Mass: Harvard University Press.

Barney, J. B. (1991), "Firm resources and sustained competitive advantage," *Journal of Management 17*, pp. 99–120.

Bartlett, C. G. and Ghoshal, S. (1989), *Managing Across National Borders: The Transnational Solution*, Cambridge, Mass.: Harvard Business School Press, pp. 23–46.

Barlett, C. G. and Ghoshal, S. (1993), "Beyond the M-form: towards a managerial theory of the firm," *Strategic Management Journal 14* (1).

Blonigen, B. A. (1997), "Firm-specific assets and the link between exchange rates and foreign direct investment," *American Economic Review 87* (3), pp. 447–65.

Boddewyn, J. J. (1985), "Foreign divestment theory: Is it the reverse of FDI theory?," *Weltwirtschaftliches Archiv 119*, pp. 345–55.

Boddewyn, J. J. and Iyer, G. (1999), "International business research: Beyond déjà vu," *Management International Review 39* (2), pp. 161–84.

Brash, D. T. (1966), *American Investment in Australian Industry*, Canberra: Australian University Press.

Brewer, T. and Young, S. (1999), *The Effects on Firms' Strategic Choices of the WTO Trade Investment Regime*, paper presented to a conference on the Locational Determinants of Multinational Firms, Paris, June.

Buckley, P. J. (1996), "The role of management in international business theory: a meta-analysis and integration of the literature on international business and international management," *Management International Review 36* (1), Special Issue, pp. 7–54.

Buckley, P. J. and Casson, M. C. (1976), *The Future of the Multinational Enterprise*, London: Macmillan.

Buckley, P. J. and Casson, M. C. (1981), "The optimal timing of a foreign direct investment," *Economic Journal 91*, pp. 75–87.

Buckley, P. J. and Casson, M. C. (1985), "*The Economic Theory of the Multinational Enterprise*," London: Macmillan.

Buckley, P. J. and Casson, M. C. (1998a), "Models of the multinational enterprise," *Journal of International Business Studies 29* (1), pp. 21–44.

Buckley, P. J. and Casson, M. C. (1998b), "Analyzing foreign market entry strategies: extending the internalization approach," *Journal of International Business Studies 29* (3), pp. 539–62.

Cantwell, J. A. (1989), *Technological Innovation and Multinational Corporations*, Oxford: Basil Blackwell.

Cantwell, J. A. (ed.) (1994), "*Transnational Corporations and Innovatory Activities*," United Nations Library on Transnational Corporations, Vol. 17, London: Routledge.

Cantwell, J. A. and Piscitello, L. (1997), *The Emergence of Corporate International Networks for the Accumulation of Dispersed Technological Competence*, Reading: Department of Economics, Discussion Paper 5 in *International Investment and Management* Series B X, No. 238, October.

Caves, R. E. (1971), "Industrial corporations: the industrial economics of foreign investment," *Economica 38*, pp. 1–27.

Caves, R. E. (1974), "Causes of direct investment: foreign firms, shares in Canadian and United Kingdom manufacturing industries," *Review of Economics and Statistics 56*, August, pp. 272–93.

Caves, R. E. (1982 & 1996), *Multinational Firms and Economic Analysis*, Cambridge: Cambridge University Press, 1st and 2nd editions.

Cavusgil, S. T. (1980), "On the internationalization process of the firm," *European Research 8* (6), pp. 273–81.

Chen, Homin and Chen Tain-Jy (1998), "Network linkages and location choice in foreign direct investment," *Journal of International Business Studies 29* (3), pp. 445–68.

Chen Tain-Jy and Chen Homin (1999), *Resource Advantages and Resource Linkages in Foreign Direct Investment.* Paper Presented to 7th International Conference on the MNEs, Taipei Chinese Culture University, December.

Conner, K. (1991), "A historical comparison of resource based theory and five schools of thought within industrial organization economies. Do we have a new theory of the firm?" *Journal of Management 17*, pp. 121–54.

Conner, K. R. and Prahalad, C. K. (1996), "A resource based theory of the firm: knowledge versus opportunism," *Organizational Science 7* (5), pp. 477–501.

Cowling, K. and Sugden, R. (1987), *Transnational Monopoly Capitalism*, Brighton: Wheatsheaf.

Cushman, D. O. (1985), "Real exchange rate risk, expectations and the level of direct investment," *Review of Economics and Statistics 67*, May, pp. 297–308.

Daniels, J. D. (1971), *Recent Foreign Direct Investment in the United States*, New York: Praeger.

Dicken, P. (1998), *Global Shift* (Third edition), New York and London: The Guilford Press.

Doremus, P. N., Keller, W. W., Pauly, L. W. and Reich, S. (1998), *The Myth of the Global Corporation*, Princeton: Princeton University Press.

Dosi, G., Freeman, C., Nelson, R., Silverberg, G. and Soete, L. (eds) (1988), *Technical Change and Economic Theory*, London: Pinter Publishers.

Doz, Y. L. and Santos, J. F. P. (1997), *On the Management of Knowledge: From the Transparency of Collocation and Cosetting to the Quandary of Dispersion and Differentiation*, Fontainebleau, France: INSEAD, mimeo.

Doz, Y. L., Asakawa, K., Santos, J. F. P. and Williamson, P. J. (1997), *The Metanational Corporation*, Fontainebleau, France: INSEAD Working Paper 97/60/SM.

Dunning, J. H. (1958), *American Investment in British Manufacturing Industry*, London: George Allen and Unwin (New, revised and updated edition, London: Routledge, 1998).

Dunning, J. H. (1977), "Trade, location of economic activity and the MNE: A search for an eclectic approach," in Ohlin, B., Hesselborn, P. O. and Wijkman, P. M. (eds), *The International Allocation of Economic Activity*, London: Macmillan, pp. 395–418.

Dunning, J. H. (1980), "Towards an eclectic theory of international production: some empirical tests," *Journal of International Business Studies 11* (1), Spring/Summer, pp. 9–31.

Dunning, J. H. (1988), *Explaining International Production*, London: Unwin Hyman.

Dunning, J. H. (1993), *Multinational Enterprises and the Global Economy*, Wokingham, Berkshire: Addison Wesley.

Dunning, J. H. (1995), "Reappraising the eclectic paradigm in the age of alliance capitalism," *Journal of International Business Studies 26*, pp. 461–91.

Dunning, J. H. (1996), "The geographical sources of competitiveness of firms: the results of a new survey," *Transnational Corporations 5* (3), December 1996, pp. 1–30.

Dunning, J. H. (1997), "Technology and the changing boundaries of firms and governments," in OECD (ed.), *Industrial Competitiveness and the Global Economy*, Paris: OECD, pp. 53–68.

Dunning, J. H. (1998), "Location and the multinational enterprise: a neglected factor," *Journal of International Business Studies 29* (1), pp. 45–66.

Dunning, J. H. (1999), "Globalization and the theory of MNE activity," in Hood, N. and Young, S. (eds), *The Globalization of Multinational Enterprise Activity*, London: Macmillan, pp. 21–54.

Eisenhardt, K. M. (1989), "Agency theory: an assessment and review," *Academy of Management Review 14* (1), pp. 57–73.

Enright, M. J. (1991), *Geographic Concentration and Industrial Organization*, Cambridge, Mass: Ph.D. Dissertation, Harvard.

Enright, M. J. (1998), "Regional clusters and firm strategy," in Chandler, A. D. Jr. Hagström, P. and Sölvell, O. (eds), *The Dynamic Firm*, Oxford: Oxford University Press, pp. 315–43.

Enright, M. J. (1999), "The globalization of competition and the localization of competitive advantage," in Hood, N. and Young, S. (eds), *The Globalization of Multinational Enterprise Activity*, London: Macmillan, pp. 303–31.

Florida, R. (1995), "Towards the learning region," *Futures 27*, (5), pp. 527–36.

Flowers, E. B. (1976), "Oligopolistic reaction in European and Canadian direct investment in the United States," *Journal of International Business Studies 7*, pp. 43–55.

Forsgren, M. (1989), *Managing the Internalization Process: The Swedish Case*, London and New York: Routledge.

Foss, N. J. (1996), "Research in strategy, economics and Michael Porter," *Journal of Management Studies 33* (1), pp. 1–24.

Foss, N. J. (ed.) (1997), *Resources, Firms and Strategies*, Oxford: Oxford University Press.

Foss, N. J., Knudsen, C. and Montgomery, C. A. (1995), "An exploration of common ground: integrating resource based and evolutionary theories of the firm," in Montgomery, C. A. (ed.), *Resource Based and Evolutionary Theories of the Firm: Towards a Synthesis*, Boston and London: Kluwer Academic Publishers.

Froot, K. A. and Stein, J. C. (1991), "Exchange rates and foreign direct investment: an imperfect market's approach," *Quarterly Journal of Economics 106*, November, pp. 1191–1217.

Ghoshal, S., Hahn, M. and Moran, P. (1997), *Management Competence, Firm Growth and Economic Progress*, Fontainebleau, France: INSEAD Working Paper 97/21/SM.

Graham, E. M. (1975), *Oligopolistic Imitation and European Direct Investment in the United States*, D.B.A. Dissertation, Harvard University, unpublished.

Graham, E. M. (1990), "Exchange of threats between multinational firms as an infinitely repeated non-cooperative game," *International Trade Journal 4* (3), pp. 259–77.

Graham, E. M. (1998), "Market structure and the multinational enterprise: a game-theoretic approach," *Journal of International Business Studies 29* (1), pp. 67–84.

Gray, H. Peter. (1999), *Global Economic Investment*, Copenhagen: Copenhagen Business School Press.

Helleloid, D. (1992), *A Resource Based Theory of the Multinational Enterprise*, Seattle, Washington: University of Washington, mimeo.

Hennart, J. F. (1982), *A Theory of Multinational Enterprise*, Ann Arbor, MI: University of Michigan Press, pp. 81–116.

Hennart, J. F. (1989), "The transaction cost theory of the multinational enterprise," in Pitelis, C. N. and Sugden, R. (eds), *The Nature of the Transnational Firm*, London: Routledge.

Hirsch, S. (1976), "An international trade and investment theory of the firm," *Oxford Economic Papers 28*, pp. 258–70.

Hoover, E. M. (1948), *The Location of Economic Activity*, New York: McGraw Hill.

Hotelling, H. (1929), "Stability in competition," *Economic Journal 29*, pp. 41–57.

Hymer, S. H. (1960), *The International Operation of National Firms: A Study of Direct Investment*, Ph.D. dissertation, M.I.T. (Published by M.I.T. Press in 1976).

Isard, W. (1956), *Location and the Space Economy*, New York: John Wiley.

Jensen, M. and Meckling, W. (1976), "Theory of the firm: managerial behavior, agency costs, township structure," *Journal of Financial Economics 3*, pp. 305–60.

Johanson, J. and Vahlne, J. E. (1977), "The internationalization process of the firm – a model of knowledge development and increasing market commitments," *Journal of International Business Studies 8*, pp. 23–32.

Johanson, J. and Vahlne, J. E. (1990), "The mechanism of internationalization," *International Marketing Review 74* (4), pp. 11–24.

Knickerbocker, F. T. (1973), *Oligopolistic Reaction and the Multinational Enterprise*. Cambridge, MA: Harvard University Press.

Kobrin, S. (1998), "Development after industrialization: Poor countries in an electronically integrated economy," in Hood, N. and Young, S. (eds), *The Globalization of Multinational Enterprise Activity and Economic Development*, Basingstoke: Macmillan, pp. 133–54.

Kogut, B. (1983), "Foreign direct investment as a sequential process," in Kindleberger, C. P. and Audretsch, D. (eds), *The Multinational Corporation in the 1980s*, Cambridge, Mass.: MIT Press, pp. 38–56.

Kogut, B. (1985), "Designing global strategies: profiting from operational flexibility," *Sloan Management Review 26*, Fall, pp. 27–38.

Kogut, B. and Kulatilaka, N. (1994), "Operational flexibility, global manufacturing and the option value of a multinational network," *Management Service 40* (1), pp. 123–39.

Kogut, B. and Zander, U. (1994), "Knowledge of the firm and the evolutionary theory of the multinational corporation," *Journal of International Business Studies 24* (4), pp. 625–46.

Krugman, P. R. (1991), *Geography and Trade*, Cambridge, MA: MIT Press.

Krugman, P. R. (1993), "On the relationship between trade theory and location theory," *Review of International Economics 1* (2), pp. 110–22.

Krugman, P. R. (1998), "What's new about the new economic geography?" *Oxford Review of Economic Policy 14* (2), pp. 7–17.

Kuemmerle, W. (1999), "The drivers of foreign direct investment into research and development: an empirical investigation," *Journal of International Business Studies 30* (1), pp. 1–24.

Kuhn, T. S. (1962), *The Structure of Scientific Revolutions*, Chicago: Chicago University Press.

Laudan, L. (1977), *Progress and its Problems: Towards a Theory of Scientific Growth*, Berkeley, CA: University of California Press, pp. 73–113.

Lipsey, R. G. (1997), "Globalization and national government policies: an economist's view," in Dunning, J. H. (ed.), *Governments, Globalization and International Business*, Oxford: Oxford University Press.

Liu, S. X. (1998), *Foreign Direct Investment and the Multinational Enterprise. A Reexamination Using Signaling Theory*, Westport, Conn.: Greenwood Publishing.

Lloyd, P. and Dicken, P. (1977), *Location in Space*, London: Harper and Row.

Loasby, B. J. (1971), "Hypothesis and paradigm in the theory of the firm," *Economic Journal 81*, pp. 863–85.

Loree, D. W. and Guisinger, S. E. (1995), "Policy and non-policy determinants of US equity foreign direct investment," *Journal of International Business Studies 26* (2), pp. 281–99.

Losch, A. (1954), *The Economics of Location* (English translation by Woglom, W. H. and Stolper, W. F.), New Haven: Yale University Press.

Luostarinen, R. (1979), *Internationalization of the Firm*, Helsinki Acta Acadamie Oeconomicae, Helsinki School of Economics.

Madhok, A. (1996), "The organization of economic activity: transaction costs, firm capabilities and the nature of governance," *Organizational Science 7* (5), September/October, pp. 577–90.

Makino, S. (1998), *Toward a Theory of Asset Seeking Foreign Direct Investment*, Hong Kong: The Chinese University (mimeo).

Malmberg, A., Sölvell, O. and Zander, I. (1996), "Spatial clustering, local accumulation of knowledge and firm competitiveness," *Geographical Annals 78B* (2), pp. 85–97.

Markusen, J. R. (1995), "The boundaries of multinational enterprises and the theory of international trade," *Journal of Economic Perspectives 9* (2), pp. 169–89.

Marshall, A. (1920), *Principles of Economics*, London: Macmillan (eighth edition).

Meyer, K. (1998), *Direct Investment in Economies in Transition*, Cheltenham, UK, Lyme US: Edward Elgar.

Montgomery, C. A. (ed.) (1995), *Resource Base and Evolutionary Theories of the Firm: Towards a Synthesis*, Boston and London: Kluwer Academic Publishers.

Nelson, R. R. and Winter, S. (1982), *An Evolutionary Theory of Economic Change*, Cambridge: Belknap Press.

Nelson, R. R. (1991), "The role of firm differences in an evolutionary theory of technical advance," *Science and Public Policy 18* (6), pp. 347–52.

Oliver, C. (1997), "Sustainable competitive advantage: combining institutional and resource based views," *Strategic Management Journal 18* (9), pp. 697–713.

Pauwells, P. and Matthyssens, P. (1997), "De-internationalization: a search for a theoretical framework," paper presented at Round-table on *Globalization and the Small Open Economy*, Antwerp: Centre for International Management and Development, May 29.

Peck, F. W. (1996), "Regional development and the production of space: the role of infrastructure in the attraction of new inward investment," *Environment and Planning*, Series A *28*, pp. 327–39.

Porter, M. E. (1980), *Competitive Strategy*, New York: The Free Press.

Porter, M. E. (1985), *Competitive Advantage*, New York: The Free Press.

Porter, M. E. (1991), "Towards a dynamic theory of strategy," *Strategic Management Journal 12*, Special Issue, Winter, pp. 95–117.

Porter, M. E. (1994), "The role of location in competition," *Journal of Economics of Business I* (1), pp. 35–39.

Porter, M. E. (1996), "Competitive advantage, agglomerative economies and regional policy," *International Regional Science Review 19* (1 and 2), pp. 85–94.

Porter, M. E. (1998), "Location, clusters and the 'new' microeconomies of competition," *Business Economics 33*, Jan. pp. 7–13.

Prahalad, C. K. and Doz, Y. L. (1987), *The Multinational Mission: Balancing Local Demands and Global Vision*, New York: The Free Press.

Rangan, S. (1998), "Do multinationals operate flexibly? Theory and evidence," *Journal of International Business Studies 29* (2), pp. 217–38.

Rugman, A. M. (1979), *International Diversification and the Multinational Enterprise*, Lexington, MA: Lexington Books.

Rugman, A. M. (ed.) (1982), *New Theories of the Multinational Enterprise*, London: Croom Helm.

Rugman, A. M. (1996), *The Theory of Multinational Enterprises: The Selected Scientific Papers of Alan A. M. Rugman*, Vol. 1, Cheltenham: Edward Elgar.

Rugman, A. M. and Verbeke, A. (1998), "Multinational enterprises and public policy," *Journal of International Business Studies 29* (1), pp. 115–36.

Safarian, A. E. (1966), *Foreign Ownership of Canadian Industry*, Toronto: University of Toronto Press.

Saviotti, P. P. and Metcalfe, J. S. (eds) (1991), *Evolutionary Theories of Economic and Technological Change – Present Statistics and Future Prospects*, Chur: Harwood Academic Publishers.

Scott, A. J. (1996), "Regional motors of the global economy," *Futures 28* (5), pp. 391–411.

Sölvell, O. and Zander, I. (1998), "International diversification of knowledge: isolating mechanisms and the role of the MNE," in Chandler, A. D. Jr., Hagström, P. and Sölvell, O. (eds), *The Dynamic Firm*, Oxford: Oxford: University Press, pp. 402–16.

Southard, F. A. Jr. (1931), *American Industry in Europe*, Boston: Houghton Mifflin.

Storper, M. (1995), "The resurgence of region economies: ten years later: the region as a nexus of untraded interdependencies," *European Urban and Regional Studies 2* (3), pp. 191–221.

Storper, M. and Scott, A. J. (1995), "The wealth of regions," *Futures 27* (5), pp. 505–26.

Strong, N. and Waterson, M. (1987), "Principals, agents and information," in Clarke, R. and McGuiness, A. (eds), *The Economics of the Firm*, Oxford: Blackwell, pp. 18–41.

Tallman, S. B., Geringer, J. M. and Li, E. (1995), *A Strategic Management Model of the Multinational Enterprise* (mimeo).

Teece, D. J. (1981), "The multinational enterprise: market failure and market power considerations," *Sloan Management Review 22*, pp. 3–18.

Teece, D. J. (1984), "Economic analysis and strategic management," *California Management Review 26*, Spring, pp. 87–108.

Teece, D. J. (1992), "Competition, cooperation, and innovation: Organizational arrangements for regimes of rapid technological progress," *Journal of Economic Behavior and Organization 18*, pp. 1–25.

Teece, D. J., Pisano, G. and Shuen, J. (1997), "Dynamic capabilities and strategic management," *Strategic Management Journal 18* (7), pp. 509–33.

UNCTAD (1996a), *Incentives and Foreign Direct Investment*, Geneva and New York: UN.

UNCTAD (1996b), *World Investment Report 1998: Investment, Trade and International Policy Arrangements*, Geneva and New York: UN.

UNCTAD (1998), *World Investment Report 1997, Transnational Corporations: Trends and Determinants*, Geneva and New York: UN.

Venables, A. J. (1998), "The assessment: trade and location," *Oxford Review of Economic Policy 14* (2), pp. 1–6.

Vernon, R. (1966), "International investment and international trade in the product cycle," *Quarterly Journal of Economics 80*, pp. 190–207.

Vernon, R. (1973), *Sovereignty at Bay*, Harmondsworth: Penguin.

Vernon, R. (1974), "The location of economic activity," in Dunning, J. H. (ed.), *Economic Analysis and the Multinational Enterprise*, London: Allen and Unwin, pp. 89–114.

Vernon, R. (1979), "The product cycle hypothesis in the new international environment," *Oxford Bulletin of Economics and Statistics 41*, pp. 255–67.

Vernon, R. (1983), "Organizational and institutional responses to international risk," in Herring, R. J. (ed.), *Managing International Risk*, Cambridge, MA: Cambridge University Press, pp. 191–216.

Weber, A. (1929), *The Theory of Location of Industries* (English translation by Friedrich), Chicago: University of Chicago Press.

Weisfelder, C. J. (1998), *Foreign Production and the Multinational Enterprise: Development of a Research Tradition from 1960 to 1990*, Bowling Green Ohio: Bowling Green State University (mimeo).

Welch, L. S. and Luostarinen (1988), "Internationalization: evolution of a concept," *Journal of General Management 14*, 2, Winter, pp. 34–55.

Wernerfelt, B. (1984), "A resource-based view of the firm," *Strategic Management Journal 5* (2), pp. 171–80.

Wernerfelt, B. (1995), "The resource based view of the firm: ten years after," *Strategic Management Journal 16*, pp. 171–74.

Wesson, T. J. (1993), *An Alternative Motivation for Foreign Direct Investment*, Cambridge, Mass.: Ph.D. dissertation, Harvard University.

Wesson, T. J. (1997), "A model of asset seeking foreign direct investment," *Proceedings International Business Division. The Administrative Sciences Association of Canada 18* (8), pp. 110–20.

Wilkins, M. (1970), *The Emergence of Multinational Enterprise: American Business Abroad, From the Cololian Era to 1914*, Cambridge, Mass.: Harvard University Press.

Wilkins, M. (1974), *The Maturing of Multinational Enterprise, American Business Abroad, From 1914 to 1970*, Cambridge, Mass.: Harvard University Press.

Williamson, O. E. (1985), *The Economic Institutions of Capitalism*, New York: The Free Press.

Williamson, O. E. (1986), *Economic Organization: Firm, Markets and Policy Control*, Brighton: Wheatsheaf Books.

Williamson, O. E. (1990), *Organization Theory*, New York: Free Press.

4   Location and the multinational enterprise
A neglected factor?

Introduction

In 1986, the economist Wilfred J. Ethier, in seeking to explain the existence of multinational enterprises (MNEs), concluded that "internalization appears to be emerging as the Caesar of the OLI triumvirate" (Ethier 1986, p. 803). I did not agree with this statement then; nor do I do so now. The OLI triad of variables (ownership, location and internalization, discussed below) determining foreign direct investment (FDI) and MNE activity may be likened to a three-legged stool; each leg is supportive of the other, and the stool is only functional if the three legs are evenly balanced. In so far as the third leg completes this balancing it may be regarded as the most important, but there is no reason to suppose one leg performs this task better than another.

In the case of the eclectic paradigm, I would accept that the I component is the critical leg, if, given the O advantages of firms and the L advantages of countries, one is trying to explain why firms internalize the cross-border market for these advantages, rather than sell them or their rights to independent firms. But, I would aver it is no less correct to argue that, given its O specific advantages, the critical choice of a multi-activity firm is whether it should internalize its intermediate product markets within its home country or in a foreign country; and that the outcome of this choice is primarily determined by the costs and benefits of adding value to these products in the two locations. I say primarily because the geography of international business activity is not independent of its entry mode; nor, indeed, of the competitive advantages of the investing firms. This interdependence is particularly apparent when one examines the dynamics of knowledge-intensive MNE activity.

In the 1960s, scholars, such as Raymond Vernon and his colleagues at Harvard (see especially Vernon 1966, 1974 and Wells 1972) working on the determinants of FDI, gave pride of place to locational variables, particularly those determining the siting of US market seeking FDI by US firms in advanced industrial countries (see also the work of some European scholars, such as Bandera and White 1968 and Scaperlanda and

Mauer 1969). In the mid-1970s – apart from research on the internationalization process of firms (see, for example, Johanson and Vahlne 1977) – attention switched from the act of FDI *per se* to the institution making the investment. Here the main focus of interest was why firms should choose to set up or acquire foreign value-adding activities, rather than export the intangible assets (or the right to use these assets) underpinning such activities, directly to foreign firms (see especially the writings of Peter Buckley and Mark Casson, J. C. McManus, Jean-François Hennart, Alan Rugman, and Birgitta Swedenborg, all of which are cited in Caves 1982 and 1996).

While I would be the first to acknowledge the value of this approach in advancing our understanding of MNE, *qua* MNEs, I believe that the contribution of the internalization school has done more to explain the existence and growth of the multi-activity firm than that of the MNE *per se*. This is because, with relatively few exceptions,[1] the transaction and coordination costs identified with arm's length intermediate product markets have not, in general, been specific to cross-border markets, or, indeed, to traversing space.

The emphasis on the firm-specific determinants of international economic activity, while still driving much academic research by scholars in business schools, is now being complemented by a renewed interest in the spatial aspects of FDI; and of how these affect both the competitive advantages of firms and their modes of entry into, and expansion in, foreign markets. We believe there are two main reasons for this. The first is that the changing extent, character and geography of MNE activity over the past two decades – itself a reflection of a series of path-breaking technological, economic and political events – is demanding an explanation by international business scholars. The second is that new research agendas, particularly those of economic geographers, trade theorists and international political economists, are not only paying more attention to the spatial aspects of value-added activity, but are also seeking to incorporate these aspects into the mainstream thinking about the growth and competitiveness of firms, the relationship between trade and FDI and the economic structure and dynamic comparative advantage of regions and countries.

This chapter seeks to review some of these happenings, most of which come into prominence between the two editions of the publication of Richard Caves, *Multinational Enterprise and Economic Analysis* (1982 and 1996). To his credit, Richard Caves acknowledges many of these in his second (1996) edition. But, since much of his analysis relates to the work of scholars in the 1980s,[2] his chapter on the international allocation of economic activity (Chapter 2) does not fully embrace the events and academic research of the last decade or so. It is these which will be the main concern of this chapter. The chapter will proceed in the following way. First, it will briefly describe the changing global economic scenario in which MNE activity has been conducted since the mid-1970s, and also the various strands of intellectual thought which have sought to explain this. Second, it will examine how the micro-locational determinants of international production have changed; and how the location portfolio of MNEs may itself help promote their dynamic competitive advantages. Third, it will consider how, from a more macroeconomic standpoint, the emergence of the MNE as a leading vehicle of cross-border transactions has affected our thinking about the determinants of trade and other non-MNE related transactions.

The changing world scenario for international business activity

The last two decades have witnessed a gradual movement towards a world economy characterized by three features. The first is the emergence of intellectual capital as the key wealth creating asset in most industrial economies. In the 1990s, the market value of industrial corporations has been variously calculated (e.g., by Blair 1995, Handy 1989 and Edvinsson 1997) at between two and a half and five times the value of their tangible assets, compared with one and a half times in 1982. The annual capital expenditure on information technology by US corporations now exceeds that on production technology (Stewart 1997). The knowledge component of the output of manufacturing goods is estimated to have risen from 20 percent in the 1950s to 70 percent in 1995 (Stewart 1997); while those workers whose main task is to create new knowledge or disseminate information (viz. professional and technical workers, managers, sales and clerical workers – the so called "white collar" workers) increased their share of the American labor force from 42 percent in 1960 to 58 percent in 1990, and this share is expected to rise to more than 60 percent by 2000.

A further indicator of the rising significance of non-material assets as creators or facilitators of wealth is the growth of services, and particularly those which are, themselves, knowledge or information intensive. In 1995, on average, services accounted for 63 percent of the world's gross national product (GNP), compared with 55 percent in 1980 and 45 percent in 1965 (World Bank 1997). Insofar as knowledge intensive and knowledge supporting production has its unique spatial needs, and tends to require resources and capabilities which MNEs are particularly well suited to provide, it is not unreasonable to hypothesize that both these features will impinge on the geographical distribution of FDI and related activities.

Secondly, and even more transparent, is the increasing globalization of economic activity, made possible, *inter alia*, by advances in transport and communications technologies and the reduction in trade and investment barriers throughout the world (UNCTAD, various issues and World Bank, various issues). Over the last two decades, the growth of world trade has consistently outstripped that of world output, while in 1998, the sales of the foreign affiliates of MNEs exceeded the value of world exports of goods and non-factor services by 74 percent (UNCTAD 1999). Moreover, between one-third and one-half of trade in non-agricultural products and between one-half and three-fifths of capital and knowledge flows are currently internalized within MNEs.[3]

At the same time, the ease at which MNEs can transfer intangible assets across national boundaries is being constrained by the fact that the location of the creation and use of these assets is becoming increasingly influenced by the presence of immobile clusters of complementary value-added activities. This is particularly the case where the transaction costs of traversing distance are high, or where the transactional benefits of spatial proximity are significant.[4] Thus while globalization suggests that the location and ownership of production is becoming geographically more dispersed, other economic forces are making for a more pronounced geographical concentration of such activity both within particular regions and countries.[5] In the words of Ann Markusen (1996), these events are presenting scholars and policy makers with a paradox of "sticky places within slippery space."

The third feature of the contemporary global economy is the emergence of what may be called "alliance" capitalism (sometimes called relational, collective, stakeholder and collaborative capitalism – see Dunning (1995)). While retaining many of the characteristics of hierarchical capitalism, the distinctive feature of alliance capitalism is the growing extent to which, in order to achieve their respective objectives, the main stakeholders in the wealth-seeking process are needing to collaborate more actively and purposefully with each other. Such collaboration includes the conclusion of closer, continuing, and more clearly delineated *intra*-firm relationships, e.g., between functional departments and between management and labor; the growth of a variety of interfirm cooperative agreements,[6] e.g. between suppliers and customers and among competitors; and the recognition by governments and firms alike of the need to work as partners if the economic goals of society (for which the former are ultimately responsible) are to be best achieved.

Once again, the growing propensity of firms to engage in cross-border alliances has implications not just for the modality by which knowledge and other intangible assets are transferred across national boundaries, but for the location of value-added activities – especially high value asset-augmenting activities.

Underpinning and reinforcing each of the events just described are two other factors which also have had a profound effect on both the macro and micro geography of MNEs. The first is the advent, in the 1980s, of a new generation of technological advances which, according to Alan Greenspan (in a speech given to New York bankers in April 1997) began to bear fruit only in the mid 1990s.[7] The second factor is the renaissance of the market economy, and the consequential changes in the macroeconomic policies and macro-organizational (micro-management) strategies of many national governments. This is most vividly demonstrated by the happenings in China and Central and Eastern Europe, but, almost as far reaching, is the reappraisal of the role of the State and markets in economic development now being played out in India, and in several African and Latin American economies (World Bank 1997). Both factors have had a major impact on the economic and political risk assessment of FDI by MNEs.

The changing geography of MNE activity

The developments just described have all impacted on the geography of FDI and MNE activity (as described in more detail in Dunning (1998)). In the period 1991–1996, 64 percent of global FDI inflows were received by the developed countries, 33 percent by developing countries and 3 percent by Central and Eastern European countries. The corresponding percentages for the period 1975–1980 were 77 percent, 23 percent and less than 0.1 percent (UNCTAD 1997). No less noticeable have been the changes in the distribution of inbound FDI within these regions. While the shares of Western Europe and the United States, cf. all FDI in developed countries, have remained broadly the same,[8] those within developing countries have markedly changed. For example, between 1975–1980 and 1991–1996, South, East and Southeast Asia (including China and India) increased their share of inbound investment to developing countries from 26 percent to 62 percent, while that of Latin America and the Caribbean fell from 53 percent to 34 percent.

It is perhaps worth observing that although the share of inbound FDI to the gross fixed capital formation of the countries more than doubled between the second half of the 1970s and the first half of the 1990s (UNCTC 1988, 1996a), the changing geography of FDI parallels reasonably well that of all investment, independently of its ownership. Between 1975 and 1980, and 1990 and 1995, for example, the share of world inbound FDI accounted for by developed countries fell from 78 percent to 70 percent, while that of world gross fixed capital formation (including that part financed by foreign firms) fell from 84 percent to 73 percent. The corresponding figures for all developing economies were 21 percent and 30 percent, and 15 percent and 26 percent; and for Asia 7 percent and 19 percent, and 7 percent and 19 percent. Although there are differences in the geography of FDI which can be specifically attributed to the political or economic conditions in the host country[9] – and it is most certainly the case that the geography of outward FDI is quite strongly country specific[10] – the data suggest that many of the factors which explain the location of FDI may not be unique to its country of origin. We shall not elaborate on this point here; but it is, perhaps, worthy of more attention.

The micro-economics of the location of MNE activity

With the caveat of the last paragraph, we now consider how scholarly thinking about the location of MNEs has evolved over the last two decades. Incidentally, we suspect that the fact that this subject has not been given much attention by international business scholars is partly because scholars have believed that the principles underlying the locational decisions of firms within national boundaries can be easily extended to explain their cross-border locational preferences;[11] and partly because economists were either generally satisfied with existing explanations, or just not interested in the subject. Certainly, until the early 1990s, there was little in common between the methodologies of international trade economists and locational economists, excepting the work of Bertil Ohlin (1933) and his successors. This was primarily because the former were concerned with country-specific general equilibrium models or models under very restrictive conditions, whereas the latter were mainly interested in firm- or industry-specific partial equilibrium models with fewer constraints (Krugman 1993).

Earlier in this chapter, we identified three major developments in the global economy which have impinged upon both the capabilities and strategies of MNEs, or potential MNEs, and the locational attractions offered by particular countries to mobile investors. In particular, we emphasized first the growing significance of firm-specific knowledge-intensive assets in the wealth-creating process, and the kind of customized assets, e.g. skilled labor and public infrastructure, which needed to be jointly used with these assets if they were to be effectively harnessed and deployed;[12] secondly, the reduction of many natural and artificial impediments to trade, but the rise of other spatially related transaction costs; and thirdly, the growing need and ease with which firms are able to coordinate their cross-border activities and form alliances with foreign firms.

Some of these factors have led firms to own and concentrate particular types of value-added activities within a limited number of locations; others have led them to disperse such activities across several locations. Some have favored a realignment of MNE activity towards advanced developed economies; others have favored a location in emerging market economies. All are symptomatic of a changing international division of labor, which, because of their increasing role in the world economy, and their need to capture the economies of interdependent activities, MNEs have helped to fashion.

The literature on the locational preferences of foreign direct investors has long acknowledged that these will not only depend on the types of activities in which they are engaged, but on the motives for the investment and whether it is a new or a sequential one. Different kinds of investment incentives are needed to attract inbound MNE activity of a natural-resource-seeking, cf. that of a market- or efficiency-seeking, kind. Export-oriented FDI is likely to be less influenced by the size of local markets than is import-substituting FDI. Investment in R&D facilities requires a different kind of human and physical infrastructure than investment in assembling or marketing activities, and so on.

But, perhaps, the most significant change in the motives for FDI over the last two decades has been the rapid growth of strategic asset-seeking FDI, which is geared less to exploiting an existing O specific advantage of an investing firm, and more to protecting, or augmenting, that advantage by the acquisition of new assets, or by a partnering arrangement with a foreign firm. In some ways, such FDI is similar in intent to that of a natural resource-seeking investment in earlier times but, its locational needs are likely to be quite different. Partly this is because it is frequently motivated by strategic considerations (especially in oligopolistic industries), and partly because the availability of the assets sought, viz. technical knowledge, learning experiences, management expertise and organizational competence, tend to be concentrated in advanced industrial countries, or the larger developing countries. The growth of strategic asset-seeking FDI in recent years is best demonstrated by the increasing role of mergers and acquisitions as modalities of FDI. According to UNCTAD (1997), between 55 percent and 60 percent of FDI flows over the period 1985–1995 was accounted for by mergers and acquisitions. Most of these were concentrated within North America, Europe and Japan, and in knowledge- and information-intensive sectors.

The locational preferences of firms making more traditional forms of FDI have also changed – as, indeed, have the attitudes of recipient countries to these investments. We might mention two of these. First, as foreign affiliates have become more embedded in host countries, this has led to a deepening of their value chains, and a propensity for them to engage in higher-order (e.g. innovatory) activities. This fact has been documented in numerous studies both on the geographical distribution of R&D and on that of patents registered by MNEs (as recent examples of these, see Dalton and Serapio (1995), Almeida (1996), Dunning (1996), Kuemmerle (1999), Shan and Song (1997), and various studies of John Cantwell and colleagues, e.g. Cantwell and Harding (1998), and Bob Pearce and Marina Papanastassiou, e.g. Papanastassiou and Pearce (1997), of the University of Reading). *Inter alia*, the Cantwell and Harding study showed that between 1991 and 1995, 11 percent of the US registered patents of the world's largest firms were attributable to research locations outside the home country of the parent company. Only in the case of Japan there was not a rise in the proportion of patents registered by foreign affiliates since the early 1970s (for a more general discussion on asset-augmenting FDI see an interesting dissertation by Wesson 1993). So far, however, this tendency of engaging in higher-order activities has been largely confined to developed countries. In 1994, for example, some 91 percent of the foreign R&D undertaken by US MNEs was located in developed countries, compared with 79 percent of their total foreign sales (Mataloni and Fahim-Nadar 1996).

Second, the location-specific assets which MNEs perceive they need to add value to the competitive advantages they are exporting (via FDI) are changing as their downstream activities are becoming more knowledge intensive. Various surveys have demonstrated that, except for some labor or resource investments in developing countries, MNEs are increasingly seeking locations which offer the best economic and institutional facilities for their core competencies to be efficiently utilized. For example, in a field study by Fabrice Hatem (1997), apart from market access and market growth, economic and institutional facilities were not only valued much higher than traditional criteria of access to raw materials, cost of labor, and fear of protectionism, but in all cases they were also thought to increase in significance over the five-year period 1996–2001. There is a suggestion, too, that the presence of other foreign investors in a particular country is becoming more significant, both as an "investment-stalk" or signaling effect to other foreign firms less familiar with that country (Srinivasan and Mody 1998; Liu 1998), and as an agglomerative magnet by which firms benefit from being part of a geographical network or cluster of related activities and specialized support services. In a study of the location patterns of US MNEs between 1982 and 1988, Wheeler and Mody (1992) identified three agglomeration benefits, viz. infrastructure quality, degree of industrialization, and existing level of FDI. They found that these exhibited a high degree of statistical significance and had large positive impacts on investment (p. 66). In an analysis of Swedish outbound FDI, over the period 1975–1990, Braunerhjelm and Svensson (1995) confirmed a positive and significant statistical relationship between that variable and the presence of pecuniary externalities associated with demand and supply linkages, including the diffusion of knowledge, e.g. spillover effects, resulting from a clustering of related firms.

A more formal examination of the changing nature and significance of external economies, and of how these are leading to a more concentrated pattern of certain kinds of FDI – particularly that of strategic asset-seeking investment in knowledge-intensive-sectors – is set out in Krugman (1991). Indeed, it was his study which helped spark off the fruitful dialogue now taking place between industrial geographers, economists and business analysts. Though this dialogue is principally concerned with the role of sub-national spatial units as repositories for mobile investment, it is also offering a number of valuable insights on the changing role of transportation and communication costs as they affect the coordination and supply of end products from existing agglomerations, and the decentralization of intermediate production;[13] and also on the changing competitive advantages of regions – particularly as they impinge upon spatial transaction costs and dynamic external economies, such as those to do with complex technologies, uncertain or unpredictable markets, interactive learning, face-to-face discussions and the exchange of uncodifiable knowledge (Florida 1995; Storper and Scott 1995).

Certainly the incentives offered by regional authorities within the European Union (EU) and of states within the United States, have been shown to be a decisive factor in influencing the intraregional location of inbound MNE activity (for some interesting case studies, see, for example, Ohmae 1995, Oman 2000). There is also a good deal of casual evidence to suggest that the promotional campaigns and incentives – in the form of the speedy processing of planning applications, land grants, subsidized rents, tax holidays and generous investment allowances – offered by local or regional development agencies to attract FDI tend to resemble those of "location tournaments"[14] (Taylor 1993, UNCTAD 1996b). Again, the experiences of the United States and the EU – or, indeed, of some of the larger countries in the EU, e.g. the United Kingdom – are salutary in this respect.

In Table 4.1, we attempt to summarize some of the differences between the kind of variables posited to influence the locational decisions of MNEs in the 1970s – most of which are well documented in Chapter 2 of *Multinational Enterprise and Economic Analysis* – and those which scholars are hypothesizing, and field research is showing to influence these same decisions of MNEs in the 1990s. In doing so, we have separately classified the four main kinds of FDI identified earlier. However, we readily accept that other contextual variables, e.g. size of firm, degree of multinationality, country or region of origin and destination and industry, insofar as these have different situational needs, may be no less significant.

The contents of the table are largely self-explanatory, but we would highlight just four main findings. The first is the changing role of *spatial transaction costs*, which reflect both the liberalization of cross-border markets and the changing characteristics of economic activity. While, in general, the reduction of these costs has led to more aggressive market-seeking FDI, and has promoted a welfare-enhancing international division of labor, it has also favored the spatial bunching of firms engaged in related activities, so that each may benefit from the presence of the other, and of having access to localized support facilities, shared service centers, distribution networks, customized demand patterns and specialized factor inputs (Maskell 1996; Rees and McLean 1997).

The second finding is that the complementary foreign assets and capabilities sought by MNEs wishing to add value to their core competitive advantages are increasingly of a *knowledge-facilitating* kind, and that this is particularly the case as their affiliates become more firmly rooted in host economies (Grabher 1993). Examples include the deepening of value-added activities by Japanese manufacturing subsidiaries in Europe and North America. An exception to this finding is some low value-adding activities in the least developed areas of the world.

The third finding is that as strategic asset-acquiring investment has become more important, the locational needs of corporations have shifted from those to do with access to markets, or to natural resources, to those to do with access to knowledge-intensive assets and learning experiences, which augment their existing O specific advantages.

The fourth finding is that much of the recent FDI in developing countries is prompted either by traditional market-seeking motives (e.g. as in the case of China, Indonesia and India), or by the desire to take advantage of lower (real) labor costs, and/or the availability and price of natural resources. Yet, even there, where firms have a choice, the physical and human infrastructure, together with the macroeconomic environment and institutional framework of the host country, tend to play a more decisive role than they once did.

Macroeconomic aspects of the changing international allocation of economic activity

In the previous section, we set out some of the reasons for the changing locational patterns of MNE activity over the past two decades. We concluded that developments in the global economy over these years had not only opened up or enlarged markets for products normally supplied by MNEs, but, by affecting the production and transaction costs of FDI, had markedly influenced its industrial structure and geography. In general, the 1990s are witnessing a closer integration in the international value-added activities of MNEs. In the case of some kinds of FDI, falling material, transportation and communication costs, and rising transactional benefits arising from the common governance of interdependent activities have made for a more concentrated pattern of FDI, both between and within regions and/or countries. In other cases, however, the emergence of new – and often important – markets, and the lowering of tariff and non-tariff barriers have made for a more dispersed pattern of FDI.

We now turn to consider some macroeconomic, or country specific, issues. In particular, we wish to address two questions. First, to what extent is the changing locational pattern of FDI affecting our understanding about the determinants of the optimal international allocation of economic activity; and second, how far, in light of the growing significance and integration of MNE, does one need to reconsider the policy implications for national and regional governments as they seek to advance their particular economic and social objectives?

Until the 1950s, most explanations of the allocation of economic activity were based on the distribution of natural resources – especially labor, land and finance capital. The principle of comparative advantage espoused that countries should specialize in the production of those products which required the resources and capabilities in which they were relatively the best endowed; and trade these for those which required resources and capabilities in which they were relatively poorly endowed.

Table 4.1 Some variables influencing the location of value-added activities by MNEs in the 1970s and 1990s

Type of FDI	In the 1970s	In the 1990s
A. Resource seeking	1. Availability, price and quality of natural resources. 2. Infrastructure to enable resources to be exploited and products arising from them to be exported. 3. Government restrictions on FDI and/or on capital and dividend remissions. 4. Investment incentives, e.g. tax holidays.	1. As in the 1970s, but local opportunities for upgrading quality of resources and the processing and transportation of their output is a more important locational incentive. 2. Availability of local partners to jointly promote knowledge and/or capital-intensive resource exploitation.
B. Market seeking	1. Mainly domestic, and occasionally (e.g. in Europe) adjacent regional markets. 2. Real wage costs; material costs. 3. Transport costs; tariff and non-tariff trade barriers. 4. As A3 above, but also (where relevant) privileged access to import licenses.	1. Mostly large and growing domestic markets, and adjacent regional markets (e.g. NAFTA, EU, etc.). 2. Availability and price of skilled and professional labor. 3. Presence and competitiveness of related firms, e.g. leading industrial suppliers. 4. Quality of national and local infrastructure and institutional competence. 5. Less spatially related market distortions, but increased role of agglomerative spatial economies and local service support facilities. 6. Macroeconomic and macro-organizational policies as pursued by host governments. 7. Increased need for presence close to users in knowledge-intensive sectors. 8. Growing importance of promotional activities by regional or local development agencies.

C. Efficiency seeking	1. Mainly production cost related (e.g. labor, materials, machinery, etc.)	1. As in the 1970s, but more emphasis placed on B2, 3, 4, 5 and 7 above, especially for knowledge-intensive and integrated MNE activities, e.g. R&D and some office functions.
	2. Freedom to engage in trade in intermediate and final products.	2. Increased role of governments in removing obstacles to restructuring economic activity and facilitating the upgrading of human resources by appropriate educational and training programs.
	3. Presence of agglomerative economies, e.g. export processing zones.	3. Availability of specialized spatial clusters, e.g. science and industrial parks, service support systems, etc. and of specialized factor inputs. Opportunities for new initiatives by investing firms: an entrepreneurial environment, and one which encourages competitiveness enhancing cooperation within and between firms.
	4. Investment incentives, e.g. tax breaks, accelerated depreciation, grants, subsidized land.	
D. Strategic asset seeking	1. Availability of knowledge-related assets and markets necessary to protect or enhance O specific advantages of investing firms – and at the right price.	1. As in the 1970s, but growing geographical dispersion of knowledge-based assets and need of firms to harness such assets from foreign locations, makes this a more important motive for FDI.
	2. Institutional and other variables influencing ease or difficulty at which such assets can be acquired by foreign firms.	2. The price and availability of synergistic assets to foreign investors.
		3. Opportunities offered (often by particular sub-national spatial units) for exchange of localized tacit knowledge ideas and interactive learning.
		4. Access to different cultures, institutions and systems; and different consumer demands and preferences.

This was the basis for a general equilibrium model of trade. Its restrictive assumptions – viz. perfect competition, the immobility of factors, homogeneity of traded products, constant returns to scale and zero transportation costs – as recently reiterated by Krugman (1993), are well known. In that model, there was little or no room for innovatory activities, or for the deployment of such created assets as intellectual capital, organizational expertise, entrepreneurship and interactive learning, either by countries or firms; and even less for the distinctive characteristics of MNEs.

Over the last four decades, these restrictions have been gradually relaxed in three main ways. First, independently of the work of scholars on FDI and MNE activity, there has been a growing appreciation by trade economists of the need to incorporate such variables as economies of scale, fabricated assets, learning experiences and market structure into their models, and to recognize that the role of these varies with types of economic activity. It is, for example, now generally accepted that different parts of the value chain may be distributed between countries, or regions within countries, according to their knowledge, capital, natural resource and labor content, and to the geography of these inputs. Second, more attention is now being paid to the extent to which the external economies which arise from the clustering of related activities, may lead to a concentration of economic activity in certain countries or regions. Third, more recognition has been given to the differences in consumer tastes between countries, while, very gradually, institutional factors, such as those specific to the multi-activity or multi-firm, and to the role of governments have begun to be acknowledged.

In incorporating these changes into their thinking, the proponents of the positive theory of trade are now able to offer a more realistic explanation of the international allocation of economic activity; while, from a normative viewpoint, though dented, the principle of comparative advantage still has much going for it as a guiding light as to how best to allocate scarce resources between countries (Wood 1993). This is particularly the case when it is widened to embrace created assets, including those which are institutional, policy and culturally related (Lipsey 1997).

However, a second intellectual lacunae remains, which makes it difficult to reconcile the approaches of location theorists and international trade economists in explaining the international allocation of production. This is the presence – and the increasing presence – of the MNE, whose central feature is its common ownership of cross-border value-adding activities. Here we need to turn once again to the work of the internalization scholars. For to explain how MNEs, *qua* MNEs, affect the international location of economic activity, we need to consider how they differ from uni-national firms. Otherwise, one should be able to use the tenets of contemporary trade and/or location theory to explain such activity. It is here that research by international business scholars is particularly relevant.

An earlier section of this chapter suggested that the changes in the geography of FDI over the last two decades have been broadly in line with that of the capital expenditures of all firms. This could mean that the ownership or multinationality of firms was not a significant variable in explaining such changes; and that trade in intermediate or final products internalized, and/or controlled, by MNEs, is no differently determined than trade between independent firms, i.e. arm's length trade.

However, as copious research shows (as reviewed, for example, in Caves (1996) and Dunning (1993)), the main impact of the foreign-ness, or multinationality, of firms has not been on the *level* of economic activity and/or trade of the countries in which they operate, but on the *structure* of these variables. From the very earliest of studies on FDI, scholars have shown that the foreign affiliates of MNEs tend to be concentrated in different industrial sectors than do their indigenous counterparts. Since each sector is likely to have its distinctive locational and trading propensities, it follows that FDI will have a differential impact on the geography of economic activity. Sometimes, this impact will reflect the characteristics of the country of the investing firms, e.g. Japanese FDI in the European auto and electronics industries in the 1980s; sometimes a very unique competitive advantage, or set of advantages; and sometimes their pattern and degree of multinationality. For it is the geographical diversity of asset-augmenting and asset-exploiting FDI, and the costs and benefits associated with their common governance, which is one of the singular features of contemporary MNE activity – especially in developed countries.

Scholars, such as Bruce Kogut, recognized these specific attributes of MNEs many years ago (see, for example, Kogut 1983 and 1985), but as the degree, scope and intensity of the foreign operations of firms has increased over the last decade (as demonstrated, for example, in the annual *World Investment Reports* of UNCTAD), and as these are now used to harness new resources, capabilities and markets, as well as to exploit the existing O advantages of firms, so have these particular qualities of multinationality become more prominent.

Though such qualities can be readily embraced into location theory, they are less easily incorporated into general equilibrium trade models. Primarily, this is because, unlike industrial organization theory, trade theory has not come to grips with the multi-activity firm, or multi-plant production, or has embraced innovation into its thinking (one notable exception is that of Grossman and Helpman 1991). Recent papers by James Markusen (1995) and Markusen and Venables (1998) have made a brave attempt to integrate the OLI framework paradigm of international production and the newer models of trade (i.e. those embracing firm-specific economies of scale, product differentiation and imperfect competition), but they tend to concentrate on how the cross-border specialization of specific knowledge-intensive activities may differ from that predicated by traditional trade theory. In a similar vein, research by

Brainard (1993) and Horstman and Markusen (1992) has concluded that
MNE-related production will be in equilibrium when firm-level fixed costs
and spatial transaction costs are large relative to plant level economies.[15]
None of these approaches, however, fully takes account of the key properties of multinationality, as distinct from the foreign ownership of firms.
While embracing some of the characteristics of internalized markets for O
specific assets, they ignore others – and especially those which elsewhere
we have referred to as transaction-cost-minimizing O advantages.[16]

Considering the normative implications of the work of Markusen and
others, and using the language of traditional trade theory, we might say
that it will be to the benefit of countries if their firms engage in outward
FDI in two very different situations. The first is where the utilization of
their O specific advantages, the production of which is relatively well
suited to the resources and capabilities of the home countries, is best
undertaken in a foreign country (or countries)[17] *and within the same firm*
(i.e. the benefits of "first best" internalized intermediate product markets
exceed those of "first best" arm's length transactions). The second is when
to protect or augment their global competitive advantages, firms engage
in buying assets in a foreign country (or countries) more favorable to
their creation, but not to their deployment. By contrast, a country will
benefit from inward direct investment when it has a comparative advantage in adding value to the services of the imported created assets – again
within the investing entity – rather than producing these assets itself, or
where a foreign firm chooses to buy assets created in the country (at the
right price) and utilize these assets in a foreign country (or countries).

In most cases, given the presence of MNEs, the recipe for an optimal
allocation of economic activity between countries is quite similar to that in
a world in which there is no FDI. But, the relative roles of markets, hierarchies and governments in this recipe are likely to be different. In
conditions other than that of perfect competition, hierarchies, or heterarchies – in the guise of multi-activity and/or multinational firms – may be
a more efficient coordinator of resources and capabilities than arm's
length markets (Caves 1996). This is particularly likely to be so in a
dynamic knowledge-based economy in which some of the ingredients of
endemic market failure, and particularly those of uncertainty, irregularity,
complexity, externalities, scale economies, vertical integration, and the
interdependence of markets, are present, as it is these which tend to generate the kind of value-added activities which can be coordinated more
efficiently under a single governance. In such cases, and providing that
the final goods' markets served by MNEs are contestable, and national
governments pursue positive and non-distorting market facilitating macro-
organizational policies (Dunning 1997b), MNEs may act as surrogates for
markets. By internalizing intermediate product markets, they may help
protect or enhance, rather than inhibit, the efficiency of final goods'
markets.

While not wishing to undervalue the role of governments in curtailing the anti-competitive behavior of firms, and in pursuing market friendly macro-organizational strategies, we believe that contemporary changes in the ways in which resources and capabilities are managed are facilitating a more appropriate balance between cross-border hierarchical (i.e. internalized) and external market transactions. Perhaps, the one area for potential concern is the widespread growth of international mergers and acquisitions and strategic alliances (UNCTAD 2000). Insofar as these may assist firms to be more innovatory, entrepreneurial and competitive in global markets, they are to the good; but, where they make it easier for companies to engage in structurally distorting business practices, they need to be carefully monitored.

The unique impact of MNEs on the international allocation of production rests on the extent to which the internalization of cross-border intermediate product markets produces a different and more efficient structure of economic activity than would otherwise have occurred. Herein lies an interesting paradox. On the one hand, the liberalization of markets and the reduction of some kinds of spatial costs are easing the trans-border movement of goods, intangible assets and services. On the other, technological and organizational change, whenever it enhances the interdependence of value-added activity, is encouraging international production to be undertaken within plants and firms under the same ownership, and for at least some of this production to be spatially concentrated. It would seem that as fast as structural and distance-related market failures are removed, others, making for internalized intermediate product markets and untraded spatial interdependencies are becoming more important.

Hints of this "new" international division of labor are shown not only by the growing participation of MNEs in global production – as described earlier in this chapter – but also by their increasing share of world export markets, at least in the manufacturing sector (documented by, *inter alia*, Dunning 1993; UNCTAD 1996a and Caves 1996). Other data also suggest that the export propensity of MNEs, or their affiliates, in the sectors in which they are most active exceeds that of indigenous competitors. Except in the case of a few countries, notably Japan, the payments for the services of knowledge-intensive assets received by US MNEs from their foreign affiliates, expressed as a proportion of their total exports, is considerably greater than the equivalent proportion between US and independently owned firms. For example, in 1996, royalties and fees received by US firms from their foreign affiliates amounted to 6 percent of their exports to these affiliates. The corresponding proportion of non-affiliated royalties and fees received by all US firms as a proportion of total US exports was 3 percent (US Department of Commerce 1997). Furthermore, of all royalties and fees received by US firms from foreign-based firms in the years 1993 to 1996, 79 percent were internal to US MNEs.[18]

The extent to which MNEs promote, or gravitate to, spatial clusters within a country or region is an under-researched area. Clearly, some older clusters, e.g. the Portuguese cork industry, the Swiss watch industry, the North Italy textile industry and the City of London financial district, developed without much MNE participation. But, many of the newly established clusters, which are geared more to accessing the external economies of knowledge creation, interactive learning and the upgrading of the competitive advantage of the constituent firms, are influenced by a rather different set of costs and benefits; and a casual examination of the membership of science and technology parks, export processing zones, research and development consortia and service support centers, would certainly suggest that MNEs are actively involved – often as flagship firms. Certainly among developed regions (e.g. the European Union) and countries (e.g. United States), knowledge-intensive and export-oriented activities tend to be more geographically concentrated than other kinds of activities (see, for example, illustrations given in Porter 1990, Dunning 1997b, Dunning 1997c and Dunning 2000).

Any modern theory of international economic activity must then take account of how the common ownership of cross-border production and transactions may result in a different value-added and spatial configuration than that which would arise if such functions were separately undertaken by uni-national firms. *Inter alia*, the extra attributes comprise the spreading of firm specific overheads and risk; the intra-firm sharing and transference of knowledge, experience and markets; and the external economies arising from jointly organized innovatory, production and marketing activities. For many of these activities, there is no external market; the output of one part of the firm can only be sold as an input to another part of the same firm. However, these interdependent activities may not need to be undertaken in the same region or country. For other activities, internal markets may offer more coordinating benefits and/or less transactional costs than arm's length markets. In both cases, however, it may be preferable to think of the MNE not as a second-best substitute for the market, but as a partner with the market to promote first-best allocative efficiency within and across value chains.

The notion of efficiency-promoting internal markets needs to be more formally built into both positive and normative macro models of international economic activity. In addition to acknowledging the different geographical needs of asset-producing and asset-exploiting activities, models of trade need to incorporate the benefits of organizing the two sets of activity under common ownership *vis-à-vis* that of the external market. This, in principle, is not a difficult thing to do. Essentially, it comes down to an identification and evaluation of the country, activity and firm-specific variables which determine whether the different transactional and coordinating functions are best organized within market friendly hierarchies, or by the market *per se*. We have already argued that markets for created assets, and for the goods and services arising from them, are likely to be intrinsically more imperfect than those for natural assets and for the goods and services arising from them. In some instances, too, it may be efficiency enhancing for these markets to be internalized. We also contend, with Behrman and Grosse (1990) and Meyer (1998), that most cross-border markets are likely to be more imperfect than their domestic equivalents, and that, because of this, MNE activity *may* be more welfare enhancing than multi-plant activity within an economy. We say "most" cross-border markets, because some domestic markets, particularly in emerging developing economies, are likely to be more imperfect than those in developed countries. But issues such as foreign-exchange uncertainty, institutional and cultural differences, and the differential role of governments are obviously likely to play a more important role in affecting the workings of cross-border than domestic markets. And we say "may" be more welfare enhancing, because much will depend upon the conditions under which foreign investment takes place.

At the same time, the extent to which cross-border markets are internalized via MNE activity will itself depend on the characteristics of the trading partners and the countries involved, as well as on the types of assets, goods and services being exchanged. In their attempts to explain the alternative forms of trans-border trade, and to advance both the positive and normative theories of trade, international economists need to delve deeper into the structure of country-specific advantages in organizing trade (particularly in knowledge-related products), through FDI and inter-firm alliances, as compared with arm's length markets.

Conclusions

The previous two sections of this chapter have examined how changes in the global economy over the past two decades are affecting scholarly thinking about both the micro-economic geography of FDI and MNE activity, and the more macro-economic explanations of the international allocation of all value-added activity. In particular, we focussed on three points. The first is the growing importance of intangible assets – and particularly intellectual capital – in the wealth-creating process, and of the need of companies to harness, as well as to exploit, these assets from a variety of locations. Secondly, we emphasized the changing role of location-bound assets, which mobile investors look for as complements to their own core competencies. In doing so, we again underscored the increasing significance of created assets (and particularly those which governments, in their macro-organizational policies, can and do influence), and, also, the benefits which spatial clusters offer whenever distance-related transactions and co-ordination costs are high.

Thirdly, we argued that, to adequately incorporate the activities of MNEs within existing trade-type theories of the international allocation of economic activity, more attention needs to be given both to the specific motives, determinants and consequences of the common governance of related cross-border activities, and to the conditions in which internalizing intermediate product markets might make for a more efficient (in the sense of the "next best" realistic alternative, assuming that all cross-border avoidable structural market imperfections have been removed) spatial configuration of economic activity in the contemporary global and innovatory economy. We have also suggested that any paradigm of the geography of FDI, as contrasted to that of the investments of all firms, needs to be constructed on similar lines.

What are the implications of our analysis and findings for future international business research? First, to return to the starting point of this chapter, and in line with the thinking of Michael Porter (1994, 1996, 1999), I believe more attention needs to be given to the importance of location per se as a variable affecting the global competitiveness of firms. That is to say, the locational configuration of a firm's activities may itself be an O-specific advantage, as well as affect the modality by which it augments, or exploits, its existing O advantages. With the gradual geographical dispersion of created assets, and as firms become more multinational by deepening or widening their cross-border value chains, then, both from the viewpoint of harnessing new competitive advantages and more efficiently deploying their home-based assets, the structure and content of the location portfolio of firms becomes more critical to their global competitive positions.

Second, in seeking to make an optimal use of the existing location-bound assets within this jurisdiction, and to promote the dynamic comparative advantage of their resource capabilities, governments need to give more attention to ensuring that their actions help fashion, support and complement those of efficient hierarchies and markets. This involves a greater appreciation both of the changing locational requirements of mobile investments, and of how, in the case of those markets where endemic failure is the most widespread, governments may work in partnership with firms either to improve markets (i.e. by a "voice" strategy[19]), or to replace these markets (by an "exit" strategy). With the growing importance of knowledge-related infrastructure, and accepting the idea of sub-national spatial units as nexus of untraded interdependencies (Storper 1995),[20] this presents both new challenges and opportunities to both national and regional governments in their macro-organizational and competitive enhancing policies.

NOTES

Source: Dunning, John H. (1998) *Journal of International Business Studies*, 29, 1: 45–66.

1 Such international-specific transaction costs have recently been explicitly identified by Klaus Meyer in a volume (Meyer 1998) based upon his doctoral dissertation at the London Business School.

2 For example, of the 1,150 or so publications cited in his volume, only 13 percent are to monographs or articles published after 1990.

3 Author's estimate, based on data on the royalties paid for managerial know how; and of the relationship between foreign portfolio and foreign direct investment.

4 There have been only a few attempts to use transaction cost analysis to explain the spatial distribution of economic activity. One example is that of the industrial geographers Michael Storper and Allen Scott. See, for example, Storper (1995), Storper and Scott (1995) and Scott (1996). Yet, such analysis offers a powerful tool for explaining why firms requiring idiosyncratic inputs, e.g. tacit knowledge of various kinds, and/or those supplying idiosyncratic and uncertain markets tend to value proximity with their suppliers and/or customers. Perhaps the best illustration of a spatial cluster, or agglomeration, of related activities to minimize distance-related transaction costs, and to exploit the external economies associated with the close presence of related firms is the Square Mile of the City of London.

5 Scott (1996) gives some examples, including the growing concentration and specialization of both manufacturing and service activities in large metropolitan areas within both developed and developing countries. In an interesting recent paper, Davis and Weinstein (1997) conclude that intra-national concentration of value-added activity is likely to obey the dictates of economic geography more than that of the international concentration of such activity.

6 Estimates of such ventures vary enormously. A recent study by Booz, Allen and Hamilton (1997) has put the number of cross-border alliances (including mergers and acquisitions) formed in 1995 and 1996 to be as high as 15,000. Another assessment by Hagedoorn (1996) suggests that between 1980 and 1994, the number of newly established cross-border technology-related inter-firm agreements rose by over three times. Finally, the value of international mergers and acquisitions over the same period were estimated to have accounted for between 50 percent and 60 percent of all new FDI (UNCTAD 1997).

7 For a detailed exposition of the development of a new trajectory of technological advances, see Lipsey (1997) and Ruigrok and Van Tulder (1995).

8 Though there have been marked fluctuations in the shares within and between these periods, which reflect, *inter alia*, changes in exchange rates and the positioning of countries in their cycles of economic development. For example, during 1975–1980, the United States attracted 32 percent of FDI received by developed countries; by 1985–1990 that share had risen to 42 percent. However, it fell again to 18 percent in 1991 and 1992; but since then it has recovered, and in 1995–1996 it stood at 35 percent.

9 Japan is a classic case in point. In the period 1990–1994 it accounted for 29 percent of the world's gross fixed capital formation, but only 0.8 percent of inbound FDI flows.

10 To give just one example; in the period 1990–1994, 49 percent of US direct investment flows were directed to Western Europe, 10 percent to Asia and 25 percent to Latin America. The corresponding percentages for Japanese direct investment flows were 20 percent, 19 percent and 10 percent (UNCTAD 1997, Dunning 1998).

11 Unlike the theory of the firm; although if there had been a well-developed theory of the multi-activity firm prior to the work of scholars such as Buckley, Casson and Hennart, one wonders if this aspect of international business activity would have attracted so much attention!

12 We use the word "customized" deliberately, following the contention of Peck (1996) that host governments may sometimes need to individualize or cus-

tomize the upgrading of their physical and human infrastructure both to meet the specific needs of mobile investors, and promote the competitive dynamic advantage of the location-bound resources within their jurisdiction.

13 I am indebted to the reviewer of the paper on which this chapter is based for making this point.

14 An expression first used in David (1984), and since taken up by Wheeler and Mody (1992) and Mytelka (1996).

15 In Markusen's words "multinational enterprises in this framework are exporters of the services of firm specific assets . . . subsidiaries import these assets" (Markusen (1995), p. 175).

16 Abbreviated, Ot transaction (or coordinating) cost-minimizing advantages, cf. Oa = asset-specific advantages.

17 Which foreign country, or countries, is decided by the normal locational criteria.

18 Other data on royalties and management fees received by US firms from foreign firms are regularly published by the *United States Department of Commerce in the Survey of Current Business*, and in the *Benchmark Surveys of U.S. Direct Investment Abroad*. See also UNCTAD (1995, 1996a and 1997).

19 The concepts of "voice" and "exit" strategies as applied to MNE-related activity are explained in Dunning (1997a).

20 The idea of a region as a spatial unit which internalizes distance-related transaction costs which otherwise would fall upon its constituent firms is an interesting notion worth pursuing by international business scholars. For, like a firm, the strategies pursued by a region to provide a set of unique, non-mobile and non-imitatable locational advantages for its firms may well determine its own competitive advantages relative to those of other regions. At the same time, regions, like firms, may decline as well as prosper; but our knowledge about the focus leading to the spatial disagglomeration of related activities is woefully inadequate.

REFERENCES

Almeida, P. (1996), "Knowledge sourcing by foreign multinationals: patent citation analysis in the U.S. semi-conductor industry," *Strategic Management Journal* 17 (Winter), pp. 155–65.

Bandera, V. N. and White, J. T. (1968), "U.S. direct investments and domestic markets in Europe," *Economia Internazionale 21* (February), pp. 117–33.

Behrman, J. N. and Grosse, R. (1990), *International Business and Governments*, Columbia, South Carolina: University of South Carolina Press.

Blair, M. M. (1995), *Ownership and Control: Rethinking Corporate Governance for the 21st Century*, Washington DC: The Brookings Institution.

Booz, Allen and Hamilton (1997), *Cross Border Alliances in the Age of Collaboration*, Los Angeles, CA: Booz, Allen and Hamilton.

Brainard, S. L. (1993), "A simple theory of multinational corporations and trade with a trade-off between proximity and concentration," Cambridge, MA: NBER Working Paper No. 4269, February.

Braunerhjelm, P. and Svensson, R. (1995), "Host country characteristics and agglomeration in foreign direct investment," Stockholm: Industrial Institute for EC and Social Research (mimeo), October.

Cantwell, J. A. and Harding, R. (1998), "The internationalization of German companies R&D," *National Institute Economic Review 163*, pp. 99–115.

Caves, R. (1982 & 1996), *Multinational Firms and Economic Analysis*, Cambridge: Cambridge University Press. First and second editions.

Dalton, D. H. and Serapio, M. G. (1995), *Globalizing Industrial Research and Development*, U.S. Department of Commerce, Office of Technology Policy, Washington, DC: U.S. Department of Commerce.

David, P. (1984), "High technology centers and the economics of locational tournaments," Stanford, CA: Stanford University (mimeo).

Davidson, W. (1970), "The location of foreign direct investment activity: country characteristics and experience effects," *Journal of International Business Studies*, *11*(2), pp. 9–22.

Davis, D. R. and Weinstein, D. E. (1997), "Economic geography and regional production structure: An empirical investigation," Cambridge, MA: National Bureau of Economic Research, Working Paper Series No. 6093 (July).

Donahue, J. D. (1996), *Disunited States*, New York: Basic Books.

Dunning, J. H. (1993), *Multinational Enterprises and the Global Economy*, Wokingham, England and Reading, Mass.: Addison Wesley.

Dunning, J. H. (1995), "What's wrong – and right – with trade theory," *International Trade Journal 9*(2), pp. 153–202.

Dunning, J. H. (1996), "The geographical sources of competitiveness of firms: some results of a new survey," *Transnational Corporations 5*(3), pp. 1–30.

Dunning, J. H. (1997a), *Alliance Capitalism and Global Business*, London and New York: Routledge.

Dunning, J. H. (ed.) (1997b), *Governments, Globalization and International Business*, Oxford: Oxford University Press.

Dunning, J. H. (1997c), "The European internal market program and inbound foreign direct investment," *Journal of Common Market Studies 35* (1 and 2), pp. 1–30 and pp. 189–223.

Dunning, J. H. (1998), "The changing geography of foreign direct investment," in N. Kumar (ed.), *Internationalization, Foreign Direct Investment and Technology Transfer: Impact and Prospects for Developing Countries*, London and New York: Routledge.

Dunning, J. H. (ed.) (2000) *Regions, Globalization and the Knowledge Based Economy*, Oxford: Oxford University press.

Edvinson, L. (1997), *Intellectual Capital Development*, Stockholm: Skandia.

Ethier, W. J. (1986), "The multinational firm," *Quarterly Journal of Economics 101*, pp. 806–33.

Florida, R. (1995), "Towards the learning region," *Futures 27*(5), pp. 527–36.

Fujita, M. and Thisse, J. R. (1996), "Economics of agglomeration," Kyoto: Kyoto University, Institute of Economic Research Discussion Paper No. 430, January.

Grabher, G. (ed.) (1993), *The Embedded Firm*, London and New York: Routledge.

Grossman, G. M. and Helpman E. (1991), *Innovation and Growth in the Global Economy*, Cambridge, MA: MIT Press.

Hagedoorn, J. (1996), "Trends and patterns in strategic technology partnering since the early seventies," *Review of Industrial Organization 11*, pp. 601–16.

Handy, C. (1989), *The Age of Unreason*, London: Hutchinson.

Hatem, F. (1997), *International Investment: Towards the Year 2001*, Geneva: United Nations.

Helpman, E. and Krugman, P. R. (1985), *Market Structure and Foreign Trade*, Cambridge, MA: MIT Press.

138 *Theoretical perspectives*

Horstman, I. J. and Markusen, J. R. (1992), "Endogenous market structures in international trade," *Journal of International Economics 32*, pp. 109–29.

Johanson, J. and Vahlne, J. E. (1977), "The internationalization process of the firm – a model of knowledge development and increasing market commitments," *Journal of International Business Studies 8*, pp. 23–32.

Kogut, B. (1983), "Foreign direct investment as a sequential process," in Kindleberger, C. P. & Audretsch, D. (eds), *The Multinational Corporation in the 1980s*, Cambridge, MA: MIT Press.

Kogut, B. (1985), "Designing global strategies: corporate and competitive value added chains," *Sloan Management Review 25*, pp. 15–28.

Krugman, P. (ed.) (1986), *Strategic Trade Policy and the New International Economics*, Cambridge, MA: MIT Press.

Krugman, P. R. (1991), *Geography and Trade*, Cambridge, MA: MIT Press.

Krugman, P. R. (1993), "On the relationship between trade theory and location theory," *Review of International Economics 1(2)*, pp. 110–22.

Kuemmerle, W. (1999), "The drivers of foreign direct investment into research and development: An empirical investigation," *Journal of International Business Studies 30(1)*, pp. 1–24.

Lipsey, R. G. (1997), "Globalization and national government policies: An economist's view," in John H. Dunning (ed.), *Governments, Globalization and International Business*, Oxford: Oxford University Press.

Liu, S. X. (1998), *Foreign Direct Investment and the Multinational Enterprise. A Reexamination Using Signaling Theory*, Westport, Conn.: Greenwood Publishing.

Loree, D. W. and Guisinger, S. E. (1995), "Policy and nonpolicy determinants of U.S. equity foreign direct investment," *Journal of International Business Studies 26(2)*, pp. 281–300.

Malmberg, A., Slovell, O. and Zander, I. (1996), "Spatial clustering, local accumulation of knowledge and firm competitiveness," *Geografiska Annaler Series B, Human Geography 78(2)*, pp. 85–97.

Markusen, A. (1996), "Sticky places in slippery space: A typology of industrial districts," *Economic Geography 72(3)*, pp. 293–313.

Markusen, J. R. (1995), "The boundaries of multinational enterprises and the theory of international trade," *Journal of Economic Perspectives 9(2)*, pp. 169–89.

Markusen, J. R. and Venables, A. (1995), "Multinational enterprises and the new trade theory," *Journal of International Economics 46*, pp. 183–203.

Maskell, P. (1996), "Local embeddedness and patterns of international specialization," Copenhagen: Copenhagen Business School (mimeo).

Mataloni, R. and Fahim-Nader, M. (1996), "Operations of U.S. multinational companies: preliminary results from the 1994 benchmark survey," *Survey of Current Business* (December), pp. 11–37.

Meyer, K. (1998), *Direct Investment in Economies in Transition*, Cheltenham, UK, Lyme U.S.: Edward Elgar.

Mytelka, L. K. (1996), "Locational tournaments, strategic partnerships and the state," Ottawa: Carleton University (mimeo).

Ohlin, B. (1933), *Inter-regional and International Trade*, Cambridge, MA: Harvard University Press, revised edition 1967.

Ohmae, K. (1995), *The End of the Nation State: The Rise of Regional Economies*, London: Harper.

Oman, C. P. (2000) *Policy Competition for Foreign Direct Investment,* Paris: OECD Development Centre.

Papanastassiou, Marina and Pearce, Robert (1997), "Technology sourcing and the strategic role of manufacturing subsidiaries in the UK: local competencies and global competitions," *Management International Review 37.*

Peck, F. W. (1996), "Regional development and the production of space: the role of infrastructure in the attraction of new inward investment," *Environment and Planning 28,* pp. 327–39.

Porter, M. E. (1990), *The Competitive Advantage of Nations,* New York: The Free Press.

Porter, M. E. (1994), "The role of location in competition," *Journal of Economics of Business 1*(1), pp. 35–39.

Porter, M. E. (1996), "Competitive advantage, agglomerative economies and regional policy," *International Regional Science Review 19*(1 and 2), pp. 85–94.

Porter, M. E. (1999) *On Competition,* Cambridge, MA: Harvard Business School Publishing.

Rees, D. and McLean, T. (1997), "Trends in location choice," in A. Jolly (ed.), *European Business Handbook 1997,* London: Kogan Page (for CBI).

Ruigrok, W. and Van Tulder, R. (1995), *The Logic of International Restructuring,* London and New York: Routledge.

Scaperlanda, A. and Mauer, L. J. (1969), "The determinants of U.S. direct investment in the EEC," *American Economic Review 59* (September), pp. 558–68.

Scott, A. J. (1996), "Regional motors of the global economy," *Futures 28*(5), pp. 391–411.

Shan, W. and Song, J. (1997), "Foreign direct investment and the sourcing of technological advantage: evidence from the biotechnology industry," *Journal of International Business Studies 28*(2), pp. 267–84.

Srinivasan, K. and Mody, Ashoka (1998), "Location determinants of foreign direct investment: an empirical analysis of U.S. and Japanese investment," *Canadian Journal of Economics 31*(4), pp. 778–97.

Stewart, T. A. (1997), *Intellectual Capital,* London: Nicholas Bradley.

Storper, M. (1995), "The resurgence of region economies: ten years later: the region as a nexus of untraded interdependencies," *European Urban and Regional Studies 2*(3), pp. 191–221.

Storper, M. and Scott, A. J. (1995), "The wealth of regions," *Futures 27*(5), pp. 505–26.

Taylor, J. (1993), "An analysis of the factors determining the geographical distribution of Japanese manufacturing investment in the UK, 1984–91," *Urban Studies 30*(7), pp. 1209–24.

U.S. Department of Commerce (1997), "U.S. international sales and purchases of private services," *Survey of Current Business,* October, pp. 95–138.

UNCTC, (1988), *Transnational Corporations and World Development,* New York: UN.

UNCTAD (1995), *World Investment Report 1995: Transnational Corporations and Competitiveness,* New York and Geneva: UN.

UNCTAD (1996a), *World Investment Report 1996: Transnational Corporations, Investment, Trade and International Policy Arrangements,* New York and Geneva: UN.

UNCTAD (1996b), *Incentives and Foreign Direct Investment,* New York and Geneva: UN.

UNCTAD (1997), *World Investment Report 1997: Transnational Corporations, Market Structure and Competition Policy,* New York and Geneva: UN.

UNCTAD (2000) *World Investment Report 2000: Cross-border Mergers and Acquisitions and Development,* New York and Geneva: UN.

Vernon, Raymond (1966), "International investment and international trade in the product cycle," *Quarterly Journal of Economics 80*, pp. 190–207.

Vernon, Raymond (1974), "The location of economic activity," in John H. Dunning (ed.), *Economic Analysis and the Multinational Enterprise,* London: Allen and Unwin, pp. 89–114.

Wells, L. T. (ed.) (1972), *The Product Life Cycle and International Trade,* Cambridge, MA: Harvard University Press.

Wesson, T. J. (1993), "An alternative motivation for foreign direct investment." Ph.D. dissertation, Harvard University.

Wheeler, K. and Mody, Ashoka (1992), "International investment and location decisions: the case of U.S. firms," *Journal of International Economics 33*, pp. 57–76.

Wood, A. (1993), "Give Heckscher and Ohlin a chance." Sussex: University of Sussex, Institute of Development Studies (mimeo).

World Bank (1997), *World Development Report: The State in a Changing World,* Oxford and New York: Oxford University Press.

5 Toward a general paradigm of foreign direct and foreign portfolio investment

Introduction

Until the early 1960s, the theory of foreign investment was essentially a theory of international portfolio or indirect capital movements. Capital flowed across national borders, mainly (though not exclusively) through the intermediation of the international capital market; and it did so in search of higher interest rates (discounted for exchange and other risks) and/or higher profits relative to those which could be earned at home. The types of financial device that were involved in these cross-national flows of capital were bonds and notes from the public and private sectors, equities, money market instruments and financial derivatives.[1]

Capital also crossed borders in the form of direct investments (FDI). FDI historically has been the dominant form of international *private* capital transfers and has represented a significant proportion of all investment. As can be seen in Figure 5.1 and Appendix A5.1,[2] from 1980 to 1995, FDI accounted for 38.7 percent of all inbound foreign investment to all countries in the International Monetary Fund's *Balance of Payments Statistics Yearbook*, with a slightly higher proportion (43.4 percent) occurring in the first half of the period than in the second half (32.6 percent).[3]

Figures 5.2 and 5.3, and Appendix A5.2 show that the vast majority of FDI and foreign portfolio investment (FPI)[4] is directed towards developed countries. During the early 1980s, FDI to developing countries was quite small and showed little sign of growth; it has only been in the late 1980s through 1995 that FDI to developing countries has trended upward and has been increasing relative to FDI to developed countries. A similar pattern appears for foreign portfolio investment (FPI), although the proportion of FPI going to developed countries is much higher than that for FDI. This phenomenon is due in large part to the inclusion of government securities as well as equities in the IMF data on portfolio investment, both of which have large, well-developed markets in developed countries.

Traditionally, FDI has been differentiated from FPI in four ways. The first is that, unlike FPI, FDI involves the transfer of non-financial assets, notably technology and intellectual capital, in addition to financial assets.

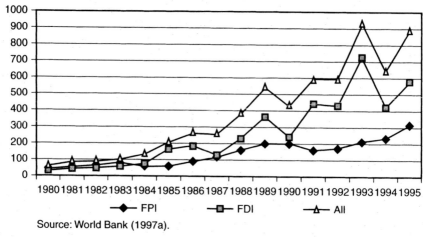

Source: World Bank (1997a).

Figure 5.1 Inbound foreign investment, 1980–1995

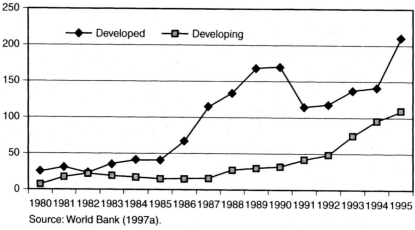

Source: World Bank (1997a).

Figure 5.2 Inbound foreign direct investment, 1980–1995

The second is that, in the case of FPI, there is a change in ownership of the assets transferred; this is not so in the case of FDI. Third, FDI is more lumpy (or indivisible) and less fungible than FPI, and is undertaken mainly by corporations, which control the deployment of the assets transferred, rather than by individuals and institutions, which exercise little control or influence over those assets. Fourth, unlike FPI, which is primarily prompted by higher foreign interest rates, FDI is motivated by the opportunity of achieving a better economic performance than that currently earned by competitor firms. For this to be achieved, the investing firms need to have some

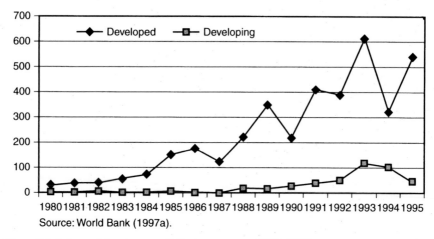

Source: World Bank (1997a).

Figure 5.3 Inbound foreign portfolio investment, 1980–1995

competitive advantage, either prior to, or in consequence of, their foreign activities, over and above that possessed by their foreign rivals, and for this advantage to be transferable across national boundaries.

There is now a well-established body of theory of FDI which, for the most part, is not concerned with explaining intrafirm capital movements per se, but rather that of the foreign value-adding activities of firms in which they have a financial stake sufficient enough to allow them some control or influence over such activities. While, de jure, such control is only achievable with a majority equity ownership, in practice most national authorities take a 25 percent, or even, in some cases a 10 percent equity stake, as indicative of some influence on the decision-making of the invested-in firm by the investing firm.[5]

Unlike the theory of FPI, that of FDI is concerned chiefly with explaining why firms extend their territorial boundaries outside their home countries, and why they do so by setting up new subsidiaries or acquiring existing foreign value-added activities, rather than by exports from their domestic production units, or by selling the right to use their competitive advantages, especially non-financial assets, through intermediate product markets. In doing so, it draws upon and integrates several branches of economic theory, including the theory of the firm and those of trade, of location and of market structure (Dunning 1993a, 1999 and 2000).

Yet, in their discussion of why firms should wish to internalize cross-border intermediate product markets, economists have been almost exclusively concerned with real, rather than financial, assets (as for example summarized in Dunning (1993b) and Caves (1996)). For example, while much has been written on the reasons why firms prefer to exploit a particular technological advantage (e.g. the ownership of patents), themselves, rather than license another firm to do so, virtually no attention has been given to why firms prefer to internalize the market for international capital (i.e. engage in foreign direct investment, rather than in foreign indirect investment). This, we believe, is partly because the two phenomena have been treated largely as substitutes for each other, but also because they have been considered as quite different and independent modalities of capital exports.

It is the contention of this chapter that this is a mistaken view and that, in our contemporary globalizing economy, portfolio and direct foreign investment can best be considered as components of a common paradigmatic approach to explain all kinds of private capital flows. We believe that, although essentially a financial act, FPI can be viewed in the same way as arm's length trade of any other asset; and that in discussing its relative merits, *vis à vis* FDI, one can use many of the tenets of internalization theory, first put forward to explain the intra- rather than interfirm (or market) exchange of non-financial assets.

However, there is a more important reason for our search for a general paradigm of private foreign investment. This is the growing interconnectedness between FDI and FPI – particularly when one takes a dynamic perspective. Historically, FPI – both private and public – has tended to precede FDI. Much of the early nineteenth-century European investments in the United States took the form of loans or minority equity stakes by institutions and/or individuals to one of the United States, and loans or minority equity stakes in publicly owned utilities or privately owned railroads, rather than by the direct ownership of United States assets by European firms (Wilkins 1989). Yet, as the United States economy matured, often with the help of inbound direct investment, its own capital markets evolved to absorb new portfolio capital inflows by European institutional and individual investors. In this way, history is now repeating itself in the emerging economies of Asia and Latin America, as successful FDI is helping to foster domestic capital markets, which, in turn, draw in more portfolio investment.

The current interconnections between FDI and FPI are, however, a good deal more complex than those of the nineteenth century. Thus, the FDI by a Chinese multinational enterprise (MNE) in an Australian mining venture may be financed by a loan to the former by a foreign bank, or an international lending agency or a foreign government. An acquisition of a French telecommunications company by a United States corporation may – if successful – lead to an inflow of FPI into the acquired company. A strategic alliance between a Canadian and a Brazilian company in which, in exchange for Canadian processing knowledge, the Brazilian company will share its marketing and distribution capabilities with the Canadian firm, may be accompanied by a minority investment of the former in the latter company.

To illustrate this point further, consider three hypothetical cases.

Case 1

Company A, a consumer products company, wants to expand globally and has targeted country X, an emerging market with demand for the products company A has to offer, as a likely place to start. Inside country X is company B, a distributor of consumer products with a strong regional presence in the most populated, economically developed area of the country. Company B would like to expand but is short of capital. Company A's strategic analysts agree that it is expensive to establish a greenfield distribution network and that it would be difficult to compete with company B in its regional market because of its extensive local knowledge and experience. Company A approaches company B about a cooperative venture in which company A will utilize B's distribution system and help expand it nationally by providing the necessary financing. This financing is made through a loan from company A to company B. The transaction does not alter company B's ownership structure, nor is a separate company established to house the venture.

Case 2

A consortium of three technology companies has developed a new generation of processing micro-chips and is looking for a location in which the chips can be mass produced at competitive costs. Country D, with a highly skilled but relatively cheap labor pool, has a state-owned chip processing plant with significant overcapacity. To attract foreign capital, country D has embarked on a privatization programme. The consortium and country D's government reach an agreement whereby the consortium acquires 48 percent of the company's stock (each member of the consortium acquires 16 percent) and sets up a management structure to control the newly privatized company.

Case 3

A diversified global conglomerate has targeted country Y as a location for expansion of one of its businesses. To test the market, this business acquires 100 percent of a small domestic company. Because the acquired company seems to be run efficiently and profitably, and is similar in most respects to other companies owned or managed by the acquiring company, no changes are anticipated in the way the acquired company is run. If it looks like the business can be expanded in country Y, the acquiring company intends to invest more capital. If expansion does not appear to be profitable, the acquired company will be sold.

For all intents and purposes, Case 1 is a direct investment by company A. However, it does not fit the prevailing definition of a direct investment and could be interpreted as a portfolio investment by company A. Case 2, on the other hand, is a clear example of a direct investment. Case 3, on paper, also is an example of direct investment, but, as far as management is concerned, it is entirely portfolio in nature.

At the same time, some FDI is increasingly taking on the characteristics of FPI. Thus, a firm rich in liquid assets may acquire the ownership, or part ownership, of a foreign corporation purely as a financial investment (i.e. there is no transfer of non-financial assets). Many of the capital exports by oil-rich countries to Europe and the United States in the 1970s were of this kind. Much more significant, however, is the strategic asset-seeking FDI of the late 1980s and 1990s, the purpose of which is less to exploit a particular competitive advantage of the investing firm by adding value to it in a foreign location, and more to protect or augment that advantage. Here, there is a direct parallel to FPI, viz. to tap into the resources and capabilities of foreign firms; although one of the main differences between FDI and FPI investment remains, viz. that the former transfers ownership rights to the investor while the latter does not.

The character of FPI is also changing as, increasingly in a knowledge-based global economy, *de facto* control over asset creation and asset usage rests less on the ownership of finance capital and more on that of all kinds of intellectual capital. Thus, in the last 15 years or so, in addition to FDI as a mode of exploiting or augmenting the competitive advantages of firms, we have seen a huge growth in cross-border non-equity alliances and networking relationships. The motives for such alliances are many and varied (for recent studies of alliances, see Duysters and Hagedoorn (1995), Hagedoorn (1985) and Beamish (1998)) but they all have one thing in common, viz. they involve the international transfer of assets – both financial and non-financial – without any FDI on the part of the parties to the alliance or the participants in the network. Sometimes the alliances are intended to exploit a competitive advantage of the contracting firm by way of a written or tacit agreement with a foreign partner, e.g. franchising in the hotel and fast-food sector, licensing agreements in the flat-glass industry, a turnkey project in the petrochemicals industry, and subcontracting arrangements in the textiles, shoe and electronics industries. Each of these collaborative ventures usually involves: (i) an ongoing non-equity association between two or more firms of different nationalities; and (ii) a transfer of assets or rights between the partners to the association.

In other cases, however, strategic alliances, like strategic asset-seeking FDI, may be geared towards accessing new knowledge or new sources of capital, or better exploiting a foreign market. Sometimes, too, they may be motivated by the need to share financial and non-financial assets and/or speed up the process of efficient asset creation or usage.

The critical feature of the plethora of cross-border arrangements now spanning global commerce is that each involves the transfer and/or governance of a single asset or combination of assets without the formal ownership rights afforded by FDI. Yet, *de jure*, while each transaction is akin to an arm's length or portfolio transfer of wealth creating assets or rights – *de facto* they may have many of the governance characteristics of FDI.[6]

All these examples point to two main conclusions, the analysis and implications of which are the main topic of this chapter. The first is the growing complementarity between FDI and FPI as agents of economic growth and development. Sometimes, this complementarity may be simultaneous; in other cases it may be sequential. But, whatever the time scale might be, the value of the one is enhanced by the other. Hence it is appropriate that, at least at one level of analysis, the determinants of each are considered as part of a whole, rather than separately.

The second conclusion is that, with the increasing cross-border mobility of many firm specific assets, or rights to assets, and the ever widening channels by which such assets are transferred, the boundaries between FDI and other modalities of asset transfer, including FPI, are becoming more difficult to delineate. Because of this, we believe there is some merit in considering whether a more holistic explanation of international asset movements – in this case FDI and FPI – is appropriate to those currently offered by the literature.

The rest of this chapter proceeds as follows: The next section discusses the changing characteristics of private FDI and FPI over the past century, and particularly over the last two decades. It goes on to offer a general paradigm within which it is suggested that more specific, or operational, explanations of FDI and FPI may be accommodated. Then, it goes on to give examples of how FDI and FPI have interacted in the past, and interact today, with each other. This is followed by a description of capital flows between the United Kingdom and the United States, both past and present, and another look at what is happening in emerging economies. The conclusion sets out some general hypotheses which we believe emerge from the "new" paradigm of foreign investment.

FDI and FPI: are they really different phenomena?

Earlier in this chapter we identified the main analytical differences between FDI and FPI. FDI essentially represented a modality by which a package of created assets[7] is transferred across national boundaries within the jurisdiction of the transferring firm. From a balance-of-payments viewpoint, outbound investment flows embrace all new equity and loan capital supplied by the investing company in the foreign organization over which it has a *de facto* controlling interest,[8] plus the reinvested profits of the foreign subsidiary and intracompany financial transfers.[9] The stock of FDI is more easily defined. It consists of the share of the total assets (usually valued at book value, but sometimes at replacement value) of the foreign

subsidiary owned or financed by the investing company less its current lia-
bilities. It, therefore, comprises both equity capital and long-term debt
financed from foreign sources.

Private FPI includes the flow of both equity and long-term debt (bonds
and loans) between individuals and/or institutions domiciled in different
countries.[10] This is achieved either indirectly through the capital market,
or directly in a foreign company, as long as the financial stake is below
that which constitutes a direct investment. Such investment may be channelled across national boundaries in several different ways. Historically,
the most common of these was through the international capital market,
and, in recent years, as the section "The sequential relationship between
FPI and FDI" below will show, there has been a marked increase in the
flow of FPI from and between developed countries, and the emergence of
developing countries as new players in that market. Second, FPI might
take the form of minority equity investments of one corporation in
another and/or loans made between two or more corporations. Third,
capital may be directly invested by institutions and/or individuals in non-
publicly quoted private companies and/or in public or semi-public bodies.

While, in the last two examples of FPI, there is a direct transfer of
funds, the *de jure* right to deploy the capital loaned or invested is transferred to the recipient institution. *De facto*, however, as we have already
seen and will demonstrate in more detail in the section on the sequential
relationship between FPI and FDI, depending on the amount of the
minority equity capital[11] and/or the terms and conditions attached to it or
to any loan, the investing individual or institution may be able to exert
considerable influence over the use made of that capital, for example as
part of a franchising, technical service, or subcontracting agreement. As
these, and other contractual agreements are becoming an increasingly
important component of the global exploitation and harnessing of
resources and capabilities, the *de facto* line between FDI and FPI is becoming an increasingly difficult one to draw.[12] Because of this, and the fact
that sequentially FDI and FPI may be closely linked to each other, this
chapter seeks to see how far it is possible to establish a general framework
for determining both forms of foreign capital transfer. It is important to
keep in mind that for the most part, we do not view FPI as being in
competition with FDI. Rather, we see the two as sometimes complementary or, possibly, alternative modes of investment that are, as a result,
capable of being described under a common paradigm.

Towards a general paradigm of foreign investment

We start our analysis by reiterating one of the most widely accepted paradigms of FDI – or more particularly the value-added activities resulting
from FDI. The eclectic paradigm (Dunning 1977, 1988, 1993a, 1995,
1998a, 1999 and 2000) avers that the amount and pattern of foreign

production by firms – i.e. production financed by FDI – will depend on the value of three sets of variables:

1   The competitive advantage of the investing (or potentially investing) firms, which are specifically the result of the nationality of their ownership (so-called ownership or O specific advantages), relative to those possessed by firms of other nationalities of ownership; and the ability of the investing firms to transfer, exploit or augment these advantages outside their national boundaries.

2   The absolute and relative attractions of different spatial areas (e.g. a country or region within a country) as a location (L specific advantages), both for the creation or acquisition of new O advantages, and for the usage of the O specific advantages. Essentially, the L specific advantages of particular spatial areas rest on the ability of national or subnational markets, and of governments, to provide a unique set of immobile assets necessary for investing firms – both domestic and foreign – to optimize the deployment of their mobile assets.

3   The relative merits, to the investing firms, of coordinating their O specific advantages with the L advantages of particular spatial areas, via arm's length markets, or internally through their own hierarchies, or by some intermediate route (e.g. an interfirm alliance or network of alliances). Where a firm chooses to replace the market for these advantages, or the rights to them by its own administrative fiat (i.e. via the modality of FDI), it is presumed to possess internalization (I) advantages. Where some form of alliance capitalism is preferred to the external market, or internal hierarchies, when it may or may not involve some FPI, it is presumed that their advantages rest with quasi-internalized or quasi-market interfirm transactions.

The eclectic, or OLI, paradigm suggests that the greater the O and I advantages possessed by firms and the more the L advantages of creating, acquiring (or augmenting) and exploiting these advantages from a location outside its home country, the more FDI will be undertaken. Where firms possess substantial O and I advantages but the L advantages, as described above, favor the home country, then domestic investment will be preferred to FDI, and any foreign markets will be supplied by exports. Where firms possess O advantages which are best acquired, augmented and exploited from a foreign market, but by way of interfirm alliances or by the open market, then FDI will be replaced by both a transfer of at least some of the assets normally associated with FDI (e.g. technology, capital, management skills, etc.) and a transfer of ownership of these assets or the right to their use. One of these assets is the equity or loan capital which comprises FPI.

The extent to which the OLI configuration favors FDI, or some other mode of international economic involvement, will be strongly dependent on a number of contextual variables, and it is when the eclectic paradigm is explicitly related to these variables that the paradigm can be translated into a number of operationally testable theories. These contextual variables are essentially fourfold. The first is the *raison d'être* for the FDI. Four motives, or types of FDI, are usually distinguished in the literature[13] – each is designed to further the economic prosperity of the investing firm [see, for example, Dunning (1993a)].

The first is to seek and secure natural resources, e.g. minerals, raw materials, or unskilled labor for the investing company (i.e. resource seeking FDI), the second is to identify and exploit new markets for its finished products (i.e. market seeking FDI); the third is to restructure its existing investments (of the first and/or second kind) so as to achieve an efficient allocation of international economic (i.e. rationalized or efficiency seeking FDI); and the fourth is to protect or augment its existing O specific advantages in order to sustain or advance its global competitive position (strategic asset seeking FDI). The *components* and *configuration* of the OLI advantages facing firms falling into each of these categories is likely to be very different; so, too, then will be the explanatory variables contained in any operationally testable theory of FDI.

Second, within the eclectic paradigm, the determinants of FDI may be different according to the home countries making the FDI (cf., e.g. Japan with Canada) and the host countries receiving the FDI (cf., e.g. Nigeria with Switzerland). Third, the precise configuration of the OLI variables explaining FDI is likely to be sector or activity specific. Thus, for example, the importance of patents, wage rates, government intervention, cross-border transport costs, and agglomerative economies in influencing the extent and pattern of MNE activity in the computer software and pharmaceutical sectors is likely to be very different from that in the iron and steel or building and contracting industry. Fourth, even within the same industry, the extent and structure of the OLI advantages of particular firms, and their response to particular OLI configurations may vary according to such contextual variables as their size, history, product range, degree of vertical integration, and location of their foreign operations; and also, too, to their managerial strategy (e.g. with respect to knowledge creation and market penetration). Clearly, then, the eclectic paradigm, though a tool offering an analytical foundation to explaining FDI, needs a good deal of contextualization before its principles can be subject to empirical testing.

It will be observed that – like its near counterpart, the internalization theory or paradigm – the eclectic paradigm of FDI is concerned with the extent to which, and the form in which, firms allocate their assets across national boundaries. Indeed, it is not a theory of FDI per se.[14] Rather, it draws upon and integrates several separate strands of microeconomic theory – most notably the resource and evolutionary theories of the firm,[15] the theory of location, the theory of economic organization (including the theory of internalization), the theory of international trade, and the theory of risk management. Implicitly or explicitly, it also incorporates a theory of business strategy, i.e. how firms might respond to a given OLI configuration, in terms of the alternative product-marketing innovation strategies open to them.[16] By contrast, the theory of FPI has traditionally drawn on macroeconomic financial variables, notably interest rate differentials and exchange-rate fluctuations. If, however, indirect investment is viewed as a transfer of wealth similar to that of an arm's length transfer of technology, plant and equipment, or human capital, then it would be legitimate to consider its determinants, *vis à vis* an internalized transfer of capital, in exactly the same way as the third component of the eclectic paradigm, viz. the I component, the purpose of which is to distinguish between the relative advantages of FDI and the market (or quasi-market) as a vehicle for transferring and coordinating the use of non-financial assets.

This, indeed, will be the underlying thrust of this chapter, viz. to treat FPI[17] as the cross-border transfer of assets through the open market, or by a non-equity interfirm agreement, rather than within the investing institution; and to see how far one can use the microeconomic and/or strategy-related theories of FDI to explain FPI – and, by inference, foreign investment in toto. This we do in the full recognition that there are certain features about FPI – notably its divisibility into small financial units – which FDI, almost by definition, cannot possess.

Let us, first, consider the three main tenets of the OLI paradigm and see how far we can apply them to FPI.

(1) O specific advantages

It is self-evident that for FPI to occur the lending, or investing, entity must have capital to invest. This, in itself, may be regarded as an advantage over other entities that do not possess that asset, or do not possess as much of it. In addition, unless perfect markets exist, and assuming that the advantage is sustainable over time, the entity must have some knowledge about both the prospects of the firm or firms in which the investment is being made and that of alternative foreign investment opportunities and their likely success. Where an intermediary is being used (e.g. an investment broker or mutual fund), such knowledge would also include that about competent sources of advice.

Such O specific advantages are the minimum required for successful FPI in cases where the investment is unconditional and the investing entity has no influence over the outcome of the investment. It embraces most individual and institutional loans, and minority equity investments channelled through the international stock market. However, as we have already seen, in other cases, FPI may be part and parcel of a package of assets transferred (e.g. as in the case of a franchising agreement) or have terms and conditions over its use set by the lending or investing entity, even though the foreign investor has no controlling equity ownership of the recipient entity's capital. In such cases, the O advantages attached to the FPI may be similar to those associated with (some kinds of) FDI. Thus, for example, in the hotel sector, long-term loans may be made by a hotel chain to a foreign hotel with which the chain has concluded a franchising agreement or management contract. The FPI is then conditional upon the terms of the agreement or contract, which will normally involve some non-equity transfer of technology, managerial skills and marketing expertise from the contractor to the contractee. O advantages associated with that kind of FPI may then be similar to those associated with a full-fledged FDI by the same hotel chain in a foreign hotel.[18] In other words, in such cases, FPI cannot be considered as an arm's length or a stand alone transfer of financial capital, but as part of a more systemic or integrated package of resource transference – but one which does not involve an equity stake which constitutes an FDI.

(2) L specific advantages (of countries or regions)

If the "how is it possible" for FPI to occur rests upon the possession of capital, knowledge about investment opportunities, the extent and structure of existing investments, and, in some cases, O advantages of a non-financial kind, the "where" of FPI will reflect the likely opportunities for securing a good rate of return (in the form of interest, dividends and capital appreciation) of the capital loaned or invested. Where the expected rate of return, discounted for risk,[19] is higher in the home country than elsewhere, domestic investment will be preferred to foreign investment. Where the reverse is the case, the choice between different foreign locations can be assessed by exactly the same criteria as those used to evaluate the choice of location for FDI, with the sole exception that in the case of FPI one is looking at L advantages from the angle of how they affect the prosperity of the recipient entity, rather than that of the investing company – as in the case of an FDI.

We do not propose to rehearse the locational attractions of particular countries, or regions within countries, to domestic corporations in which, directly or indirectly, there is some FPI. For the most part, these will be similar to those facing the subsidiaries of MNEs, except that their industry composition may be different, as may be their respective "embeddedness" (e.g. with respect of research and development activity), in the local economy, and their propensity to engage in international transactions. But variables such as raw material and labor costs, taxes, quality of infrastructure, size and character of the local market and managerial efficiency, as they affect the prosperity of indigenous firms, are as much likely to affect the location of inbound portfolio investment as that of direct investment.

At the same time, it may be hypothesized that FPI will be more responsive to changes in the value of L specific variables of countries and regions than will FDI. This is partly because the latter tends to be both more indivisible and spatially "sticky"[20] than the former,[21] and partly because international capital markets are likely to be more volatile than are the internal workings of TNCs. Indeed, it is this very volatility[22] which may lead to the replacement of these markets by FDI or some form of inter-firm agreement in the first place.

(3) The internalization theory of FDI

This theory (see, for example, Buckley and Casson (1976 and 1985) and Hennart (1982 and 1986)) argues that the foreign production of firms arises because of the failure of cross-border markets to transact intermediate goods and services at a cost below that which would be achieved if these transactions were undertaken within the same firm. The market most commonly taken to illustrate the *raison d'être* for FDI is that of intangible assets, and especially technology and all kinds of information. Thus, for example, technology will be bought and sold on the open market, i.e. externalized, as long as the net costs of doing so are less than those of organizing the transactions within the same firm. This, in fact, is only likely to be the case where the technology is reasonably standardized, where there are large numbers of buyers and sellers, and where there is little information asymmetry or avenues for opportunism. But, as often as not, these conditions do not exist, in which case the market will either be internalized or be translated into a specific agreement between the parties to the exchange.

In principle, there is no reason why (the services of) finance capital should not be treated like that of any other intangible asset, or part of a group of intangible assets.[23] In practice, of course, finance capital is more fungible (i.e. can be put to many uses), than can intangible real assets, although this fungibility may be constrained where conditions or terms are placed on its deployment. It is also more divisible; hence the large number of individuals engaging in FPI. Such fungibility and divisibility, together with the homogeneity of finance capital (in the sense that one dollar or pound sterling is identical to another), are just some of the reasons why the market for FPI is likely to involve fewer transaction or coordination costs than that of the market for real intangible assets; and why, indeed, the volume of FPI greatly exceeds the value of cross-border interfirm flows of the latter assets (as opposed to claims to intangible assets).

Although in reality [e.g. where they are undertaken by different investors (such as individuals compared to institutions)] or to achieve different goals, FPI and FDI may not be viable alternatives for each other, the internalization paradigm may still offer a robust analytical framework for evaluating the choice of one kind of investment over another; and this is so notwithstanding the fact that the composition and value of the individual I specific variables determining that choice may be different from those used to explain the mode by which other intangible assets are transferred across national boundaries.

To further consider the relationship between FDI and FPI, we first identify the major actors involved in FPI; second, how the OLI variables facing direct investors need to be modified to explain FPI; and third, how the particular advantages available to private portfolio investors are translated into an FPI. Table 5.1 sets out the major actors and their objectives. The actors are placed in three categories – viz. mutual funds; banks; and other investors such as corporations, investment banks, insurance companies, pension funds and individuals other than those channelled through the first two actors. Table 5.2 cross-references the objectives with the ownership, location and *externalization* advantages (OLE) of FPI identified earlier, and Table 5.3 describes how the advantages are manifested in actions.

While each type of lender or investor has similar objectives, the criteria each uses in making its investment decisions are likely to be different. Diversification, for instance, will have a different meaning for each investor, depending on the structure of the portfolio and the diversification strategies used. An international bond fund will diversify differently from an international stock fund, and both will diversify differently from, say, a single product high-technology firm looking for a minority interest in a foreign firm to help it find new markets for its existing product lines. It is quite possible, of course, that each of these investors may hold the same kind of investment. In fact, if direct investment is included, all types of investor might hold the same asset. In case 2 above, for instance, this

Table 5.1 Major actors and their objectives in private portfolio investment

Investor	Objective
Institutional investor	Yield
	Capital gain
	Diversification
	Speculation
	Market knowledge/access
Bank holding companies	Yield
	Capital gain
	Market knowledge/access
	Diversification
Non-financial firms	Yield
	Capital gain
	Speculation
	Market knowledge/access
	Diversification

Table 5.2 A description of ownership, location and externalization (OLE) variables for foreign portfolio investment

Ownership (origin of investment)	Location (direction of investment)	Externalization (reason for using external markets rather than internal markets for transferring capital)
Size of investible funds	Political stability of countries in which investments are made	Correlation of returns with other markets, especially home markets
Number of different funds, such as geography-based or sector-based[a]	Commitment to a market economy	Lower transaction costs
Access to new/additional investible funds	Degree of market openness and integration with global or regional markets[b]	Divisibility, transparency, fungibility of finance capital
Ease of transferability of investment among funds	Level of market sophistication or maturity	Possession of propietary or non-public information
Research capabilities and access to information about other markets/countries	Level of government support for portfolio investment	
Experience and capabilities of fund managers	Ease with which returns or gains can be repatriated	
Client preference for and attitude about risk	Ease of capital repatriation and/or dividend remission	
Risk-management capabilities, including use of derivative products	Condition of financial market infrastructure (e.g. banking system)	
Electronic funds transfer and communication capabilities	History of or prospects for economic growth	

Notes
a The institutionalization of savings on OECD countries in the last decade is an example of this. Where and how these savings are invested is dependent on many other factors within the OLE framework.
b The liberalization of financial markets, particularly in emerging and developing economies, has expanded the location options of FPI.

situation could occur if the government of country D continues to privatize its 52 percent interest in the company. As a result, and as cases 1, 2 and 3 illustrate, little can be known about the intent of an investment just by looking at what it is.

As a framework for later discussion, let us first identify the ownership, location and externalization advantages specifically applicable to portfolio investors. Ownership advantages include the size of the portfolio, the investment, risk management and learning capabilities and experience of the portfolio managers, the existing stock of FPI,[24] and market information and knowledge (or the ability to access/acquire market information). All of these are things that can (and do) differ from investor to investor. Location advantages refer both to those provided by the home base and foreign locations (actual or desired). Thus, access to funds and a

Table 5.3 The execution of OLE advantages in foreign private portfolio investment

Advantage	How executed
Ownership	Choice of investment (e.g. debt or equity), including amount, term, yield, location (geographic and sector), and covariance with other similar investments in other locations.
Location	Investment made to pursue firm and client diversification objectives, as well as to meet client preferences for country and/or sector exposure. Knowledge-gathering investment. To take advantage of favourable tax and/or dividend/repatriation policies.
Externalization	Selective participation in countries, geographic regions or sectors to pursue portfolio structure objectives, as well as the movement among and between countries, regions and sectors.

regulatory and policy-framing environment that is conducive to the mar-
shalling and investing of funds domestically and abroad are locational
advantages. Externalization advantages – the counterpart of internalization advantages of FDI – of using markets to support ownership and location advantages, include the ability to take advantage of investments
whose returns have limited covariance with the existing stock of investments; the ability of the market to provide the necessary information of
investors to exercise their preferred options and investment strategies;
and also the lower costs of managing a large number of relatively standard
transactions, cf. those incurred by firms.

Diversification, as used in Table 5.1, refers to the diversification (reduction) of risk as well as the structure of the entire investment portfolio.
This can be achieved by diversifying the type of investment made (e.g.
stocks in different industries, bonds from different countries, mixing
stocks and bonds, etc.) or by selecting investments that have little covariance within and across sectors. The expertise and market knowledge of
portfolio managers, displayed in the ability of portfolio managers to
research, locate and act upon investment opportunities, and the ability to
marshal funds to invest, determine in large part how much the portfolio
can be diversified. It is an ownership advantage because that expertise,
market knowledge and access to funds can be unique to each type of
investor.

The location advantage of having easy access to investible funds and a
regulatory, financial and economic environment that eases the mar-
shalling of funds for investment help a mutual fund seek other markets
outside its home market. This is not the same thing as simply investing
foreign source funds from investors, which would represent a capital
outflow from those foreign sources. Rather, it is establishing a foreign
base in which those foreign source funds are accumulated for real investment. The mode in which the base is established can take the form of

direct investment (e.g. setting up a branch office), portfolio investment (e.g. purchasing a minority interest in a domestic fund in return for access to funds and/or clients), or an arm's length transaction (e.g. buying funds). Access to funds is not the same thing as the ownership advantage of having investible funds. For instance, all mutual funds in the United States share the same locational advantage created by the regulatory and investment climate of the United States, but not all mutual funds have the same level of assets, the same investment objectives and the same mix of investors.

The same rationale for market-seeking actions applies to banks and other investors. Banks, however, also engage in client-following and client-seeking investment behavior. The role locational advantage plays here is clear: the institutions want to be near their clients and would like to attract new clients. Given the highly regulatory nature of the banking industry, the most effective way foreign banks can get close to existing and potential clients is by being where the clients are (see Sagari 1989). This could be accomplished through direct investment (branch offices) or portfolio investment (joint ventures or partnerships with domestic banks). Both of these advantages could enhance an existing ownership advantage, the former by strengthening ties with clients and attracting more investible funds, and the latter by attracting more investible funds.

One could argue with a fair amount of strength that certain other investors, such as investment banks, also engage in client-following and client-seeking behavior. For investment banks, however, once capital is mobile across borders, the incentive for them to establish a foreign office simply to be near their existing clients is weakened. A better way to characterize their behavior, and that of other investors such as pension funds, is resource seeking. Functionally, resource-seeking behavior is the same as the client-seeking behavior of banks in that the objective (i.e. securing more investible funds) is similar. The distinction is in the underlying purpose of using the locational advantage. For banks, it is primarily in establishing a relationship that may result in funds to invest; for non-banks, on the other hand, it is gaining access to funds. As with the client-seeking and client-following behavior of banks, the resource-seeking behavior of non-banks can be achieved through either direct or portfolio investment.

Because the advantages of using the international capital market rather than internalizing that market are defined in terms of portfolio structure and strategic outlook (attitude towards risk), they will influence the yield-seeking and capital gain-seeking behavior of all three types of investor. The overall return of an entire portfolio will be affected by the degree of covariance among the assets (see Markowitz 1959). Volatility of returns will be greater when covariance is high. The amount of total risk in a portfolio therefore will depend a great deal on the level of covariance. Investors comfortable with volatility (risk seeking) will build a portfolio of assets differently from risk-averse investors who are not comfortable with such greater volatility, but both will build portfolios in accordance with the desired structure of those portfolios.

The possibility of a link between diversification and yield-seeking and capital gain-seeking behavior comes immediately to mind. Obviously, the overall yield of a portfolio and the amount of risk inherent in it will depend on how much the portfolio is diversified and how much covariance is present. In a sense, then, the ultimate performance of a portfolio will depend on the interplay of the various ownership, locational and externalization advantages. The size, type and nature of a portfolio and the way it is managed from a cash-flow and risk-perspective (ownership) depends on the assets in the portfolio. The way in which new assets are acquired to meet specific growth objectives (for the individual portfolio or the investing company) depends on the use to which locational advantages are put. Performance (yield and capital gains) objectives, which in turn influence the type of asset acquired or sought, then depend on the strategic outlook of the investor.

The variables and contexts identified in Tables 5.1 and 5.2 are self-explanatory. Each is firmly grounded in the theory of FDI, of portfolio capital movements, and of locational economics. From these, and taking a medium- to long-term perspective, it is possible to formulate a series of operationally testable hypotheses as to: (a) when FDI and FPI are complements to each other; and (b) if they are substitutes, or are independent of each other, what are the variables likely to determine the final choice or modality of financial asset transfer. While we shall offer some hypotheses later in this chapter, we shall not seek to formally test them. Instead, we shall offer some illustrations of how, in the past, and in today's globalizing economy, FDI and FPI have been, and are, related to other, in terms of their respective – sometimes similar, sometimes different – OLI or OLE configurations.

The sequential relationship between FPI and FDI

While, at a given moment of time, FPI and FDI may appear to be independently determined and undertaken for different reasons, it is quite possible that over time they may be closely related to each other. History is full of examples of FPI, both in developed and developing countries, laying the ground work for FDI. Usually, and especially in the case of infrastructure investment in countries subject to political or economic volatility, the FPI will be financed by public authorities or international agencies (e.g. the World Bank), or protected by an investment guarantee scheme. In other instances (e.g. as on the American continent in much of the nineteenth century), private foreign capital was steered, mainly through the international capital market, to state governments and/or to state-supported ventures. No less today do foreign direct investors expect host countries to provide the human, technological and institutional infrastructure with which their O specific intangible assets may be successfully combined. Frequently, however, especially in some developing and transitional economies, local savings are insufficient to finance these assets and the capital has to be imported, usually by grants from foreign governments, by foreign loans, and/or (minority) equity investments from international agencies and corporations.

At the same time, it is clear by the emergence and dramatic growth of domestic capital markets in several Asian and Latin American countries, that FPI may follow, as well as precede, FDI. But most post-FDI portfolio capital flows are quite differently sourced and directed than are pre-FDI portfolio flows. Whereas the former tend to be financed by national governments and international lending agencies and directed to infrastructural projects – and hence are not our immediate concern – the latter are primarily initiated by individual and institutional investors and are directed to (potentially) profitable and/or growth-oriented sectors in the recipient countries – including some infrastructure projects. Furthermore, while pre-FDI portfolio capital flows normally precede the presence of a flourishing domestic economy and capital market, post-FDI flows are drawn largely by these phenomena.

In today's global economy, however, the sequential interaction between FPI and FDI can be both more indirect and more varied than that just described. For example, it is perfectly possible that part of inbound portfolio capital flows may be used to finance outbound direct investment[25] or, for FDI, in a particular sector, to stimulate competitors to seek FPI – often jointly with other intangible assets to upgrade their own core competencies. In their global search for resources and capabilities, MNEs themselves frequently draw on loan capital from both national and international capital markets; and, in the case of alliances with foreign firms, they may exchange loans and/or equity stakes. Sometimes, too, foreign-owned banks will make long-term loans to indigenous firms, which are used to finance their own international operations; or, in the case of wholesale traders and distributors, to help finance a joint venture with a foreign exporting company. Renewed confidence in an economy, or in a particular sector or region in an economy, which may have been greatly assisted by the activities of foreign subsidiaries, may lead to more FPI in that economy, sector and industry.[26] By contrast, lack of confidence in an economy, region or sector, as demonstrated for example by falling stock prices, might lead not only to a reduction of FPI, but – in the longer run – of FDI as well. More generally, there is some suggestion that, over time, the economic progress of an economy, region or sector will parallel all kinds of foreign and domestic investment quite closely.[27]

The following two sections illustrate the changing interaction between FDI and FPI, using the framework of the eclectic paradigm. The first considers the evolving form and structure of capital flows between the United

Kingdom and the United States over the past century or more; and the second does the same – but for a more recent period, viz. 1972 to 1995 – in respect of foreign capital flows into two emerging regions, East Asia and Latin America.

United Kingdom–United States capital flows

The history of foreign investment in the United States up to 1914 has been well documented by Mira Wilkins (1989). Here we will seek to emphasize a few highlights of that history from the perspective of United Kingdom FDI and FPI.

Applying the concept of the investment development path[28] (Dunning and Narula 1996), most of the created assets (e.g. capital, technology and organizational capacity, etc.) for the economic development of colonial America initially came from Europe and especially the United Kingdom. Partly, by way of migration of human and physical capital, partly by grants and loans from the mother country, and partly by some embryonic American businesses financed by foreign direct or portfolio investment, foreign assets, when combined with the rich natural resources of the Eastern seaboard, helped create the colony's own location (L) advantages, and its firms to generate a unique set of O specific competencies.[29]

In the post-revolutionary period, foreign capital flowed into the United States. The first half of the century was a time when the new Republic was both making huge investments of roads, canals, ports and railroads, and evolving its own distinctive economic structure, based largely on the comparative advantage of its natural assets and its emerging created assets, the latter being primarily designed to upgrade the value of the former (Wright 1990). Such circumstances combined to create an OLI (or OLE) configuration in which the major vehicles for transferring financial and real assets (or rights) between the United Kingdom and the United States were: (a) migration of human capital; (b) the transfer of knowledge via the export of goods and licensing agreements; and (c) the international capital market (see Wilkins (1989)). In 1853, according to a United States Treasury Department Survey, of the $222 million of foreign investment stocks held in the United States, 72 percent was directed to government securities and another 21 percent to the bonds of railroad, canal and navigation companies. The main FDIs of the time were confined to trading and banking and insurance activities. There was also some United Kingdom ownership of the early railroad companies, but FDIs in manufacturing industry were, according to Mira Wilkins (1989), "few and far between" (p. 88).

The marked preference for United Kingdom and other European indirect, rather than direct, investments in the United States reflected primarily the (relatively) efficient workings of the international capital market, and partly the (relatively) high trans-Atlantic transaction and coordination costs of operating a United States subsidiary of a United Kingdom company. In addition, the most capital-intensive sectors in the United States economy were those in which foreign companies were reluctant to hold a major equity stake (viz. public utilities). By contrast, FPI in United States government securities was generally thought to be a relatively safe investment, particularly when they were recommended by a leading United Kingdom merchant banking house.

Technological and organizational advances of the 1870s and the maturing of many United States enterprises dramatically changed the scenario for inbound foreign investment. Although, right up to the First World War, the bulk of such investment was portfolio, rather than direct,[30] the advent of managerial capitalism and the lowering of intracompany spatial transaction and coordination costs favoured the territorial expansion of foreign firms into the United States, particularly in those sectors in which they were perceived to have an O advantage over their United States counterparts. At the same time, there was a great deal of syndicated FDI in these years,[31] which, in its intent at least, has more in common with FPI. By 1910 too, the sectoral preference of United Kingdom investors had switched from government securities to railway stocks and bonds and commercial ventures. According to Sir George Paish (1911), the former accounted for 85.2 percent of the $3.3 billion of United Kingdom investments in the United States in 1910, while investments in industrial companies, mining, land and public utilities accounted for most of the balance. Of these latter investments, about two thirds took the form of direct investments, as it was in these sectors that the net transaction costs of markets, relative to administrative hierarchies, were most evident.[32]

During and after the First World War, a sizeable proportion of United Kingdom investments in the United States were sold, while the late 1920s saw the collapse of the international capital market. However, while United Kingdom investors lost some of their O advantages as suppliers of finance capital, United Kingdom firms continued to lead the outflow of FDI, and by 1938 they accounted for two fifths of global FDI. During these years, however, United Kingdom firms lost ground to their United States counterparts, particularly in FDI intensive sectors, while new locational attractions were being offered by Commonwealth countries, notably Canada and Australia. The net result of these events was that although the flow of United Kingdom investment into the United States did recover somewhat in the 1930s, this recovery was almost wholly the result of new FDI designed to exploit the growth of the United States market and overcome trade and transaction related barriers.

For much of the first 20 years following the end of the Second World War, there was very little United Kingdom portfolio investment in the United States capital market. Indeed, it was only in 1958 that sterling became fully convertible. FDI was also limited because of the lack of competitive advantages of United Kingdom, cf. United States, firms and because of the high costs of production in the United States relative to those in the United Kingdom. Gradually, however, United Kingdom industrial competitiveness recovered, often aided by the capital, technology and managerial skills transferred via FDI from the United States to the United Kingdom (Dunning 1958); and by the early 1980s. United Kingdom and continental European FDI in the United States was rising at twice to three times the rate of United States FDI in Europe (Dunning 1993b, chap. 7). By 1982, the United Kingdom FDI stake in the United States once more exceeded that of the United States in the United Kingdom, and by the early 1990s it was one half as much again.

While part of this renewed interest by United Kingdom MNEs in the United States can be explained by the extant theories of FDI, since the early 1980s an increasing proportion of FDI has taken the form of takeovers and mergers which has been geared less to exploiting the existing competitive advantages of the investing companies and more to augmenting these advantages.[33] To this extent, the motives of United Kingdom FDI in the United States have begun to parallel those of FPI – viz. to invest in the economic strength of a foreign company, country or region in a country. This has been particularly well demonstrated in the high technology sectors, where FDI by United Kingdom firms in the United States has been complemented by interfirm alliances between United States and United Kingdom firms. Sometimes such alliances have involved an export of loan or equity capital from the United Kingdom to the United States; but, more usually, the main vehicle of financial involvement by individual and institutional investors in the more competitive United States sectors has been through the capital market, for example, by the purchase of unit trusts, mutual funds, and by purchases of stock of United States companies or of United Kingdom MNEs with FDIs in the United States.

Table 5.4 sets out the trend of United Kingdom FDI flows in the United States and the United States gross national product from 1972 to 1995. We have presented the data as three-year moving averages to iron out at least some of the sharp changes in foreign investment brought about by mergers and acquisitions and/or short-term speculative reasons. Table 5.5 presents the trend of all FDI and FPI flows to the United States and the United States' gross national product over the same period, also as three-year moving averages. The figures show, first, that both kinds of foreign investment have increased at a faster rate than gross national product; second, that FPI and FDI have broadly parallelled one another, but especially so since the early 1980s; and third, that, although for the period as a whole, the share of FPI in total foreign investment has risen, it has also fluctuated more noticeably than FDI.

In terms of the eclectic paradigm, the rising share of foreign investment in the United States' gross national product – and incidentally of the total gross fixed capital formation in the United States[34] – is consistent with two somewhat conflicting propositions. The first is that the O specific advantages of foreign-owned firms are rising relative to those of United

Table 5.4 FDI flows from the United Kingdom into the United States, 1972–1995 ($ billions)

Years	FDI	Percent growth	GNP	Percent growth
1972–1974	0.36		1,350	
1973–1975	0.56	55.9	1,478	9.5
1974–1976	0.58	2.4	1,619	9.5
1975–1977	0.63	9.9	1,792	10.7
1976–1978	0.76	19.8	2,011	12.2
1977–1979	1.26	66.7	2,257	12.2
1978–1980	2.04	61.9	2,506	11.0
1979–1981	3.20	56.6	2,776	10.8
1980–1982	4.26	33.1	2,995	7.9
1981–1983	4.52	6.2	3,226	7.7
1982–1984	5.08	12.4	3,472	7.6
1983–1985	4.86	−4.3	3,763	8.4
1984–1986	6.22	28.0	4,044	7.5
1985–1987	10.35	66.2	4,292	6.1
1986–1988	15.05	45.5	4,577	6.6
1987–1989	19.19	27.5	4,900	7.1
1988–1990	14.51	−24.4	5,227	6.7
1989–1991	9.71	−33.1	5,503	5.3
1990–1992	2.10	−78.4	5,839	6.1
1993	13.23	530.8	6,564	12.4
1994	11.12	−15.9	6,932	5.6
1995	22.08	98.5	7,247	4.5

Source: Calculated from various issues of United States Department of Commerce, *Survey of Current Business*. These data include reinvested profits from existing investments.

Note: Data are not available on United Kingdom FPI into the United States.

States' owned firms, and hence the firms' ability to invest in the United States is that much greater. The second is that the foreign firms are investing in the United States to protect or augment their existing competitive advantages. This second proposition is consistent with the view of portfolio investors that the United States' economy is a good place in which to invest their capital. Clearly, which of these two propositions is most applicable is likely to be industry and, indeed, firm specific. But from a casual examination of the comparative growth and profitability data on the leading United States and United Kingdom firms (Dunning and Pearce 1985), and data from the United States Department of Commerce and the industrial distribution of the United Kingdom FDI in the United States – including FDI in research and development ventures – it would seem that, while the former proposition may hold good for the less knowledge- but more marketing-intensive industries (especially food, drink and tobacco), the latter proposition better explains the growth of the United Kingdom (and for that matter other European and Japanese) FDI in the high-technology industries, noticeably the biotechnology and the telematics industries).

Table 5.5 Trends in all FDI and FPI flows into the United States, 1972–1995
($ billions)

Period	FDI	Percent change	FPI	Percent change	All foreign Investment	Percent change
1972–1974	2.8		5.9		8.7	
1973–1975	3.4	19.8	3.0	−48.6	6.4	−26.4
1974–1976	3.9	15.0	2.9	−3.8	6.8	6.3
1975–1977	3.6	−8.9	11.0	278.3	14.6	114.7
1976–1978	5.3	49.3	12.0	8.6	17.3	18.5
1977–1979	7.1	33.8	11.4	−4.8	18.5	6.9
1978–1980	11.5	61.8	6.8	−40.1	18.3	−1.1
1979–1981	17.3	50.7	9.3	37.1	26.6	45.4
1980–1982	18.7	8.0	11.7	25.2	30.4	14.3
1981–1983	17.1	−8.8	8.7	−25.3	25.8	−15.1
1982–1984	17.1	−0.1	12.2	38.9	29.3	13.6
1983–1985	18.8	10.3	31.5	159.3	50.3	71.7
1984–1986	26.1	38.4	58.2	84.7	84.3	67.6
1985–1987	31.6	21.2	70.8	21.7	102.4	21.5
1986–1988	44.3	40.2	73.0	3.0	117.3	14.6
1987–1989	55.7	25.6	77.6	6.4	132.3	12.8
1988–1990	57.6	3.6	63.9	−17.8	121.5	−8.2
1989–1991	45.9	−20.4	58.4	−8.5	104.3	−14.2
1990–1992	29.2	−36.4	50.5	−13.5	79.7	−23.7
1993	43.0	47.4	111.0	119.7	154.0	93.2
1994	49.8	15.7	139.5	25.7	189.3	22.9
1995	60.2	21.0	236.2	69.4	296.4	56.6

Source: IMF (1996), *Balance of Payments Statistical Yearbook, 1996* (Washington, D.C.: IMF).

Over the last two or more decades, the L advantages of United States-based assets have been most evident in two kinds of activity. The first, as witnessed especially by Japanese FDI in the United States, has been in those industries in which the global O advantages of the foreign investors are particularly evident, yet which are best exploited from a United States location. The second have been in those industries in which foreign firms perceive they need a presence in the United States to gain access to specific resources and capabilities, including institutional capital, and/or to augment their own advantages by acquiring, or engaging in an alliance with, United States firms. This latter kind of FDI has been particularly noticeable in research and development, knowledge-intensive manufacturing and in the service industries. It is also worth observing that both foreign and domestic investment in these industries has tended to favor particular states in the United States – notably California, Massachusetts, New Jersey, South Carolina and Texas – each of which has an above average share of knowledge-intensive manufacturing and service industries.

For the most part, then, we conclude that, normalizing for industry and firm-specific differences, discounting short-term factors affecting stock market performances and apart from differences in cross-border transaction and transport costs which only affect FDI, that the L advantages of the United States in attracting inbound portfolio and direct investment are broadly the same. However, within the United States, there is some suggestion that foreign subsidiaries do portray different locational preferences than their indigenous competitors (Ulgado 1996; Shaver 1998).

While in some cases the premises of the internalization paradigm can be used to explain why FDI is preferred to FPI, much of United Kingdom FPI now directed to the United States is not directly substitutable for FDI, but rather is complementary to it. This is primarily because it is undertaken by different economic agents and the unit size of the investment is, on average, much smaller. In the case of individual (i.e. personal) lenders or investors, for example, the choice is not between FPI and FDI, but between FPI in the United States[35] or in United States firms, and that in other countries or in non-United States firms; this, for example, especially applies to FPI in United States Government securities. At the same time, indirectly and over time, there is some suggestion that FDI and FPI are sometimes alternative and sometimes complementary ways of achieving this goal. Certainly since the late 1980s they have tended to parallel the fortunes of the United States economy. Many non-equity United Kingdom–United States strategic alliances are also part of the global strategy of foreign firms with major foreign interests in the United States, and are intended to protect or add to the value of these interests. At the same time, FPI invested in United States MNEs may help such firms not only to finance (say) joint research and development or marketing ventures with foreign firms, but to better penetrate new foreign markets, either by way of outbound direct investment or by some form of interfirm collaboration.

FDI and FPI in emerging economies

The last two decades have seen a remarkable increase in the level of private capital flows into developing countries, with the fastest growth occurring in FPI. The entire period from 1975–1995 can be divided up into three seven-year subperiods, 1975–1981; 1982–1988, and 1989–1995. These periods coincide roughly with three stages of private capital flows: the pre-debt crisis stage (1975–1981); the debt-crisis and its aftermath stage (1982–1988); and the recovery and boom stage (1989–1995). Table 5.6 presents data on the annual average inbound flows of FDI and FPI during these stages for all developing countries, and shows the proportional share of FDI in these flows.[36] The initial stage is indexed at 100.0 to provide a gauge for the changing magnitude of each type of investment. (Further details on the year-to-year FDI and FPI to all developing countries are provided in Appendix Table A.5.2.)

The effect of the debt crisis on FPI from 1982–1988 resulted in a slightly negative ($169 million) net flow. Two factors caused the downturn

Table 5.6 Net flows of private investment to all developing countries in three stages, 1975–1995 ($ billions)

Stage	FDI	Index Stage 1 = 100	FPI	Index Stage 1 = 100	Total	FDI as percent of total
1: 1975–1981	7,035	100.0	7,866	100.0	14,901	47.2
2: 1982–1988	11,764	167.2	−169	−2.1	11,595	101.5
3: 1989–1995	53,037	753.9	35,671	453.5	88.707	59.8

Source: Calculated from World Bank (1997a).

Table 5.7 Private investment in East Asia and Latin America as compared to that in all developing countries during three stages, 1975–1995 ($ billions)

Stage	FDI	Percent of all FDI	FPI	Percent of all FPI	Total	Percent of total
1: 1975–1981	5,679	80.7	6,212	79.0	11,891	80.0
2: 1982–1988	8,519	72.4	−475	281.4	8,044	69.4
3: 1989–1995	41,264	77.8	29,439	82.5	70,704	79.7

Source: Calculated from World Bank (1997a).

in private FPI. First, some private debt was either restructured or was converted to public debt, which, in turn was guaranteed by a third party (such as the United States Treasury Department or the IMF) to both forestall economic collapse of the debtors and to protect the lenders.[37] Second, the flow of new private debt slowed as the effects of the debt crisis spread across developing countries, making lenders cautious about extending credit until conditions improved.[38] Net flows of FDI, on the other hand, increased by 167 percent during the debt crisis stage.

These private investment flows, however, were not spread uniformly across developing countries. As can be seen in Table 5.7, two geographic regions – East Asia and Latin America – attracted the largest share of private investment throughout the entire period.[39] From 1975 through 1995, these two regions averaged over 77 percent of all FDI directed to developing countries, and well over 100 percent of all FPI (around 80 percent, excluding the debt crisis stage) directed to developing countries. In terms of combined private flows, and considering that FPI in Latin America during the debt crisis saw a net outflow, these two regions averaged 76 percent of all private flows going to developing countries from 1975 through 1995. Table 5.8 describes the effect these two regions had on the changes in flows from stage to stage, and Table 5.9 indexes FDI and FPI flows to the first stage for East Asia, Latin America and all other regions.

The main features of Tables 5.6 through 5.9 can be summarized as follows:

- In the initial, pre-debt crisis stage, average FPI actually exceeded average FDI in all developing countries, $7.9 billion versus $7.0 billion.
- Most of this FPI is presumed to be in the form of commercial bank loans rather than bonds or equity.
- The proportion of all FDI to all private foreign investment has risen from stage to stage, taking into account the impact of the debt crisis.
- The proportion of FDI to all private foreign investment is generally higher in East Asia than Latin America.
- Following the debt crisis, average FDI, $41.3 billion, exceeded average FPI, $35.7 billion, for all developing countries.
- Of the stage-to-stage change in average flows of FDI, 60.1 percent went to East Asia and Latin America from stage 1 to stage 2, and 79.3 percent from stage 2 to stage 3.
- Of the stage-to-stage change in average flows of FPI, 116.3 percent of the change from stage 1 to stage 2 was explained by flows to East Asia and Latin America, and 81.3 percent from stage 2 to stage 3.
- East Asia experienced higher indexed growth rates than all developing countries in FDI and FPI across all stages.
- Latin America experienced lower indexed growth rates than all developing countries in FDI and FPI across all stages (except for the debt crisis stage).

The last two points indicate that although East Asia and Latin America combined have attracted the largest share of private foreign investment going to developing countries, the pattern of flows to each region differs. Comparing data in Tables 5.7, 5.8 and 5.9 shows that, in terms of indexed growth, both FDI and FPI in Latin America lagged behind East Asia and all developing countries in stages 2 and 3. Even so, the share of average FDI going to Latin America in stages 2 and 3 was 42.3 percent and

Table 5.8 Change in private investment in East Asia and Latin America from stage 1 to stage 2 and stage 2 to stage 3 as compared to that in all developing countries ($ billions)

East Asia and Latin America					
Stage	*Change in FDI*	*Percent of all change*	*Change in FPI*	*Percent of all change*	*Change in total*	*Percent of total change*
From 1 to 2	2,840	60.1	−6,687	83.2	−3,847	116.3
From 2 to 3	32,746	79.3	29,914	83.5	62,660	81.3

All developing countries		
Stage	*Change in FDI*	*Change in FPI*	*Change in total*
From 1 to 2	4,728	−8,035	−3,307
From 2 to 3	41,273	35,839	77,112

Source: Calculated from World Bank (1997a).

Table 5.9 Net flows of private investment to East Asia and Latin America in three stages, 1975–1995 ($ billions)

Stage	FDI	Index Stage 1 = 100	FPI	Index Stage 1 = 100	Total	FDI as percent of total
East Asia						
1: 1975–1981	1,174	100.0	843	100.0	2,017	58.2
2: 1982–1988	3,539	301.4	938	111.3	4,477	79.0
3: 1989–1995	26,592	2,264.5	13,011	1,544.3	39,603	67.1
Latin America						
1: 1975–81	4,518	100.0	5,370	100.0	9,887	45.7
2: 1982–88	4,980	110.2	−1,413	−26.3	3,567	139.6
3: 1989–95	14,672	324.8	16,429	306.0	31,101	47.2

Source: Calculated from World Bank (1997a).

35.6 percent, respectively (versus 30.1 percent and 36.5 percent for East Asia), and the share of average FPI was 46.1 percent in stage 3, versus 36.5 percent for East Asia.[40] The reasons for this difference are two-fold. First, Latin America started from a much higher base in both FDI and FPI than did East Asia; in 1975, it attracted $3.3 billion in FDI and $3.0 billion in FPI, compared to East Asia's $1.0 billion in FDI and FPI (see Appendix Table A.5.3). Second, more markets were opening up to FDI in East Asia than in Latin America, particularly from 1989 to 1995, the years in which China began to open its markets to foreign participation.[41]

Another feature distinguishing the East Asian and Latin American regions is their deeper and richer history of foreign capital inflows as compared to other regions. This being so, they offer a useful case study of how the extension of the eclectic paradigm to embrace FPI might help explain the changing composition of inbound foreign investment in the last 20 years.

If we start with the premise that the ownership variables for portfolio investors described in Table 5.2 already are present, the choice of outlet for FPI would depend on location (L) and externalization (E) variables. Several studies of FPI in East Asia and Latin America have concluded that a broad range of macroeconomic reforms and conditions (such as the realignment of exchange rate and monetary controls, reduced restrictions on capital flows and a commitment to a market economy, including privatization) have helped pull portfolio investment to those areas (Lim and Siddall 1997; Chudnosky 1997; Frischtak 1997; World Bank 1997a and 1997b) These pull factors coincide with a reconfiguration of the location variables for FPI set out in a section on the general paradigm of foreign investment (Chuhan, Claessens and Mamingi 1993; Bekaert 1995; and Fernandes-Arias and Montiel 1995). At the same time, declining interest rates in developed economies, particularly the United States, and higher expected rates of return in the developing markets of East Asia and Latin America, combined with a low correlation of returns between developed and developing markets, helped push FPI to those markets in which attractive investment opportunities were present (Harvey 1995; Calvo, Leiderman and Reinhart 1993 and 1996). These push factors are consistent with those found in the externalization variable explaining FPI.

The amount of direct and portfolio investment in East Asia and Latin America during the first stage of the past two decades, viz. 1975 to 1981, can be used as a base from which changes in the pattern of investment flows within and between regions can be assessed. From Table 5.9 it is evident that Latin America provided more opportunities for both FDI and FPI than did East Asia in that stage, which is consistent with the former's broader and deeper level of economic development, especially in Mexico, Brazil and Argentina.[42] Given this higher base, it would be likely that the relative rate of increase in FDI and FPI in East Asia would be higher than that found in Latin America even if, in absolute terms, the level of both kinds of flows is higher in Latin America.

In both regions, the increase in L specific advantages sought by foreign MNEs, coupled with the appropriate O and I specific advantages, led to increases in FDI. As might be expected, the rate of increase in FDI in East Asia has been considerably higher than in Latin America, particularly in stage 3 (1989–1995), which saw the opening up of China as a major new location for FDI.

At the same time, FPI in many East Asian economies grew rapidly in response to the combination of the increasing openness of their political regimes and their rapid industrialization. The differing pattern of FPI flows in East Asia and Latin America is also worth discussing. In stage 2, growth in FPI in East Asia, as indexed to stage 1, outpaced FPI growth in Latin America.[43] Given the Mexican debt crisis and its impact on other Latin American countries in the 1980s, it is not surprising that FPI in Latin America was negative. It is interesting to note, however, that the outflow in FPI from Latin America was not matched by a corresponding increase in FPI either in East Asia or any other region.

This phenomenon can be explained within the context of the eclectic paradigm as applied to FPI. Using the terminology of L specific variables in the section on the general paradigm of foreign investment, this crisis was sparked off by a deterioration in basic financial infrastructure, which was exacerbated by over-borrowing and foreign-exchange problems. The degree to which replacements to the "lost" investment in Latin America could be found elsewhere rested on the opportunities for such investment. However, the fact that developing countries as a whole experienced a net outflow of FPI in stage 2, and that FPI was only marginally higher than stage 1 in East Asia, points to the apparent lack of suitable locational advantages found in other developing countries and regions.[44]

The different pattern of FPI flows in East Asia and Latin America from stage 2 to stage 3 also can be described within the context of the eclectic paradigm if one first thinks about how ownership and location advantages for FPI are exercised. The modality of FPI is one of externalization – viz. using the financial markets to pursue the objectives enabled by ownership and location advantages – as opposed to internalizing them as in the case of FDI. As financial markets develop and mature in more places, outlets for potential direct and/or portfolio investment should increase, as should the volume of investible funds. One should expect, therefore, an increase in both types of investment.

How FDI and FPI change in relation to each other depends in large part on the forces of supply and demand. It can be argued that the supply of opportunities for FDI will begin to decline before similar opportunities for FPI begin to decline. Presumably, then, the volume of FPI flows should increase relative to FDI, and perhaps, at some point, surpass it. Taking into consideration that stage 1 FPI consisted mostly of bank loans rather than the "purer" bond and/or equity form of FPI, and the effect of the 1980s debt crisis, this relationship between FPI and FDI has been the case in East Asia and Latin America. In the former region, the ratio of FDI to FPI declined from roughly 4 to 1 in the 1980s to roughly 2 to 1 in the 1990s; in the latter the ratio of FDI to FPI was about 7 to 8. And in both regions the volume of FDI grew dramatically, by a factor of nearly 8 in East Asia from stage 2 to stage 3, and by a factor of around 4 in Latin America. In other words, the evidence strongly suggests that the factors favoring the externalization of the market for O specific advantages have increased faster than those favoring internalization.

While this analysis uses data prior to the Asian financial crisis of 1997, brief reference to that crisis should be made. In a nutshell, the Asian financial crisis was caused and exacerbated by financial systems that were neither as strong nor as secure as they seemed, and the over-extension of those financial systems that FPI helped to cause. In particular, unlike the Mexican debt crisis some years earlier, the Asian crisis was initiated by the calling in of a very large number of debts over a short period of time (i.e. it was a liquidity crisis). To some extent, this helps support the arguments made here about the applicability of the eclectic paradigm to portfolio investment. For what has happened in Asia, as in Latin America in the 1980s, has been a change for the worse in a key location variable which has resulted in the decision to not externalize existing ownership or other L specific advantages in the form of portfolio investment.[45]

Summary and conclusions

This chapter has sought to extend one of the mainstream themes of FDI, viz. the eclectic paradigm of international production, to embrace FPI, and in particular to examine the situations in which FPI and FDI are substitutable or complementary forms for exploiting or augmenting the ownership specific advantages of investing institutions and/or individuals. After setting out an analytical framework for discussing these issues and offering up some tentative suggestions about the real determinants of FPI, the chapter went on to illustrate how, first, in the role of foreign (and particularly United Kingdom) investment in the development of the United States economy, and second, in the recent explosive growth in FDI and the emergence of domestic capital markets in some developing countries, FDI and FPI have interacted with each other, and how such interaction may be at least partly explained by the tenets of the eclectic paradigm.

In particular, the eclectic paradigm would seem to provide a good analytical framework for explaining (a) the level and pattern of long-term FPI – and particularly that undertaken by corporations and by institutions and private investors investing in commercial institutions, and (b) the choice between FPI and FDI – and particularly where FDI is made to augment existing corporate competitive strengths, and where FPI is part and parcel of a transfer of other real resources.

In addition, this chapter has offered some casual, statistical and other evidence which suggests that inbound FPI tends to follow FDI as countries proceed along their IDPs. At some point in that path, however, the flows appear to be more complementary to each other as countries become increasingly integrated through both intra- and inter-firm transfers of global resources and capabilities across national boundaries.

The ability to test our assertions in the previous section about the patterns of FDI and FPI in the more advanced emerging economies will depend on further study and more refined methods of collecting data. In particular, detailed analysis of capital transfers, including the type of transfer and the parties involved, is needed to determine, for instance, how much a firm or sector receiving FDI flows also makes use of FPI flows. Because developing countries will continue to be a target for FDI and FPI, and as a result of the problems in East Asia during the summer of 1997, these flows will attract greater attention, which means that more and better data should become available. A more rigorous analysis of our conclusions, therefore, will be possible.

Finally a word about the policy implications of this chapter. While, in some cases, national or subnational governments, seeking foreign resources and capabilities to help them advance their economic objectives might view FPI (combined with inter-firm technology *et al.* transfers) and FDI as competitive modalities, increasingly they would be advised to take a more holistic stance towards their competitive-enhancing strategies and to arrange their domestic economic affairs so as to attract (the right kind of) both FPI and FDI. This is because, as we have shown, FPI and FDI are becoming increasingly complementary to each other, both in their determinants and in their effects. In general, recent economic events have shown that the key economic role of governments in a globalizing knowledge-based economy is first to facilitate an efficient market-based economic system, and second to ensure that the appropriate legal, institutional, and moral infrastructure is in place for this to be accomplished.

APPENDIX

Table A.5.1 All inbound foreign investment, 1980–1995 ($ billions)

Year	FDI	Portfolio	Total	Percent direct
1980	29.1	30.1	59.2	49.1
1981	45.6	39.9	85.4	53.3
1982	44.0	39.2	83.1	52.9
1983	48.9	55.7	104.6	46.8
1984	53.7	74.4	128.1	41.9
1985	51.0	153.8	204.8	24.9
1986	78.8	177.9	256.8	30.7
1987	126.9	125.4	252.3	50.3
1988	156.8	226.3	383.1	40.9
1989	193.8	356.7	550.6	35.2
1990	201.2	236.1	437.3	46.0
1991	153.8	442.2	596.0	25.8
1992	165.9	434.1	599.9	27.6
1993	210.3	727.5	937.7	22.4
1994	231.0	417.4	648.4	35.6
1995	316.4	583.7	900.2	35.2

Source: IMF, *Balance of Payments Statistical Yearbooks*, 1987–1996.

Table A.5.2 Distribution of inbound FDI and FPI between developed and developing countries, 1980–1995 ($ billions)

Year	FDI						FPI					
	Developed	Percent	Developing	Percent	Total	Percent	Developed	Percent	Developing	Percent	Total	Percent
1980	23.8	81.8	5.3	18.2	29.1	100.0	28.6	95.0	1.5	5.0	30.1	100.0
1981	29.9	65.6	15.7	34.4	45.6	100.0	37.2	93.2	2.7	6.8	39.9	100.0
1982	24.2	55.1	19.7	44.9	43.9	100.0	35.0	89.5	4.1	10.5	39.1	100.0
1983	33.3	68.1	15.6	31.9	48.9	100.0	53.1	95.3	2.6	4.7	55.7	100.0
1984	38.5	71.6	15.3	28.4	53.8	100.0	71.6	96.2	2.8	3.8	74.4	100.0
1985	38.5	75.5	12.5	24.5	51.0	100.0	149.5	97.2	4.3	2.8	153.8	100.0
1986	66.4	84.3	12.4	15.7	78.8	100.0	177.0	99.4	1.0	0.6	178.0	100.0
1987	113.2	89.2	13.7	10.8	126.9	100.0	124.9	99.6	0.5	0.4	125.4	100.0
1988	132.1	84.2	24.8	15.8	156.9	100.0	216.8	95.8	9.4	4.2	226.2	100.0
1989	166.5	85.9	27.3	14.1	193.8	100.0	349.9	98.1	6.8	1.9	356.7	100.0
1990	169.6	84.3	31.6	15.7	201.2	100.0	213.6	90.5	22.5	9.5	236.1	100.0
1991	112.9	73.4	40.9	26.6	153.8	100.0	410.9	92.9	31.3	7.1	442.2	100.0
1992	117.7	70.9	48.2	29.1	165.9	100.0	385.3	88.8	48.8	11.2	434.1	100.0
1993	136.5	64.9	73.8	35.1	210.3	100.0	613.4	84.3	114.1	15.7	727.5	100.0
1994	139.5	60.4	91.4	39.6	230.9	100.0	316.2	75.7	101.3	24.3	417.5	100.0
1995	208.9	66.0	107.5	34.0	316.4	100.0	541.5	92.8	42.2	7.2	583.7	100.0

Source: IMF, *Balance of Payments Statistical Yearbooks*, 1987–1996.

Table A.5.3 Annual flows of FPI and FDI to all developing countries, 1975–1995 ($ billions)

Year	FDI	FPI
1975	7,309.7	4,857.2
1976	3,461.0	3,979.6
1977	6,107.2	5,527.2
1978	7,015.7	5,564.7
1979	7,429.3	7,248.6
1980	5,092.3	9,216.0
1981	12,832.6	18,668.5
1982	11,335.3	5,706.7
1983	8,424.3	451.2
1984	9,129.3	(998.0)
1985	11,103.4	(1,695.4)
1986	9,464.3	(1,407.8)
1987	13,506.7	(1,388.5)
1988	19,382.4	(1,849.8)
1989	23,168.0	3,847.0
1990	24,549.0	13,285.0
1991	33,478.0	15,740.0
1992	43,644.0	30,704.0
1993	67,214.0	63,931.0
1994	83,716.0	56,548.0
1995	95,489.0	65,639.0

Source: World Bank (1997a).

Note: brackets () means negative flows.

Table A.5.4 Annual flows of FDI and FPI to East Asia and Latin America, 1975–1995 ($ billions)

Year	East Asia				Latin America			
	FDI	Percent of total	FPI	Percent of total	FDI	Percent of total	FPI	Percent of total
1975	969.1	13.3	971.0	20.0	3,274.0	44.8	3,039.0	62.6
1976	962.0	27.8	787.0	19.8	1,760.0	50.9	2,130.0	53.5
1977	983.0	16.1	762.0	13.8	3,159.0	51.7	2,872.0	52.0
1978	979.0	14.0	162.9	2.9	4,082.0	58.2	3,089.0	55.5
1979	920.0	12.4	563.6	7.8	5,205.0	70.1	4,625.0	63.8
1980	1,312.0	25.8	1,030.0	11.2	6,148.0	120.7	6,000.0	65.1
1981	2,001.0	15.6	1,620.9	8.7	7,996.0	62.3	15,833.0	84.8
1982	2,403.0	180.0	1,532.3	26.9	6,345.0	475.2	4,020.0	70.4
1983	2,820.0	33.5	1,481.8	328.4	3,614.0	42.9	(1,917.0)	NM
1984	2,837.0	31.1	1,067.3	NM	3,234.0	35.4	(2,035.0)	203.9
1985	2,949.0	26.6	373.0	NM	4,373.0	39.4	(2,079.0)	122.6
1986	3,115.0	32.9	(83.5)	5.9	3,556.0	37.6	(1,877.0)	133.3
1987	3,908.0	28.9	554.2	NM	5,788.0	42.9	(2,229.0)	160.5
1988	6,740.0	34.8	1,640.2	NM	7,949.0	41.0	(3,773.0)	204.0
1989	8,330.0	36.0	5,370.0	139.6	8,138.0	35.1	(2,296.0)	NM
1990	10,179.0	41.5	9,022.0	67.9	8,121.0	33.1	3,603.0	27.1
1991	12,706.0	38.0	7,150.0	45.4	12,504.0	37.3	8,921.0	56.7
1992	20,923.0	47.9	9,351.0	30.5	12,740.0	29.2	18,739.0	61.0
1993	38,128.0	56.7	16,692.0	26.1	14,066.0	20.9	39,779.0	62.2
1994	44,105.0	52.7	18,366.0	32.5	24,238.0	29.0	24,531.0	43.4
1995	51,776.0	54.2	25,123.0	38.3	22,897.0	24.0	21,724.0	33.1

Source: World Bank (1997a).

Note: brackets () means negative flows.

NOTES

Source: Dunning, John H. and Dilyard, John R. (1999), *Transnational Corporations*, vol. 8, no. 1, pp. 1–52.

1 The latter have been included in the IMF's *Balance of Payments Statistics Yearbook* (IMF, various years) only recently and are recorded only for the 1990s. They represent a small fraction of total portfolio capital.
2 Prior to 1980, the IMF recorded portfolio investment as the net of inbound and outbound investment, even though records of direct and portfolio investment go back to 1970. Also, data from IMF sources differ from that used by the World Bank (and used elsewhere in this paper) for two reasons. First, although economists in both institutions continually analyse the data for accuracy and make adjustments as necessary, the World Bank data goes further back in time. Second, portfolio investment includes public-sector securities and other investments, in addition to the private investments that are focused on later.
3 Inbound investment reflects all direct and portfolio investment, including government bonds and other public debt, that is going into a country and is therefore a better measure of investment flows than outbound investment, which reflects the source of investment flows. The vast majority of outbound investment comes from developed countries.
4 *Editor's note:* In balance-of-payments statistics, foreign investment consists of three components: direct portfolio and *other* investment. In this article, the authors treat portfolio and other investments together as one single entity, and call this entity "portfolio investment".
5 The World Bank, for example, distinguishes between direct and portfolio (or indirect) investment by using the 10 percent ownership rule. It is not the purpose of this chapter to debate the appropriate level of equity ownership by which a portfolio investment becomes a direct one. In any event, the vast majority – probably 80 percent–90 percent of all FDI takes place in enterprises in which the foreign investor has a majority, i.e. 51 percent or above equity shareholding.
6 As, for example, are written into many management contracts in the hotel sector, or franchising agreements in the case of franchisors in the fast food sector, e.g. McDonalds or Kentucky Fried Chicken.
7 For a distinction between created assets, e.g. capital, knowledge, technological capacity, entrepreneurship and natural assets, e.g. land and unskilled labour, see Dunning (1992).
8 Which, itself, is made up of outflows of capital to finance acquisitions and/or greenfield investment, and/or changes in intercompany capital transaction.
9 Although not all countries report such data.
10 Including loans with bonds and equity as a form of portfolio investment is done for two reasons. First, the credit circumstances of firms or the condition of domestic financial markets (especially in developing countries) may be such that loans are the only available source of long-term debt. Second, prior to 1989, data from the World Bank do not distinguish between loan and bond categories of private long-term debt on a consistent basis, categorizing it as loans only.
11 I.e. up to 49 percent or the total equity stake.
12 Both absolutely and relative to that of other portfolio investors.
13 E.g. to advance its overall profitability, long-term growth, market share, etc.
14 A point frequently make by some commentators, notably Robert Aliber (1970, 1971).
15 As these theories have evolved over the past two decades or so. On the resource-based theory see especially Penrose (1959), Barney (1991), Collis (1991), Peteraf (1993). On the evolutionary theory, see Nelson and Winter (1992), Dosi *et al.* (1988), and Cantwell (1989). On the concept of the eclectic

paradigm being an "envelope" of several economic and business context-specific theories, see Dunning (2000).

16 Strategy is a variable which need only be introduced when time and uncertainty enter into the determinants of FDI. For our own interpretation of how this variable may be incorporated into the eclectic paradigm, see Dunning (1993b), chapters 3 and 4.

17 Portfolio knowledge is that transferred on the open market or between independent buyers and sellers (i.e. inter-firm transfers), as opposed to knowledge transferred within the same firm (i.e. intra-firm transfers).

18 To the best of our knowledge, there have been no estimates made of the kind of FPI being described.

19 Which may differ between companies according to their managerial strategies, time preferences and attitude toward risk and uncertainty. In theory, however, it is possible to use financial formula, e.g. net present value or other formulae of the discounted rate of return, to collate alternative locations.

20 *Inter alia* because of its investment in firm-specific fixed assets.

21 Exceptions include some kinds of footloose manufacturing investment and some non-capital intensive service investment. Of course, as a last resort an FDI can always be sold to an indigenous firm.

22 *Inter alia* because of its investment in firm-specific fixed assets.

23 We specifically mention groups of products as very rarely does FDI internalize the market for a specific product, but rather a package of complementary intangible assets (e.g. technology, entrepreneurship, organization skills, learning experience, marketing expertise).

24 It is possible also that investment portfolios will include domestic investments as well.

25 For example, a joint Chinese/Australian venture for mineral exploitation in Australia is being financed partly by a loan from the World Bank to the Chinese partner. For other examples, see Zhan (1995).

26 As, for example, has occurred in the United Kingdom auto industry since the mid-1980s.

27 As shown, for example, in the stock prices of publicly quoted companies in the world's capital markets, GNP data and trends in foreign investment and domestic capital formation. See also Chapter 7 of this volume.

28 The investment development path suggests that as countries develop their propensity to engage in FDI, or be invested in by foreign firms, changes. At an early stage of development, countries tend to be substantial net importers of FDI; later, as the competitive advantages of their own firms increase, they also become capital exporters.

29 Here, it is worth distinguishing between two separate economies in colonial America, viz. that of the North, based on textiles, shipbuilding and the fishing industry; and that of the South, based on cotton and tobacco plantations.

30 Estimates of the relative significance of FDI vary a great deal. According to Cleona Lewis (1938), some 86 percent of United Kingdom investments in the United States in 1914 represented the purchase of United States securities and the balance was direct investments in controlled enterprises. Elsewhere (Dunning 1988) we have estimated that $1,450 million, or 21 percent, of the stock of all long-term foreign investments in the United States were FDIs. For an alternative assessment of the portfolio composition of FDI see Svedberg (1978).

31 For example, in brewing and distilleries, and in the flour milling sector.

32 For a more detailed analysis of United Kingdom investments in the United States in 1910–1914, see Corley (1994a and b).

33 For example, by harnessing new technologies and/or management

capabilities, fostering synergistic economies, planning the financial risks and reducing the time of innovatory activities, enabling economies of scale and scope to be both exploiting, strengthening global marketing networks, etc.

34 In 1976–1980, the ratio of all inbound FDI flows to gross fixed capital formation in the United States was 2.0 percent, by 1981–1985 it had risen to 2.9 percent, by 1984–1989 to 5.8 percent and by 1990–1994 to 41 percent (Dunning 1997; UNCTAD 1996).

35 Including that in United Kingdom mutual funds specializing in United States securities.

36 The reader may note a difference in the level of flows reported in this table versus that in Appendix Table A.5.1. The data shown in the tables of this section represent inbound flows to developing countries only. Appendix Table A.5.1 presents inbound flows to all countries from all countries and as such includes investments made in developed countries as well as developing countries.

37 This does not mean that net flows of public or guaranteed debt increased during this period. Rather, this category of debt fell virtually steadily from a high of $60.3 billion in 1982 to $41.4 billion in 1988. Also, some FPI was converted to FDI as part of the debt restructuring (World Bank 1997a).

38 This overall decline in private debt was not universal and was confined mostly to Latin America. Some regions, such as East Asia, actually saw an increase in the average flow of private debt from the pre-debt crisis period.

39 The World Bank divides all developing countries into six geographic regions: East Asia and the Pacific; Latin America; South Asia; Eastern Europe and Central Asia; Middle East and North Africa; and, sub-Saharan Africa. *Editor's note:* The World Bank definition of developing countries differs substantially from the definition used by UNCTAD. The most notable difference is that, in UNCTAD's categorization, Central and Eastern Europe does not belong to the developing world.

40 In stage 2, the high level of average net outflows of FPI in Latin America, $1.4 billion, was greater than all average net inflows to all other regions.

41 FDI to China increased from $3.4 billion in 1989 to $35.8 billion in 1995, growing from 41 percent to 69 percent of all FDI going to East Asia. FPI to China in 1995, on the other hand, totalled only $3.3 billion, or only 13 percent of all FPI to East Asia (World Bank 1997a).

42 East Asian flows exclude Singapore and Taiwan Province of China, both of which are excluded from the World Bank definition of developing countries.

43 Stage 2 actually saw a net outflow of FPI from Latin America, but some of this outflow was caused by the conversion of private debt to public or publicly guaranteed debt.

44 Interestingly, the 1997 financial crisis in East Asia also has its root in the financial services industry. While the effects of the crisis have been felt most profoundly in East Asia, the threat of contagion is more widespread than that found in the Mexican/Latin America debt crisis. This is partly due to a greater degree of market integration between the Asian markets and other developed and developing markets caused by the FPI in that region.

45 In the last 18 months, primarily due to actions taken by their governments, the L advantages of several Asian countries, and especially Korea, have improved considerably. As a result FDI has been stable and FPI, to some extent, has started to flow back into the region. For further details see UNCTAD (1999).

REFERENCES

Aliber, R. Z. (1970), "A theory of foreign direct investment," in C. P. Kindleberger, (ed.), *The International Corporation*, Cambridge, MA: MIT Press.

Aliber, R. Z. (1971), "The multinational enterprise in a multiple currency world," in J. H. Dunning, (ed.), *The Multinational Enterprise*, London: Allen & Unwin.

Barney, J. B. (1991), "Firm resources and sustained competitive advantage," *Journal of Management*, 17, pp. 99–120.

Beamish, P. W. (ed.) (1998) *Strategic Alliances*, Cheltenham: Edward Elgar, pp. 49–56.

Bekaert, Geert (1995), "Market integration and investment barriers in emerging equity markets," *The World Bank Economic Review*, 9, 1, pp. 75–107.

Buckley, P. J. and Casson, M. C. (1976), *The Future of the Multinational Enterprise*, London: Macmillan.

Buckley, P. J. and Casson, M. C. (1985), *The Economic Theory of the Multinational Enterprise*, London, Macmillan.

Calvo, Guillermo A., Leiderman, L. and Reinhart, C. M. (1993), "Capital inflows and the real exchange rate appreciation in Latin America: the role of external factors," *IMF Staff Papers*, 40, 1, pp. 108–51.

Calvo, Guillermo A., Leiderman, L. and Reinhart, C. M. (1996), "Inflows of capital to developing countries in the 1990s," *Journal of Economic Perspectives*, 10, 2, pp. 123–39.

Cantwell, J. (1989), *Technological innovation and multinational corporations*, Oxford: Blackwell.

Caves, R. E. (1996), *Multinational Enterprise and Economic Analysis*, Cambridge: Cambridge University Press.

Chudnovsky, D. (1997), "Beyond macro-economic stability in Latin America," in J. H. Dunning and K. A. Hamdani (eds), *The New Globalisation and Developing Countries*. Tokyo and New York: United Nations University Press.

Chuhan, Peter, Claessens, S. and Mamingi, N. (1993), "Equity and bond flows to Asia and Latin America," Working Paper 1160, Policy Research Department. Washington, D.C.: World Bank.

Collis, D. J. (1991), "A resource based analysis of global competition: the case of the bearings industry," *Strategic Management Journal*, 12, pp. 49–68.

Corley, T. A. B. (1994a), "Foreign direct investment and British economic deceleration 1870–1914," in H. Pohl (ed.), *Transatlantic Investment from the 19th Century to the Present*, Stuttgart: Franz Steiner Verlag.

Corley, T. A. B. (1994b), "Britain's overseas investments in 1914 revisited," *Business History*, 36, 1, pp. 71–87.

Dosi, G., Freeman, C., Nelson, R., Soete, L. and Silverberg, G. (eds) (1988), *Technical Change and Economic Theory*, Cambridge: Cambridge University Press.

Dunning, J. H. (1958), *American Investment in British Manufacturing Industry*, London: Goerge Allen and Unwin.

Dunning, J. H. (1977), *United Kingdom Transnational Manufacturing and Resource Based Industries and Trade Flows in Developing Countries*, Geneva: UNCTAD.

Dunning, J. H. (1988), *Explaining International Production*, London: Unwin Hyman.

Dunning, J. H. (1992), "The global economy, domestic governance, strategies and transnational corporations; interactions and policy recommendations," *Transnational Corporations* 1, 3, pp. 7–46.

Dunning, J. H. (1993a), *Multinational Enterprises and the Global Economy*, Wokingham: Addison Wesley.

Dunning, J. H. (1993b), *The Globalization of Business*, London and New York: Routledge.

Dunning, J. H. (1995), "Reappraising the eclectic paradigm in the age of alliance capitalism," *Journal of International Business Studies*, 26, 3, pp. 461–93.

Dunning, J. H. (1997), "Globalization and the new geography of foreign direct investment," *Oxford Development Studies*, 26, 1, pp. 47–69.

Dunning, J. H. (1998a), "Location and the multinational enterprise: a neglected factor?," *Journal of International Business Studies*, 29, 1, pp. 45–56.

Dunning, J. H. (2000), "The Eclectic Paradigm as an Envelope for Economic Business Theories of MNE Activity," *International Business Review* 9, pp. 163–90.

Dunning, J. H. (1999), "Globalization and the theory of MNE activity," in N. Hood and S. Young (eds), *The Globalization of Multinational Enterprise*, London: Macmillan.

Dunning, J. H. and Narula, R. (eds) (1996), *Foreign Direct Investment and Governments*, London and New York: Routledge.

Dunning, J. H. and Pearce, R. D. (1985), *The World's Largest Industrial Enterprises 1962–83*, Farnsborough: Gower.

Duysters, G. and Hagedoorn, J. H. (1995), "Strategic groups and inter-firm networks in international high-tech industries," *Journal of Management Studies*, 32, 3, pp. 359–81.

Fernandes-Arias, E. and Montiel, P. J. (1995), "The surge in capital inflows to developing countries," World Bank Policy Research Working Paper, 1473 (June).

Frischtak, C. R. L. (1997), "Latin America," in J. H. Dunning (ed.), *Governments, Globalization and International Business*, Oxford: Oxford University Press, pp. 431–54.

Hagedoorn, J. H. (1986), "Trends and patterns in strategic partnering since the early seventies," *Review of Industrial Organisation*, 11, pp. 601–16.

Harvey, Campbell R. (1995), "The risk exposure of emerging equity markets," *The World Bank Economic Review*, 9, 1, pp. 19–50.

Hennart, J. F. (1982), *A Theory of Multinational Enterprise*, Ann Arbor, MI: University of Michigan Press.

Hennart, J. F. (1986), "What is internalization?," *Weltwirtschaftliches Archiv*, 122, pp. 791–804.

International Monetary Fund (IMF) (various years), *Balance of Payments Statistics Yearbook*, Washington, D.C.: IMF.

Lewis, C. (1938), *America's Stake in International Investment*, Washington, D.C.: Brookings Institution.

Lim, Linda Y. C. and Siddall, N. S. (1997), "Investment dynamism in Asian developing countries," in J. H. Dunning and K. A. Hamdani (eds), *The New Globalisation and Developing Countries*, Tokyo and New York: United Nations University Press, pp. 79–124.

Markowitz, Harry M. (1959), *Portfolio Selection: Efficient Diversification of Investments*, New Haven: Yale University Press.

Nelson, R. and Winter, S. (1992), *An Evolutionary Theory of Economic Change*. Cambridge, MA.: Harvard University Press.

Paish, G. (1911), "Great Britain's capital investments in individual colonial and foreign countries," *Journal of the Royal Statistical Society*, 74, pt 2, pp. 167–211.

Penrose, E. T. (1959), *The Theory of the Growth of the Firm*, Oxford: Basil Blackwell.

Peteraf, M. (1993), "The cornerstones of competitive advantage: A resource based view," *Strategic Management Journal*, 14, pp. 179–91.

Rugman, A. M. (1980), "Internalization as a general theory of foreign direct investment, a reappraisal of the literature," *Weltwirtschaftliches Archiv*, 116, 2, pp. 365–79.

Rugman, A. M. (1986), "European multinationals: an international comparison of size and performance," in K. Macharzina and W. H. Staehle (eds), *European Approaches to International Management*, Berlin and New York: Walter de Gruyter.

Sagari, S. (1989), "U.S. direct investment in the banking sector abroad." Washington, D.C.: World Bank, mimeo.

Shaver, J. M. (1995), "Do foreign-owned and U.S.-owned establishments exhibit the same location pattern in United States manufacturing industries?," *Journal of International Business Studies*, 29 (3), pp. 469–92.

Svedberg, P. (1978), "The portfolio direct composition of private foreign investment in 1914 revisited," *Economic Journal*, 88, pp. 763–77.

Ulgado, F. (1996), "Location characteristics of manufacturing investments in the United States: a comparison of American and foreign based firms," *Management International Review*, 36, 1, pp. 7–26.

UNCTAD (1996), *World Investment Report 1996: Investment, Trade and International Policy Arrangements*. New York and Geneva.

UNCTAD (1997), *World Investment Report 1997: Transnational Corporations, Market Structure and Competition Policy*. New York and Geneva.

UNCTAD (1999), *World Investment Report 1999: Foreign Direct Investment and the Challenge of Development*. New York and Geneva.

United States Department of Commerce (various years), *Survey of Current Business*, Washington, D.C.: Department of Commerce.

Wilkins, M. (1989), *The History of Foreign Investment in the United States to 1914*, Cambridge, MA: Harvard University Press.

World Bank (1996), *World Debt Tables, Volumes I and II*, Washington, D.C.: The World Bank.

World Bank (1997a), *Global Development Finance, Volumes I and II*, Washington, D.C.: The World Bank.

World Bank (1997b), "Financial flows and the developing countries," quarterly reports, mimeo.

Wright, G. (1990), "The origins of American industrial success, 1879–1940," *American Economic Review*, 80, pp. 651–68.

Zhan, J. X. (1995). "Transnationalization and outward investment: the case of Chinese firms," *Transnational Corporations*, 4, 3, pp. 67–100.

Part III

Regions and globalization

6 Regions, globalization and the knowledge economy

The issues stated

Introduction

The purpose of this chapter is to offer an analytical framework for evaluating the implications of recent economic events on the spatial distribution of economic activities; and of the role played by multinational enterprises (MNEs)[1] and cross-border inter-firm coalitions[2] of firms on the international and intra-national division of labor. In particular, we shall be concerned with the parallel, yet apparently antithetical, forces towards the geographical dispersion of asset augmenting and asset exploiting activities,[3] and the concentration of such activities in limited spatial areas; or what Ann Markusen (1996) has referred to as the paradox of "sticky places within slippery space."

The theme of this chapter is of increasing interest to businesses practitioners and to policy makers alike; and to the academic community. To business practitioners, research is revealing that, as the core competencies of firms become more knowledge-intensive, yet more mobile across space, so the choice of location in the production, organization and use of those assets is becoming a more critical competitive advantage.[4] To the national or regional policy makers, the challenge is to offer, both to indigenous and foreign-owned firms, the spatially anchored resources and capabilities within their jurisdiction, which are perceived by these firms to be at least as attractive complements to their own ownership specific advantages as those offered by other countries or regions. To the academic scholar, locationally related studies are at the cutting edge of interdisciplinary research, and of the intersection of research being undertaken by trade, FDI and evolutionary economists, by economic geographers, by industrial sociologists and by business strategists.

The chapter proceeds in the following way. First, it identifies and describes the main features of four of the critical events of the past two decades which have affected the global locational options available to firms, and their choice between these options. Second, it examines and explains the trend towards the closer and deeper economic interdependence between, and among, countries, which is the critical characteristic of both (macro-)regionalization[5] and globalization. The third section looks more closely at the nature of clustering and agglomeration of related value-added activities; and whether it is possible to offer a paradigm of why particular kinds of asset augmenting and asset exploiting foreign direct investment (FDI) are attracted to certain countries and micro-regions. Fourth, the chapter examines the ways in which the growth of MNE related activity has affected, and is affecting, both the international and intra-national location of production; and of our thinking about its determinants and effects. Fifth, we shall analyze some of the consequences of our findings and our theorizing both for national and regional policy makers, and for business practitioners. Finally, a concluding section will discuss some of their implications for scholarly research – and particularly that which draws together the different approaches to the issues under discussion.

The changing world economic scenario: the mid-1970s to the late 1990s

In this section, we identify four main events of the last two decades which we believe have had a profound impact on both the nature and composition of global economic activity, on its ownership and location, and on its organizational modes. These are:

1   The increasing importance of all forms of intellectual capital in both the asset creating and asset exploiting activities of firms.
2   The growth of co-operative ventures and alliances between, and within, the main wealth creating institutions.
3   The liberalization of both internal and cross-border markets.
4   The emergence of several new major economic players in the world economy.

We shall deal with each of these in turn.

The knowledge economy

Over the last three centuries, the main source of wealth[6] in market economies has switched from natural assets (notably land and relatively unskilled labor),[7] through tangible created assets (notably buildings, machinery and equipment and finance), to intangible created assets (notably knowledge and information of all kinds) which may be embodied in human beings, in organizations or in physical assets. It has, for example, been estimated that, whereas in the 1950s, 80 percent of the value added in US manufacturing industry represented primary or processed foodstuffs, materials or mineral products, and 20 percent knowledge, by 1995, these proportions had changed to 30 percent and

70 percent respectively (Stewart 1997). No less significant, the book value of the tangible assets of corporations is becoming a decreasing component of their market value. One estimate (Handy 1990) put this at between 25 percent and 33 percent in the mid-1980s, while Leif Edvinson (1997) has more recently calculated that, for most organizations, the ratio of their intellectual capital[8] to that of their physical and financial capital is between 5 to 1 and 16 to 1.

Between 1975 and 1995, expenditure on all kinds of research and development in the OECD economies rose three times the rate of output in manufacturing industry (OECD 1997). Over the same period, while the number of patents registered in the US increased from 76,800 to 113,600, i.e. by 48 percent, those in the more knowledge-intensive sectors,[9] rose from 16,827 to 47,533, i.e. by 182 percent (US Patent and Trademark Office 1997). The proportion of the age group 15–24 engaged in higher education increased from 35 percent in 1980 to 56 percent in 1993 (World Bank 1997). Finally, capital spending on information technology, which, in 1965, was only one-third of that on production technology, now exceeds it. Throughout economic activity, created intangible assets are replacing natural or created tangible assets as the main source of wealth augmentation in industrial societies. *Inter-alia*, this is demonstrated by the rising contribution of services, relative to goods, in the gross national output (GNP) of most countries.[10]

These data all tell a consistent story, viz. the trend towards the cross-border augmentation of assets by cross-border FDI and strategic alliances as an important instrument for increasing economic wellbeing. They also suggest that, in evaluating the economic prosperity of societies, scholars need to give more attention to the dynamics of asset seeking FDI. Most theories of the firm, of industrial organization and of location are still caught in a static web; and are mainly interested in how existing assets may be deployed – and located – in the most efficient way. The advent of the knowledge-based economy demands that scholars should give at least as much attention to a scenario in which assets, far from being largely fixed and immobile as in bygone days, are now eminently increasable and mobile. This may require a fundamental re-think of the relevance of the leading paradigms and theories of the 1970s and early 1980s in explaining the contemporary spatial distribution of economic activity.

Intellectual capital is different from other forms of capital in its deployment in another way. While, to be effective, one piece of land, or a particular machine, or even "x" dollars of financial assets, is (or are) largely independent of another piece of land, machine or "x" dollars of financial assets, this is not the case with a unit of knowledge and other forms of intellectual capital. Not only is knowledge a heterogeneous commodity and can be put to multiple uses; often, one kind of knowledge needs to be combined with several other kinds to produce a particular good or service. With the development of two of the key "engines" of the knowledge economy, viz. the microchip and the computer, the distinction between "high" and "low" technology industries, as proxied by the final output they produce, is becoming less and less meaningful. In their use of knowledge, parts of the textile, food processing, retail construction and health care industries are just as technologically advanced as the elec-tronics, pharma-ceutical, financial services and management consultancy sectors.

The intellectual capital needed both to augment and to exploit assets is then complex; and it is rarely the property of only one firm. For a firm to increase or deploy its own knowledge effectively, it may have to comple-ment this knowledge with that of other firms; and more often than not, by way of some kind of collaborative agreement.[11]

There are, of course, several reasons for the growth of inter-firm collab-oration which will be further discussed in the next section. Here we would offer just three observations about the nature of contemporary knowl-edge. First, it can be highly expensive; the cost of the next generation of micro-chips or a new generic drug frequently runs into billions of dollars. Second, the outcome of much investment in augmenting knowledge, e.g. by research and development (R&D), is highly uncertain. Third, many kinds of knowledge (and particularly those which can be imitated) obso-lesce quite speedily. Together, with its increasing complexity, these fea-tures of intellectual capital – coupled with its competitive protecting or enhancing imperatives – have very considerable implications for both the location and the organization of firms; and, indeed, for the character and composition of micro-regions.

Alliance capitalism

One of the particularly interesting features of the leading market economies of recent years has been the extent to which the hierarchical form of governance of both private and public organizations has been complemented with, and in some cases replaced by, a variety of inter-organizational co-operative agreements. This has caused scholars to suggest that the present stage of capitalism may best be described as alliance capitalism.[12] These alliances may, and do, take a variety of forms, and involve a large number of institutional entities. They may be between the different stakeholders of the firm and/or between the various opera-tional or functional units, making up a firm's value chain (viz. *intra*-firm alliances). They may be between one firm and another – for example, between a firm and its competitors, suppliers or customers (viz. *inter*-firm alliances).[13] They may be between a private firm and a public institution; between public institutions, notably between regional and national gov-ernments. They may also be between various interest groups, e.g. con-sumers, environmentalists and labor unions and so on.

Inter-corporate alliances may be formed to promote asset augmenting or asset exploiting activities. In the former case, partners are normally sought to access synergistic or complementary knowledge-intensive assets, learning and organizational capabilities, and markets. Technology advancing alliances may also be concluded to share the cost of R&D and to speed up the innovatory process. In the latter case, alliances are usually formed to increase the efficiency of existing asset deployment, by, for example, facilitating economies of scope and scale, and by making better use of existing managerial and marketing capabilities. In such cases, firms may engage in coalitions to protect or strengthen their competitive positions versus other firms; while, unless precluded from doing so by anti-trust legislation, one firm may acquire another to increase its market power and gain additional economic rents.

The growth of knowledge capitalism has led to an explosion of inter-firm alliances. Data on mergers and acquisitions (M&As) and collaborative non-equity coalitions suggest that, whether by FDI or by cross-border licensing, franchising *et al.* agreements, alliances have been most pronounced, and increased the most, in knowledge-intensive sectors (UNCTAD 2000); and have been predominantly concluded between MNEs and other corporations in advanced industrial countries.[14]

Liberalization of markets

Perhaps the most dramatic and most transparent economic event of the last two decades has been the growing liberalization of both national and international markets. Though most vividly demonstrated by the removal of the Berlin Wall in 1989, and the opening up of the People's Republic of China to inbound FDI, the reconfiguration of national economic policies of most Latin American countries, India and some African economies, and the move towards closer macro-regional integration in various parts of the world, have all contributed to the renewed vitality of the market system as the main instrument for the harnessing and deployment of scarce resources and capabilities throughout the world.

Since the early 1980s, artificial barriers to trade have tumbled – particularly at the macro-regional level. At the same time, both transport and communication costs have dramatically fallen,[15] as have the intra-firm costs of doing business within and across national boundaries. As a result, the share of trade and FDI, as a proportion of the GNP of the great majority of countries, has sharply risen.[16]

Several other indices of the growing openness of countries to the rest of the world point to the same conclusion. Most dramatic of these has been the spectacular expansion of cross-border financial flows, and of the extent and depth of international financial integration. For example, foreign portfolio investment flows rose from $56.2 billion in 1984 to $412.5 billion in 1995 (IMF vd), while the increase in international bank loans have consistently outpaced that of both world exports and FDI for most of the 30 years prior to 1994 (Perraton *et al.* 1994). Relatedly, the average daily trade in the foreign exchange market rose from $15 billion in 1973 to $880 billion in 1992 and $1300 billion in 1995, while cross-border sales and purchases of financial assets rose from less than 10 percent of GDP in 1980 in the US, Germany and Japan to 135 percent, 170 percent and 85 percent respectively in 1993 (Kozul Wright 1997).

Even more impressive is the recent increase in the use of cross-border communications media. In 1990, the minutes per capita spent on international telephone calls for all countries in the world was 6.3; by 1998 it was 15.3. In 1990, there were 2.6 million Internet users and 11 million mobile cellular subscribers: by 1999 the corresponding figures were 257 million and 472 million (International Telecommunications Union 2000).

Finally, we might mention the great increase in cross-border people traffic over the last two decades. Though part of this, e.g. the trebling of tourist expenditure, and the quadrupling of the number of passengers on international airlines[17] cannot be put solely at the door of the liberalization or deregulation of markets, these and other people movements (e.g. migration, employment of foreigners, cross-border travel to work, etc.) have most certainly been aided, directly or indirectly, by the reduction in obstacles to the movement of goods, assets, services and people.

Emerging markets

The last and most gradual – but by no means the least important – event (or trend is, perhaps, the better word) is the take-off of several developing economies as major players on the world economic scene. Most of these are in Asia and Latin America; and most are commonly referred to as "newly industrializing" economies. Three, e.g. Hong Kong, Singapore and South Korea, were among the wealthiest 30 countries in the world in 1997 (World Bank 1998).

The clearest expression of the significance of the emerging economies, both as locations of production and as markets is their share of the world's GNP. In 1980, Latin American, South East and East Asian developing countries accounted for 24.1 percent of the world's GNP; the corresponding figure for 1995 was 26.8 percent (World Bank vd). Comparable figures for the share of world exports were 18.4 percent and 28.9 percent; for the share of the world's inward foreign direct investment *stock*, 16.7 percent and 23.5 percent (UNCTAD 1998); for the share of the world's inward foreign portfolio investment flows, 1.7 percent and 12.6 percent (IMF vd)[18]; for the share of commercial energy use, 19.2 percent and 29.7 percent; for the share of the world's patents registered in the US, 0.4 percent and 3.5 percent (US Patent and Trademark Office 1999); and for the share of the world's telephone lines, 17.8 percent and 43.8 percent (UN vd).

Coupled with the economic events earlier described – all of which are intensifying the competitive pressures between corporations, and are leading to a reconfiguration of their product and innovation strategies – the emergence of new economies is helping to fashion a new North–South and South–South division of labor. Although, as they move along their investment development paths (Narula 1995; Dunning and Narula 1996), the economic structure of industrializing countries tends to move closer to that of their more advanced industrialized counterparts. The more knowledge-intensive asset augmenting activities tend to still remain very heavily concentrated in the latter countries;[19] and, indeed, in micro-regions within these countries.[20] We shall take up this point in "Localization, clusters and the concept of 'sticky' places," below.

Globalization: extending and deepening the economic interdependence between nations

What then is the impact of the events described on the location of economic activity? Location theory has long since asserted that a profit maximizing firm will site its value-added activities where it perceives this particular goal is best advanced.[21] Such profits represent the differences between revenue (a demand related variable) and costs (a supply related variable), plus taxes and duties, less allowances and subsidies. Costs are of four main kinds, viz. design and development, production, transportation and transaction. Taxes, duties, allowances and subsidiaries may be direct or indirect, general or specific. In imperfect – and particularly oligopolistic – markets, firms will also take account of the locational strategies of their competitors.

Each of these broad locational determinants, are to some extent product, activity and country (or region) specific. Besides the availability and costs of factor and intermediate inputs, the main supply related variables influencing whether a firm concentrates or disperses its asset augmenting or asset exploiting activities over space are, on the one hand, the extent to which such activities can benefit from scale economies, and, on the other, the spatially related transaction costs involved. As George Stigler (1951) pointed out many years ago – as did Adam Smith before him – division of labor, i.e. the specialization of economic activity, is limited by the size and geography of the market. Today, we might add to this variable the *character* of the market (and in particular the extent to which it is customized), and the transaction costs of exchanging goods and services between different political and cultural regimes.

We make these fairly obvious introductory points, as it is worth emphasizing, that the extent, form and pace of globalization is not uniformly spread across the planet, nor across different value-added activities. Some goods and services, for example, are non-tradable, i.e. they are immobile across space. Some are produced in their entirety in only one or a few countries, and are exported across the globe. Some are replicated in their entirety in several countries, but only sold in their country of production. Some parts of the global activities of firms (e.g. research and development) tend to be concentrated in a few countries and regions, while others are spread more widely.

What then is economic globalization? We will not dwell on this well-researched topic, save to give (what we believe to be) an excellent interpretation by a political scientist – Anthony McGrew (1992).

> Globalization refers to the multiplicity of linkages and interconnections between the states and societies which make up the present world system. It describes the process by which events, decisions, and activities in one part of the world come to have significant consequences for individuals and communities in quite distant parts of the globe. Globalization has two distinct phenomena: scope (or stretching) and intensity (or deepening). On the one hand, it defines a set of processes which embrace most of the globe or which operate worldwide: the concept therefore has a spatial connotation. On the other hand it also implies an intensification on the levels of interaction, interconnectedness or interdependence between the states and societies which constitute the world community. Accordingly, alongside the stretching goes a deepening of global processes.
>
> (Anthony McGrew 1992, p. 23)

In short, globalization is a process leading to the structural transformation of firms and nations. It represents a discontinuity in the process of internationalization in the sense that it creates new and deeper cross-border relationships and dependencies. Sometimes, the transformation takes place at a regional level: much of the integrated production networks of MNEs is so focused. Sometimes, it occurs at a global level. For example, the advent of electronic commerce is dramatically truncating distance in financial and foreign exchange markets (Stopford and Strange 1991). One scholar has gone as far as to aver that the emergence of the Internet and global financial integration is heralding "the end of geography" (O'Brien (1992)). Sometimes, however, globalization, while facilitating the cross-border movement of intermediate products, notably technology, is also leading to the widespread replication of end products.

We have already identified some of the forces "pushing" or "pulling" in the direction of regionalization and globalization. We now set out a few additional facts, particularly as they relate to the growth of MNE related activity

1   Over the last decades the growth of world trade has consistently outpaced that of world output – usually by a ratio of 2 to 1; while in 1998 the sales of the foreign affiliates of MNEs exceeded that of world trade by 74 percent (UNCTAD 1999).

2   The majority of the global sales of MNEs are in knowledge or information sectors, or in sectors supportive of these activities.

3   Between one-third of cross-border trade in non-agricultural goods and

services, and between one-half and three-fifths of all capital and technology flows is now internalized within MNEs.

4   There have been two important trends in MNE related activity (FDI and alliance formation) over the past two decades. The first is the spectacular growth of asset seeking mergers and acquisitions (M&As) and strategic alliances within the triad countries, or within regions of the US, Japan and Western Europe.[22] The second has been the no less dramatic growth of asset exploiting FDI in some emerging markets, notably China,[23] an increasing part of which has been supplied from other Asian developing countries.[24]

5   A rising proportion of FDI in both developed and developing countries is in services – particularly information intensive services.[25]

6   An increasing proportion of the total R&D expenditures is accounted for by their foreign subsidiaries.[26] Moreover, it is growing faster than that of other forms of MNE related production,[27] and also than that of the indigenous firms of the countries in which MNE subsidiaries are located.[28] Furthermore, an increasing proportion of the foreign R&D activities of MNEs is directed to augmenting their home based intellectual capital – often by tapping into foreign R&D facilities – rather than to more effectively deploying their existing R&D capabilities (Kuemmerle 1999).

Localization, clusters and the concept of "sticky" places

We have already suggested that globalization does not necessarily mean that all wealth creating activities are dispersed uniformly throughout the world. Far from it. If, indeed, the specialization of economic activity is limited by the size of the market, then it would be proper to hypothesize that globalization will be accompanied by more, rather than less, specialization; and hence, by implication, will lead to further spatial concentration of such activity. Much, of course, will depend on how the production, transportation and transaction costs imposed by artificial barriers to trade, vary with size of output produced. The "where" of concentration will depend on the national and micro-regional specific characteristics influencing such costs, and also on the spatial proximity of related activities (clusters), which generate both static and dynamic external economies.

In examining the proposition that some types of wealth creating activities are becoming more concentrated in sub-national clusters, it may be useful to distinguish between traditional and contemporary trade and location models. Traditional, i.e. Heckscher-Ohlin, type trade models were primarily designed to explain the optimum (i.e. the most efficient) patterns of trade between countries, based on the distribution of immobile factor endowments. Location theories were similarly concerned with the optimum siting of asset exploiting activities, i.e. those designed to maximize the static efficiency of the investing firms; but, unlike trade theories, they explicitly acknowledged the role of the transaction costs (and benefits) of spatially proximate activities.[29]

Contemporary trade and location theories are more contextual than their predecessors.[30] While those just described are still a robust explanation of some kinds of cross-border division of labor – particularly of natural resource intensive activities between developed and developing countries – they are less comfortable in explaining the distribution of knowledge-intensive activities, and particularly those between and within advanced countries and under the governance of MNEs. Such activities are not only likely to incur substantial overhead costs, and thus need non-decreasing returns to scale and the necessary volume to cover these; but, as already indicated, they frequently involve multiple and interrelated technological inputs.[31] To minimize distance related transaction costs, and to maximize the benefits of dynamic learning economies, it frequently pays firms to concentrate their activities within a limited spatial area. Hence, the concept of the learning region (Florida 1995); and with it, the significance of dynamic agglomerative economies as a locational pull to firms – and particularly those seeking to augment their resources and capabilities.

Globalization may then lead to a dispersion of knowledge-intensive production between and within countries; and to a convergence in cross-border economic structures. It may equally lead to a concentration of such production in particular countries, and in micro-regions within those countries, in which case economic structures of the countries and micro-regions will tend to diverge from, than converge with, each other.

In fact, both trends are discernible, but it is the contention of this chapter that: (i) the greater the degree of knowledge intensity of a particular activity; (ii) the easier it is for labor to migrate across regions or countries; (iii) the lower the distance related costs; and (iv) the more firms engage in FDI and alliance related activities to augment, rather than exploit, their existing assets; then, the more likely is it that national and micro-regional economies will develop specialized centers of excellence.[32] At the same time, it is quite evident that the main competitors to some micro-regions in attracting and retaining mobile investment are not other micro-regions in the same country, but micro-regions in other countries.[33]

This observation is consistent with the growing sophistication of both intra-industry trade and intra-industry FDI between countries and/or micro-regions. Such sophistication is not confined to the types of products produced. Rather, it extends to the innovatory milieu of the competing locations, and, in particular to the opportunities of firms within that milieu, to tap into and learn from the resources, capabilities and entrepreneurship of each other, i.e. augment their core competencies.[34]

These opportunities, and the benefits of spatial clustering, clearly vary between industries and firms; and they may be exploited through a variety of organizational routes – e.g. arm's length markets, non-equity alliances and FDI. Which modality is chosen will depend on the extent and character of the relevant *dynamic* spatially specific transaction costs, e.g. those associated with innovatory activities. In general, one might predict that: (i) the less complex and/or independent the knowledge required for the production of a particular good or service; (ii) the more codifiable (i.e. less tacit) or idiosyncratic that knowledge is; (iii) the less the information symmetry there is between the related firms; (iv) the fewer the chances there are for opportunistic behavior; (v) the less uncertain the outcome of any relationship is; and (vi) the more widely located the customers are, then the lower the spatial transaction costs, and the less the economies of agglomeration are likely to be.[35]

Clustering is, therefore, likely to be strongly activity specific; and to be most marked where the critical decision takers in firms need to be in close physical proximity to exchange, or share, tacit knowledge. The City of London is a classic example of an agglomeration of interdependent firms each producing part of a final product.[36] Globalization and technological change have combined to strengthen such clustering, and also to upgrade the knowledge intensity of the constituent firms. At the same time, the increasing mobility of firm specific assets and the growing complementarity between different kinds of technology has fostered more diversity of economic activity, often with beneficial consequences for innovatory output (Feldman and Audretsch 1999).

So far, we have tended to concentrate on supply-related reasons why firms cluster. We have argued that while the original Marshallian reasons for clustering[37] still hold good, those to do with a variety of "soft" locational factors and access to knowledge and learning capabilities have become more important[38] (Florida 1995; Giersch 1996). At the same time, clusters may be fashioned by the needs of consumers, and some of these also possess all, or at least, most, of the characteristics so far identified. Such clusters are particularly noticeable in the consumer services sectors; they tend to be city oriented and include airline offices, car rental agencies, film distributors, medical services and fast food chains.

The role of MNEs in affecting the location of economic activity

So far in our analysis, we have not considered the unique role of MNEs in affecting the location of economic activity. To this we now turn. What is distinctive about this particular organizational form? As defined earlier, a MNE is an institution which owns or controls value activities in at least two countries. Many of the larger MNEs own or control value-added activities in a large number of countries; and do so via both FDI and cross-border alliances. To what extent is the locational pattern of such activities different than it would be than if each of them had been separately and independently owned? Does the common ownership of production in two or more countries affect our theorizing about the geography of asset augmenting or asset exploiting investment, and its tendency to be concentrated or dispersed?

The multi-domestic MNE

To answer this question, let us consider two types of governance structures of MNEs.[39] The first is the *multi-domestic* or "stand-alone" structure, which most MNEs, outside the natural resource based sectors, adopted until the 1960s. The main feature of the multi-domestic MNE is that it treats its foreign subsidiaries as autonomous wealth creating units. Each subsidiary tends to replicate – albeit often on a truncated scale – the asset exploiting activities of its mother company; and to supply its products to local and/or closely adjacent markets. Though the parent organization may export intangible assets (e.g. technology, managerial and marketing expertise) and other intermediate products (e.g. materials, components and parts) to its affiliates, for the most part, there is likely to be little trade in finished products between the parent company and its affiliates, or among its affiliates. In short, the multi-domestic MNE engages in little integrated production and little cross-border product or process specialization.

Frequently, in the past, the multi-domestic or "stand-alone" MNE has been prompted to engage in FDI to overcome tariff barriers and other restrictions to trade, or to be near to critical supply facilities and/or to the special needs of foreign consumers. *De facto*, this kind of defensive market seeking FDI often replaces trade, and does little to promote a more efficient regional or global division of labor. However, there are also some kinds of *aggressive* market seeking MNE activity which, while not replacing trade, do little to promote it. Examples include FDIs in some service sectors, e.g. in fast food chains, building and construction, railroads, public utilities, and the regional offices of MNEs.

Yet, though globally dispersed, multi-domestic MNEs may still favor particular locations *within* a country. Moreover, these are not always the same as those chosen by domestic firms. Several studies on the intra-national distribution of inbound from 1958 onwards[40] investment have shown that foreign affiliates of MNEs tend to be located in or near large conurbations, and/or be adjacent to leading ports. They also tend to favor subnational clusters of related activities, and to be more sensitive to the regional policies of governments[41] (Yannopoulos and Dunning 1976).

One other frequently voiced need of first-time foreign investors is to reduce the costs of producing in an unfamiliar environment as much as possible. Several country based studies[42] have shown that in various countries, either the presence of indigenous firms has attracted FDI into the same micro-region, or the establishment and growth of one investor has had a positive signaling affect on other foreign investors (Liu 1997).[43] On the other hand, there is also some evidence that foreign owned firms prefer to establish *de novo* clusters of related activities. Examples include the surge of biotechnology investments in California in the 1980s, and major new investments by the Japanese auto companies – Nissan in North East England, Toyota in Derby – in the 1990s (UNCTAD 1995).

The globally (or regionally) integrated MNE

The main feature of this kind of MNE is that it adopts a systemic and holistic approach towards its global operations, and treats its foreign affiliates as part of a network of interrelated activities, designed to promote the interest of the MNE *in toto*. Where possible, the integrated MNE will take full advantage of the geographical distribution of natural and created assets, of spatially related agglomerative economies, and of liberalized markets. This means it is likely to engage in more rationalized and efficiency seeking FDI than is its multi-domestic counterpart, and to source its inputs and augment its resources and capabilities from across the globe. It is also likely to engage in a good deal of intermediate and final product trade between its parent company and its affiliates, and among its affiliates – especially within regionally integrated areas. The activities of the globally integrated MNE are then likely to promote both trade and FDI.

The globally integrated MNE is very much a creature of the late twentieth century; and each of the events described in "The changing world economic scenario," above have helped foster such integration. Broadly speaking, the integrated MNE promotes three kinds of cross-border specialization. The first is *horizontal* specialization in which each of the products supplied by the same firm are produced in different regions or countries. The primary rationale of this specialization is to take advantage of the economies of scale and differentiated consumer needs; although where the products require a different mix of natural resources and capabilities, it may be of the H-O type. The second is *vertical* specialization where different stages of the value-added chain of a particular product are undertaken in different locations. The main object of this type of specialization – which predominantly (though not exclusively) occurs between developed and developing countries – is to take advantage of differences in factor costs and consumer tastes, although the opportunity to gain scale economies may also be relevant.

The third kind of specialization – asset augmenting specialization – is an amalgam of the first two; but it is different in that it is designed less to advance the static efficiency of the MNE, and more to enhance its future wealth creating capabilities in a cost learning effective way. The geography of this kind of labor is mainly confined to the advanced industrial countries, and geared to either promoting the efficiency of the MNEs global R&D capabilities,[44] or gaining access to foreign created assets which will best protect or enhance its competitive advantages.[45] It is this kind of specialization which is being increasingly fashioned by the imperatives of the knowledge-based global economy; and by the need of firms located in one country to complement their core competencies with those of firms located in another country.[46]

To what extent is the globally integrated MNE likely to prefer to locate the three kinds of cross-border specialization in particular micro-regions of host countries? The evidence is mixed. The primary issue with respect to horizontal and vertical FDI is the extent to which "static" spatial transaction costs favor its proximity to a cluster of related firms, so it can exploit the benefits of "untraded interdependencies" (Storper 1995). However, over time, most of these clusters have evolved their own nexus of innovating and learning capabilities; in other words, they also generate dynamic externalities to the participating firms.

Examples of both horizontal and vertical clusters abound.[47] The former include the watch industry of Geneva, the cork industry of Northern Portugal, the woolen textile industry of Prato and Biellia in Northern Italy, the film industry of Hollywood, the diamond industry of Amsterdam, the tomato canning industry of Campania, Southern Italy, the cutlery industry of Solignen, and the financial services industry of the City of London and Wall Street (New York). Examples of vertical clusters include the large number of export zones set up in developing countries – especially in Asia – to house relatively labor intensive stages of the value chain by MNEs, in such manufacturing sectors as textiles, leather goods and consumer electronics, and, more recently, in services such as insurance, shipping, shared support centers and computer software.[48] In more advanced countries, the Boeing agglomeration of related firms in the Seattle region and the Toyota complex of firms in the Tokyo region are examples of vertically integrated clusters, in which a flagship firm producing an end product, which comprises a large number of components and parts, is surrounded by a satellite of its suppliers.

It is our contention that the dynamic externalities associated with these horizontal and vertical clusters are becoming more important as intellectual capital becomes more sophisticated, idiosyncratic, tacit, complex and context dependent. Furthermore, as the main repositories of such knowledge, and certainly the principal organizing unit for accessing and leveraging geographically dispersed units (Doz, Asakawa, Santos and Williamson 1997), MNEs are not only drawn to regional clusters, but, by their presence and impact, to influence their character and growth.[49] Historical examples include the chemical and cotton thread industries of New Jersey (Wallace 1998) and the office machinery industry of mid-Scotland (Dunning 1958, 1998). More recent cases include clusters of the Japanese consumer electronics affiliates in South Wales (Strange 1993), and a bevy of MNEs in the Bangalore software sector (Balasbramanyam and Balasbramanyam 2000).[50]

It is, however, the third type of industrial specialization and clustering which is increasingly engaging the attention of scholars; and it is one, too, in which both national and micro-regional authorities are watching carefully. The spectacular development of business, industrial and science parks, and specialized service sectors, are all testimony to the belief that the asset augmenting activities of firms benefit from being part of a knowledge creating milieu – in which private firms, universities, technical colleges, and government research institutions are all involved. Many of these clusters were initially initiated by micro-regional authorities to help upgrade the resources and capabilities under the jurisdiction; and, sometimes, they were targeted specifically at mobile investors.[51] For the most part, such clusters tend to be concentrated in the triad regions or nations; and as intellectual capital becomes more geographically diffused and cross-border innovatory competition becomes more intense, firms from one part of the triad are finding it increasingly desirable to establish an R&D presence, and/or conclude technology enhancing alliances with firms, in another part.[52]

But more than this; as firms increasingly scan the globe for knowledge capital, they are engaging in FDI specifically to tap into, and harness, country and firm-specific resources, capabilities and learning experiences.[53] Such assets may be synergistic with their core assets, or complementary to them. They can be harnessed by the acquisition of, or merger with, foreign firms and/or by the conclusion of non-equity coalitions with them. MNEs may also use their foreign affiliates or partners as vehicles for seeking out and monitoring new knowledge and learning experiences; and as a means of tapping into national innovatory or investment systems more conducive to their dynamic competitive advantages (Doremus, Keller, Pauly and Reich 1998). In such cases, a presence in the innovating heartland of the sectors will help lower the transaction costs involved in such a task. Thus, firms are likely to be attracted to pockets of intellectual capital in a foreign economy, and in so far as they are allowed to do so, to participate in joint research and development and collective learning experiences (Florida 1995).

There is some casual evidence that the R&D activities of firms tend to be more spatially concentrated in a country, than do other activities;[54] and are more likely to be drawn to centers of academic excellence and to industrial and science parks. There is also some suggestion that the major metropolitan areas and their surrounding hinterlands are becoming the loci of agglomerative knowledge enhancing activities. Indeed, according to Allen Scott (1998), as sources of new employment, they are not only growing faster than the national average,[55] but are becoming the leading regional motors of technological change.

In summary, then, the changing geography of MNE related activity is a microcosm of that of the world economy. On the one hand, MNEs are conducting a rising proportion of their value-added activities outside their home countries;[56] and also in more countries.[57] For the most part, too, their affiliates are becoming more embedded in their local environments; and are helping to foster the dispersion of at least some kinds of intellectual capital. MNEs from developing countries also tend to locate their activities away from the large industrial concentrations originally favored by their developed countries' counterparts. For example, FDI in Europe by Korean auto and electronics MNEs has been more concentrated in Central and Eastern Europe and in the less prosperous areas of the UK and other EC countries than has FDI by US and Japanese MNEs (UNCTAD 1995, 1997, 1998). The numbers of cross-border M&As and strategic alliances have also risen faster than their domestic counterparts (Booz, Allen and Hamilton 1997).

On the other hand, MNEs and their affiliates are being increasingly drawn to a network of "sticky" places for their wealth creating activities; and there is a strong suggestion that the events of the last two decades, and particularly the deepening of the knowledge-based economy and the growing interdependence between cutting edge technologies, have increased the spatial costs of related economic transactions. This has prompted MNEs to locate their R&D and production units in a geographical area large enough to accommodate a concentrated nexus of competitors, suppliers, customers, and/or of firms using common support services, but small enough to maximize the benefits of "untradable interdependencies" (Storper and Scott 1995).

We may infer then that there is no real paradox of geographical space; and that globalization and localization are opposite sides of the same coin.[58] This section of the chapter has further suggested that, because of their unique characteristics, MNEs are likely to display a different geography of economic activity than that of their uni-national counterparts. In part, this is a reflection of the products they produce; but mostly it arises from their capabilities to harness and utilize resources, capabilities and markets from throughout the world, and to do so within their own governance structures. Such advantages, we believe, make for more globalization and more spatial clustering, than would occur if all the cross-border value-added activities, owned and controlled by MNEs, were undertaken by independent firms; and if all trade was conducted at arm's length prices. But much more research is needed if this suggestion is to be more than just a suggestion!

We would briefly make one further point. There is some evidence (see, for example, OECD 1996) to suppose that industrial clusters, particularly of small and medium size (SME) firms, tend to generate the kind of external economies, which assist at least some of the clustering firms to internationalize their markets and/or production. In particular, several of the country studies in OECD (1996) reveal a close correlation between the export success of firms, and their participation in cross-border alliances, and their involvement in domestic networks.

A regional perspective

We now turn to consider some of the implications of recent economic events for the role of micro-regions as spatial entities, and for the governance of those regions. Is it the case, as some writers (e.g. Ohmae 1995) has suggested, that micro-regions are replacing the nation state as the principal spatial mode of governance; or is the more temperate view of geographers such as Allen Scott, and business strategists such as Michael Porter, that such regions will become increasingly important milieus for competitive enhancing activities of mobile investors, and as engines of national economic growth, a more persuasive one?

Much research has been conducted over the past 30 years on the role of FDI and MNE related activity in advancing the economic wellbeing of nation states,[59] but relatively little on how it has affected that of micro-regions.[60] In principal, one would expect the results to be very similar, and particularly so when the micro-regions are the size of small countries (cf. the impact of FDI on the economy of Baden Württemberg with that of Belgium, or that of Northern Ireland with that of Denmark). While, traditionally, scholars have always distinguished between intra- and international economic activity, and have generally assumed that the sovereignty of sub-national governments is more constrained than that of national governments, contemporary economic events are demanding a reappraisal of these views. This is particularly so in the case of countries which have become part of macro-regional integration schemes.

Nevertheless, *de facto*, the economic governance of most micro-regions is shared and executed by a range of authorities – micro-regional, national, and supranational. The exact role of each will vary from macroregion to micro-region, country to country and over time. In many respects, the relation of micro-regional to national governance may be likened to that of a subsidiary of a MNE to its parent company. The subsidiary has its own goals and agenda for achieving these goals; so does the parent company. The amount of decision taking responsibility devolved to the subsidiary is likely to depend on such variables as the functions performed by it, its size, age and experience, the respective capabilities of the managers of the parent organization and those of the subsidiary, and the extent to which the managers of the latter, while promoting their own goals, are perceived to advance those of the MNE of which they are a part.

The same principle of "subsidiarity" may be applied to understanding how much sovereignty is decentralized from national to micro-regional governments.[61] But, from the perspective of the regional government, its economic tasks are clear cut. These are, first, to promote the full and most efficient usage of the resources and capabilities within its jurisdiction; and second – in so far as is within its power – to provide the supportive infrastructure for its existing resources and capabilities to be upgraded, and for its indigenous firm to be competitive in world markets.

The contribution of inbound mobile investment is normally judged by these criteria. However, the questions of particular interest to the contributors to this volume are: first, whether in the contemporary globalizing, knowledge-based economy, such investment is likely to make a more, or less, significant contribution to regional economic welfare; second what should be the policies of regional governments to ensure that such a contribution is an optimum one; and third, how far are these policies supported by, or reconcilable with, those pursued by national, and/or supra-national, governments, which seek to promote a broader canvass of interests.

The governments of micro-regions are like the managers of firms in another respect. They compete with each other for resources, capabilities and markets. An increasing role of many sub-national authorities, in recent years, has been directed to providing as many cost-effective incentives and as few obstacles as possible to the kind of mobile investment the region perceives it needs to promote its dynamic comparative advantage. Many of these incentives have taken the form of investment grants, tax holidays, free or subsidized land, customized public utilities, the aggressive pursuance of which by some micro-regions, e.g. some states in the US, has led some scholars to refer to them as locational tournaments (Mytelka 1996).

But no less significant have been the concentrated efforts of some micro-regional governments to provide, or ensure that the private sector provides, the kind of location bound assets which investors – be they from the region or elsewhere – perceive they need if they are to best exploit their more mobile core competencies. However, it is becoming clear that regional authorities need to do more than this, simply because many of these assets (e.g. cost-efficient utilities, educational facilities, transport and communication infrastructure) are either provided, or can be fairly easily replicated, by their competitors.[62] This suggests that they need to offer mobile investors a unique set of spatially fixed competitive advantages, which are either customized to their individual needs (Peck 1996), or are not easily imitated by other regional governments. There is also need for strategic collaboration between the different levels of sub-national governance to minimize both private and public transaction costs.[63] Finally, local administrations, in conjunction with local co-operative and/or trade associations, educational and innovatory institutions need to create an environment, which not only helps promote the agglomeration of related activities, but one in which mobile investors can accumulate resources and capabilities, yet from which they may find it difficult to exit (Harrison 1992)![64] This, more often than not, is an extremely difficult thing to do, although some micro-regions, e.g. Silicon Valley in California and some small countries, e.g. Singapore and Hong Kong, have done so very successfully.[65]

What also is becoming increasingly clear is that, to advance their economic objectives, micro-regional governments need to give as much attention to providing the right milieu for asset augmentation activities of their resident firms – be they domestic or foreign – as for asset-exploiting activities. Once again, the idea of the dynamic learning region comes to the fore; and, with it, the need for local administrations to adapt their infrastructural systems to best meet the demands of the global economy[66] to work together with the private sector to minimize any structural distortions and transaction costs which might impede both the redeployment and upgrading of local resources and capabilities.

It is within this context that the role of micro-regional clusters needs to be evaluated. To what extent is regional prosperity advanced if the agglomeration of vertically or horizontally related activities is encouraged – or, at least, not inhibited – by regional governments?[67] If such spatial networks are to be facilitated, how best might this be accomplished and what form should the clusters take?

It is possible to identify several kinds of spatial clusters.[68] These are likely to vary according to their scope, density, pattern of activities, growth potential, innovatory capacity and governance structures (Enright 1998). In this chapter, we shall confine our discussion to six types of clusters. The first of these are "hub-and-spoke" clusters, in which a hub or nucleus of flagship firms generate a circle of satellite (or spoke) firms. In this case (the Boeing complex around Seattle, the Toyota complex around Tokyo, the Pohang Steel complex around Pohang in Korea, and the newly emerging Jenoptak electronics complex at Jena in Eastern Germany are good examples) the success of the cluster is likely to rest on the capability of the flagship firm to leverage and develop a network development of suppliers and customers which are able to gain external economies not only from the hub firm but from each other.[69]

The second kind of cluster is that exemplified by the Northern Italian textile industry, the Portuguese cork industry, the Cambridge (New Zealand) horse breeding industry and the Geneva watch industry, and was first identified by Alfred Marshall (1920).[70] It comprises a concentration of enterprises engaged in similar economic activities, so that each can draw from such external economies as the availability of a common pool of natural resources and transportation facilities. The third type of cluster, like the second, consists of a complex of firms producing similar goods and services. The difference is that while, in the former case, the main cluster-specific benefits arise from a reduction of static distance related transaction costs, and from internalizing static external economies; in the latter they primarily take the form of institution building learning economies and the sharing of collective knowledge. The R&D laboratory is, in fact, a major component in the success of the latter, but not the former cluster, as is the interchange of tacit knowledge and ideas between the constituent firms and local universities and technical colleges.

The fourth type of industrial district is that which arises from an agglomeration or of government publicly sponsored institutions. Examples include a congregation of aerospace military and other research establishments which are concentrated around Farnborough and Aldershot in South East England,[71] around Colorado Springs in the US, and around San Jose dos Campos in Brazil;[72] and which generate a satellite of subcontractors in adjacent regions. The willingness and capacity to create and develop such spatial networks in obviously strongly dependent on national, rather than on regional, priorities and policies. In general, the most regional governments can do is to provide the human and physical infrastructure required to make them a success. State governments in several countries, notably the US, however, have played an important role in encouraging tertiary education. For example, state funded universities explain much of the growth of cities such as Durham, Chapel Hill, Ann Arbor, Austin and Madison in the US, which rank among the fastest growing US conurbations (Markusen and Gray 1999).

The fifth type of cluster is that typified by export processing zones in developing countries. Here, often tempted by tax *et al.* incentives offered by national and/or regional governments, foreign MNEs have set up primarily export oriented labor intensive activities; and, *via* the signaling affect, have encouraged the agglomeration of like firms. However, if such clusters are to be anything but enclaves, and fully benefit the local economy, a national or regional policy which promotes the continuous upgrading of indigenous resources, and the establishment of backward or forward linkages with local firms, is essential (McIntyre, Narula and Trevino 1996).

The sixth type of cluster is specifically directed at encouraging all forms of asset augmenting activities.[73] Science and technology parks are primary examples of such clusters. To be successful, they need an up to date and sophisticated institutional infrastructure, and an innovative milieu which helps generate the fluidity of knowledge, learning externalities and social capital, demanded by the participating firms (Putman 1993). As we have already indicated, such clusters are usually, though not exclusively, located in the major metropolitan areas or in university towns and cities in advanced industrial countries.

We have suggested that foreign MNEs may, and frequently do, play a major role in the formation, structure and development of the third, fifth and sixth types of cluster; in some cases, too, they may initiate the first type of cluster. In the second and fifth types of cluster, foreign MNEs would normally be expected to engage in resource-seeking, market-seeking or efficiency-seeking investment; in the first, third and sixth kinds, in addition to asset exploiting activities, foreign investors may also be aiming to augment their existing competitive advantages. Some recent research by Birkinshaw and Hood (1997) on Canadian, Scottish and Swedish MNEs suggests that, while, historically, the role and influence of foreign affiliates has been more pronounced in "branch plant" clusters, in the future they are likely to make a contribution to the character and content of "leading edge" (i.e. innovating) clusters.

While, as we have already indicated, scholarly research has generally concluded that, in the absence of structural market distortions, the economic welfare of recipient countries has been advanced by asset exploiting FDI, there have been few studies on the affects of asset augmenting FDI on either national or regional economic welfare. Back in the 1960s, there was a good deal of concern in Europe about the possible "poaching" of intellectual capital by US inbound investors in some knowledge-intensive sectors, notably the pharmaceutical industry. This concern was especially marked as and when US firms acquired European companies and transferred some of their innovatory activities back to the US (Dunning 1970). Strangely enough, the huge wave of intra-triad M&As which have occurred over the last decade do not seem to have sparked off the same kind of anxiety. It is possible, although we think improbable, that this is because it is perceived that the price paid for such resources and capabilities is a socially acceptable one.[74] A more likely explanation is the fact that the recent spate of cross-border M&As and strategic alliances has been a two-way phenomenon; certainly European and US purchases of foreign firms have been fairly evenly matched by the foreign acquisitions of European and US firms[75] (DeLong, Smith and Walter 1996; UNCTAD 1998).

At the same time, there has been some reluctance by national administrations to allow foreign owned firms to participate in domestic R&D consortia – and particularly those publicly funded. Examples include the outlawing or limited participation of foreign owned firms in SEMATECH – a US consortium of semi-conductor firms; and, indeed, the somewhat ethnocentric attitude of successive US governments to the ownership of innovatory activities undertaken in the US.[76] By contrast, the European authorities take a more relaxed attitude to the foreign membership of such consortia, as, indeed, does the Japanese government.

The social benefits of inbound asset augmenting investment deserve further study; and particularly, at a regional level, of the distribution of its benefits between the parent companies (and countries) of the foreign affiliates and the micro-regions in which the latter are located. Case studies of the consequences of such FDI, which is deliberately designed to acquire intellectual capital from the host locations, are sorely needed. In particular, is the price paid by the foreign investor for such capital, compared with that which might have been paid by a domestic firm, sufficient to compensate for any "leakages" of proprietary knowledge to the investing country? Do the foreign firms bring other benefits to the micro-region; or, should one not be concerned with the issue at all – particularly where host regions to FDI are also home regions to outbound MNEs – and let the market make the appropriate decisions?

Some managerial implications

The final section of this chapter will identify some of the possible implications of recent economic events for managers of MNEs à *propos* their location decisions. The first point we would emphasize is that making the right location choice for a particular FDI, and attaining the right portfolio of locations for all FDIs by a particular firm can, itself, be an important competitive advantage. Moreover, as firms become more multinational, as firm-specific assets become more mobile, and as the options for locating most kinds of FDI widen, so, achieving the optimum mix of locations for the harnessing and deployment of geographically dispersed resources and capabilities, for the procurement of inputs, and for the supplying of their products to end markets, is becoming more critical.

At the same time, this issue has been largely ignored in the managerial literature. My guess is that for every 50 treatises, monographs and papers published on the strategic management of resources and capabilities, and the appropriate entry mode into foreign markets, there has been only one on the impact of locational choice on firm specific competitiveness. Maybe business scholars consider this outside their domain, and that locational decisions are taken only on purely economic grounds.[77] Yet even in the 1920s, it was being postulated that, in oligopolistic industries at least, one firm's locational choice was likely to be influenced not only by the existing location of other firms, but by how the latter might react to its own choice (Hotelling 1929). And certainly one of the central themes of the Multinational Enterprise Project led by Ray Vernon of Harvard in the 1960s[78] was "why" and "where" US, European and Japanese businesses preferred to site their manufacturing business outside their home countries. In 1974, Vernon wrote a classic paper on the "Location of Economic Activity" (Vernon 1974), in which he specifically differentiated between the locational strategies of large asset exploiting MNEs at different stages of their product cycles.[79] Though Vernon did not specifically couch his analysis in terms of the locational competitiveness of the investing firms, this, in fact, was his main interest.

For much of the last 30 years, academic interest in the geography of economic activity has been mainly confined to economists and economic geographers. While some of the earlier oligopolistic type models have been extended and refined,[80] they still do not address head-on the locational issues of critical concern to scholars of business strategy. In the last decade or so, however, three new research thrusts have emerged. The first is the influential work of Paul Krugman (1991, 1993 and 1995) on the determinants of the geographical concentration of economic activity. The second is the extension of Michael Porter's earlier studies (Porter 1985, 1990) on the competitive advantage of firms to embrace a spatial dimension (Porter 1994, 1996, 1998). The third is the growing attention being given by MNEs to the dynamic interaction between the competitive (or

ownership-specific) advantages of firms and the competitive (or locational) advantages of countries, particularly in respect of asset augmenting
FDI (Gray 1996; UNCTAD 1996; Dunning 1997, 1998); and also the
acknowledgement by some scholars (e.g. Oliver 1997) that the resource-
based theory of the firm might be usefully widened to incorporate variables external to firms, and, in particular, the local institutional environment in which they operate.

We have already suggested that one of the unique competitive advantages of the large MNE in a knowledge-based, globalizing economy is its
ability to identify, access, harness and effectively coordinate and deploy
resources and capabilities from throughout the world. This must surely
include an explicit and appropriate locational strategy. Such a strategy
should embrace not only all the activities of the MNE, but also those of its
competitors, suppliers and customers, over which it has some influence
and/or control. On the one hand, decisions about the acquisition and use
of technology, those about the cross-border sourcing of inputs, the siting
of R&D and production, and the servicing of global markets, are becoming increasingly complex. On the other, as the product and production
strategies of MNEs in any particular industrial sector are tending to converge,[81] their locational choices could become more critical to their
overall competitive advantages. And this applies no less to their search for
the right micro-region(s) in which to site their investments as to their
search for the right country(ies).

Conclusions

In this chapter, we have sought to describe and analyze the impact which
recent economic events have had on the location of value-added activities,
and particularly on those of MNEs. More specifically, we have focussed
attention on the centrifugal forces making for the macro-regionalization
and globalization of FDI and inter-firm alliances, and on the centripetal
forces making for a more concentrated geographical pattern. We have
also distinguished between those value-added activities embodying largely
location bound resources and capabilities and those embodying mobile
resources and capabilities.

The chapter has also identified the differences between the kind of
international division of labor fostered by multi-domestic MNEs and globally (or regionally) integrated MNEs; and how each, and the growing significance of micro-specific agglomerative economies, is affecting the
intra-national, as well as the cross-border, allocation of innovatory and
productive activities.

In our analysis of these issues, we distinguished between the asset augmenting and asset exploiting motives for MNE related activities, and their
different locational needs. In particular, we discussed the notion of distance related transaction costs; and argued that, in the contemporary

knowledge-based economy, dynamic transaction costs, e.g. those to do with learning and the co-ordination of innovation-related tasks, were at least as, if not more, important in influencing locational decisions as were their static counterparts. This led on to an examination of the drawing power of clusters of related firms in micro-regions; and how MNEs have both responded to, and influenced, the form of these clusters. Empirical evidence suggests that, whereas in the case of asset exploiting FDI, MNEs are most active in clusters involving below average knowledge-intensive activities, in the case of asset augmenting FDI they are increasingly gravitating to above average knowledge-intensive activities.[82]

One of the key conclusions of this chapter is that a carefully planned and executed locational strategy of MNEs is becoming an increasingly important factor influencing their global competitiveness. Inter alia, such a strategy should comprise the siting of firm specific, but mobile intangible assets, in countries and/or micro-regions which offer the most congenial complementary immobile assets. This conclusion applies equally to asset seeking and to asset exploiting FDI. Since, too, the distance costs of the more idiosyncratic knowledge-intensive transactions are probably increasing – as are the number and complexity of these transactions – the advantages of the spatial clustering of related activity increase – and this is in spite of the huge advances in telecommunications and distance learning facilities.

A second critical conclusion of our analysis is that the growing mobility of firm specific core competencies is placing increasing responsibility on micro-regional authorities to ensure the availability and quality of location bound complementary assets to attract the right kind of mobile investment. Moreover, as we have said, such a competitive advantage depends not only on the regional provision of general supportive assets (e.g. basic infrastructure), but on the identification and promotion of a set of the specific and unique advantages which cannot be easily imitated by other regions. These latter advantages and the policies of micro-regional authorities necessary to secure and augment them – may well include the promotion of distinctive clusters of related activities which, as shown in "The role of MNEs" above, may be of very varied forms.

This chapter has also identified various lacunae in our scholarly knowledge about the ways in which MNEs might affect the economic prosperity of host micro-regions – particularly where the objective of the former is to protect or add to their asset base. The changing relationship between micro-regional, national and supra-national governmental regimes, as each affects both the competitiveness of micro-regions and the behavior of MNEs investing, or likely to invest, in those regions, is also an underresearched area. More attention, too, needs to be given by students of business strategy on the significance of locational choice as a competitive advantage of firms; and how it may impact on their resource base, learning capabilities, values and entrepreneurial behavior.

Finally, if it is true that micro-regions are increasingly becoming one of the leading motors of economic development (Scott 1998), and the gateways of countries to the global marketplace (Ohmae 1995), does it not make sense to view the MNE, not only as one of the critical channels for organizing cross-border asset seeking and asset exploiting activities not only between different nation states, but also between micro-regions within different nation states. Is it, indeed, not the case that the economic linkages between Silicon Valley in California and Silicon Glen in mid-Scotland, or between the New York and London financial districts, are at least as significant as those between the UK and the US as factors determining the international location of economic activity, and patterns of cross-border trade?

NOTES

I am grateful to H. Peter Gray for his comments on an earlier draft of this chapter.

1 Defined as enterprises which own or control foreign owned value-added activities, and which internalize cross-border intermediate product markets.
2 Such as a variety of non-equity co-operative agreements, e.g. strategic alliances, licensing, franchising, sub-contracting, turnkey agreements and so on.
3 By asset augmenting activities we mean those directed to increasing the existing stock of resources and capabilities within the domain of firms or countries; by asset exploiting activities we mean those directed to utilizing existing assets in order to produce added value from them.
4 See, for example, some recent contributions by Michael Porter (Porter 1994, 1996, 1998) on this subject.
5 Throughout this chapter, we will define macro-regions as a grouping of nation states located in geographically bounded but proximate space. A classification of a macro-region may vary according to the purposes of that classification. Examples of macro-regions include the European Union (EU), the North American Free Trade Agreement (NAFTA), MERCUSOR, APEC and ASEAN. By contrast, we shall use the term micro-regions to embrace sub-national spatial units. These units may be large, e.g. states within the US; or very small, e.g. cities, industrial estates and science parks.
6 We use this expression to embrace all activities, both asset augmenting and asset exploiting which create an income stream.
7 A clear exception must be made of craftsmanship, which dates back to the Middle Ages and beyond.
8 This is a generic expression embracing all kinds of knowledge and competition embodied in both human, physical and organizational capital. For further details, see Edvinson (1997).
9 Chemicals and pharmaceuticals, machinery and electrical equipment, computers and office equipment, industrial and scientific instruments.
10 In 1995, on average, services (excluding those part of primary or secondary production) accounted for 63 percent of the world's GNP compared with 53 percent in 1980 and 45 percent in 1965). For further details see World Bank (1997), Tables 11 and 12.
11 The knowledge content of a firm may be likened to a completed jigsaw puzzle. The central pieces represent its core competencies, which are usually created

by itself. However, to obtain the complete picture, these pieces need to be locked into others. These, while representing the resources and capabilities of other firms have to be shaped so as to fit into the central pieces.

12 Sometimes referred to as "relational," "collective," "collaborative and associational" and "stakeholder" capitalism. For a review of these and similar concepts, see Dunning (1997a) and Cooke and Morgan (1998).

13 Cooke and Morgan (1998), for example, distinguish between the principal-agent and trustee models of corporate governance; between hierarchical (M form) and heterarchical (N form) modes of organization; between stand-alone, or linear, and integrated approaches to innovation; between coercive and participatory forms of work organization; and between adversarial and collaborative supply chain relationships.

14 Estimates of alliances vary considerably. A recent study by Booz, Allen and Hamilton has put the number of all cross-border alliances and M&As in 1995 and 1996 as high as 15,000 (Booz, Allen and Hamilton 1997). Another estimate by Hagedoorn (1996) is that between 1980 and 1994 the number of newly established cross-border technology alliances (which are mainly directed at asset augmenting activities) rose by over three times. Finally, the value of international M&As between 1991 and 1997 has increased by four times, and accounted for around three-fifths of all FDI flows over the same period (UNCTAD 1998).

15 Between 1920 and 1970 average ocean freight and port charges (per short ton of cargo) fell from $25 to $5; the average air transport costs per passenger mile fell from $0.68 to $0.11; while the cost of a three-minute telephone call from New York to London fell from $244.7 to $3.3 (Hufbauer 1991).

16 For example, between 1980 and 1996 the combined exports and imports as a percentage of GNP $\times$ 2 of the US rose from 9.1 percent to 12.0 percent. Corresponding figures for the UK were 22.5 percent and 29.6 percent; for Germany 23.2 percent and 22.2 percent; for Korea 34.2 percent and 34.4 percent; and for Venezuela 25.5 percent and 29.0 percent. The relevant figures for FDI stock as a percent of GNP were 5.8 percent and 9.4 percent for the US, 13.6 percent and 25.6 percent for the UK, 5.5 percent and 9.2 percent for Germany, 1.0 percent and 2.7 percent for Korea and for Venezuela 1.3 percent and 9.1 percent (IMD 1998).

17 For further details, see UNCTAD (1998).

18 Averaged over the years 1979 and 1994–96.

19 To give just one example, in 1996, of the worldwide research and development expenditure of around $580 billion, 91 percent was concentrated in the advanced industrial countries. (Author's estimate, calculated from data contained in IMD 1998, Table 7.01.)

20 Some evidence for this assertion in respect of changes in the location of economic activity in the European Community consequential upon the completion of the internal market is given in Dunning (1997b). In a more recent paper, Cantwell and Iammarino (1998) have shown that between 1969 and 1995 some 60.8 percent of the R&D activities by foreign owned firms in the UK was concentrated in the South East of England, compared with 41.7 percent for all large firms.

21 NB usually, but not always, those of its individual value-adding units.

22 Overall, between 1985 and 1997 the value of cross-border M&As, as a proportion to FDI flows averaged 55 percent, while between the early 1980s and 1996 the number of inter-firm technology agreements increased by 2 to 3 times (UNCTAD 1998, pp. 19 and 23).

23 The share of new FDI directed to developing countries rose from 19.6 percent in 1983–88 to 29.6 percent in 1989–94 (UNCTAD 1995).

24 Thus, in 1995 it was estimated that 75 percent of the foreign direct investment stock in China was from other Asian countries.

25 In 1993, 11.7 percent of the sales of US foreign affiliates was in services (other than trade) and 7.9 percent in finance and business services. The corresponding figures for 1982 were 8.1 percent and 4.4 percent (US Dept of Commerce, 1985 and 1995).

26 US Department of Commerce data reveal that, in 1994, the R&D performed by US foreign affiliates amounted to 13.0 percent of that of their parent companies. The corresponding percentage in 1982 was 7 percent and in 1989 9 percent (US Department of Commerce 1985, 1998; Dunning 1993).

27 Further details are set out in various articles and books. See especially Granstrand, Hakanson and Sjolander (1992), OECD (1997a and b), Archibugi and Iammarino (1998) and Cantwell and Harding (1998).

28 For example, the share of patents registered in the home countries of OECD member states accounted for by non-resident firms doubled between 1984 and 1994, as did the share of patents registered abroad by firms from those countries.

29 Initially by Adam Smith (1776) and Alfred Marshall (1920) and then by most economic geographers and spatial economists.

30 For a review of some of these see Audretsch (1998) and other papers contained in a special issue of the *Oxford Review of Economic Policy 14* (2), Summer 1998.

31 As acknowledged and explored by James Markusen in his various writings. See especially Markusen (1995).

32 For a summary of the main factors which facilitate intra-national and intra-regional agglomeration, see Ottavinano and Puga (1997). For an analysis of why spatial clustering is more likely to occur *within* countries rather than *between* countries see Davis and Weinstein (1997).

33 Thus, for example, Silicon Valley in California, as well as competing with some other (but not all) regions in the US for mobile knowledge-intensive investment, may also compete with, e.g. Silicon Glen in Scotland and similar micro-regional complexes in Japan, Germany and Italy. The main competitor to the Sheffield cutlery industry is not another UK region, but Solingen in Germany. For other examples see Enright (1998).

34 Such research as has been conducted (see, for example, Baptista and Swann (1994)) suggests that firms which are located in strong clusters in the UK are more likely to innovate than those in other regions.

35 However, a recent study on inter-firm alliances in the US semi-conductor industry suggests that the "optimum" spatial area associated with such economies may be larger than is commonly supposed (Arita and McCann 1998).

36 As documented in some detail by Dunning and Morgan (1971).

37 Notably, the access to a pool of flexible skilled labor, common support services and availability of non-tradable specialized inputs, the capturing of information spillovers, a more competitive and/or entrepreneurial environment, and a common set of shared values and ideologies.

38 According to Giersch, as the economic variables affecting production costs in different countries converge, so the non-economic variables affecting transaction costs become a more significant determinant of locational competition. Such variables include the ethics of property and contracts, attitudes to technical progress, and economic and civic morality modes of corporate and individual behavior and cultural assets.

39 As described by Michael Porter (1986). In practice, however, most large modern MNEs exhibit aspects of each of these structures.

40 See, for example, Dunning (1958) (reprinted with a statistical update 1998), Hill and Munday (1992), Mariotti and Piscitello (1995) and Cantwell and Iammarino (1998).

41 Thus in the UK, for example, the proportion of post-World War II FDI located in areas of above average unemployment or below average rates of growth has been considerably higher than that of indigenous firms (Dunning 1958 (1998)).

42 Notably those of Srinivasan and Mody (1997), and Braunerhjelm and Svensson (1995).

43 A recent example is the "follow my leader" strategy of Japanese MNEs in the consumer electronics industry in South Wales. Since Sony first invested in a Newport factory, several other Japanese companies have located in the same area.

44 An example in the pharmaceutical industry to undertake R&D on tropical medicines in the tropical countries and advanced biotechnology in the triad countries.

45 As in the case of much of Japanese FDI in the European pharmaceutical sector – an internationally oriented sector in which currently Japanese firms have a competitive *dis*advantage.

46 This is not to deny there may be restrictions placed on foreign owned firms from accessing some kinds of capital. This point is taken up further in the section headed: "A regional perspective."

47 For a recent catalogue of some of these, see Enright (1998).

48 Note that not all of these clusters are based on semi-skilled labor; for example, the comparative advantage of a Bangalore computer software complex is based on the created availability of highly skilled and professional labor.

49 For example by encouraging "follow my leader" tactics by other firms (Knickerbocker 1973). In his study of the inter-state distribution of FDI in the US, Miles Shaver (1996) showed that this was positively correlated to their separate agglomeration measures.

50 However, there are other clusters which have developed without the presence of MNEs. The City of London financial district, the North Italian woolen textile industry, and even (initially at least) the electronics industry, Silicon Valley are all cases in point.

51 In a recent paper, Enright (1998) gives several examples of foreign firms being drawn into spatial clusters by the presence of knowledge enhancing facilities. Nissan, he observes, does a substantial part of its new design work in Southern California, a leading center of auto design. Several European chemical and pharmaceutical companies do the bulk of their biotechnology research in biotechnology clusters in the US. The established financial centers of London, New York and Tokyo, far from losing their competitive advantage in high value activities, seem to be consolidating this advantage. At the same time, banking and financial MNEs are being increasingly drawn to new financial clusters in Hong Kong and Singapore (Enright 1998, p. 5).

52 For some evidence of the increasing role played by the subsidiaries of MNEs in innovatory activities, see Pearce (1999) and Pearce and Papanastassiou (1996) and Papanastassiou (1999). In this latter paper, the authors also point to the role played by supportive institutions in the UK, e.g. universities, scientific institutions, etc., in influencing the amount and character of R&D undertaken by foreign affiliates in that country.

53 There is widespread support for this statement. For a summary of the literature, see Dunning 1996, 1998 and Makino (1998). Both papers also offer an interpretation of the theory of asset seeking investment.

54 For example, where in 1993, 68.4 percent of the Japanese owned R&D laboratories were concentrated in four US states, viz. California, Michigan, New Jersey and Massachusetts, only 32.8 percent of Japanese owned manufacturing establishments were so located (Florida and Kenney (1994)). In the UK, between 1969 and 1995 60.8 percent of patents registered by the subsidiaries of foreign firms, were attributable to research undertaken in London and South East England (Cantwell and Iammarino 1998a). In Italy, over the same period, 67.2 percent of patents registered by such firms were attributable to research undertaken in two districts – Piedmonte and Lombardia (Cantwell and Iammarino 1998b)

55 In his paper, Scott shows that the growth of the value added in manufacturing in the 40 metropolitan areas in the US with more than one million people was 30.6 percent between 1972 and 1992 (after discounting for inflation) – well above the national average of 20.3 percent. However, he also shows that the fastest rate of growth (81.5 percent) occurred in the "sunbelt" group of metropolitan areas, which, not only did not have the industrial heritage of the other, e.g. areas in the North East, but made a focussed effort to build their economies on knowledge- and information-intensive manufacturing and service sectors.

56 Clearly this varies between countries and according to the respective investment opportunities offered by home and foreign countries. Over the last decade or so, for example, the proportion of the sales of the foreign affiliates of US corporations has remained around 30 percent; but in the case of several European countries, e.g. UK and Germany and most Asian countries (especially Japan) it has markedly increased (UNCTAD 1997, 1998).

57 The spread of MNEs into more countries is particularly noticeable in the service sectors.

58 For a more detailed examination of this theme, see Enright (1998).

59 See especially Caves (1996) and Dunning (1997a).

60 One recent exception is that of Wallace (1998), who has recently completed a Ph.D. dissertation on FDI in New Jersey.

61 We recognize, of course, there are many layers of micro-regional governance, e.g. from states, to countries, to districts, to cities, to businesses *et al.* parks.

62 This is not to deny there may be some "X" inefficiencies in the actions of regional government in providing these services, or in promoting a "hassle free" business environment; or, indeed, of publicizing the benefits of the resources and capabilities within their jurisdiction to foreign investors as well, or aggressively, as they might. For a discussion of such policies pursued by US state governments, see Donahue (1998).

63 For an examination of the importance of this kind of collaboration, and of the need for a reconstruction of some local institutions in the light of the increasing importance of mobile investment, see an interesting case study of the Korean MNE LG in South Wales (Phelps and Tewdwr-Jones 1998 and Phelps, Lovering and Morgan 1998).

64 Enright (1998), for example, gives details of the specific needs of different kinds of clusters for complementary assets, some of which are under the governance of regional authorities. These include "effluent treatment facilities for specific industries (Catalan leather), dedicated water (Malaysian electronics) or electricity lines (Venezuelan metals) and specialized port (Hong Kong trading) or airfreight facilities (Dutch flowers), specific training programs in software (Bangalore), motion pictures (Los Angeles), materials science (Sassuolo), wine making (Napa Valley), and electronics (Singapore) among others" (Enright 1998, p. 7).

65 See, for example, a very interesting paper entitled "Singapore Incorporated" by Haley, Low and Toh (1996).

66 For a careful analysis of the role of institutional systems in minimizing the transaction costs of economic activity and maximizing the benefits of special-ization and the agglomeration of related firms see Kasper and Streit (1998). Although the authors do not address the specific problems and challenges of micro-regional governments, much of what they write is directly relevant to them.

67 Michael Porter, in his 1990 book, argued that the main role of national gov-ernments was to do nothing which would prevent, retard or distort cluster for-mation. In his latest thinking, Porter (1996, 1998) assigns a more positive role for micro-regional governments; and particularly that of promoting "specializa-tion, upgrading and trade among regions" (Porter 1996, p. 88). Porter goes on to assert that cluster formation can be encouraged by *specialized* infrastructure and institution in areas where factor endowments, past industrial activities, or even historical accidents have resulted in concentration of economic activity.

68 See Park (1996), Markusen (1996) and Markusen and Gray (1998).

69 For a detailed analysis of the Seattle hub-and-spoke district see Gray, Golob and Markusen (1996). In his review of clusters, Park (1998) distinguishes between supplier and customer, and advanced supplier and advanced cus-tomer hub and spoke clusters.

70 And, indeed, before that by Adam Smith (1776) as recently highlighted by Ozawa (2000).

71 And documented by Hall *et al.* (1987).

72 As documented by Diniz and Razavi (1997).

73 As viewed from the perception of the micro-region.

74 See Dunning (1970) for a discussion of the social and private price of domestic assets acquired by foreign firms.

75 Between 1990 and 1997 the combined foreign acquisitions by European and US firms amounted to $1,134 billion, while the foreign purchases of European and US firms totaled $957 billion (UNCTAD 1998).

76 The relationship between US technology policy and the competitiveness of US firms and inbound foreign direct investment is explored by Ham and Mowery (1997).

77 Sometimes as modified by the personal preferences or prejudices of the main decision taker(s)!

78 Most particular as explored by Knickerbocker (1973) in his "follow my leader" hypothesis and Graham (1978) in his exchange of threats hypothesis.

79 Most noticeably from the innovatory through the mature to the senescent stage.

80 See, for example, Graham (1990) and Cantwell and Randaccio (1992).

81 Although we accept that firms might continue to differentiate their products from those supplied by their competitors – and, indeed, to do so even more intensively than in the past.

82 See an interesting paper by Birkinshaw and Hood (1997) which distinguishes between two kinds of clusters, viz. "leading edge" cluster, e.g. Silicon Valley, and a "branch plant" cluster, e.g. Scotland's electronics industry. They con-clude that, historically, FDI has tended to be concentrated and has had the most influence on structure and development of the latter kind of cluster. They accept, however, that the advent of the globalizing economy may lead to more FDI in the leading edge clusters.

REFERENCES

Archibugi, D. and Iammarino (1998), *Innovation and Globalization, Evidence and Implications*, Reading: University of Reading Discussion Papers in International Investment and Business, March.

Arita, T. and McCann, P. (1998), *Industrial Alliances and Firm Location Behavior: Some Evidence From the US Semiconductor Industry*, Reading: University of Reading Discussion Papers in Urban and Regional Economies, No. 130, March.

Audretsch, D. B. (1998), "Agglomeration and the location of economic activity," *Oxford Review of Economic Policy 14* (2), pp. 18–29.

Baptista, R. and Swann, P. (1994), *Do Firms in Clusters Innovate More? An Exploratory Study*, London: London Business School (mimeo) (1994).

Birkinshaw, J. and Hood, N. (1997), *Foreign Investment and Industry Cluster Development: The Characteristics of Subsidiary Companies in Different Types of National Industry Clusters*, Stockholm School of Economics and Strathclyde University (mimeo).

Booz, Allen and Hamilton (1997), *Cross Border Alliances in the Age of Collaboration*, Los Angeles: Booz, Allen and Hamilton.

Braunerhjelm, P. and Svensson, R. (1995), *Host Country Characteristics and Agglomeration in Foreign Direct Investment*, Stockholm: Industrial Institute for Economic and Social Research (mimeo) October.

Cantwell, J. A. and Harding, R. (1998), "The internationalization of German companies R&D," *National Institute Economic Review 16* (3), pp. 99–115.

Cantwell J. A. and Iammarino, S. (1998), *Multinational Corporations and the Location of Technological Innovation in the UK Regions*, University of Reading Discussion Papers in International Investment and Management, No. 262, December.

Cantwell, J. and Sanna Radaccio, F. (1992), "Intra-industry direct investment in the European Community," in Cantwell, J. C. (ed.), *Multinational Investment in Modern Europe: Strategic Interaction in the Integrated Community*, Aldershot (Hants) and Brookfield (Vermont): Edward Elgar.

Caves, R. (1996), *Multinational Firms and Economic Analysis* (Second edition), Cambridge: Cambridge University Press.

Cooke, P. and Morgan, K. (1998), *The Associational Economy*, Oxford: Oxford University Press.

Davis, D. R. and Weinstein, E. (1997), *Economic Geography and Regional Production Structure: An Empirical Investigation*, Cambridge, Mass.: NBER Working Paper No. 6093.

DeLong, G., Smith, R. C. and Walter, I. (1996), *Global Merger and Acquisition Tables 1995*, New York: Salomon Center (mimeo).

Diniz, C. C. and Razavi, M. (1997), "State Anchored Dynamos: São José Dos Campos and Campinos, Brazil," in Markusen, A. and Lee, Yong Sook, *Second Tier Cities: Explaining Rapid Growth in Brazil, Korea, Japan and the United States*, Minneapolis: University of Minnesota Press, pp. 97–123.

Donahue, J. D. (1998), *Disunited States*, New York: Basic Books.

Doremus, P., Keller, W. W., Pauly, L. W. and Reich, S. (1998), *The Myth of the Global Corporation*, Princeton, NJ: Princeton University Press.

Doz, Y. L., Asakawa, K., Santos, J. F. P. and Williamson, P. J. (1998), *The Metanational Corporation*, Fontainebleau, France: INSEAD Working Paper 97/60/SM.

Dunning, J. H. (1958, 1998), *American Investment in British Manufacturing Industry*, London: Allen & Unwin (1998 edition published by Routledge, London and New York).

Dunning, J. H. (1970), *Studies in International Investment*, London: Allen & Unwin.

Dunning, J. H. (1993), *Multinational Enterprises and the Global Economy*, Wokingham, England and Reading, Mass.: Addison Wesley.

Dunning, J. H. (1996), "The geographical sources of competitiveness of firms: the results of a new survey," *Transnational Corporations 5* (3), December, pp. 1–30.

Dunning, J. H. (1997a), *Alliance Capitalism and Global Business*, London and New York: Routledge.

Dunning, J. H. (1997b), "The European internal market program and inbound foreign direct investment," *Journal of Common Market Studies 35* (1 and 2), pp. 1–30 and 189–223.

Dunning, J. H. (1998a), "Globalization and the theory of MNE activity," paper presented to a conference on *Multinational Enterprise Activity and Economic Development*, Strathclyde, Scotland, May.

Dunning, J. H. (1998b), "The changing geography of foreign direct investment," in Kumar, K. (ed.), *Internationalization, Foreign Direct Investment and Technology Transfer: Impact and Prospects for Developing Countries*, London and New York: Routledge.

Dunning, J. H. and Narula, R. (eds) (1996), *Foreign Direct Investment and Governments*, London and New York: Routledge.

Dunning, J. H. and Morgan, E. V. (eds) (1971), *An Economic Study of the City of London*, London: Allen & Unwin.

Edvinson, L. (1997), *Intellectual Capital Development*, Stockholm: Skandia.

Enright, M. J. (2000), "The globalization of competition and the localization of competitive advantage: policies toward regional clustering," in Hood, N. and Young, S. (eds), *Globalization of Economic Activity and Economic Development*, Basingstoke, Hampshire: Macmillan, pp. 303–31.

Feldman, M. P. and Audretsch, D. (1999), "Innovation in cities: science based diversity, specialization and localized competition," *European Economic Review 43*, pp. 409–27.

Florida, R. (1995), "Towards the learning region," *Futures 27* (5), pp. 527–36.

Florida, R. and Kenney, M. (1994), "The globalization of Japanese R&D: the economic geography of Japanese R&D investment in the United States," *Economic Geography 70*, pp. 343–69.

Giersch, H. (1996), "Economic morality as a competitive asset," in Hamlin, A., Giersch, H. and Norton, A., *Markets, Morals and Community*, St Leonards, Australia: Center for Independent Studies Occasional Paper No. 59.

Graham, E. M. (1978), "Transatlantic investment by multinational firms: a rivalistic phenomenon," *Journal of Post Keynesian Economics 1*, pp. 82–99.

Graham, E. M. (1990), "Exchange of threats between multinational firms as an infinitely repeated non-cooperative game," *International Trade Journal 4* (3), pp. 259–77.

Granstrand, O., Hakanson, L. and Sjolander, S. (eds) (1992), *Technology, Management and International Business: Internationalization of R&D and Technology*, Chichester (UK): Wiley.

Gray, H. P. (1996), "The eclectic paradigm: the next generation," *Transnational Corporations 5* (2), pp. 51–66.

Gray, M., Golob, E. and Markusen, A. (1996), "Big firms, long arms, a portrait of a 'hub and spoke' industrial district in the Seattle region," *Regional Studies 30* (7), pp. 651–66.

Hagedoorn, J. (1996), "Trends and patterns in strategic technology partnering since the early seventies," *Review of Industrial Organization 11*, pp. 601–16.

Haley, U. C. V., Low, L. and Toh, Mun-Heng (1996), "Singapore Incorporated: reinterpreting Singapore's business environments through a corporate metaphor," *Management Decision 34* (9), pp. 17–28.

Hall, P., Breheny, M., McQuaid, R. and Hart, D. (1987), *Western Sunrise*, London and Boston: Allen & Unwin.

Ham, R. and Mowery, D. (1997), "The United States," in Dunning, J. H. (ed.), *Governments, Globalization and International Business*, Oxford: Oxford University Press, pp. 283–321.

Handy, C. (1990), *The Age of Unreason*, London: Hutchinson.

Harrison, B. (1992), "Industrial districts: old wine in new bottles," *Regional Studies 26* (5), pp. 469–83.

Hill, S. and Munday, M. (1992), "The UK regional distribution of foreign direct investment: analysis and determinants," *Regional Studies 26*, pp. 534–44.

Hotelling, H. (1929), "Stability in competition," *Economic Journal 29*, pp. 41–57.

Hufbauer, G. (1991), "World economic integration: the long view," *Economic Insights 30*, pp. 26–27.

IMD (1998), *The World Competitive Yearbook 1998*, Lausanne: IM.

IMF (vd), *Balance of Payments Statistical Yearbook* (annual publication), Washington: IMF.

International Telecommunications Union (2000) *Telecommunications Industry at a Glance: Mobile Driving Growth of Telecommunication Markets*, Geneva: ITU.

Kasper, W. and Streit, M. (1998), *Institutional Economics, Social Order and Public Policy*, Cheltenham, UK: Edward Elgar.

Kuemmerle, W. (1996), "The drivers of foreign direct investment into research and development: an empirical investigation", Journal of International Business Studies *30* (1), pp. 1–24.

Knickerbocker, F. T. (1973), *Oligopolistic Reaction and the Multinational Enterprise*, Cambridge, MA: Harvard University Press.

Kozul-Wright, R. (1997), "The size of nations: small economies in a globalizing world," *Development and International Cooperation XIII* (24 and 15), pp. 105–38.

Krugman, P. R. (1991), *Geography and Trade*, Cambridge, MA: MIT Press.

Krugman, P. R. (1993), "On the relationship between trade theory and location theory," *Review of International Economics 1* (2), pp. 110–22.

Krugman, P. R. (1995), *Development, Geography and Economic Theory*, Cambridge, MA: MIT Press.

Liu, S. X. (1998), *Foreign Direct Investment and the Multinational Enterprise. A Reexamination Using Signaling Theory*, Westport, Conn.: Greenwood Publishing.

Makino, S. (1998), *Toward a Theory of Asset Seeking Foreign Direct Investment*, Hong Kong: The Chinese University (mimeo).

Mariotti, S. and Piscitello, L. (1995), "Information costs and location of FDIs within the host country: empirical evidence from Italy," *Journal of International Business Studies 26* (4), pp. 815–41.

Markusen, A. (1996), "Sticky places in slippery space: a typology of industrial districts," *Economic Geography 72* (3), pp. 293–313.

Markusen, A. and Gray, M. (1999), "Clusters and regional development in New Jersey," in J. H. Dunning (ed.), *New Jersey in a Globalizing Economy*, Newark: Rutgers University, CIBER.

Markusen, J. R. (1995), "The boundaries of multinational enterprises and the theory of international trade," *Journal of Economic Perspectives 9* (2), pp. 169–89.

Marshall, A. (1920), *Principles of Economics*, London: Macmillan (eighth edition).

McGrew, A. G. (1992), "Conceptualizing global politics" in McGrew, A. G. and Lewis, P. G. (eds), *Global Politics: Globalization and the Nation State*, Cambridge: The Polity Press.

McIntyre, J. R., Narula, R. and Trevino, L. J. (1996), "The role of export processing zones for host countries and multinationals: a mutually beneficial relationship?," *International Trade Journal 10*, pp. 435–66.

Mytelka, L. K. (1996), *Locational Tournaments, Strategic Partnerships and the State*, Ottawa: Carleton University (mimeo).

Narula, R. (1995), *Multinational Investment and Economic Structure*, London and Boston: Routledge.

National Science Foundation (1997), *Patenting Activity in the US*, Washington: National Science Foundation.

O'Brien, R. (1992), *Global Financial Integration: The End of Geography*, London: Pinter Publishers.

OECD (1996), *Networking Enterprises, Local Development*, Paris: OECD.

OECD (1997a), *Science and Technology Indicators*, Paris: OECD.

OECD (1997b), *Internationalization of Industrial R&D: Patterns and Trends*, Paris: Group of National Experts on Science and Technology Indicators, OECD.

Ohmae, K. (1995), *The End of the Nation State: The Rise of Regional Economies*, London: HarperCollins.

Oliver, C. (1997), "Sustainable competitive advantage: combining institutional and resource based views," *Strategic Management Journal 18* (9), pp. 697–713.

Ottavinano, G. and Puga, D. (1997), *Agglomeration in the Global Economy: A Survey of the New Economic Geography*, London Centre for Economic Performance, Discussion Paper No. 356.

Ozawa, T. (2000), "Small and medium size MNC, industrial clusters and globalization: the Japanese experience", in Hood, N. and Young, S. (eds), *Globalization of Multinational Enterprise Activity and Economic Development*, Basingstoke, Hampshire: Macmillan.

Papanastossiou, M. and Pearce, R. D. (1999) *Multinationals, Technology and National Competitiveness*, Cheltenham: Edward Elgar.

Park, S. O. (1996), "Networks and embeddedness in the dynamic types of industrial districts," *Progress in Human Geography 20* (4), pp. 476–93.

Pearce, R. D. (1998) "The evolution of technology in multinational enterprises: the role of creature subsidiaries," *International Business Review 8*, pp. 125–48.

Pearce, R. D. and Papanastassiou, M. (1996), *R&D Networks and Innovation: Decentralized Product Development in Multinational Enterprises, R&D Management 26* (4), pp. 315–33.

Peck, F. W. (1996), "Regional development and the production of space: the role of infrastructure in the attraction of new inward investment," *Environment and Planning 28*: pp. 327–39.

Perraton *et al.* (1994), "The globalization of economic activity," *New Political Economy 2* (2).

Phelps, N. A. and Tewdwr-Jones, M. (1998), "Institutional capacity building in a strategic vacuum: the case of the Korean company LG in south Wales," *Environment and Planning C: Government and Policy 16*, pp. 735–55.

Phelps, N. A., Loverin, J. and Morgan, K. (1998), "Tying the firm to the region or tying the region to the firm?" *European Urban and Regional Studies 5* (2), pp. 119–37.

Porter, M. E. (1985), *Competitive Advantage*, New York: The Free Press.

Porter, M. E. (ed.) (1986), *Competition in Global Industries*, Boston: Harvard Business School Press.

Porter, M. E. (1990), *The Competitive Advantage of Nations*, New York: The Free Press.

Porter, M. E. (1994), "The role of location in competition," *Journal of Economics of Business I* (1), pp. 35–39.

Porter, M. E. (1996), "Competitive advantage, agglomerative economics and regional policy," *International Regional Science Review 19* (1 and 2), pp. 85–94.

Porter, M. E. (1998), "Location, clusters and the 'new' micro-economies of competition," *Business Economics 33*, Jan. pp. 7–13.

Putman, R. D. (1993), *Making Democracy Work: Civic Traditions in Modern Italy*, Princeton: Princeton University Press.

Schoenberger, E. (1988), "Multinational Corporations and the new international division of labor: a critical appraisal," *International Regional Science Review 11* (2), pp. 105–19.

Scott, A. (1998), *Regional Motors of the Global Economy*, Newark: Rutgers University, CIBER Distinguished Lecture Series No. 1, March.

Shaver, J. M. (1996), *Industry Agglomeration and Foreign Greenfield Investment Survival in the United States*, New York: Stern School of Business (mimeo).

Smith, A. (1776), *An Inquiry into the Nature and Causes of the Wealth of Nations* (London, reprinted in Cannon, E. (ed.), New York, 1937).

Solvell, O. and Bengtsson, M. (1997), *The Role of Industry Structure Climate of Competition and Cluster Strength*, Stockholm Institute of International Business, Stockholm, School of Economics (mimeo).

Srinivasan, K. and Mody, A. (1998), "Location determinants of foreign direct investment: an empirical analysis of US and Japanese investment," *Canadian Journal of Economics 31* (4), pp. 778–97.

Stewart, T. A. (1997), *Intellectual Capital*, London: Nicholas Bradley.

Stigler, G. (1951), "The division of labor is limited by the extent of the market," *Journal of Political Economy LIX*, pp. 185–93.

Stopford, J. and Strange, S. (1991), *Rival States, Rival Firms: Competition for World Market Shares*, Cambridge: Cambridge University Press.

Storper, M. (1995), "The resurgence of region economies: ten years later: the region as a nexus of untraded interdependencies," *European Urban and Regional Studies 2* (3), pp. 191–221.

Storper, M. (1997), *The Regional World*, London: Guilford Press.

Storper, M. and Scott, A. J. (1995), "The wealth of regions," *Futures 27* (5), pp. 505–26.

Strange, R. (1993), *Japanese Manufacturing Investment in Europe*, London and New York: Routledge.

UN (vd), *Annual Statistical Yearbook*, New York: UN.

UNCTAD (1993), *World Investment Report 1993: Transnational Corporations and Integrated International Production*, New York and Geneva: UN.

UNCTAD (1995), *World Investment Report 1995: Transnational Corporations and Competitiveness*, New York and Geneva: UN.

UNCTAD (1996), *Investment Incentives*, New York and Geneva: UN.

UNCTAD (1997), *World Investment Report 1997: Transnational Corporations, Market Structure and Competition Policy,* New York and Geneva: UN.

UNCTAD (1998), *World Investment Report 1998: Trends and Determinants,* New York and Geneva: UN.

US Patent and Trademark Office (1997), *Patenting Trends 1997,* Washington: US Patent and Trademark Office.

US Patent and Trademark Office (1999), *Patent Counts by Country/State and Year,* Washington: US Patent and Trademark Office, Washington, March.

US Dept. of Commerce (1995), *U.S. Direct Investment Abroad. Provisional Results 1993,* Washington: US Government Printing Office.

US Dept. of Commerce (1985), *U.S. Direct Investment Abroad 1982 Benchmark Survey Data,* Washington, Government Printing Office.

US Dept. of Commerce (1991).

US Dept. of Commerce (1998) *U.S. Direct Investment Abroad 1994 Benchmark Survey Data,* Washington, Government Printing Office.

Vernon, R. (1974), "The location of economic activity," in Dunning, J. H. (ed.), *Economic Analysis and the Multinational Enterprise,* London: Allen and Unwin, pp. 84–114.

Wallace, L. (1998), *Foreign Direct Investment and the New Jersey Economy,* Newark, NJ: Ph.D. Thesis, Rutgers University, Faculty of Management.

World Bank (1997), *World Development Report,* Oxford: Oxford University Press.

World Bank (1998), *World Development Report,* Oxford: Oxford University Press.

Yannopoulos, G. N. and Dunning, J. H. (1976), "MNEs and regional development: an exploratory paper," *Regional Studies 10* (5) pp. 389–401.

7 Globalization and the new geography of foreign direct investment

Introduction

In this chapter, we shall identify, and suggest reasons for, the changing geography of foreign direct investment (FDI) by multinational enterprises (MNEs)[1] between 1975–1980 and 1990–1996.[2] In pursuing this task, we shall consider the main changes which have occurred in the global economy over the past two decades, and in particular, how these have affected: (i) the competitive or ownership specific (O) advantages of firms; (ii) the competitive or location specific (L) advantages of countries; and (iii) the modalities by which firms coordinate their mobile O specific advantages with the immobile L specific advantages of countries (i.e. whether firms choose to buy or sell assets, or rights to assets through intermediate product markets and/or network relationships, or whether they prefer to internalize (I) the market for these assets or rights).[3]

More particularly, we shall argue that it is the thrust of recent international political and economic events, and technological advances, which, through their impact on the configuration of OLI advantages facing MNEs, has been the predominant determinant of the changing geography of FDI.[4] We shall also suggest that these same events have caused a fundamental – and possibly an irreversible – shift in the relative significance of the individual O, L and I variables (e.g. as set out in Dunning 1995a and 2000), as they influence both the strategy of MNEs toward FDI and the location of their value-added activities. In so doing, we will give especial attention, first, to the distinction between the perceived need of firms to exploit, i.e. capture the economic rent, on existing O specific advantages, and that directed to protecting or augmenting these advantages,[5] and second, to the growing importance of high-value FDI, as witnessed by, for example, the significant expansion of research and development (R&D) activities undertaken by the foreign affiliates of MNEs, particularly, but not exclusively, in advanced industrial countries.[6]

The chapter proceeds in the following way. The following section describes the changes in the geography of FDI inflows between two periods, 1975–1980 and 1990–1996. The next section then offers some explanations for the changes identified. This is followed by a section that discusses how the new geography of MNE activity varies according to the strategy of the investing firms, the activities in which they engage and the countries from which they originate. The final section summarizes the main findings of the chapter.

The new geography of foreign direct investment

Table 7.1 portrays the changing distribution of the flows of FDI by region and country of destination between the second half of the 1970s and the first six years of the 1990s.[7] For the first period, we have taken a six-year annual average, and for the second, a seven-year annual average of flows, which we believe to be a sufficiently long period to even out any "lumpy" merger and acquisition (M&A) activity. We have chosen to use FDI flow, rather than stock data, mainly because the former are regularly compiled by the IMF and UNCTAD,[8] and are reasonably comparable over time.

Table 7.1 suggests there have been quite significant shifts in the geography of FDI over the past two decades. A comparison of the data in columns 2 and 4, as well as that set out in column 5, shows that, of the major regions of the world, South, East and South East Asia and Central and Eastern Europe have spectacularly increased their share of inbound investment, while Japan and the European Union (EU)[9] have posted more modest gains. On the other hand, while other developed economies, the Americas, West Asia and Africa have also recorded absolute increases in inward investment – and, in the case of the US, substantial increases[10] – they have lost some of their earlier attractions, relative to those of other regions or countries.[11]

Table 7.2 gives details of the leading recipients of inward direct investment in the two periods in developed and developing countries. Overall in 1975–1980, the ten largest recipient countries accounted for 74.1 percent of all FDI flows; with just over one-half being directed to the United States, the United Kingdom, France and the Netherlands. By the first half of the 1990s, this geographical concentration had decreased to 66.5 percent, although four leading countries, viz. the United States, the United Kingdom, France and China, still accounted for 46.4 percent of the total FDI flows.

Table 7.2 also shows that among the most significant changes in the distribution of inbound FDI between developing countries over the past two decades have been, first, the rise of China to the second largest recipient; and second, the declining drawing power of Brazil and one of the leading oil exporting countries in the 1970s – Egypt. There has been some shifting in the ranking of the leading recipients of FDI. Among the developed countries, France, Spain and Canada have both increased their share of FDI over the past two decades, while, of the developing countries, Singapore, Argentina and Thailand have considerably strengthened their positions.

Table 7.1 The distribution of FDI inflows by host region and country, 1975–1980 and 1990–1996 ($ millions)

	1975–1980 Annual average	Percent	1990–1996 Annual average	Percent	Index of FDI growth 1975–1980 = 100
Total inflows	32,183	100.0	234,724	100.0	729.3
Developed economies	24,642	76.6	153,381	65.3	622.4
Western Europe	13,874	43.1	92,295	39.3	665.2
of which: European Union[a]	13,190	41.0	83,947	35.8	636.4
North America	8,757	27.2	50,942	21.7	581.7
of which: US	7,895	24.5	44,757	19.1	566.9
Japan	152	0.5	1,013	0.4	666.7
Other developed economies	1,859	5.7	9,169	3.9	493.2
of which: Australia	1,271	3.9	5,805	2.5	456.7
Developing economies	7,539	23.4	74,778	31.9	991.9
Africa	810	2.5	3,498	1.5	431.9
Latin America and Caribbean	4,014	12.5	22,536	9.6	561.4
of which: South America	2,377	7.4	12,824	5.5	539.5
Asia	2,489	7.7	48,075	20.5	1931.5
of which: South, East and South East Asia	1,971	6.1	45,857	19.5	2326.6
West and Central Asia[b]	518	1.6	2,217	0.9	428.1
Other developing economies[c]	226	0.7	668	0.3	295.8
Central and Eastern Europe	3	Neg.	6,565	2.8	218,847.6

Source: UNCTC (1988), UNCTAD (1995a, 1998).

Notes
a Includes the 12 member countries of the European Union in 1994.
b Including the Middle Eastern countries.
c The Pacific and developing Europe.
Neg. = negligible.

It is worth noting that there are some leading developed and developing economies which did not receive as much FDI as one might have expected. Japan is the most obvious example; it accounted for only 0.6 percent inflows into the developed countries in 1975–1980 and 0.9 percent in 1990–1996. Of the larger European countries, Italy received only one-quarter of the share of France in the first period and one-fifth in the second period, while some of the more populated newly industrial countries (NICs) of Asia, viz. Indonesia, Korea, Taiwan and the Philippines, attracted only modest (though increasing) amounts of new capital inflows.

The cases of India – and even more spectacularly, that of some Central and East European countries – are interesting in that, although their share of total inward FDI remains very small, the rate of growth of investment directed to these countries over the last two decades has been well above average.[12] On balance, however, there has been a slight trend towards a more even geographical distribution of FDI. In the case of

Table 7.2 The largest recipients of inward FDI 1975–1980 and 1990–1996 (annual averages)

Developed countries

Country	1975/80 $m	Percent[b]	Country	1990/96 $m	Percent
USA	7,894.0	32.0	USA	44,757.1	29.2
UK	5,795.4	21.1	UK	19,613.4	12.8
France	2,127.3	8.6	France	19,080.1	12.4
Netherlands	1,276.6	5.2	Belgium	10,012.1	6.5
Australia	1,271.4	5.2	Spain	8,579.3	5.6
Belgium[d]	1,203.1	4.9	Netherlands	7,770.9	5.1
Germany	1,052.6	4.3	Canada	6,185.3	4.0
Spain	970.5	3.9	Australia	6,118.9	4.0
Top 8	20,991.6	85.2	Top 8	122,117.1	79.6
All	24,642.0	100.0	All	153,380.9	100.0

Developing countries[a]

Country	1975/80 $m	Percent[c]	Country	1990/96 $m	Percent[c]
Brazil	1,835.8	24.4	China	22,424.7	30.0
Mexico	1,023.5	13.5	Singapore	7,081.7	9.5
Malaysia	524.3	7.0	Mexico	5,622.1	7.5
Singapore	502.0	6.7	Malaysia	4,289.0	5.7
Egypt	376.1	5.0	Argentina	3,690.3	4.9
Iran	315.5	4.2	Brazil	3,222.7	4.3
Indonesia	289.9	3.8	Indonesia	2,842.6	3.8
Hong Kong	241.1	3.2	Thailand	2,179.9	2.9
Top 8	5,108.2	67.8	Top 8	51,353.0	68.7
All	7,539.1	100.0	All	74,777.6	100.0

Source: UNCTC (1988), UNCTAD (1995a, 1998).

NB: In the years 1975–1980, the 10 largest recipients of FDI identified in the above table accounted for 74.1% of all FDI inflows, and in 1990–1994 they accounted for 68.8%. In the former period, Japan accounted for only 0.6% of all inflows into developing countries; and in the latter for 1.0%.

Notes

a Bermuda was, in fact, ranked higher – sixth – but we have excluded the tax haven from our rankings.
b Of all developed country investment.
c Of all developing country investment.
d And Luxembourg.

developed countries, the standard deviation around the mean amount of inbound FDI of $1,265 million in the 1975–1980 period was $1,995 million; and for developing countries around a mean of $195 million, it was $354 million. The corresponding means and standard deviations for the average annual amount of FDI in the 1990–1994 period were $6,609 million and $8,848 million for developed countries, and $950 million and $1,335 for developing countries.

Explaining the changes in the geography of MNE activity

In explaining the changes in the geographical composition of FDI over the last 20 years, let us first consider the main changes in the global political and economic scenario over this period. Although there is no clear watershed date which initiated the changes, we believe that the beginning of the administrations of Margaret Thatcher in the UK (in 1979) and Ronald Reagan in the US (in 1980) offers as good as a dividing line between the two eras of FDI as any other. As these changes are fairly well known, we will do more than set them out in Table 7.3. We have done so sequentially, although we fully appreciate that many of these changes are interdependent of each other. It is, however, their combined effects on (a) the mobile competitive advantages of enterprises, and (b) the immobile locational attractions of countries, and on how these impact on the organization and geography of MNE activity, to which we wish to give special attention.

(a) The changing character of the O specific advantages of firms

Prior to the late 1970s, the main competitive advantages possessed by the foreign affiliates of MNEs over their indigenous counterparts (some of which, themselves, were MNEs) were their privileged access to specific intangible assets, e.g. technology, management and organizational skills, access to markets, etc. Elsewhere, we have termed these Oa advantages (Dunning 1993).[13] For the most part, too, the core competencies of MNEs reflected the resource endowments of their home countries, rather than those of the host countries in which they operated. Few MNEs, at that time, practiced globally integrated production or marketing strategies, although, within the European Union, there was some product and process specialization, and some intra-firm trade, particularly among US affiliates. While the propensity of MNEs to increase the foreign component of their total value-added activities was leading to more sequential or efficiency seeking FDI (Kogut 1983), the majority of firms pursued multidomestic strategies towards their global operations; and most foreign subsidiaries outside the resource based and labor intensive manufacturing sectors operated on a "stand alone" basis and traded little with each other.

In the 1970s scenario, in so far as the geography of FDI reflected the

Table 7.3 Some features of the changing world economic scenario: late 1970s to mid-1990s

---

1   The renaissance of the market economy, as the predominant form of economic organization by most countries. Along with such renaissance has come the liberalization, deregulation and privatization of markets which have lowered the artificial or man-made costs of the movement of goods, services and assets.

2   In the light of 1, the reorientation of the macro-economic and macro-organizational philosophies of national governments towards more market-enabling and less market-distorting policies – at least as far as wealth creating activities are concerned.

3   The coming on-stream of a new generation of technological advances, and particularly those in telecommunications, which has hastened the trend towards knowledge-based capitalism; and which, for the most part, has lowered the costs of transversing space, of assets, goods and people.

4   In the light of 1–3 above, the promotion of many regional economic schemes (notably the completion of the internal market in Europe, NAFTA, and ASEAN)

5   In the light of 1–4 above, the growing competition among firms – including firms of different nationalities. In a real sense, regional and global competition for resources and markets is replacing national competition – particularly in international industries

6   In the light of 1–5 above, firms have reorganized and restructured the range and composition of their value-added activities. Sometimes this has resulted in down-sizing and disinternalization of intermediate product markets; in other cases, it has prompted more M&As so that firms can better capture the benefits of economies of scale and scope; and acquire competitive-enhancing assets.

7   Partly as a consequence of 1–6, and the emergence of China, the newly industrializing countries (NICs) and some Central European economies, as important actors in the global market economy – each of which has different propensities both to be invested in – by foreign firms and to engage in outward foreign investment, the geography of FI has undergone some major changes since the mid-1970s.

---

distribution of the O specific advantages among firms of different nationalities, these also tended to reflect the structure of the natural and created assets, and the markets, of their home countries. There is ample empirical evidence, both of the geography of outward FDI, and of that of recipient countries attracting inward FDI, to support this assertion.[14] Moreover, these same O advantages help to explain at least some contemporary FDI – and particularly European and US FDI in Japan (Dunning 1997), Japanese FDI in the US (Hennart and Park 1994), and that by third-world MNEs (Dunning, van Hoesel and Narula 1998).

Over the last two decades, the nature and character of the competitive advantages of MNEs has changed. In general, their country of ownership has become a less important determinant, and their degree of multi-nationality – which is a firm-specific variable – a more important one. Moreover, although part of the core-competencies of firms continues to be the exclusive or privileged possession of specific assets, it is the way in which these assets are governed and co-ordinated with the assets of other firms, and with the L specific endowments of countries or regions in which they operate, which is increasingly driving the global strategy of MNEs, and the location of their various value-added activities.

The benefits of the common governance of inter-related cross-border operations embrace both lower transaction costs and greater co-ordinating benefits than those incurred or offered by external markets; and are particularly well demonstrated in the case of knowledge or learning-based firms with multiple home bases (Porter 1990). It is these firms which are best positioned to benefit from the liberalization of markets and regional integration; and, to foster an international division of labor based, not on the spatial disposition of natural resources, but on that of created assets. Often such a geography has very different implications for the location of MNE activity; this is because the critical determinants of the former, e.g. the quality and cost of natural resources and semi-skilled labor, are replaced by the availability of a supportive and sophisticated physical and human infrastructure, and the ease of access to global markets.[15]

In, perhaps, no other area of value-added activity have the changing O advantages of firms more affected the geography of FDI than that of research and development (R&D). Prior to the 1970s, there was comparatively little R&D – and particularly fundamental R&D – undertaken by MNEs outside their home countries; although there were some exceptions, e.g. that by MNEs from the UK, Canada and some smaller European nations, and in sectors such as food, beverages and pharmaceuticals, where local supply or demand conditions made it desirable for some R&D to be decentralized. However, even in these cases, the predominant motive for foreign-based innovatory activity was to adapt home-based R&D and create peripheral products and processes – i.e. what Kuemmerle (1999, p. 9) refers to as "home based exploiting R&D."

Over the last two decades, not only has the percentage of innovatory activity undertaken by MNEs outside their home countries risen sharply,[16] but the reasons for conducting such activity – at least in industrialized countries – have broadened to include both the creation of new core products and/or processes, and the acquisition of R&D facilities necessary to advance the productivity of domestic R&D; or, as Kuemmerle (1999) puts it, to "augment home based R&D." Such a strategy has very different locational implications than that of exploiting home-based R&D advantages; and, indeed, it suggests a more concentrated geographical pattern of FDI to take advantage of clusters of technological expertise and expense. Certainly, what little empirical evidence we have[17] supports this contention; and indicates that, in spite of the increase in the share of FDI directed to developing countries in recent years, the share of R&D activity so directed by MNEs may well have fallen.[18] This is not to say that MNEs are undertaking less R&D in developing countries, but that innovatory related FDI has not followed the same locational pattern as has that of other kinds of FDI.

(b) The changing character of the L advantages of countries

Not only has the widening and deepening of MNE activity from market-seeking and natural resource-seeking FDI to embrace efficiency and strategic asset-seeking FDI[19] required firms to reappraise their locational strategies, but world economic events have had a direct impact on the structure and character of the competitive advantages of countries.

In the 1970s, the locational advantages of countries lay primarily in their favored possession of natural resources and unskilled or semi-skilled labor, and their ease of access to markets for finished products. It was such L specific endowments which inbound foreign investors were seeking in order to add value to their mobile O specific advantages. Traditional location theory tended to classify the variables affecting the siting of foreign production into three groups, viz. those which were cost related, revenue related and profit related (Guisinger and associates 1985). Government imposed taxes or subsidies might be deployed to affect one or other of these variables, the significance of which depends on the type of FDI and the country in which it was being made. Most of the variables affecting FDI were common to foreign and domestically owned firms, although some, notably tax holidays, limitations on capital repatriation, and some performance requirements were specific to foreign investors (UNCTAD 1995a).

In some sectors, and for rationalized (i.e. efficiency-seeking) FDI, factors, which belong to the generic category of transaction costs and benefits, were also of some importance; and particularly those which offered the best opportunities to firms to exploit the economies of scale and scope, and to capture the benefits of the common governance of related activities. In the high technology and knowledge intensive sectors too, MNE affiliates, already well embedded in host countries, were attracted less by low cost labor and more by knowledge intensive labor to add value to the O specific assets being transferred from their home countries; and this was particularly so where the affiliates were responsible for complete product lines of their own. These same firms also made stronger demands on the local physical infrastructure, especially transport and communications, and frequently valued the presence of sub-national clusters of value-added activities related to their own.

Over the last two decades, this latter type of FDI activity has become increasingly significant, partly because the increasing degree of multinationality of many foreign investors has encouraged subsidiaries to engage in vertical or horizontal specialization, and partly because of the elimination, or reduction, of distance related transaction costs, especially between countries which are part of a customs union or free trade area, e.g. the

European Community. The growth of intra-firm, intra-regional trade has well outpaced that of inter-firm, inter-regional trade (UNCTAD 1995a, 1996, 1998). It is fashioning a geographical composition of FDI similar to that of intra-industry trade, and is less determined by the country-specific costs of factor endowments or size of local markets, and more by those variables which facilitate firm and/or plant economies of scale and scope,[20] and the effective exploitation of regional and/or global markets.

Most efficiency-seeking FDI in developing countries tends to be vertically integrated, with investors seeking locations which offer an adequate supply of cost-effective semi-skilled or skilled labor, a good physical infrastructure, government policies which are market friendly, and minimal distance related transaction costs. The external economies of clustering may also offer a locational attraction, particularly in countries whose overall industrial base leaves something to be desired. Such agglomeration economies, first explicitly identified by Alfred Marshall (1920), enable the participating firms to draw upon a common infrastructure, a specialized pool of labor or customers, develop mutually beneficial relations with their suppliers, and learn from local producer associations and their competitors. Hence, the development of export processing or free trade zones, and the deliberate attempts by local or central governments to facilitate industrial districts of one kind or another.[21] Examples of such economic activity in developing countries abound.[22] They are particularly numerous in those countries now attracting the bulk of new FDI in East Asia, viz. China, South Korea, Malaysia and Indonesia, and in Singapore, which, in effect, is a "city state."

By contrast, most horizontally integrated FDI is concentrated in the advanced industrial economies; and it is in these economies – and particularly in some of the knowledge intensive sectors – that one observes not only regional clusters of economic activity, but that FDI is especially drawn to these clusters. Again, as Chapter 6 has shown, there are many examples of recently formed clusters.[23] They include, in the US, an agglomeration of biotechnology and semi-conductor firms in the Silicon Valley/Bay area of California, and pharmaceutical and telecommunications firms in New Jersey; in the UK, a range of high-technology firms along the M4 corridor (particularly between Slough and Swindon), and financial services in the City of London; and in Japan, the clustering of the primal R&D plants semi-conductor firms in the Tokyo or Osaka Metropolitan regions (Arita and Fujita 1996).

There has, however, been another reaction of firms to recent economic events – and particularly the liberalization of markets and technological advances – which has had a no less critical impact on the spatial pattern of FDI, particularly among industrial countries. That has been the dramatic increase in the number of cross-border M&As and strategic alliances specifically aimed at protecting or enhancing the global profitability and/or market share of the participating firms. Between 1985 and 1996, for example, it is estimated that world-wide cross-border M&As accounted for around 55 percent of FDI outflows; and nearly four-fifths of those between developed countries (UNCTAD 1994, 1998). Similarly, the number of international inter-firm technology agreements concluded annually doubled between 1980–1983 and 1992–1996[24] (UNCTAD 1998).

The spatial implications of FDI by firms wishing to sustain or augment their existing O specific advantages, is that they will tend to acquire, or merge with, firms in other locations with a broadly similar, or more sophisticated, structure of natural and created assets to that of their own. Certainly, this applies to M&As and alliances designed to strengthen or complement the technological base of the investing companies, or to accelerate the innovating process. Such asset-seeking ventures, together with those aimed at facilitating access to unfamiliar markets, have accounted for a great majority of all cross-border liaisons in recent years (Hagedoorn 1993 and 1996; Narula and Dunning 1999).

By contrast, in the newly emerging markets, notably China, wholly or jointly owned greenfield ventures have been the main mode of entry by MNEs. According to UNCTAD (2000), over the last decade only one-fifth of cross-border M&As' activities took place in developing countries; although this ratio is now sharply increasing.[25] Indeed, one suspects – although there are few hard facts to support this suspicion – there has been more strategic asset-seeking FDI by Korean, Taiwanese, Malaysian, Thai and Brazilian firms in Europe and the US than there has been of European and US MNEs in Asia or Latin America; and that this has been particularly the case in the first part of the 1990s.

(c) Some changes in the modality of organizing the competitive advantages of firms

Finally, in this section of the chapter, we briefly consider the extent to which the geography of FDI may have been affected by changes in the modes by which firms co-ordinate their cross-border value activities. Our reading of the impact of recent world economic events on the organizational strategies of firms is that, notwithstanding the shedding of some activities by firms and the growth of inter-firm collaborative arrangements, FDI, as a vehicle for both exploiting and augmenting O specific advantages, has continued to rise in significance. But, in so far as we believe this to be the case for both developed and developing countries, the impact of the increased I advantages of firms may have had little impact on the geography of their value-added activity.[26] For, corresponding to the growth of efficiency-seeking FDI and asset-seeking M&As in developed countries, there has been a much more relaxed attitude to the foreign ownership of domestic assets in other parts of the world, notably in the erstwhile socialist regimes and several Asian and Latin American countries, e.g. Malaysia, Korea, Mexico and Chile. At the same time, the trend towards a reduction of intra-regional barriers to trade, and more integrated cross-border production networks – particularly by Japanese and other Asian MNEs in South and East Asia and by US MNEs in Latin America – is further accelerating the pace of FDI in these parts of the world.

So much, then, for our suggested reasons for the recent changes in the geography of FDI, which we have couched in terms of the OLI paradigm of international production. Table 7.4 summarizes our conclusions on this matter, which, as yet, have not been subject to any formal statistical testing.

Some country, sectoral and firm-specific factors affecting the geography of FDI

The impact of global economic events of the last decades on the OLI configuration of MNE activity is likely to differ according to their countries of origin, the range and nature of their value-added activities, and a variety of firm-specific structural and strategic-related variables. This means that, *inter alia*, changes in the geography of FDI may be the outcome of changes in the value of these contextual variables. Thus, it is possible – and, indeed, it is the case! – that the share of China of inbound FDI has increased because one of the major source countries – Hong Kong – has increased its FDI in China relative to that of other countries. Similarly, if high-value banking and financial services are primarily located in advanced industrial countries, then, if MNE activity in such services is growing relative to that in other sectors, *ceteris paribus*, one would expect the geography of FDI as a whole to favor those countries. Developing countries, on the other hand, appear to be the main recipients of capital inflows arising from privatization schemes and a revival of interest by foreign firms in infra-structural development projects (UNCTAD 1996).

Let us now consider some of the ways in which the changing composition of the main capital exporting countries, that of the sectoral pattern of economic activity and that of the characteristics and strategy of the leading MNEs has affected the spatial distribution of FDI over the past two decades.

(a) The structure of source countries

As Table 7.5 shows, the main change in the geographical composition of the stock of outward direct investment between 1973 and early 1996 was a 23.2 percent drop in the share of the US, which was matched by a 3.4 percent increase in the share of Japan, an 11.2 percent increase in that of Western Europe and other developed market economies, and a 7.6 percent increase in that of developing countries. Of the other developed countries, most increased their share of outbound FDI – and France,

Table 7.4 The new geography of FI: some suggested explanations couched in terms of the changing OLI configurations facing investing firms

	1975–1980	1990–1996
O advantages (of firms)	• Those associated with the possession of, or privileged access to, country-specific intangible assets, viz. technology, trademarks, managerial expertise, entrepreneurship; and access to factor, intermediate product or final goods markets	• Those associated with multinationality *per se* (Ot) • Organizational learning, and ability to seek out and exploit complementary assets • Ability to achieve an optimum portfolio of assets and to combine own O advantages with L specific endowments of foreign countries

L advantages (of countries)	• Traditional L specific variables related to
	  i domestic factor costs,
	  ii market size and growth, and
	  iii transport costs and tariff or other economic and psychic barriers
	• Government imposed incentives or obstacles to FDI, including performance requirements
	• A market facilitating macro-economic and/or macro-organizational environment offered by host governments
	• A stable political and economic regime
		• The provision of location-bound resources and capabilities which help firms both to exploit and to augment their existing competitive advantages
		• The continual upgrading of location bound assets so as to promote increasingly high-value FDI

I advantages (of firms)	• Those arising from the imperfect markets for specific intangible assets; and from learning experiences and governance of interrelated value-added activities, mainly in the domestic market	• Those arising from the ownership and/or control of interrelated activities in different geographical areas. These include spreading of political and environmental risks, and the holistic integration of disparate functions and strategies

Table 7.5 Stocks of FDI by major home countries and regions, 1973–1996

	1973 $b	Percent	1980 $b	Percent	1990 $b	Percent	1996 $b	Percent
Developed economies	205.0	98.5	508.0	98.8	1,614.6	95.9	2,830.9	90.9
Western Europe	82.6	39.7	236.6	46.0	853.9	50.7	1,584.8	50.9
of which: UK	27.5	13.2	80.4	15.6	230.8	13.7	355.1	11.4
France	8.8	4.2	23.6	4.6	110.1	6.5	202.2	6.5
Germany	11.9	5.7	43.1	8.4	151.6	9.0	291.7	9.4
Italy	3.2	1.5	7.3	1.4	56.1	3.3	107.5	3.5
Netherlands	15.8	7.6	42.1	8.2	109.1	6.5	192.8	6.2
Sweden	3.0	1.4	5.6	1.1	49.5	2.9	70.9	2.3
Switzerland	7.1	3.4	21.5	4.2	65.7	3.9	144.7	4.6
Other	5.5	2.6	13.0	2.5	81.0	4.8	173.4	5.6
North America	109.1	52.4	242.8	47.2	514.1	30.5	917.7	29.5
of which: US	101.3	48.7	220.2	42.8	435.2	25.8	793.0	25.5
Canada	7.8	3.7	22.6	4.4	78.9	4.7	124.7	4.0
Japan	10.3	4.9	19.6	3.8	204.7	12.2	258.6	8.3
Other developed countries	2.9	0.4	6.8	1.3	41.9	2.5	69.8	2.2
of which: Australia	1.0	0.5	2.3	0.4	30.1	1.8	46.0	1.5
Developing economies	3.0a	1.4	6.1	1.2	69.4	4.1	281.6	9.0
Central and Eastern Europe	Neg.	Neg.	0.1	Neg.	0.2	Neg.	3.3	0.1
Total	208.1	100.0	514.2	100.0	1,684.1	100.0	3,115.8	100.0

Source: UNCTC (1988), UNCTAD (1998).

Neg. = negligible

Note

a Calculated by deducting FDI outflows 1974–1979 from 1980 stock data (UNCTC 1988).

Germany, Italy, Australia, Spain and Belgium substantially so – but a few, notably the Netherlands, South Africa and the UK decreased theirs.

Two questions now arise. The first is: to what extent is the geography of FDI of the countries increasing their share of total FDI different from that of those decreasing their share? The second is: how far has this influenced the overall geography of FDI between 1975–1980 and 1990–1996?

Table 7.6 sets out some details on the geography of FDI of Western Europe, Japan and the US[27] for the latter half of the 1970s and for the first six years of the 1990s. What do they show? First, in both periods, they depict some major differences in the geography of FDI of the three regions or countries. Between 1975 and 1980, Japanese MNEs directed a considerably higher proportion of their investments to developing countries, and especially Asia, than did their European or US counterparts; by contrast, their share of the increased stock of FDI in Western Europe was less than one quarter of that of either US or European firms.[28]

Second, and perhaps more interestingly, one observes very different changes in the geography of FDI of the three major investors since the late 1970s. While Japanese MNEs have increased their foreign activities most sharply in the developed countries (and particularly in the US in the 1980s and Europe in the 1990s), US MNEs have reoriented their interests away from other developed countries. European investors, on the other hand, have been increasingly attracted to locations nearer home, especially since the initiation of the Internal Market Program of the European Community (EC) (Dunning 1997). Although not documented in Table 7.6, there was also a reorientation of FDI by third-world countries away from other developing countries – towards the advanced industrialized countries, in the 1980s (Dunning, Van Hoesel and Narula 1997); but in the 1990s, other developing countries, and especially China, have absorbed the great bulk of such investment (UNCTAD 1998).

Third, when comparing the spatial distribution of FDI of the three regions with that of all countries, it needs to be appreciated that the relative weight of the three regions as sources of FDI has shifted. As Table 7.5 has shown, taken as a group, Western Europe, Japan and the developing countries have increased their share of all FDI. Since in both periods, Japan and the Asian developing countries directed a much greater proportion of their FDI to other Asian countries, it is not surprising that the percentage of total FDI going to Asian developing countries – and China in particular – has risen so sharply. On the other hand, as the structure of the Japanese economy has moved closer to that of the leading European economies over the last two decades, so the industrial composition of its FDI has changed (Ozawa 1996); and it has changed in a way which has favored the advanced industrial countries as a location for both production and pre-production (e.g. R&D) activities.

We conclude: the data set out in Tables 7.5 and 7.6 suggest that the changing composition of total FDI reflects the changing geography of the

Table 7.6 Geographical distribution of changes in outward FDI stock, 1975–1980, and FDI flows, 1990–1996: USA, Western Europe and Japan

	1975–1980				1990–1996			
	USA	Western Europe[1]	Japan	All countries[2]	USA	Western Europe[6]	Japan	All countries[2]
Developed countries	78.2	81.1	45.7	76.6	63.1	62.8	65.5	77.2
Western Europe	48.4	40.7	9.2	43.1	49.2	45.7	15.5	38.5
(of which UK)	15.9	n.a.	n.a.	16.9	(16.9)	(5.7)	(7.0)	(9.4)
North America	20.4	32.8[3]	26.9[3]	27.2	7.9	15.4	46.3	20.3
(of which USA)	–	(32.8)	(26.9)	(24.5)	–	(14.2)	(44.7)	(18.1)
Japan	3.0	0.7	–	0.5	1.6	0.5	–	4.4
Other developed countries	6.4	13.7[4]	9.6[4]	5.7	4.5	1.1	3.7	7.0
(of which Australia and New Zealand)	(3.4)	(10.5)	neg.	(3.9)	(4.3)	(0.9)	(3.5)	(2.6)
Developing countries	21.8	18.9	53.9	23.4	35.9	36.8	34.2	21.5
Asia	2.8	6.3	27.7	6.2	9.8	2.1	24.0	15.2
(of which China)	(Neg.)	(Neg.)	(Neg.)	(Neg.)	(1.0)	(0.2)	(6.8)	(5.1)
Latin America	14.1	7.7	15.4	12.5	22.8	12.5	8.4	5.2
Africa	N/A	N/A	N/A	2.5	0.3	0.7	0.4	0.9
Other	4.9[5]	4.8[5]	10.8[5]	2.2	3.0	6.1	1.4	0.1
Central and Eastern Europe	neg.	0.1	0.3	neg.	1.0	0.5	0.2	1.4
Total	100.0	100.0	100.0	100.0	100.0	100.0	100.0	100.0
[Share of each region in total FI stock 1980 and 1996]	[42.0]	[45.0]	[3.7]	[100.0]	[25.4]	[50.9]	[8.3]	[100.0]

Source: 1975–1980 – changes in both stocks: UNCTC (1988). 1990–1994 FDI flows: OECD (1998).

Notes
1 UK, Germany and the Netherlands in 1980 accounted for between 70% and 75% of the total Western European outward FDI stock. The UK data are for 1974–1980 and the German data are for 1976–1980.
2 FDI flows of all countries for both periods. These data are not directly comparable with changes in stock data, and occasionally anomalies occur, e.g. as in the case of the Japanese data, where the US Department of Commerce estimates of changes in stock are considerably in excess of those derived by the IMF from Japanese balance of payments accounts.
3 US data.
4 Including Canada.
5 Including Africa and unallocated.
6 For UK, Germany, France, Italy, Netherlands, Switzerland and Sweden which accounted for 79.3% of the Western European outward FDI stock in 1996.
Neg. = negligible
N/A. = not applicable

leading source countries or regions, and their significance as foreign direct investors. Yet, to quite a large extent, these changes have cancelled themselves out. Thus, while Japanese investors have focused more attention on Europe and the US, US investors have been more attracted to the developing economies. Western European investors have continued to favor other industrialized nations, but some of the earlier appeal of the US has lessened, and particularly since 1989. And, while China has emerged as one of the three top recipients of FDI since 1990, the greater part of this inflow has originated, not from first-world MNEs, but from Chinese ethnic communities elsewhere in East Asia.

(b) The industrial composition of MNE activity

As the previous paragraphs have implied, the geographical patterns of Western European, US and Japanese MNE activity are, at least, partly based on the comparative resource endowments and market conditions of their home countries. Until very recently,[29] most scholars have opined that FDI is likely to be concentrated in sectors characterized by (one or more of three) features, viz.: (i) capital and/or knowledge intensity; (ii) product differentiation; and (iii) the provision of services which are supportive of other kinds of FDI, or information intensive, or are "branded" in some way or another. For much of the post-war period, the growth of FDI has been concentrated in these sectors – notably oil, autos, electronics and electrical equipment, office machinery, pharmaceuticals, packaged foods, banking and finance, business consultancies and trade related services; and, indeed, until the late 1980s, the share of the sales of foreign affiliates to the global sales of MNEs in these sectors continued to rise. It is, thus, understandable that countries which display a dynamic comparative advantage in those activities are those which have recorded the largest rise in their inbound FDI.

At the same time, over the last 20 years, a series of critical technological and organizational advances have affected not only the sectoral pattern of economic activity, but the very system within which the production of goods and services takes place. The features of this new production system – variously called "flexible," "lean" and "organcentric" production or Toyotaism – and how it differs from that which it is partly replacing, viz. "mass" production "scale" and "machinecentric" or Fordism, has been the subject of a large number of monographs and scholarly papers.[30] Sufficient for our purposes to observe that these systemic changes, coupled with the growing porosity of national boundaries, the increasingly generic and non-specific nature of many innovations, and the convergence of learning capabilities among networking firms, tending to blur the distinction between economic activities likely to be trade or FDI intensive and those which are not.

So far, these changes, which have been largely concentrated in the advanced industrial economies, have had only a limited affect on the geography of FDI. But, comparing the period 1990–1996 with that of 1975–1980, we might highlight two important developments. The first is the extension of the cross-border vertical division of labor to embrace higher value activities, and to take advantage of speedier, more efficient and less costly transportation and communication networks. The contemporary textile and clothing industry is an excellent example of a sector which has embraced a wide range of cross-border organizational arrangements, the success of which rests on the application of the latest technological advances, e.g. in computer aided design and manufacturing techniques; in the, near instantaneous, transfer of information, e.g. designs, specifications, process technologies and marketing schedules, by use of the Internet, fax or e-mail. Other traditional sectors also being upgraded and becoming more FDI intensive include building and construction, while the liberalization of markets and privatization schemes and the increasing tradability of many services[31] are resurrecting FDI as a delivery mode for a whole range of infrastructural products, notably telecommunications and public utilities, as well as those previously tightly regulated, e.g. banking and financial services, insurance and some professional services.

The second important development is the growing significance of intermediate and final services to foreign direct investors. In 1980, for example, 39 percent of the total FDI stock by US MNEs was in the tertiary sector, and 49 percent in the manufacturing sector; and the corresponding percentages for (the leading) European and Japanese MNEs were 40 percent and 37 percent, and 47 percent and 34 percent. By 1996, the percentages of all FDI accounted for by the tertiary sector had risen to 54 percent in the case of the US firms, 51 percent in the case of European firms, and 66 percent in the case of Japanese firms;[32] and that of manufacturing had fallen to 35 percent, 49 percent and 27 percent respectively (OECD 1998). On average, between 1980 and 1995, services accounted for a little over three-fifths of all new MNE activity; and, if one was also to include the services component of the goods produced in the manufacturing sector – and particularly knowledge-intensive goods – this proportion would probably rise to two-thirds, or even higher in the case of US MNE activity.

Statistical data on the geography of FDI in services are extremely patchy. We do know, however, that the strongest growth in MNE activity in services over the last 20 years has been among the triad nations. In the case of the country attracting the largest amount of FDI over this period, viz. the US, the share of the increase in the FDI stock directed to the tertiary between 1986 and 1997 was 53.0 percent (OECD 1998). Most of these new capital imports were from Western Europe and Japan; and they comprised both M&As and greenfield investments. Indeed, apart from in a few manufacturing sectors, notably autos and consumer electronics and electrical goods – Japanese MNEs have concentrated their foreign activities in financial, trading and transportation services and real estate.[33]

Between 1986 and 1994, no less than 72 percent of the increase in the FDI stock of Japanese firms was directed to the tertiary sector (UNCTAD 1993a; OECD 1998). In the EC too, over the last decade, the share of intra- and extra-EC FDI in services – particularly high-value services – has increased quite dramatically.

In many developing countries, too, the growth of inbound tertiary FDI has outpaced that of manufacturing FDI.[34] However, unlike service related MNE activity in the developed countries (apart from that of first time investors) much of that attracted to the developing world has taken the form of trade enhancing activities, or infrastructural investment, both of which are frequently a prelude to FDI, in the primary or secondary sectors. Thus, for example, since the late 1980s, in China and parts of Latin America, FDI inflows have been increasingly directed to privatization schemes in such services as electric power, telecommunications, hotels, and building and construction. Recent deregulation of some public utilities and parts of the financial services sector in India seems set to open the door to more service related MNE activity in that country.

In conclusion, while the implementation of new production systems and the move towards knowledge-based capitalism in the advanced industrial economies is reorienting the locational preferences of MNEs towards these economies; the emergence of powerful new nations in the third-world, and the liberalization and privatization of the markets for infrastructure and trade supporting services is resulting in a counteracting shift in the location of FDI towards the middle and lower income economies. At the moment, the net effect of these forces is favoring the industrialized countries, although one suspects that the current trend could well be reversed if, and when, the third-world countries increase their share of the world's output.

(c) *The changing profile of the leading MNEs*

The third contextual variable likely to influence the geography of FDI is that of the distinctive characteristics of the MNEs – once one has normalized for sector and country-specific differences. Such characteristics are of two main kinds. The first comprise the structural attributes of firms, e.g. their age, size, degree of multinationality, product range, innovating capabilities, degree of vertical integration and so on; and the second comprise their strategic actions or reactions towards the ownership and management of their core competencies, and the location of the value-added activities arising from, or associated with, these.

Because of space constraints, we shall confine ourselves to offering a few carefully selected facts about the geography of FDI of particular firms, and some speculation about the reasons for them, and the extent to which they might help explain the data set out in earlier tables. In our desire to control – as best as we can – for (source) country and sector differences, we shall limit our analysis to just six sectors – viz. oil refining, food products, chemicals, electronics, computers and autos. In the first two, we shall consider the FDI profile of US and European MNEs; the third, European MNEs; the fourth, Japanese and European MNEs; the fifth, US MNEs; and the sixth, MNEs from the US, Europe and Japan.

Table 7.7 sets out the details using an index of multinationality devised by UNCTAD (1995).[35] It presents a mixed picture. Take, first, the degree of multinationality of US firms in 1996. In the petroleum sector, the index varies from 23.4 percent to 72.7 percent, but there is high correlation between the degree of multinationality and size of enterprise (one of the structural variables earlier identified). The same is true of the three top US auto producers, although the variation in the degree of multinationality is somewhat less. In the food products and computer sectors, the degree of multinationality does not seem to be size related; rather, in this instance, one suspects it is the distinctive strategy of the firms – and particularly that of the chief executives of the firms towards foreign markets, which is the more important explanation. The multinationality index for European firms in food products, chemicals and electronics sectors shows a fairly uniform pattern, but here the *size* (e.g. population) *of the investing country* enters into the picture. In the chemicals sector, for example, Solvay, a Belgian firm and AKCO, a Dutch firm, exhibit well above the average multinationality ratio of the eight firms considered; while, in the electronics sector, Philips, from the Netherlands, and ABB (Asea Brown Boveri), a Swiss/Swedish firm, exhibit very high ratios indeed. More generally, normalizing for size of country, the UNCTAD data show a positive correlation between size of firm and degree of multinationality; while, in Western Europe, normalizing for size of firm, there is a negative correlation between size of country and degree of multinationality.

The multinationality of Japanese firms partly reflects their lateness in the internalization process; and partly that their average size (in 1996) was generally smaller than that of their European and US counterparts. Apart from Sony, all the Japanese electronics MNEs recorded lower indices of multinationality than their European competitors. In the auto industry, however, each of the Japanese producers registered average or above average degrees of multinationality compared to those of their US or European rivals.

Since the late 1970s, the growing significance of the foreign operations of the world's leading 100 industrial MNEs has largely mirrored that of the countries and sectors of which they are part. That of the Japanese firms has expanded the most (admittedly from a very low base), followed by that of Western European firms – and particularly those from Germany and France. On average, the degree of multinationality of US MNEs has changed very little – and has hovered around the 30 percent level (UNCTAD 1998).

However, within countries and sectors, some firms stand out above

Table 7.7 A selection of the largest MNEs classified by sector, country, size[1] and index of multinationality[2] (IM) 1985 and 1996

Petroleum refining

		IM 1985	IM 1996
(a) US			
Exxon	(4)	59.0	72.7
Mobil	(10)	57.2	62.3
Chevron	(45)	n.a.	35.3
Texaco	**(51)**	**42.6**	**44.6**
Amoco	*(66)*	*16.8*	*25.5*
Atlantic Richfield	*(93)*	*5.0*	*23.4*
(b) European			
(UK/N) Royal Dutch Shell	(2)	60.0	66.6
(F) Elf Aquitaine	*(13)*	*43.0*	*56.6*
(UK) BP	(25)	66.3	75.8
(I) ENI	*(27)*	*n.a.*	*63.8*
(F) Total	*(29)*	*n.a.*	*33.5*

Food products

		IM 1985	IM 1996
(a) US			
Philip Morris	(28)	28.0	47.8
Pepsico	**(88)**	**29.8**	**30.4**
Sara Lee (1995)	(90)	26.3	51.7
RJR Nabisco (1995)	**(90)**	**31.9**	**34.4**
(b) European			
Nestlé	**(11)**	**98.0**	**95.3**
(UK/N) Unilever	(18)	n.a.	87.1
(UK) Grand Metropolitan	**(69)**	**38.0**	**76.2**

Chemicals

		IM 1985	IM 1996
(a) European			
(G) Bayer	*(14)*	*50.0*	*79.9*
(G) Hoescht	*(15)*	*41.5*	*65.6*
(F) Rhone Poulenc	*(33)*	*32.9*	*67.4*
(C) Ciba Geigy (1995)	**(38)**	**66.5**	**58.2**
(G) BASF	(35)	30.2	59.2
(B) Solvay	(83)	89.5	92.2
(N) Akco	(79)	65.0	73.2
(Ny) Norsk Hydro (1994)	**(99)**	**73.6**	**43.5**

Electronics

		IM 1985	IM 1996
(a) Japanese			
Matushita	(53)	5.5	28.3
Sony	(24)	*20.7*	*60.5*
Hitachi	(60)	*15.0*	*20.0*
Toshiba	(91)	*6.0*	*24.0*
NEC (1995)	(93)	7.5	18.6
(b) European		1985	1996
(S) *ABB*[3]	(12)	*60.0*	*96.1*
(F) *Alcatel Alsthom*	(23)	*n.a.*	*62.9*
(N) **Philips**	(20)	**93.6**	**84.9**
(G) *Siemens*	(22)	*28.0*	*50.4*

Computers

		IB 1985	IB 1996
(a) US			
IBM	(6)	41.5	54.3
Hewlett Packard	(41)	37.1	50.0
Digital (1994)	(81)	*38.0*	*57.2*

Autos

		IM 1985	IM 1996
(a) US			
Ford	(3)	**41.0**	**37.7**
General Motors	(5)	**30.8**	**30.3**
Chrysler	(80)	16.0	16.3
(b) European		1985	1996
Volkswagen	(8)	*29.0*	*55.3*
Daimler Benz	(19)	*21.0*	*41.9*
Fiat	(17)	25.0	38.2
Renault	(30)	**31.8**	**43.2**
Volvo	(67)	*38.0*	*58.5*
Bosch	(47)	*25.0*	*62.4*
BMW	(37)	*15.0*	*59.1*
(c) Japan			
Toyota	(7)	*12.5*	*35.0*
Nissan	(16)	*n.a.*	*50.4*
Honda	(36)	*21.1*	*56.6*

Notes

Italic: below average growth of IM. Bold: above average growth of IM. Plain text: around average growth of IM.

1 Ranked (by size of foreign assets) of the 100 leading MNEs.

2 Defined as the average of the percentage of global assets, sales and employment of MNEs accounted for by their foreign affiliates.

3 Asea and Brown Boveri.

European country codes: B, Belgium; F, France; G, Germany; I, Italy; N, Netherland; Ny, Norway; S, Sweden; C, Switzerland; UK, United Kingdom.

others in the aggressiveness with which they pursue their FDI strategies. Of those listed in Table 7.7, those worthy of especial mention (their names are printed in italics) include the (relatively) smaller US oil refining companies Amoco and Atlantic Richfield; Volkswagen, Volvo, Bosch and BMW among the European auto companies; Hoescht, Rhone Poulenc, BASF and Bayer among the European chemical companies; ABB and Siemens among the European electronics companies; and Matushita, Sony and Toshiba among the Japanese electronics companies. In other sectors, Digital and IBM (US – computers), Philip Morris (US – tobacco), Glaxo (UK – pharmaceuticals), Grand Metropolitan (UK – food products) and Sara Lee (US – food products) each recorded substantial increases in their foreign participation ratios. It is, perhaps, worth observing that the growth in these ratios has been accomplished both by purchases of existing foreign firms, e.g. Grand Metropolitan's acquisition of General Mills in the US, and the merger between Asea and Brown Boveri to form ABB; and by aggressive greenfield investments, e.g. those undertaken by IBM, BMW and the Japanese electronics and auto companies in Europe and the US.

By contrast, in the case of those firms in bold print in Table 7.7, the index of multinationality has either declined or not kept pace with the average of the sector of which they are part. As far as MNEs from small countries are concerned, e.g. Sandoz, Ciba Geigy and Nestlé (Switzerland), Philips of Eindhoven (the Netherlands) and Solvay (Belgium), this is because the foreign, *vis à vis* the domestic component of their operations, was already very substantial indeed, in the early 1980s. Other MNEs have re-focused their attention on their domestic markets. For example, faced with intensive competition from their Japanese counterparts, US auto MNEs – and especially Ford and GM – completely reconfigured their domestic production systems in the late 1980s and early 1990s, and have since regained much of the US market they lost in earlier years. Domestic M&As have had an ambivalent effect, depending on the geography of the acquired firm's investment. Among the leading 100 MNEs whose index of multinationality has fallen, or has not kept pace with the average for their sector for this reason, are BAT Industries (UK – tobacco, cosmetics and insurance), AT&T (US – telecommunications equipment and services), Xerox (US – scientific and photographic equipment) and RTR Nabisco (US – food and tobacco products).

What, now, of the consequences of these shifts in the FDI profiles of some of the world's largest companies on the geography of FDI? Data constraints enable us to perform only the most superficial exercise. However, by comparing changes in the geography of the sales, assets or employment of firms according to the extent to which they had increased their index of multinationality in particular sectors and countries, we can gain a hint of the contribution of firm-specific factors to the changing spatial distribution of FDI.

We took our data from the 1980 and 1992 editions of *The World Directory of MNEs* (Stopford, Dunning and Haberich 1980; Stopford 1992). We calculated – in so far as the data allowed – the average rates of FDI growth for two groups of firms, in each of the main regions of the world. To obtain our groups, we simply divided the total number of firms into two and took the top and bottom growers in each industry/country subgroup.

The results of our exercise were somewhat inconclusive. While there is some suggestion that the MNEs with above average rates of growth grew relatively faster in Europe and North America than MNEs with below average rates of growth, this was not so in the case in developing countries; indeed, in Asia, the slower growing MNEs increased their share of total MNE activity.[36] However, since the number of sample observations was only very small (56), we believe more broader based research is necessary before we can draw any reasonable conclusions about the role of firm-specific factors in influencing the changing geography of FDI.

Summary and conclusions

The principal objective of this chapter has been to describe and offer some explanations for the changing geography of FDI between the second half of the 1970s and the first five years of the 1990s. The two periods were chosen to reflect the years immediately preceding the introduction of a series of critical and far reaching economic, political and technological events; and those after the most dramatic of these events – viz. the collapse of the command economic system of the Central and Eastern European economies – came into effect.

Our conclusions may be classified into two groups, viz. (1) those relating to the facts, and (2) those relating to the explanation of the facts.

In group (1), the main changes in the geography of the leading investing regions or countries between 1975–1980 and 1990–1996 are, first, the emergence of China as the second largest recipient of FDI. This surge of inbound FDI to the People's Republic explains a large part of new MNE activity directed to the developing countries since the late 1970s. Second, and more significant than the changing share of North/South FDI flows have been the changes in the distribution of North/North, and North/South flows. Thus, Western Europe – and, in particular, France and Spain – have gained as FDI recipients at the expense of Canada and the US; while the NICs of South and East Asia have become more attractive locales relative to most countries in Latin America. Third, while Africa continues to be of marginal interest to foreign investors, Central and Eastern Europe, and especially the Visegràd countries,[37] have begun to emerge as quite important recipients. Fourth, some of the traditional resource-based recipients of FDI, viz. Canada and Australia, have lost ground to the faster growing industrialized countries. Fifth, inward FDI going to Japan has increased only marginally over the last two decades. Sixth, there has been a slight fall in the geographical concentration of FDI among developed countries; and a slight rise of that among developing countries. However, excluding China, there has been a sharp reduction in the concentration of FDI among developing countries.

In group (2), in our explanations of these facts, we concentrated on five main factors:

(a) Changes in the geography of FDI, and/or the degree of multinationality of the investing firms, can be usefully explained by viewing the impact of global political and economic events on the configuration of OLI advantages facing foreign investors or potential foreign investors. After identifying these events, we concluded that both the core competencies of firms and the locational advantages of countries had undergone a number of profound changes (as summarized in Table 7.4); as, indeed, had the organizational modalities by which firms spatially reconfigured the creation and usage of their core competencies. In particular, we observed the rising importance of asset acquiring or augmenting FDI, particularly among triad countries; and of the need of firms to site their foreign activities in countries and/or regions which offered the quantity and quality of L bound created assets which best complemented their own O specific advantages. These developments have affected the geography of FDI in as much as firms increasingly favor locations which offer these facilities – the nature of which will vary to the type of value-added activity undertaken by MNEs, and particularly its technological and knowledge intensity.

(b) As might be expected, recent changes in the geography of FDI have reflected the composition of the countries of origin, the nature of the economic activities undertaken, and the structure and strategies of the participating firms. Between 1975–1980 and 1990–1996, the most significant growth in outward FDI was recorded by MNEs from Japan and from third-world countries (especially from ethnic Chinese communities); by contrast, the US MNEs achieved only a modest growth in their foreign activities. Since, as Table 7.3 shows, the geography of FDI by the faster and slower growers was quite different – especially within the developing economies – it is clear that part of the changes in its spatial distribution can be put down to the differential rate of growth of the leading outward investors. A good case in point is that of China – where three-quarters of the inward FDI over the past 15 years has originated from other Asian countries. By contrast, the decreasing share of US-owned MNE activity has meant a fall in the share of the total FDI directed to Latin America – an area in which US firms tend to invest proportionately more than those of MNEs from other countries.

(c) We have suggested that changes in the sectoral composition of economic activity have had a more ambiguous affect on the geography of FDI. This is because, on the one hand, the growth of the technology and knowledge industrial sectors and high-value service sectors have encouraged more FDI in the most advanced economies; on the other, the liberalization of many infra-structural service sectors, and the need by fast growing emerging economies for resource-based and/or market-seeking FDI has revitalized Heckscher-Ohlin type investment flows. This section of the chapter also stressed some of the (no less ambiguous) implications of the relatively faster growth in services FDI for the geography of FDI; and also those of the trend towards more flexible production systems, which, we suggested, favored the growth of small and medium size MNEs, and also the upgrading of both manufacturing and service activities in developing countries.

(d) We finally took a brief look at the implications for the geography of FDI of the different rates of growth of some of the leading MNEs from six industries and three groups of investing countries (or regions). While we could find no satisfactory comprehensive explanation for the changing locational strategies of the faster, cf. the slower, growing MNEs, we were able to conclude that, first the larger firms of the leading 100 industrial MNEs generally demonstrated a higher index of multinationality than their smaller counterparts; and second, that firms with the lower indices of multinationality in 1980 tended to record higher than average rates of FDI growth over the following decade. Both of these facts tend to support our earlier proposition that the strategic response of MNEs to the emerging global economy is to increasingly integrate their sourcing value-added and marketing activities, and to harness their resources and capabilities from throughout the world.

(e) Finally, it is worth pointing out that much of the data set out in this chapter do not include the effects of the Asian crisis of 1997 and 1998.

NOTES

Source: This chapter contains material originally presented at a workshop on *Foreign Investment and Economic Development* in Maastricht in November 1996, which was organized by UNITECH. A longer, but less contemporary, version of this chapter was included in an edited volume by Kumar (1998).

1 Throughout this chapter, FDI stocks or flows are used as proxies for the value-added activities of firms which own or control such activities outside their national boundaries (i.e. MNEs). Though an imperfect measure of these activities, the FDI data, published by all the major countries in the world are broadly comparable. This is not the case with other data, e.g. sales, net output or employment.

2 At the time of writing, 1996 was the latest year for which detailed data on FDI stock and flows are available. These do not fully take into account the effects of the East Asian crisis nor the problems of the Russian economy. However, preliminary data for 1997 suggest that FDI inflows to South East and South Asia were 6.2 percent higher than those for 1996, which in turn were 16.6 percent above those for 1995. By contrast, foreign portfolio capital inflows dropped

dramatically; indeed there was a net exodus of capital from the region in 1997. FDI outflows from the region in 1997 were also marginally higher than those in 1996 ($50.2 billion, cf. $47.4 billion). Rather surprisingly, FDI inflows into the Russian Federation more than doubled from $2.5 billion to $6.2 billion in 1997 (UNCTAD 1998).

3 The OLI configuration, explaining the extent and pattern of the foreign value-added activities was first put forward by the author in the mid-1970s. For a recent exposition of the eclectic paradigm of international production, see Dunning (1995a, 2000).

4 Of course, we accept that there are other modalities than FDI in promoting the cross-border mobility of goods, services and assets. Indeed, it is likely – though this is very difficult to quantify – that non-equity strategic alliances and networking have become increasingly important vehicles for the transfer of assets, particularly intangible assets, over the past two decades. See particularly, in this connection, the work of John Hagedoorn and his colleagues at MERIT and the University of Limburg.

5 These latter we have termed strategic asset-acquiring advantages (Dunning 1993). In the last decade, FDI of this kind – particularly that by firms investing in advanced industrialized countries by way of M&A – has become one of the dominant factors affecting the geography of FDI.

6 For further details, see Section 3, p. 9 and Kenney and Florida (1993, 1994).

7 We chose the former period as this was immediately prior to the wave of liberalizing markets, and the current generation of technological advances.

8 See, for example, IMF (vd), UNCTAD (1996).

9 Previously called the European Community. We have taken the composition of the EU to be that existing on 1st January 1995 for all years discussed in this chapter.

10 The US, in particular, substantially increased its share of worldwide FDI in the 1980s. Between 1983 and 1989 it accounted for 42.6 percent of all inflows, compared with 24.5 percent in 1975–1980. However, between 1990 and 1996, its share fell back to 19.1 percent.

11 In the case of both Africa and West Asia, it was the oil exporting countries which recorded the least gains, and, indeed, in the 1990s, the flow of new investment has been less than one-half that of the second half of the 1980s.

12 India, for example, recorded a nine-fold increase in direct investment inflows between 1990–1992 and 1994–1996. The Central and Eastern European countries recorded a five-fold increase.

13 a standing for assets.

14 The kind of O advantages which scholars, in the 1970s, used to explain FDI are set out in Dunning (1993) and Caves (1996). The ones which consistently offered the greatest explanatory power were proprietary knowledge and product differentiation, and access to markets. For a more extensive examination of the role of country specific variables in affecting the O specific advantages of firms, see Dunning (1990).

15 So called O_t advantages (t standing for transactions) in the literature.

16 In 1993, US firms conducted 13.0 percent of their R&D outside their home country; the Japanese were increasingly establishing R&D facilities in Europe; while in the US, foreign firms accounted for 15.5 percent of total R&D expenditures in 1991, compared with 4.8 percent in 1977 (Dunning and Narula 1995).

17 Also by USA MNEs in the UK. For examples, see Dunning (1958).

18 One of the reasons for this is that part – and probably an important part – of the growth of foreign-based R&D has taken the form of acquisition rather than of greenfield R&D. In the US, almost four-fifths of the total investment outlays by foreign direct investors in the 1980s was through the purchase of existing US businesses.

19 We accept there are certain parallels between the kind of FDI designed to acquire natural resources in the nineteenth and early twentieth century, and that designed to acquire created assets, notably technology, information and learning experience of the 1980s and 1990s. Both were (or are) aimed at facilitating, or enhancing, the use of the existing O advantages of the investing companies; and both were (or are) frequently prompted by aggressive, or defensive, production, marketing and innovatory strategies of large oligopolists.

20 For a recent review of the interaction between trade and location theory see a special edition of the *Oxford Review of Economic Policy 14* (2), Summer 1998. For an examination of the evolving relationship between modern trade and FDI theory, see Dunning (1995b), Markusen (1995) and Markusen and Venables (1995); and for a discussion of the changing locational attributes sought after by MNEs see Kozul-Wright and Rowthorn (1998) and Dunning (1998).

21 For a description of the various kinds of industrial districts, see Harrison (1992), Gray, Golog and Markusen (1996), Park and Markusen (1995), Enright (1998) and Saxenian (1994). See also Chapter 6 of this volume.

22 See, for example, Park and Markusen (general) (1992), Park and Markusen (Korea) (1995), Ohmae (China) (1995) and Balasubramanyan and Balasubramanyan (India) (1996).

23 Industrial clusters are, of course, not confined to high technology firms. Examples of the concentration of more traditional industries are to be found in Porter (1990), Enright (1998, 1999) and Harrison (1994). However, one's sense is that, in the contemporary global economy, these clusters are becoming more, rather than less, important.

24 I.e. from 280 to 631. For further details of strategic alliances in higher technology sectors see Hagedoorn (1993 and 1996) and Narula and Dunning (1999).

25 In 1996 and 1997 cross-border M&A sales involving developing countries amounted to $178,656 million compared with $133,729 in 1994–1995 and $89,844 million in 1992–1993 (UNCTAD 1998, p. 413).

26 We would emphasize that our assertion that FDI continues to be a major mode for exploiting or acquiring the O specific advantages of firms in no way negates the proposition that firms need to engage in more co-operative ventures in order to best protect or enhance these advantages. In practice, however, many of these co-operative ventures will be between institutions *within* particular countries rather than *across* countries.

27 These data are culled mainly from OECD (1998), UNCTC (1988) and UNCTAD (1995 and 1998). In turn, these data were initially obtained from those published by the IMF (vd), based on balance of payments statistics and those directly provided by national authorities of FDI stocks and/or flows.

28 Unlike its US and Japanese counterparts, Western Europe FDI *includes* intra-regional FDI – which, as the table reveals, has increased substantially over the last 20 years. Were such FDI *excluded* from the data, its pattern of FDI would look very different indeed.

29 We write "very recently" as it has only been in the last five years that substantial MNE activity has occurred in sectors in which there was previously no, or little, foreign investment. For an examination of the recent surge in FDI in infrastructure development, see UNCTAD (1996).

30 We will not even attempt to catalogue these, but one very recent analysis of the interface between the new system and the globalization of economic activity is that by Ruigrok and van Tulder (1995).

31 The increasing tradability of services is a two-edged sword as far as FDI is concerned. On the one hand, it opens doors for trade in services previously

closed; on the other, it facilitates the kind of FDI which, itself, makes for more intra-country (and intra-firm) trade in services.

32 1994 data.

33 The retrenchment in Japanese FDI in the US since the early 1990s explains why between 1994 and 1997 the share of new FDI in the service sector fell to 47.8 percent (OECD 1998).

34 Although, as a proportion of total FDI, it is still below that of most developed countries. In 1993, for example, 33 percent of the stock of inbound FDI in Taiwan was in the tertiary sector (compared with 20 percent in 1980). The corresponding percentages for Korea were 37 percent and 21 percent (UNCTAD 1995).

35 This essentially represents an average of three measures of multi- or trans-nationality, viz. share of foreign sales to total sales, share of foreign assets to total assets, and share of total employment. This index was calculated for the top 100 MNEs in 1994, its total employment, ranked by their foreign assets.

36 This, for example, the average ratio between the 1990 and the 1978 share of the sales (and or employment) of foreign affiliates in Europe, relative to all foreign sales of MNEs in the top half of the industry/country groupings, was 1.15; and for MNEs with below average it was 1.05; corresponding ratios for North America were 1.97 and 1.31. For developing countries, the ratios for Asia were 0.94 and 1.35; and for Latin America 0.93 and 0.90. It will be observed that the time period chosen for this exercise was that in which the share of all FDI in the US increased sharply.

37 Viz. the Czech Republic, Hungary and Poland. These countries accounted for 69 percent of the region's stock on inbound FDI in 1994 (UNCTAD 1995, p. 100).

REFERENCES

Arita, T. and Fujita, M. (1996), *Local Agglomeration and Global Networks of the Semiconductor Industry: A Comparative Study of US and Japanese Firms,* University of Pennsylvania and Kyoto University (mimeo).

Balasubramanyan, V. N. and Balasubramanyan, A. (1996), *Software in South India,* The Management School: Lancaster University.

Caves, R. (1996), *Multinational Firms and Economic Analysis* (2nd edn.), Cambridge: Cambridge University Press.

Dunning, J. H. (1958), *American Investment in British Manufacturing Industry,* London: George Allen and Unwin, reprinted by Arno Press, New York 1958. (Updated and revised edition published by Routledge: London and New York in 1998.)

Dunning, J. H. (1990), *The Globalization of Firms and the Competitiveness of Nations,* Lund, Sweden: University of Lund (The Crafoord Lectures 1989), pp. 9–57.

Dunning, J. H. (1993), *Multinational Enterprises and the Global Economy,* UK: Addison Wesley.

Dunning, J. H. (1995a), "Reappraising the eclectic paradigm in the age of alliance capitalism," *Journal of International Business Studies 26* (3), pp. 461–91.

Dunning, J. H. (1995b), "What's wrong – and right – with trade theory?", *International Trade Journal IX* (2), pp. 153–202.

Dunning, J. H. (1996), "Explaining foreign direct investment in Japan: some theoretical insights," in M. Yoshitomi and E. Graham (eds), *Foreign Direct Investment in Japan,* London: Edward Elgar, pp. 8–63.

Dunning, J. H. (1997), "The European Internal Market Program and inbound foreign direct investment," *Journal of Common Market Studies 35* (1), pp. 1–30.

Dunning, J. H. (1998), "Location and the multinational enterprise: a neglected factor," *Journal of International Business Studies 29* (1), pp. 45–66.

Dunning, J. H. (2000), "The eclectic paradigm as an envelope for economic and strategic theories of MNE activity", *Business Review 9*, pp. 163–90.

Dunning, J. H. and Narula, R. (1995), "The r&d activities of foreign firms in the US," *International Studies of Management and Organization 25*, Nos 1–2, Spring–Summer, pp. 39–75.

Dunning, J. H., van Hoesel, R. and Narula, R. (1996), "Explaining the new wave of outward FDI from developing countries," Maastrict MERIT, occasional paper 2/96013.

Enright, M. J. (1998), "Regional clusters and firm strategy," in Chandler Jr., A. D., Hagström, P. and Sölvell, Ö. (eds), *The Dynamic Firm, The Role of Technology, Strategy, Organization and Regions,* Oxford: Oxford University Press, pp. 315–42.

Enright, M. J. (1999), "The globalization of competition and the localization of competitive advantage: policies towards regional clustering," in Hood, N. and Young, S. (eds), *The Globalization of Multinational Enterprise Activity,* London: Macmillan, pp. 303–31.

Gray, A., Golog, E. and Markusen, A. (1996), *Big Firms, Long Arms, Wide Shoulders: The Hub and Spoke Industrial District in the Seattle Region, Regional Studies* 30(7), pp. 651–66.

Guisinger, S. E. (1985), and associates, *Investment Incentives and Performance Requirements,* New York: Praeger.

Hagedoorn, J. (1993), "Strategic technology alliances and modes of cooperation in high technology industries," in Grabher G. (ed.), *The Embedded Firm,* London and Boston: Routledge, pp. 116–37.

Hagedoorn, J. (1996), "Trends and patterns in strategic technology partnering since the early seventies," *Review of Industrial Organization 11*, pp. 601–16.

Harrison, B. (1992), "Industrial districts: old wine in new bottles," *Regional Studies 26* (5), pp. 469–83.

Harrison, B. (1994), *Lean and Mean: The Changing Landscape of Corporate Power in the Age of Flexibility,* New York: BasicBooks.

Hennart, J. F. and Park, Y. R. (1994), "Location, governance and strategic determinants of Japanese manufacturing investment in the US," *Strategic Management Journal 15*, pp. 419–36.

IMF, *Balance of Payments Yearbook* (summary tables) (Washington: IMF, vd).

Kenney, M. and Florida, R. (1993), "The organization and geography of Japanese R&D: results from a survey of Japanese electronics and biotechnology firms," *Research Policy 23*, pp. 305–23.

Kenney, M. and Florida, R. (1994), "The globalization of Japanese R&D: the economic geography of Japanese R&D investment in the US," *Economic Geography 70* pp. 344–69.

Kogut, B. (1983), "Foreign direct investment as a sequential process," in Kindleberger, C. P. and Audretsch, D. B. (eds), *The Multinational Corporation in the 1980s,* Cambridge, MA: MIT Press.

Kozul-Wright, R. and Rowthorn, R. (1998), "Spoilt for choice? Multinational corporations and the geography of international production," *Oxford Review of Economic Policy 14*, 2, pp. 74–92.

Kuemmerle, W. (1999), "The drivers of foreign direct investment into research and development: an empirical investigation", *Journal of International Business Studies 30* (1), pp. 1–24.

Kumar, N. (1998), *Globalization, Foreign Direct Investment and Technology Transfers* (ed.), London and New York: Routledge, in collaboration with United Nations Press.

Markusen, J. R. (1995), "The boundaries of multinational enterprises and the theory of international trade," *Journal of Economic Perspectives 9* (2), pp. 169–89.

Markusen, J. R. and Venables, A. (1920), *Multinational Firms and the New Trade Theory,* Cambridge, MA: NBER Working Paper No. 5036, February (1995).

Marshall, A. *Principles of Economics,* 8th edn. London: Macmillan.

Narula, R. and Dunning, J. H. (1999), "Technocratic-corporate partnering, extending alliance capitalism," in Boyd, G. and Dunning, J. H. (eds), *Structural Change and Cooperation in the Global Economy,* Cheltenham, UK and Northampton, MA, USA: Edward Elgar.

OECD (1998), *International Direct Investment Statistics Year Book 1998,* Paris: OECD.

Ohmae, K. (1995), *The End of the Nation State: The Rise of Regional Economies,* London: Harper.

Ozawa, T. (1996), "Japan: the macro-IDP, meso-IDPs and the technology development path (TDP)," in Dunning, J. H. and Narula, R. (eds), *Foreign Direct Investment and Governments,* London and New York: Routledge, pp. 142–73.

Park, S. O. and Markusen, A. R. (1992), *New Industrial Districts: A Critique and Extension from the Developing World* (paper presented at the Symposium of the IGU Commission on Industrial Change, Time, Space, Competition and Contemporary Industrial Change, Florida, August.

Park, S. O. and Markusen, A. R. (1995), "Generalizing new industrial districts: a theoretical agenda and an application from a non-Western economy," *Environment and Planning A 27,* pp. 81–104.

Porter, M. E. (1990), *The Competitive Advantage of Nations,* New York: The Free Press.

Ruigrok, W. and Val Tulder, R. (1995), *The Logic of International Restructuring,* London and New York: Routledge.

Saxenian, A. L. (1994), *Regional Advantage: Culture and Competition in Silicon Valley and Route 128,* Cambridge, MA: Harvard University Press.

Stopford, J. M. (1992), *The World Directory of Multinational Enterprises* (1992 edn.), Basingstoke: Macmillan.

Stopford, J. M. (1980), Dunning, J. H. and Haberich, K. O. *The World Directory of Multinational Enterprises,* Basingstoke: Macmillan.

UNCTAD (1993a), *World Investment Report 1993: Transnational Corporations and Integrated Production,* New York and Geneva: UN.

UNCTAD (1993b), *World Investment Directory Vol. III: Developed Countries,* New York: UN.

UNCTAD (1994), *World Investment Report 1994: Transnational Corporations, Employment and the Workplace,* New York and Geneva: UN.

UNCTAD (1995), *World Investment Report 1995: Transnational Corporations and Competitiveness,* New York and Geneva: UN.

UNCTAD (1996a), *World Investment Report 1996, Transnational Corporations, Investment, Trade and International Arrangements,* New York and Geneva: UN.

UNCTAD (1996b), *Incentives and Foreign Direct Investment,* Geneva and New York: UN.

UNCTAD (1998), *World Investment Report 1998: Trends and Determinants,* New York and Geneva: UN.

UNCTAD (2000), *World Investment Report 2000: Cross Border Mergers and Acquisitions and Development,* New York and Geneva: UN.

UNCTC (1988), *Transnational Corporations and World Development,* New York: UN.

8 Globalization and FDI in Asian developing countries

Introduction

This chapter seeks to do three main things. First it examines the extent to which Asian developing countries have participated in the trend towards a globalizing world economy over the past two decades or so. Second, it looks more specifically at the ways in which one of the main engines of globalization, viz. inbound investment by foreign institutions and individuals in Asia and outbound investment by Asian multinational enterprises (MNEs) and individuals have contributed towards a deepening economic interdependence between Asian countries and the rest of the world. Third, it presents some recently published data on trends of European foreign direct investment (FDI) in Asian developing countries, and of how some 310 leading MNEs and international experts, view future corporate investment priorities up to the year 2001.

Where possible, we shall adopt a three-fold classification of Asian developing countries, which corresponds to that used by the UNDP,[1] viz. high human development (HHD), medium human development (MHD) and low human development (LHD) countries. The Human Development Index, compiled by the UNDP, while incorporating gross domestic product (GDP) per capita, also embraces other variables such as life expectancy and adult literacy. A list of the Asian countries assigned to each group is set out in Appendix 1. We are aware that there are other criteria for classifying Asian developing countries, apart from their stage of human development. For example, in some situations, size is a critical variable; and, where appropriate, we shall distinguish between small and medium to large Asian countries.

The contents of this chapter will be mainly descriptive, and no formal econometric analysis of the data will be undertaken. However, we will attempt to relate our statistical findings to the main body of extant theory; and also offer some additional hypotheses of our own.

Globalization and developing countries

Our interpretation of the term globalization, and of how it differs from internationalization is contained in a quotation by Anthony McGrew in a jointly edited book *Globalization and the Nation State* which was first published in 1992:

> Globalization refers to the multiplicity of linkages and interconnections between the states and societies which make up the present world system. It describes the process by which events, decisions, and activities in one part of the world come to have significant consequences for individuals and communities in quite distant parts of the globe. Globalization has two distinct phenomena: scope (or stretching) and intensity (or deepening). On the one hand, it defines a set of processes which embrace most of the globe or which operate world-wide: the concept therefore has a spatial connotation On the other hand it also implies an intensification on the levels of interaction, interconnectedness or *interdependence* between the states and societies which constitute the world community. Accordingly, alongside the stretching goes a deepening of global processes.
>
> (McGrew and Lewis 1992, p. 23)

In short, then, globalization is leading to the structural transformation of firms and nations, and is creating new relationships and new dependencies. Sometimes, the transformation takes place at a regional level: much of the integrated production networks of MNEs is so focused. Sometimes, it occurs at a global level. For example, the contemporary global financial system is one in which national markets throughout the world, though physically separate, operate as if they are in the same place (Stopford and Strange 1991). One scholar has put it even more dramatically by averring that global financial integration is "the end of geography."[2]

The main causes of globalization are well known. I shall focus on just two. The first is the pressure on firms – by consumers and competitors alike – to continually innovate new products and upgrade the quality and/or reduce the price of existing goods and services. At the same time, the escalating costs of research and development, coupled with ever shortening product life cycles, are compelling firms both to curtail the scope of their value-added activities and to search for wider markets. Moreover, in order to effectively and speedily exploit their core competencies, firms are finding they need to combine these with the core competencies of other firms and those of governments. Hence, the emergence of strategic alliances and networks which, together with FDI, are the main instruments fashioning deep economic interdependence.

The second cause of globalization – which in many ways is better described as a removal of an obstacle – is the renaissance of market supporting policies pursued by national governments; and the growth of market led regional integration. In the last five years alone, more than 30 countries have abandoned central planning as the main mode of allocating scarce resources; while, as we shall see later, over 80 have liberalized their inward FDI policies. The privatization of state-owned enterprises, the liberalization and deregulation of markets – especially for services – and the removal of a bevy of structural distortions, have all worked to stimulate cross-border corporate integration, both within MNEs and between independent firms, or groups of firms.

In this chapter we will consider just eight indices of globalization and Table 8.1 sets out how these vary between the three groups of Asian developing economies, other developing countries, developed countries and all countries. These indices are:

1   Trade as a percent of GDP in 1996.
2   Changes in (1), 1980–1996.
3   Share of world exports of "growth" products, 1995.
4   Changes in (3), 1980–1995.
5   Inward plus outward direct investment stock as a percentage of GDP, 1996.
6   Changes in (3), 1980–1996.
7   Inward plus outward foreign portfolio investment as a percentage of GDP, 1996.
8   Changes in mergers and acquisitions, 1990–1996.
9   Use of international communications media, 1994.

The findings of Table 8.1 are self-evident. Briefly highlighted they are:

- Asian economies are more globalized than other developing economies; and enjoy a larger share of the exports of "fast growth" products of the OECD. As might be expected, smaller Asian countries tend to be more globalized than their larger counterparts.
- The propensity of Asian economies to be more deeply integrated into a global economy tends to increase as economic development proceeds. As other research (Dunning 1981, 1986 and Dunning and Narula 1996) has shown, there is a GNP per capital threshold before a country is able to attract substantial amounts of inward direct investment and another threshold before it engages in outward direct investment. These thresholds are also seen to vary with the size, industrial structure and general economic environment of the developing countries, but, as identified in Table 8.1, only Group 1, Asian and a handful of Latin American countries are experiencing "balanced" globalization – by which we mean they are: (a) sharing in export growth of dynamic products; (b) are engaging in outward as well as inward and outward FDI and merger and acquisition activity; and (c) make good use of international communications facilities.

Table 8.1 Indices of globalization of Asian economies, 1980–1996

	Trade				Foreign investment				International communications	
	% of GDP 1996	Change % 1980–1996 trade[a]	% of growth trade[a]	Change % of growth trade	FDI as % of GDP 1996	Change % 1990–1996	FPI as % of GDP 1996	Change M&As 1990–1996	Int. Tel.[b] Calls 1994	Internet[c] Users 1994
1. Asian developing economies	72.1	489.1	384.6	134.8	26.7	1,196.9	19.5	491.7	32.9	16.6
a. Group 1	114.5	580.3	596.4	47.3	31.5	1,246.3	26.5	302.9	97.2	49.6
b. Group 2	45.2	419.5	381.4	293.1	25.9	2,123.3	10.7	317.9	1.2	0.2
c. Group 3	20.3	190.9	176.0	64.1	3.1	721.4	2.8	7,005.5	0.4	0.0
2. Latin American economies	24.8	106.9	122.1	72.6	18.8	586.8	34.1	164.2	N/A	N/A
3. African economies	134.1	29.53	−47.7	N/A	44.9	443.9	N/A	996.1	N/A	N/A
a. Sub-Sahara	N/A	N/A	−29.3	N/A	29.4	112.1	N/A	200,094.1	1.4	N/A
b. Other	N/A	N/A	4.6	N/A	12.1	300.5	N/A	896.1	N/A	N/A
4. All developing economies	62.1	178.4	92.8	N/A	20.5	853.8	25.6	358.8	2.5	1.5
5. All industrial economies	25.4	165.9	186.8	N/A	17.7	462.2	46.5	40.4	35.1	232.2
6. All economies	36.8	170.0	157.8	N/A	21.4	515.3	50.6	71.7	9.4	60.9
7. Smaller Asian economies[1]	174.1	581.4	585.5	34.3	58.8	1,321.2	58.8	170.6	81.8	32.0
8. Larger Asian economies[2]	43.2	532.4	411.4	165.3	15.2	8,815.6	3.1	930.2	1.6	2.2

Source: World Investment Report, 1998a; World Economic Forum; The World Competitiveness Report, 1998; UNDP Human Development Report, 1997; The IMF Balance of Payments Statistics, 1985, 1998.

N/A = Not available

Notes
1 Defined as countries with a population of 20 million or less in 1996.
2 Defined as countries with a population of over 20 million in 1996.
a For 1995 data.
b Minutes per person 1994.
c Per 100,000 people 1994.

- Almost certainly part of the more outward looking stance of Asian (and other developing countries) reflects a trend towards regionalization, rather than globalization. Thus, for example, it was estimated (UNCTAD 1997) that 75 percent of all inward direct investment in Asian developing countries between 1990 and 1995 originated from elsewhere in Asia, while about the same proportion of the manufacturing exports from these same countries in 1995 went to other Asian countries. On the other hand, it is clear that Asian developing countries are gaining an increasing share of world *outward* FDI – or at least they were up to 1996[3] – as their own firms take a more global perspective on the sourcing of products such as footwear, clothing, consumer electronics, semi-conductors, toys, computer software and some kinds of technology; and as they seek to make inroads into European and US markets.
- There is some suggestion that an increasing proportion of cross-border-strategic alliances are now involving Asian firms. According to a survey of Booz, Allen and Hamilton (1997), the average value of a cross-border strategic alliance concluded by Japanese and other Asian firms was four times greater than that of US firms in the mid-1990s; while approaching two-thirds of developing Asia is viewed by the leading Western MNEs as offering the best prospects for new forms of cross-border collaboration, for acquiring complementary technological and other skills, and for exploiting new markets.

What are the main explanations for the facts just described? We might highlight just three of these. The first is the increased liberalization of markets in Asian developing countries, and a more positive attitude to the inbound investment, and a growing belief that, to be competitive in international markets, the leading Asian firms need to engage in outward direct investment. Almost certainly, one important contributor to the recent economic crises in the Far East was the imprudent haste at which both firms and governments of Asian developing countries tried to "catch up" with their Western counterparts.

The second factor is the growing competition among firms – and particularly MNEs from industrialized countries – both to protect existing and to exploit new markets, and to be more cost effective in their global sourcing and production strategies. This has fostered a new international division of labor; and, because of their favorable real costs, and investment incentives offered by their governments relative to those of their competitors, Asian developing countries have gained the lion's share of new FDI and inward strategic alliance over the last decade.[4]

The third factor is the forceful, yet market friendly, development strategies pursued by governments of Asian developing countries, which in the main have been consistent with the tenets of globalization (and increasingly so over the last decade). However, again, through zealous and incautious expansionist macro-economic policies, and the fostering of easy credit by the financial sector, Asian governments may well have contributed towards the economic downturn and growing indebtedness of their economies in the mid and late 1990s.

Foreign investment and the deepening interdependence of the Asian economies

One of the key attributes of a deepening economic dependence, or interdependence, of a country with the rest of the world is the extent to which that country is invested in by foreign institutions and individuals, and/or the extent to which its own institutions and individuals invest in other countries.

In this section we shall primarily concentrate on foreign direct investment (FDI) as a globalizing vehicle. However, in so far as the growth of inbound foreign portfolio investment (FPI) mirrors the strength and vitality of the local capital market, and the confidence with which foreign institutions view the local economy, while outbound FPI normally reflects the availability of locally generated savings, and the perceived opportunities for investing in foreign countries, we shall briefly consider this variable as well.

Table 8.2 sets out some details of the significance of inbound and outbound foreign investment to the three groups of Asian economies, and the "balance" between the two over the last two decades. In particular it examines:

1   The proportion of inward and outward FDI stock of the gross domestic product (GDP),[5] 1980 and 1996.
2   The balance between inward and outward FDI stock, 1980 and 1996.
3   The growth of inward and outward FPI flows between 1983–1989 and 1990–1996.
4   The value of shares quoted on the domestic stock-market as a proportion of GDP, 1980–1982 and 1994–1996.

What do these data show? We would highlight four main points:

•   As a proportion of their GDP, the combined inward and outward and direct stock of Asian developing countries rose from 4.4 percent in 1980 to 20.5 percent in 1996. The corresponding increases for South, East and South East Asian developing countries were 5.1 percent and 23.9 percent. These rates of increase are about the same as those for countries in South America (6.8 percent and 21.9 percent) and North Africa (3.5 percent and 12.8 percent) but not (and rather surprisingly as it is usually perceived to be marginalized in the globalization process) for Sub-Saharan Africa (4.1 percent and 23.0 percent) (UNCTAD 1998a).

Table 8.2 Foreign investment and Asian economies, 1980–1996

	FDI as % of GDP Inward		Outward		Inward/Outward FDI balance (ratio)		Growth of FPI (%)		Market Capital as a % of GDP	
	1980	1996	1980	1996	1980	1996	Outward 1990/1996	Inward 1990/1996	1980/1982	1994/1996
1. Asian developing economies	7.8	14.6	4.4	6.0	15.9	2.13	598.47	2,307.9	20.2	53.5
a. Group 1	14.9	22.9	12.5	20.5	2.5	0.88	686.47	2,430.8	54.2	114.2
b. Group 2	7.9	22.2	0.5	1.0	27.8	11.75	783.93	3,021.5	0.8	27.9
c. Group 3	0.7	8.4	0.1	0.1	17.6	19.36	NA	1,471.3	5.6	26.5
2. Latin American economies	6.4	17.4	0.4	1.5	16.2	11.73	−86.02	190.6	4.3	25.8
3. African economies	3.2	16.6	0.1	4.1	21.7	4.01	−295.08	−1,232.6	N/A	148.0
a. Sub-Sahara	3.1	22.0	0.1	4.5	30.2	1.46	N/A	N/A	N/A	N/A
b. Other	3.3	11.2	0.2	3.6	15.2	13.04	N/A	N/A	N/A	N/A
4. All developing economies	4.3	15.6	0.5	4.9	8.6	3.18	84.31	413.8	2.7	39.9
5. All industrial economies	4.8	7.6	6.5	10.1	0.7	0.75	227.34	235.3	33.5	64.9
6. All economies	4.6	10.6	4.9	10.6	0.9	0.98	217.02	236.4	24.9	70.6
7. Smaller Asian economies	15.0	31.8	8.3	31.8	2.7	0.62	686.35	2,654.8	119.0	178.3
8. Larger Asian economies	2.4	7.5	0.1	7.5	38.5	5.98	160.58	595.1	3.1	25.3

Source: As per Table 1 and Emerging Stock Markets Factbook, 1998 and 1990.

N/A = Not available

- The most pronounced trends towards globalization have occurred in China (classified as a Group 2 country), and Group 1 Asian developing countries. Most noticeably – the significance of inbound FDI has increased the most in China and some Group 3 countries, e.g. Viet Nam, Nepal and Myanmar. At the same time, Hong Kong, Taiwan, and Korea have each moved along their investment development paths to become important outward investors. It is also noteworthy that an increasing proportion of Asia outward direct investment, particularly by Group 1 countries has been directed to advanced industrial countries, outside Asia (Dunning, Narula and Van Hoesel 1996); and, in part, at least, has been geared to gaining access to new resources and markets rather than to exploit a particular competitive advantage of the investing firms.
- While, until the mid-1980s, most of new FDI in and by Asian developing countries took the form of greenfield investment, in the last decade the share in global mergers and acquisitions (M&As) accounted for by these countries has risen sharply. In 1990, for example, the total value of these M&As involving South, East and South East Asian firms as buyers or sellers was 4.9 percent; by 1997 this figure had risen to 9.0 percent (UNCTAD 1998a). However, in both years, two-thirds of the Asian firms' sales and more than four-fifths of the purchasing Asian firms were from China and Group 1 countries.
- Since the early 1980s there has been a huge increase in inbound portfolio investment into Asian developing countries – particularly in bonds and notes. In 1985 such countries accounted for 2.4 percent of global inbound FPI; by 1996 this proportion had risen to 4.2 percent. Corresponding figures for outbound FPI from Asian developing countries were 0.7 percent and 3.1 percent. In 1990 FPI into Asia was still only 2.5 percent of FDI. By 1994–1995 this proportion had risen to 50.1 percent. Partly the increase which again was strongly concentrated in China and Group 1 countries reflects the development of the capital markets in these countries. The last column of the table shows that the market value of Asian domestic capital markets was 53.5 percent of their GDPs in 1996, compared with 39.9 percent for all developing countries.

What are the explanations for these facts? In terms of the OLI paradigm of international production (Dunning 1993, 1995), the marked increase in inbound FDI reflects the rising locational advantages of Asian, cf. other developing countries; and/or a greater propensity of foreign direct investors to internalize the markets for their competitive (i.e. ownership specific) advantages. The opening up of several markets into which FDI had been previously restricted (e.g. in Korea) and the gradual upgrading of indigenous, but location bound, created assets (especially skilled labor, the institutional framework and technological infrastructure) needed by foreign firms to exploit their own particular core competencies, explain much of the growth of inward FDI. At the same time, Asian firms have come to evolve their own unique competitive advantages, which together with rising domestic wage rates, and encouragement, both from the indigenous banking system and their home governments, explain the upsurge in outbound investment over the last decade or so.

Of course, the opening up of the People's Republic of China to inbound FDI was the greatest single stimulus to that country's entry into the global market economy. In 1997, that country accounted for 41.1 percent of the inbound foreign direct investment stake into South, East and South East Asian developing economies. Hong Kong was responsible for nearly one-half of such investment and Singapore and Taiwan another third between them. However, it is estimated that more than two-thirds of that investment went to mainland China – i.e. was symptomatic of a trend towards regionalization rather than globalization. Whether one prefers Ozawa's "stages of economic development" (Ozawa 1992, 1996) or our own "investment development path" explanation of the dynamics of FDI in and out of developing countries, the deepening of the structural integration between Asian economies and the rest of the world, and the continual upgrading of indigenous resources facilitated by both inward and outward FDI, have exhibited an entirely predictable pattern over the last two decades. Moreover, in explaining why Asian developing countries – be they in Groups 1, 2 or 3 have generally recorded higher levels of FDI than those of other developing countries – particularly in the last decade – one finds the more export and market oriented friendly approach of Asian governments, a more entrepreneurial culture and the Confucian ethic of the Asian people, and a greater quality control and a consensus approach to decision taking by Asian firms, have all helped these economies to embrace the challenges and opportunities of the global economy more easily than their counterparts in Africa and Latin America.

While recent economic events are most certainly slowing down the pace of globalization in East Asian countries,[6] the demands on Asian firms to become even more competitive in their home and foreign markets is likely to become even more pressing. And though outbound FDI is likely to be curtailed until the early 2000s, and some expansion plans shelved,[7] it is also likely that the depreciating currency of several Asian countries (notably Malaysia, Hong Kong, Korea and Indonesia) will lead to more inbound FDI – particularly from Europe and the US – including some acquisitions of, or alliances with Asian firms now facing financial difficulties. In the longer run, however, we anticipate a renewed upgrading in the resources and capabilities of the Asian "tigers," particularly in sectors which, if they are to be internationally competitive, their firms also need to be part of a global network of valued-added activities.[8]

European FDI in developing Asian economies

With these thoughts in mind let me now turn to consider recent, and likely future, trends of European FDI in Asia. In doing so I shall rely very heavily on a European Commission/UNCTAD report, *Investing in Asia's Dynamism, European Union Direct Investment in Asia*, published in 1996, an UNCTAD/Invest in France/Arthur Anderson study on *International Investment: Towards the Year 2001* and a study by the European Round Table of Industrialists on *Investment in the Developing World*, both of which were published in 1997.

Table 8.3 presents some data on FDI by European Union (EU) countries in selected Asian countries between 1980 and 1993, and compares it with that of other triad investors. This reveals that, over this period, the EU's stock of all FDI in the named Asian countries fell from 16.4 percent to 12.9 percent, but that this mainly reflected a rise in non-triad (mostly intra-Asian) FDI in the region. In the case of the Group 1 countries and most Group 2 countries about which data are available, the increase in the European stake more or less kept pace with that of the US and Japanese stake. However, in China, Europe – and to a lesser extent the US – MNEs have lagged well behind their Asian counterparts; and this pulled down the share of all EU FDI in Asia quite considerably.

When one looks at individual Asian countries, one sees the share of European FDI – relative to that of US and Japanese FDI – being the highest in Singapore and Malaysia – countries in which the UK and/or other European investors have long had cultural, ethnic, political or economic links. By contrast in the Philippines, and Thailand, the US has a larger than average stake, while the Japanese presence is seen to be most marked in Indonesia and Korea, and that of mainland China is concentrated in Hong Kong and Taiwan. Again this picture is largely consistent with traditional FDI theory. What, however, is perhaps a little surprising is the increase in the share of the EU since the 1980s in countries with strong US or Japanese connections, e.g. the Philippines and Korea, and a decrease in their relative participation in countries in which they have strong historical ties, viz. Singapore and Malaysia. It would seem then there has been some convergence in the geographical origin of triad FDI in the Asian countries over the last decade, and that is paralleling the trend in other parts of the world, e.g. the US and Europe.

Part of the explanation for these changing shares of EU FDI is that, while the pre-1980s patterns of FDI strongly reflected the competitive advantages, psychic ties and natural resource needs of the investing countries, in more recent years, most FDI has been in sectors in which competitive advantages tend to be more *firm* than *country* specific, and in which large MNEs from each of the triad countries are well represented. The auto, chemical, electronics, clothing and footwear, and telecommunications industries are cases in point. It is our belief that both the geo-

Table 8.3 FDI by the triad nations in developing Asia, 1980–1993 ($ millions and percentage)

	Stocks						Flows			
	1980		1985		1993		1985–1987		1990–1993	
	Value	Share of total FDI	Value	Share of total FDI	Value	Share of total FDI	Value	Share of total FDI	Value	Share of total FDI
Hong Kong										
European Union	N/A	N/A	182	12.4	647	12.3	33	17.2	17	12.5
Japan	N/A	N/A	308	21.0	1,788	34.1	84	44.2	67	49.5
United States	N/A	N/A	788	53.7	1,474	28.1	80	42.2	15	10.7
Triad total	N/A	N/A	1,278	87.2	3,910	74.6	197	103.6	99	72.8
All countries	N/A	N/A	1,466	100.0	5,244	100.0	190	100.0	135	100.0
Korea, Republic of										
European Union	123	6.6	241	6.6	2,220	19.8	31	7.4	360	34.8
Japan	1,026	55.0	1,002	52.3	4,466	39.8	224	53.6	226	21.8
United States	491	26.3	1,073	29.5	3,259	29.1	120	28.7	333	32.2
Triad total	1,640	87.9	3,216	88.5	9,945	88.7	375	89.6	919	88.8
All countries	1,866	100.0	3,634	100.0	11,209	100.0	419	100.0	1,034	100.0
Singapore										
European Union	1,342	39.6	2,040	30.4	5,271	26.9	147	16.5	342	16.3
Japan	567	16.7	1,600	23.9	6,167	31.5	355	39.8	489	23.3
United States	1,001	29.6	2,440	36.4	6,851	35.0	268	30.0	572	27.3
Triad total	2,910	85.9	6,081	90.7	18,289	93.4	771	86.2	1,404	66.9
All countries	3,387	100.0	6,708	100.0	19,581	100.0	894	100.0	2,098	100.0
Malaysia										
European Union	1,720	26.6	2,264	26.6	5,842	17.1	84	10.3	837	15.2
Japan	1,135	17.6	1,602	18.8	7,435	21.8	284	34.7	1,142	20.7
United States	413	6.4	604	7.1	3,586	10.5	65	7.9	709	12.9
Triad total	3,268	50.6	4,470	52.5	16,864	49.5	144	17.6	2,688	48.8
All countries	6,462	100.0	8,510	100.0	34,091	100.0	818	100.0	5,508	100.0

Table 8.3 continued

	Stocks				Flows					
	1980		1985		1993		1985–1987		1990–1993	
	Value	Share of total FDI	Value	Share of total FDI	Value	Share of total FDI	Value	Share of total FDI	Value	Share of total FDI
Group 1										
Countries Total										
European Union	3,185	27.2	4,727	23.3	13,980	19.9	295	12.7	1,556	17.7
Japan	2,728	23.3	4,512	22.2	19,856	28.3	947	40.8	1,924	21.9
United States	1,905	16.3	4,905	24.1	15,170	21.6	533	23.0	1,629	18.6
Triad total	7,818	66.7	15,045	74.0	49,008	69.9	1,487	64.1	5,110	58.2
All countries	11,715	100.0	20,318	100.0	70,125	100.0	2,321	100.0	8,775	100.0
Indonesia										
European Union	851	8.3	2,672	17.4	9,967	14.7	269	25.7	1,205	13.4
Japan	3,462	33.7	5,009	32.6	13,937	20.6	329	31.4	1,379	15.3
United States	437	4.3	974	6.3	3,701	5.5	123	11.7	450	5.0
Triad total	4,750	46.2	8,655	56.4	27,605	40.8	721	68.8	3,034	33.7
All countries	10,274	100.0	15,353	100.0	67,625	100.0	1,047	100.0	8,999	100.0
Philippines										
European Union	114	9.3	349	13.5	748	17.1	15	12.3	71	21.7
Japan	206	16.8	362	14.0	890	20.3	12	9.5	111	33.7
United States	669	54.6	1,461	56.6	1,937	44.1	79	65.2	55	16.7
Triad total	988	80.7	2,172	84.2	3,576	81.5	105	87.1	237	72.1
All countries	1,225	100.0	2,580	100.0	4,389	100.0	121	100.0	329	100.0
Thailand										
European Union	156	15.9	350	15.8	1,484	10.7	24	9.2	210	10.3
Japan	285	29.0	622	28.0	4,579	32.9	100	38.5	602	29.4
United States	322	32.8	721	32.5	2,412	17.3	69	26.7	311	15.2
Triad total	762	77.7	1,693	76.2	8,476	60.9	193	74.4	1,122	54.8
All countries	981	100.0	2,221	100.0	13,918	100.0	259	100.0	2,050	100.0

China										
European Union	300	13.6	584	8.3	2,018	3.5	113	5.5	300	2.6
Japan	128	5.8	502	7.2	4,288	7.5	245	12	782	6.7
United States	372	16.9	1,106	15.8	4,680	8.2	312	15.2	830	7.1
Triad total	800	36.3	2,192	31.2	10,986	19.2	670	32.7	1,911	16.4
All countries	2,202	100.0	7,015	100.0	57,172	100.0	2,048	100.0	11,631	100.0
Group 2										
Countries total										
European Union	1,421	9.7	3,955	14.6	14,217	9.9	421	12.1	3,501	10.5
Japan	4,081	27.8	6,495	23.9	23,694	16.6	686	19.7	5,316	15.9
United States	1,800	12.3	4,262	15.7	12,730	8.9	583	16.8	3,686	11.0
Triad total	7,300	49.7	14,712	54.1	50,643	35.4	1,689	48.6	12,502	37.3
All countries	14,682	100.0	27,169	100.0	143,104	100.0	3,475	100.0	33,473	100.0

Source: UNCTAD, Division on Transnational Corporations and Investment, FDI database.

N/A = Not available

graphical origin and the industrial structures of inbound investment – particularly in Group 1 Asian developing countries – will continue to converge,[9] and reflect as much the degree of multinationality or strategies of the investing firms as their countries of origin.

Other data on the sales of foreign affiliates in Asia and exports to Asia from the three triad countries or regions, suggest that, in the mid-1990s, EU firms exported slightly more to Asia than their Asian subsidiaries produced and sold. This was in contrast to the rest of the world, where the main modality of servicing foreign customers was through FDI rather than exports. In the case of US and Japanese firms, too, the relative significance of deep integration was higher in other regions than developing Asia.

Economists usually distinguish between different kinds of trade and FDI according to their *natural resource* and/or *created asset* intensity.[10] Table 8.4 shows quite clearly the growing importance of capital and technology-intensive trade and investment, relative to more traditional natural resource and labor-seeking FDI. It also shows that relative to their share of all manufacturing FDI, that of European Union MNEs in technology/capital-intensive FDI has increased the most, and that their "revealed" comparative advantage[11] in both this kind of FDI is higher than that for the US and Japanese.

Table 8.4 Shares of developing Asia in world manufacturing FDI stock and manufactured exports of the European Union, Japan and the United States by industry groups, 1985 and 1993 (percentage)

Item	European Union		United States		Japan	
	1985	*1993*	*1985*	*1993*	*1985*	*1993*
Outward FDI						
Resource intensive[1]	4.9	1.9	1.8	5.2	28.9	29.1
Labor intensive[2]	1.6	2.1	1.8	4.1	50.4	34.8
Technology/capital intensive[3]	3.4	4.7	5.1	9.8	25.3	27.3
All manufacturing	3.4	3.7	3.7	7.5	30.8	29.1
Exports						
Resource intensive	2.0	3.8	12.5	15.0	45.5	65.1
Labor intensive	4.2	5.8	13.9	13.2	30.9	44.6
Capital/technology intensive	5.8	7.4	13.7	20.1	22.0	33.5
All manufactured exports	4.1	6.2	13.4	18.0	26.1	37.4

Source: UNCTAD, Division on Transnational Corporations and Investment, FDI database; and UNCTAD trade statistics database.

Notes
1 Food, beverages and tobacco, paper and wood products, coal and petroleum products, rubber products, non-metallic mineral products and metals. Coverage of industries varies, to some extent, for the different categories in FDI and exports.
2 Textiles and "other manufacturing."
3 Chemicals, mechanical equipment, electrical and electronic equipment, motor vehicles and other transport equipment.

Turning now to recent surveys of European business and their attitudes towards investing in Asia, we would make three points:

(1) The regulatory environment in most Asian countries – and particularly in smaller Group 1 countries – is perceived to compare reasonably favorably with that in other developing countries, particularly in respect of alliance formation and investment protection. Of the 10 countries identified in Table 8.5, Korea was ranked the least liberal in its attitudes towards FDI. In another survey conducted by the European Round Table of Industrialists (1997)[12] (which embraced a rather different sample of developing countries) most of the Asian developing countries were classified as being "quite open" in 1996 and/or were opening up to FDI at above average speed.

(2) Of the transaction cost-related barriers to FDI in Asia, identified in Table 8.6, those related to bureaucracy, corruption and lobbying were the ones most frequently mentioned by an opinion survey of some 300 businessmen conducted by the World Economic Forum (1995, 1997). These were again most marked in Group 2 Asian countries and in India. Including developed countries in our analysis, it is clear that, as countries move along their investment development paths (Dunning and Narula 1996), the transaction cost-related barriers to inbound FDI fall. Table 8.6 also shows that relative to other developing countries, Asian counties do well on all counts identified except with respect to the quality of their local capital markets. In particular, they were perceived to have particularly good telecommunications and technological infrastructures; and their governments were thought to be more transparent at successfully communicating their intentions.

(3) A final table (Table 8.7) drawn from the Invest in France/DATAR/Arthur Anderson report (1997), compares the perceptions of some 310 MNE executives and international experts about past and future FDI intentions. The replies are categorized both by the home region of the investing companies and by the region of investment.

The table shows that, over the past five years, and among developing regions, Asian countries have been ranked the highest by all groups of foreign investors. Even more impressive it is anticipated that over the next five years, developing Asia will have a higher priority for new FDI than either Western Europe and North America.[13] As might be expected, Asian and Japanese MNEs grade the developing Asian region higher than do their US or Western Europe counterparts; however, it is the Western based firms which are most upgrading their investment expectations in Asia.

The data set out in Tables 8.4 to 8.7 suggest that historically speaking – and with a few major exceptions, Western European MNEs have generally underestimated the growth potential of the dynamic Asian economies. Partly this is most certainly due to the greater "psychic" distance between Europe and many Asian countries than as between Japan and the US and these countries; and the fact that, in engaging in low cost production

Table 8.5 Survey results on the FDI regimes in Asian developing countries[a]

Economy	Local K market* (A)	Acquisition of control (B)	Equal treatment* (C)	Employment of foreigners (D)	Strategic alliances (E)	Cross-border ventures* (F)	Investment protection (G)	Image of country* (H)	Overall assessment (I)
Group 1									
Singapore	3.8	8.2	7.6	7.6	8.4	9.0	7.3	9.0	7.6
Hong Kong	9.2	9.3	6.6	7.0	8.5	8.5	5.1	8.6	7.8
Republic of Korea	7.8	4.8	5.3	4.4	5.3	5.3	5.9	5.8	5.6
Malaysia	6.1	4.9	5.0	5.5	7.4	7.8	7.2	8.4	6.5
Thailand	7.0	5.2	7.0	5.9	7.8	7.7	6.4	7.4	6.8
Taiwan	5.8	N/A	7.6	N/A	N/A	6.7	N/A	6.8	6.7
Group 2									
Philippines	7.6	6.0	7.2	6.9	7.5	7.4	6.7	6.4	6.9
Indonesia	6.2	6.2	5.8	6.2	7.5	6.6	6.5	6.2	6.4
China	5.7	6.5	5.4	6.2	5.2	5.9	7.8	7.9	6.3
Group 3									
India	6.3	6.6	5.3	6.5	6.6	4.3	5.7	4.1	5.7
Other developing Asia	8.4	6.2	7.5	5.8	6.8	7.9	6.5	3.9	6.6
Average, 11 Asian economies	7.0	6.2	6.3	6.0	7.0	6.8	6.4	6.6	6.5
Developed countries[b]	8.1	8.1	6.7	6.9	7.3	8.3	6.1	6.4	7.2
Countries and countries in transition[c]	7.2	7.7	5.9	7.3	5.7	7.3	5.6	5.2	6.5

Source: World Economic Forum (1995, 1997).

*Indicates 1997 data

N/A = Not available

Notes

a   Survey results are scaled from 0 (least favorable to FBI) to 10 (most favorable to FBI) in terms of the items (A)–(G).
b   Average for Australia, Canada, France, Germany, Italy, Switzerland, United Kingdom and the United States.
c   Average for Argentina, Brazil, Chile, Colombia, Czech Republic, Hungary, Mexico, Poland, Russia and Venezuela.
(A)   Access to local capital is restricted for foreign companies (0)/is not restricted (10).
(B)   Foreign investors may not acquire (0)/are free (10) to acquire control in a domestic company.
(C)   Foreigners are not treated (0)/are treated (10) equally to citizens in all respects
(D)   Immigration laws prevent (0)/do not prevent (10) your company from employing foreign skills.
(E)   Strategic alliances are not common (0)/are common (10) between domestic and foreign firms.
(F)   Cross-border ventures cannot be negotiated with foreign partners without government imposed restraint (0)/can be negotiated freely (10).
(G)   Investment protection schemes are not (0)/are available for most foreign partner countries (10).
(H)   Image of your country abroad (0) hinders the development of business/ (10) supports the development of business.
(I)   Average assessment according to criteria (A)–(F).

Table 8.6 Transaction cost-related barriers to FDI in Asian developing countries[a]

Economy	Cultural barriers	Country image	State control	Trans-parency	Bureau-cracy	Corrup-tion	Lobby-ing	Distribu-tions system	Tele-communi-cations	Techno-logical infrastruc.	Labor regula-tions	Overall assess-ment
	*	*		*	*	*		*			*	
	(A)	(B)	(C)	(D)	(E)	(F)	(G)	(H)	(I)	(J)	(K)	(L)
Group 1												
Singapore	8.5	9.0	7.1	7.4	7.6	9.4	7.8	9.2	9.3	8.6	3.2	7.9
Hong Kong	8.5	8.6	9.0	6.4	7.0	6.9	6.5	8.2	9.3	6.3	8.2	7.7
Rep. of Korea	4.9	5.8	4.6	3.1	2.5	4.6	5.3	3.5	7.4	5.5	8.0	4.8
Thailand	6.6	7.4	5.1	2.9	4.1	2.6	3.7	5.5	4.9	4.3	6.9	4.9
Malaysia	6.7	8.4	5.7	6.1	5.5	4.8	4.9	7.3	7.2	5.3	7.9	5.8
Taiwan	8.5	6.7	N/A	4.6	4.0	4.4	N/A	6.2	N/A	N/A	4.9	N/A
Group 2												
Indonesia	7.3	6.2	4.4	4.2	3.6	2.3	3.6	4.5	5.9	4.0	5.8	4.6
Philippines	8.8	6.4	4.7	4.8	2.8	2.0	3.6	3.9	3.7	3.1	5.6	4.1
China	6.7	7.8	4.1	5.8	1.8	2.5	4.5	3.7	5.3	2.7	5.0	4.2
Group 3												
India	7.4	4.1	4.0	2.7	2.7	1.9	3.9	3.3	4.0	3.8	2.8	4.1
Other Asia	8.0	3.9	5.9	2.6	3.0	2.4	4.1	5.8	6.3	6.3	7.2	5.6
Average, 11 Asian economies	7.6	5.7	4.6	4.0	2.8	2.2	3.9	4.2	5.0	4.0	5.9	4.5
Developed countries[b]	7.3	6.7	6.1	5.0	3.9	7.0	4.5	7.4	7.8	6.5	4.9	6.3
Developing countries and countries in transition[c]	8.0	5.2	5.1	3.5	2.5	2.7	4.2	4.8	4.9	3.5	4.8	4.6

Source: World Economic Forum (1995, 1997).

N/A = Not available

Notes:
a Survey results are scaled from 0 (least favorable to FDI) to 10 (most favorable to FDI) in terms of the items (A)–(L).
b Average for Australia, Canada, France, Germany, Italy, Switzerland, United Kingdom and the United States.
c Average for Argentina, Brazil, Chile, Colombia, Czech Republic, Egypt, Hungary, Mexico, Peru, Poland, Russia and Venezuela.
* Indicates 1997 data.

(A) National culture is closed (0)/open (10) towards foreign cultures.
(B) Image of your country abroad is distorted (0)/reflects reality accurately (10).
(C) State control of enterprises distorts (0)/does not distort (10) fair competition in your country.
(D) The government does not often communicate its intentions successfully (0)/is transparent towards citizens (10).
(E) Bureaucracy hinders (0)/does not hinder (10) business development.
(F) Improper practices (such as bribing or corruption) prevail (0)/do not prevail (10) in the public sphere.
(G) Lobbying by special interest groups distorts (0)/does not distort (10) government decision making.
(H) Distribution systems are generally inefficient (0)/efficient (10).
(I) Telecommunications infrastructure does not meet (0)/meets business requirements very well (10).
(J) Technological infrastructure is developed slower (0)/faster (10) than in competitor countries.
(K) Average assessment according to criteria (A) – (K).
(L) Labor regulations are (0) too restrictive/(10) are flexible enough.

Table 8.7 Investment priorities by region: past, present and future (Opinion of 310 MNEs and international experts)

	Home Country		Western Europe[1]		North America[1]		Japan[1]		Developing Asia[1]		Latin America		Africa		Central-Eastern Europe	
	Past	Future	Past	Future	Past	Future	Past	Future	Past	Future	Past	Future	Past	Future	Past	Future
By home region																
North America	7.6	6.8	5.8	5.6	4.4	4.4	2.5	2.8	4.1	6.7	3.5	4.5	0.6	0.9	1.9	3.4
Asian NIEs	5.7	5.3	2.9	3.7	3.8	4.4	2.2	1.7	7.0	7.5	1.7	2.1	0.6	0.8	1.6	2.1
Japan	7.7	7.4	4.4	4.7	5.9	5.7	0.0	0.0	6.7	7.6	1.8	3.1	0.7	1.0	1.7	2.9
Western Europe	6.9	6.0	5.6	5.5	3.7	4.0	1.4	1.7	4.0	5.5	2.5	3.7	1.0	1.1	3.2	4.4
By size of revenue																
>10 billion $	6.9	6.2	5.6	5.3	4.2	4.3	2.2	2.6	5.3	7.1	3.3	4.5	1.2	1.3	3.3	4.5
1 to 10 billion $	6.7	5.9	5.7	5.4	4.4	4.5	2.0	2.1	4.4	6.2	2.6	3.8	0.9	1.0	2.7	3.8
<1 billion $	7.1	6.3	4.6	5.0	3.5	4.0	1.0	1.5	4.5	5.8	2.0	2.7	0.5	0.8	1.6	2.7
NA	7.7	6.7	4.6	4.7	4.2	4.5	1.6	2.1	4.7	6.3	2.6	3.7	0.7	0.9	2.7	4.0
By industry																
Manufacturing	7.0	6.2	5.3	5.2	4.6	4.7	2.0	2.4	4.9	6.5	2.5	3.6	0.7	0.8	2.5	3.7
Services	7.1	6.2	5.0	5.2	3.0	3.5	1.1	1.5	4.2	5.7	2.4	3.5	0.9	1.1	2.5	3.7
By type of respondent																
Companies	6.7	6.0	5.4	5.2	4.2	4.3	1.8	2.2	4.8	6.3	2.7	3.9	0.9	1.1	2.7	3.9
Expert	7.6	6.6	4.6	5.0	3.9	4.3	1.3	1.7	4.5	6.3	2.4	3.2	0.6	0.8	2.2	3.3
Total	7.0	6.2	5.2	5.1	4.1	4.3	1.7	2.0	4.7	6.3	2.6	3.7	0.8	1.0	2.5	3.7

Sources: Invest in France Mission/DATAR/Arthur Anderson (1997).

Note

1 Excluding home country. Past = Last five years. Future = Next five years (1996–2001). Scale from 0 to 10.0. 0 = no priority. 10 maximum priority. Average of answers.

outside their home countries, European MNEs have preferred to use neighboring regions (e.g. Southern Europe and North Africa) rather than most distant locations. Partly too, European MNEs are (or perceive they are) at a competitive disadvantage in supplying goods to Asian markets *vis-à-vis* their Japanese or Asian counterparts. More recently, the "benign" neglect[14] of Asia by European MNEs has been exacerbated by the further liberalization of trade and FDI in the European Union and by the partial renaissance of the market economy in Central and Eastern Europe.

While the increased attention now being given by European MNEs to Asia suggests some reprioritization of their geographical preferences – as witnessed, for example, by a sharp increase in approved new projects by European investors in India, and an increasing number of bilateral and tax treaties concluded between European Union member states and Asian countries in the first half of the 1990s[15] – it is too early to judge whether, over the next decade or so, they can make substantial inroads to markets already largely secured by Asian and US MNEs. Perhaps the best opportunities lie in the penetration of the giant Chinese and Indian markets and of the newly emerging economies of the Indian subcontinent (including Myamar).[16] For historical and cultural reasons, India, perhaps, offers the greatest opportunities; although relative to other Western investors, the European presence in Malaysia and Indonesia has always been quite strong. Clearly, too, more needs to be done in creating additional new and closer Asia/European trade, technology and FDI networks; particularly in the light of closer trans-Pacific links likely to follow as APEC gets under steam. It is here, in particular, that the European Commission and the European Investment Bank can provide useful institutional support and financial help, particularly to small firms as they seek both to evaluate and exploit opportunities for FDI, and for alliance formation between European and Asian firms.

Conclusions

This chapter has demonstrated that over the last decade many Asian developing countries have been at the forefront of the globalization process; and that the more advanced of these are becoming important outward investors, not only elsewhere in Asia but in industrialized Western nations. It has further shown that inbound FDI is playing an increasingly important role in helping Asian developing economies to upgrade their economic structures in tune with the demands of the international market place; and to help them gain access to foreign resources and markets (UNCTAD 1996). In this connection the recent export performance of US manufacturing subsidiaries in Asia is most impressive.[17] The emergence and growth of domestic capital markets has also facilitated the inflow of FPI,[18] which has further stimulated both investment and exports by indigenous firms.

A final section of the chapter showed that, except in Asian countries which have close historical and cultural ties, European FDI in developing Asian countries has lagged behind that of other countries. This is partly because European investors have given Asia a lower investment priority than other regions; and partly because other Asian and US MNEs had already gained an export foothold in these markets. On the other hand, in the last five years there has been a slight shift in the geography of new European FDI (notably from the UK) towards developing Asia; and according to the European industrialists' survey, this shift is likely to accelerate over the next five years.

Finally, while the events of the latter 1990s will undoubtedly slow down the globalization process of the Asian economies – and particularly the outbound FDI by their MNEs – we do not anticipate this will lead to a major shift in the economic philosophy or outward looking stance of these countries. We would agree with *The Economist* (1998) that the remedy for the current bout of Asian "economic flu" lies in more prudent monetary and debt policies, a further liberalization of domestic financial systems, stricter bank regulation and supervision, exchange rate flexibility and a restructuring of some of the larger Asian, e.g. the Korean chaebols. In turn, these reforms, coupled with a continuation of market facilitating macro-organizational strategies should lead to leaner, fitter and more stable Asian economies, and even more competitive Asian MNEs. It is this – as much as any short-term repercussions of the crisis – which the Western industrialized nations should be most concerned about. And one way they may be able to capitalize on the current weakness of Asian currencies is for their own corporations to gain a further foothold (via FDI and alliance formation) in what, after all, remains, and is likely to remain one of the most dynamic growth regions in the world.

APPENDIX

Table A.8.1 FDI inflows by selected regions, 1990–1997 ($ billions)

	1990	1991	1992	1993	1994	1995	1996	1997 (p)	Growth(%) 1990–1994	1994–1997
Africa	2.3	2.8	3.2	3.7	5.3	4.8	4.6	4.4	130.4	17.0
Central and Eastern Europe	1.2	2.5	4.4	6.3	5.9	14.3	12.4	14.4	391.7	144.1
Latin America and the Caribbean	9.3	15.3	16.2	18.2	29.6	31.1	41.8	53.0	218.3	79.0
South, East and South East Asia	20.1	21.2	27.7	47.6	56.4	66.1	83.1	86.2	180.6	52.8

p = provisional

Source: Geneva: FDI/TNC Data Base.

Table A.8.2 FDI inflows by host region and country, 1986–1997

South, East and South East Asia	1986–1991 Annual Av.	1992	1993	1994	1995	1996	1997
High human development							
Singapore	3,592	2,204	4,686	5,480	6,912	9,440	10,000
Malaysia	1,605	5,183	5,006	4,342	4,132	5,300	3,754
Hong Kong	1,711	2,051	1,667	2,000	2,100	2,500	2,600
Thailand	1,325	2,114	1,730	1,322	2,003	2,426	3,600
Korea, Republic of	863	727	588	809	1,776	2,308	2,341
Taiwan	1,034	879	917	1,375	1,559	1,402	2,248
Brunei Darussalam	–	4	14	6	7	9	5
Total	10,130	13,162	14,608	15,334	18,489	23,385	24,548
Medium human development							
China	3,105	11,156	27,515	33,787	35,849	42,300	45,300
Indonesia	1,777	1,777	2,004	2,109	4,348	7,960	5,350
Vietnam	68	385	523	742	2,000	2,156	1,200
Philippines	501	228	1,238	1,591	1,478	1,408	1,253
Sri Lanka	41	123	195	166	63	170	140
Maldives	5	7	7	6	5	7	10
Total	5,497	13,676	31,482	38,401	43,743	54,001	53,253
Low human development							
India	177	233	574	1,314	1,929	2,587	3,264
Pakistan	188	335	347	419	639	690	800
Cambodia	–	33	54	69	151	350	200
Myanmar	68	171	149	91	115	100	80
Bangladesh	6	4	14	11	2	9	145
Nepal	2	1	4	6	5	5	20
Mongolia	–	2	8	7	10	5	7
Korea, Democratic People's Rep.	95	42	6	7	3	4	2
Total	536	777	1,142	1,910	2,841	3,741	4,518

Source: UNCTAD, World Investment Report 1998a.

Table A.8.3 FDI outflows by host region and country, 1986–1997

South, East and South East Asia	1986–1991 Annual Av.	1992	1993	1994	1995	1996	1997
High human development							
Hong Kong	2,373	8,254	17,713	21,437	25,000	26,356	26,000
Singapore	658	1,317	2,021	3,104	3,906	5,900	5,900
Korea, Republic of	923	1,208	1,361	2,524	3,529	4,670	4,287
Taiwan	3,191	1,869	2,451	2,460	2,678	3,843	5,222
Malaysia	311	514	1,325	1,817	2,575	3,700	3,100
Thailand	92	147	233	493	886	931	500
Brunei Darussalam	–	–	–	–	–	–	–
Totals	7,548	13,309	25,104	31,835	38,574	45,400	45,009
Medium human development							
China	745	4,000	4,400	2,000	2,000	2,114	2,500
Indonesia	7	52	356	609	603	512	2,400
Philippines	−1	5	374	302	399	136	136
Sri Lanka	2	2	7	8	7	8	8
Vietnam	–	–	–	–	–	–	–
Maldives	–	–	–	–	–	–	–
Totals	753	4,059	5,137	2,919	3,009	2,770	5,044
Low human development							
India	3	24	41	83	117	239	100
Pakistan	12	−12	−2	1	6	3	3
Cambodia	–	–	–	–	–	–	–
Myanmar	–	–	–	–	–	–	–
Bangladesh	–	–	–	–	–	–	–
Nepal	–	–	–	–	–	–	–
Mongolia	–	–	–	–	–	–	–
Korea, Democratic People's Rep.	–	–	–	–	–	–	–
Totals	15	12	39	84	123	242	103

Source: UNCTAD, World Investment Report 1998.

Table A.8.4 Countries associated with high, medium and low human development categories

High human development
  Hong Kong
  Singapore
  Korea, Republic of
  Brunei Darussalam
  Thailand
  Malaysia
  Taiwan

Medium human development
  Sri Lanka
  Philippines
  Indonesia
  China
  Vietnam

Low human development
  Myanmar
  India
  Pakistan
  Cambodia
  Nepal
  Bangladesh

NOTES

1 United Nations Development Program.
2 O'Brien (1992), quoted in Kobrin (1993).
3 For example, South and South East Asian countries accounted for 14.2 percent of global outward direct investment in 1996, compared with 8.7 percent in 1992. This share, however, dropped back to 11.8 percent in 1997.
4 See especially the Appendices in UNCTAD (1997).
5 This measure is preferred to that of foreign direct investment flows to gross domestic capital formation partly because FDI flows sometimes include reinvested projects and sometimes they do not; and partly because FDI flows are essentially a financial measure whereas capital formation is a real expenditure measure.
6 Both indirectly and as a result of the rippling affects these events have on the rest of the world. For example, in December 1997, the IMF revised downwards its projections for world economic growth (GDP) by a one percentage point in 1997 and 0.8 percentage point in 1998, with particular sharp reductions for the Asian economies of 3.8 percent for Korea, 5.4 percent for Indonesia and Malaysia and 7.0 percent for Thailand (IMF Survey 1998). In 1997, the outward direct investment flow from Korea was $4,287 million, compared with $4,670 million in 1996. The corresponding figures for Malaysia and Thailand were $3,100 million and $3,700 million and $500 million and $931 million respectively (UNCTAD 1998a). See also Appendix Table A.8.3 to this chapter.
7 For example, in 1998, a number of Korean MNEs including Hyundai and Samsung Electronics announced they were postponing or shelving expansion plans for their UK subsidiaries.
8 At the same time it is possible that the ownership and/or control structure of

Asian globalization might change; and that Western firms may play a more important role than they have done up to now.

9 At least at a two or even three digit SIC level. However, within these industries, the principle of comparative advantage still holds good and different countries tend to specialize in the production of different kinds of products.

10 The former is sometimes referred to as Heckscher-Ohlin (H-O) trade, and the latter as Schumpterian (S) trade.

11 Obtained by dividing the share of a particular type of FDI or exports by the share of all FDI and exports.

12 The European Industrialists' survey excluded Singapore and Hong Kong from the Asian developing countries, but included Bangladesh, Viet Nam, Pakistan and Sri Lanka.

13 This survey was undertaken between June and October 1996. A later survey published in 1998 confirms the high rating given to both China and the Asia/Pacific region, right up to the year 2002. See Invest in France Mission/Arthur Anderson.

14 An expression coined by the European Commission (see UNCTAD 1996, p. 59).

15 According to the European Commission/UNCTAD 1997 (pp. 64–65) survey, by November 1994, 109 such tax treaties and 103 investment treaties had been concluded.

16 Where in December 1996, European Union countries accounted for 40 percent of the (approved) FDI stocks (Mason 1997).

17 In 1993, for example, US manufacturing subsidiaries in Asian developing countries exported 69.9 percent of their sales. The corresponding proportion for Latin American subsidiaries was 41 percent, for African subsidiaries 50.4 percent and for subsidiaries in all countries 51.1 percent (US Department of Commerce 1995).

18 Between 1983–1989 and 1990–1995 the annual average flows of inward portfolio investment to Asian countries increased nearly eight times (from $1,840m to $14,512m). However, due primarily to substantial privatization schemes in Brazil, Mexico and Argentina, and in Central Europe, the inflow of portfolio capital to other developing countries over the same period of time was 28-fold (from 8,719m to $20,048).

REFERENCES

Booz, Allen and Hamilton (1997), *Cross Border Alliances in the Age of Collaboration*, Los Angeles: Booz, Allen and Hamilton.

Cuyvers, L. De Lombaerde, P. and Van Den Bulcke, D. (1994), European Round Table of Industrialists (ERT), *Investment in the Developing World*, Brussels: ERT.

Dunning, J. H. (1986), "The investment development cycle revisited," *Weltwirtschaftliches Archiv 122*, pp. 667–77.

Dunning, J. H. (1981), "Explaining the international development path of countries: towards a dynamic or developmental approach," *Weltwirtschaftliches Archiv 119*, pp. 30–64.

Dunning, J. H. (1993), *Multinational Enterprises and the Global Economy*, Wokingham, England and Reading, Mass.: Addison Wesley.

Dunning, J. H. (1995), "Reappraising the eclectic paradigm in an age of alliance capitalism," *Journal of International Business Studies XXVI* (3), pp. 461–91.

Dunning, J. H. and Narula, R. (1996), *Foreign Direct Investment and Governments*, London and New York: Routledge.

Dunning, J. H., Narula, R. and Van Hoesel, R. (1996), *Explaining the New Wave of Outward FDI from Developing Countries*, Maastricht MERIT, occasional paper 2/96–013.

Economist (1998), "Keeping the hot money out," *The Economist*, Jan. 24, 1998, pp. 85–6.

European Commission/UNCTAD (1996), *Investing in Asia's Dynamism*. Brussels: Office for Official Publications of European Communities.

European Round Table of Industrialists (1997), *Investment in the Developing World*, Brussels, European Round Table of Industrialists.

Fry, M. J. (1993), *Foreign Direct Investment in South East Asia*, Institute of South East Singapore.

IMF (1998), "Interim Assessment revises global growth projections downwards," *IMF Survey 27*(1), January 12, 1998, pp. 1–4.

IMF (various), *Balance of Payments Statistics Yearbook Summary Tables*, Washington IMF.

Invest in France Mission/DATAR/Arthur Anderson (1997), *International Investment: Towards the Year 2001*, New York: UN.

Invest in France Mission/DATAR/Arthur Anderson (1998), *International Investment: Towards the Year 2002*, New York: UN.

Kobrin, S. J. (1993), *Beyond Geography: Inter-Firm Networks and the Structural Integration of the Global Economy*, Philadelphia: William H. Wurston Center for International Management Studies, The Wharton School, Working Paper 93–10.

Mason, M. (1997), *Foreign Direct Investment in Burma/Myanmar. Trends, Determinants and Prospects*, New Haven: Yale University (mimeo).

McGrew, A. G. and Lewis, P. G. (1992), *Global Politics: Globalization and the Nation State*, Cambridge: The Polity Press.

O'Brien, R. (1992), *Global Financial Integration: The End of Geography*, London: Pintet Publishers.

Ozawa, T. (1992), "Foreign direct investment and economic development," *Transnational Corporations 1* (1), pp. 27–54.

Ozawa, T. (1996), "Japan: The macro-IDP, meso IDPs and the technology development path," in Dunning, J. H. and Narula, R. (eds), *Foreign Direct Investment and Governments*, London and New York: Routledge, pp. 142–73.

Stopford, J. and Strange, S. (1991), *Rural States, Rural Firms*, Cambridge: Cambridge University Press.

UN (1997), *The Effect of the European Union Single Market on ASEAN: Trade and Investment Issues*, Antwerp: University of Antwerp Centre for International Management and Development Discussion Paper No. 1994/E/15.

UNCTAD (1997), *World Investment Report: Transnational Corporations, Market Structure and Competition Policy*, New York and Geneva: UN.

UNCTAD (1998a), *World Investment Report 1998: Trends and Determinants*, New York and Geneva: UN.

UNCTAD (1998b), *The Financial Crisis in Asia and Foreign Direct Investment: An Assessment*, Geneva: UN.

UNDP (1997), *Human Development Report 1997*, Oxford: OUP.

US Department of Commerce (1995), *US Direct Investments Abroad: Provisional Results*, 1993. Washington: US Department of Commerce.

World Bank (1997), *World Development Report 1997: The State in a Changing World*, Oxford: OUP.

World Economic Forum (1995), *World Competitiveness Report 1995*, Geneva: IMD and World Economic Forum.

World Economic Forum (1997), *World Competitiveness Yearbook*, Lausanne and Geneva: IMD and World Economic Forum.

9 The European Internal Market Program and inbound foreign direct investment

Introduction

This chapter considers the impact of the completion of the European Internal Market Program (IMP) on the geographical distribution of economic activity within the European Community (EC).[1] More particularly, it assesses the empirical validity of a number of hypotheses, drawn from FDI theory on the likely affect of the removal of tariff barriers on intra-EC and extra-EC trade and FDI flows, and the relationship between the two. The evidence strongly suggest that the twin forces of regionalization and localization, identified in Chapter 1, have been accelerated as a result of recent European integration; and that the balance between the two is strongly determined by the knowledge intensity and mobility of the economic activities involved.

European integration prior to 1985

During the late 1960s and 1970s, there were several scholarly attempts to assess the impact of the European Common Market (ECM) – the first phase of macro-economic regional integration within the European Community (EC), on foreign direct investment (FDI).[2] Although their results were sensitive to the data and the econometric models chosen, all the studies supported the proposition that, while the removal of intra tariffs, and the establishment of a common external tariff, increased both intra- and extra-FDI – and sometimes significantly so[3] – other determinants of FDI (e.g. market size, market growth, relative factor costs, agglomeration economies, etc.) were at least as, if not more, important, particularly once the initial (and sometimes once-for-all affects) effects of the ECM had worn off.[4]

Furthermore, the studies showed that the impact of European integration (hereafter called Mark 1 integration) on FDI was strongly conditional on the motives for such investment; and on the time frame of the analysis. Thus, while the direct, or first order, impact of the removal of tariffs was to reduce *defensive import substituting* FDI, and to replace it by exports from the investing country, it also led to the restructuring of existing intra-European FDI wherever its trade creating consequences led to a geographical concentration of production in those activities in which foreign owned firms had a competitive advantage. The indirect, or second order, effects of integration (e.g. increased competitiveness of local firms, augmented income levels and market growth) were shown to lead to more *rationalized* (or efficiency) seeking and *offensive* market seeking. While the former was also associated with an increase in trade (particularly intra-EC trade), the effects of the latter were more ambiguous.

An examination of the FDI data for the period 1957–1985[5] reveals the following main points:

1   Although, as a proportion of their total outbound FDI, that of both EC countries and of non-EC countries – particularly the US – rose quite substantially, non-EC MNEs continued to account for the majority of FDI in the EC.[6]

2   Around 90 percent of inbound extra- and intra-EC FDI prior to 1985 was concentrated in the "core" countries of the EC,[7] and, much of this (a rough estimate would be about three-fifths) was within a 500-mile radius of Frankfurt. This geographical pattern of economic activity was broadly similar for both extra- and intra-EC FDI; although the latter tended to favor the UK and Germany relatively less, and Belgium and France relatively more.

3   In the early 1980s, about one-third of all FDI from EC countries was directed to *other* EC countries; this compared with 35 percent of US FDI and 15 percent of Japanese FDI to *all* EC countries. The total share of the inbound FDI stock in the EC originating from other EC countries (i.e. the EC's *FDI-intensity* ratio) was generally higher than its share of worldwide FDI (excluding the FDI stock of the investor country).[8] Corresponding *trade-intensity* ratios for intra- and extra-EC transactions for the same year were very similar, although a little higher for intra-EC transactions (UNCTAD 1994; EAG 1998).

4   There are few reliable data on the impact of Mark 1 integration on the sectoral distribution of FDI in the EC. The best we have relate to the sales of US manufacturing subsidiaries in the EC. Here, there is some suggestion that the growth of such sales between 1972 (the year before the UK acceded to the Community) and 1985 was most pronounced in those manufacturing sectors subject to plant economies of scale; where the US firms had the most marked competitive (or ownership specific) advantages; where the pre-EC, intra-EC tariffs were highest; and where the post-EC barriers to US–EC trade were the most severe.

5   There is some casual evidence that, apart from some extra-EC defensive import substituting FDI, most intra- and extra-EC FDI was either trade neutral or trade enhancing. Molle and Morsink (1991) found

that, over the period 1973–1983, there was a direct correlation between the intensity of intra-EC trade and FDI flows, once the trade intensity index had reached a certain level. US data suggest that the ratio between the sales of US manufacturing affiliates in the EC and exports from the US to the EC increased markedly in the 1960s – and much more so than in the UK, who did not join the EC until 1973. Thereafter, this ratio fell from a peak of 5.8 to 4.9 in 1977 and to 4.0 in 1985 (UN 1993a).

However, perhaps the most dramatic affect of Mark 1 integration was on intra-EC trade between the affiliates of US firms. In 1957, 85 percent of all sales by such affiliates were to domestic purchasers, and 1 percent were exported to the US; almost all of the rest, viz. 14 percent, were to other EC countries or the UK. By 1966, the exports to countries other than the US had risen to 26.7 percent, by 1977 to 38.3 percent and by 1982 to 45.7 percent (UN 1993a); and in both 1977 and 1982, 69 percent of these exports were between US affiliates (i.e. intra-firm exports). Other data suggest that intra-EC trade was most pronounced between the core European countries, and was particularly concentrated in sectors characterized by plant economies of scale and (relatively) low or declining transport costs.

In short, the first phase of macro-regional integration in Europe was accompanied by a substantial net increase in EC related FDI and trade flows. However, the largest increases in FDI were from countries outside the EC; and the evidence strongly suggests US (and later Japanese) MNEs were able to take advantage of the removal of tariff barriers, and surmount the transaction costs of the remaining non-tariff barriers better than their EC equivalents.[9] Although, during the period 1958 to 1985, there was a sizeable increase in intra-EC FDI,[10] intra-EC trade grew much faster – and the great majority of this was between, rather than within firms. By contrast, US FDI in the EC increased more rapidly than US exports for the first 20 years of the ECM, after which (until 1985 at least) exports rose more rapidly.

European integration: 1985 to date

Some theoretical insights

In 1985, the Internal Market Program (IMP) was initiated by the European Commission in Brussels. The intention of the program was to eliminate all remaining non-tariff barriers to trade in goods, services and assets between the member countries of the EC by the mid-1990s. These barriers were classified into four main groups, viz. discriminatory purchasing procedures, border controls, differences in technical standards and differences in fiscal duties. Between 1985 and the late 1990s, it was anticipated that some 319 directives, intended to remove or drastically reduce these barriers, would have been in effect by the (then) 12 member states.

Like the eradication of tariff barriers, that of the non-tariff barriers was expected to have different consequences for individual countries, industrial sectors and firms; and for the modalities of production and servicing markets. For example, the principal consequences of Mark 1 integration was to allow member countries to better exploit their dynamic trading advantages, based both on their natural and created resource endowments and economies of scale. It also helped promote the common ownership of cross-border activities in FDI intensive sectors (Markusen 1995). In so far as the transaction costs of non-tariff barriers are different from those of tariff barriers[11] and differentially affect countries, sectors and firms, it may be expected that their impact on the modalities of production and servicing markets may also be different.

However, before proceeding to consider how EC 1992 has affected, and is affecting, FDI in the EC, it might be helpful to rehearse the kind of expectations suggested by received economic analysis. As shown in EAG (1998), economists normally draw upon two sets of analytical tools to analyze the consequence of economic integration, viz. the theory of trade and the theory of FDI, or more especially the theory of international production.[12] These should be regarded as complementary, rather than competing, theories. The theory of trade is essentially concerned with the effects of economic integration on the *location* of economic activity, and the extent to which particular markets in the integrated area are serviced by exports or by local production. However, for the most part, received trade theory pays little attention either to the nationality of ownership of economic activity, or to the possibility that such activity might be part of a diversified or multinational firm.[13]

By contrast, the theory of FDI is primarily interested in the impact of macro-regional integration on FDI, either into or out of the member states. While, in so doing, it draws upon the theory of trade, it is also concerned with identifying the consequences of the *foreign* ownership of economic activity within the integrated region on the structure and location of that activity. In other words, FDI theory examines the impact of integration on the competitive advantages of firms of different nationalities, the location of activities associated with these advantages, and the way in which these advantages are organized jointly with the resource capabilities of the host countries.[14]

There is, of course, much in common between these two approaches, if for no other reason than many of the factors which influence the location of economic activity are likely to be independent of the nationality of ownership. However, in most cases, the consequences of economic integration for trade and FDI are less predictable. For example, the increased competitive pressures arising from the removal of trade barriers, together with the improved opportunities to exploit plant economies of scale, might lead to *strategic asset augmenting FDI*. In this case, there may be a change in the *ownership* of economic activity (e.g. an investment *diversion* affect) but not its location; as a result, the consequences of trade flows – initially at least – may be quite trivial. Similarly, where integration leads MNEs to rationalize the existing value-added activities of foreign subsidiaries, this may lead to both a geographical concentration of scale-related production, and an increase in intra-EC trade, over and above that which might be expected to occur between independently owned EC firms.

To keep this chapter to manageable proportions, while attempting to address the more important economic consequences of the IMP, we shall concentrate on four generic hypotheses suggested by the trade and FDI literature.

Hypothesis 1

The first hypothesis is that the IMP will have a positive effect on *intra*-EC trade, and an ambivalent effect on *intra*-EC FDI. Depending on the form and height of existing non-tariff barriers, it is likely to have an ambivalent effect on *extra*-EC trade, but a positive effect on *extra*-FDI and on the *intra*-EC trade by the foreign affiliates of non-EC MNEs.

Both trade and FDI theory suggest that intra-EC trade *creation* will arise as a result of more efficient resource allocation within the EC; and will be most pronounced in those sectors which supply products subject to *plant* economies of scale, and which cost little to transport. At the same time, depending on the level of the external tariff, extra-EC defensive FDI will be relatively unaffected or increased, depending on the competitive enhancing affects of integration, efficiency seeking FDI may increase.[15] The IMP is also likely to affect the value of at least some of the variables determining FDI. It might, for example, be hypothesized that demand related variables, e.g. market size and growth, will become less important for integrated, cf. stand alone, EC affiliates; while supply related variables, e.g. infrastructure and agglomerative economies may become relatively more important.

Hypothesis 2

The second hypothesis is that the IMP will have an ambivalent effect on the geographical distribution of FDI *within* the EC, both by EC and non-EC MNEs.

However, while the literature suggests that the locational response of foreign investors will vary according to the country of origin of the parent companies, there is no obvious reason why the site specific factors affecting the allocation of activity between a MNE's home country and an EC country (or, in the case of intra-EC FDI, another EC country) will be very different from that as between two separately owned firms in the two countries. At the same time, Markusen and Venables (1995) have shown that, as countries become similar in size, factor endowments and technical efficiency, cross-border activity will become increasingly dominated by MNEs, which will displace trade, provided that transport costs are not insignificant. More generally, they, and other trade economists (e.g. Helpman and Krugman 1985; Krugman 1990) suggest "macro-regional integration will lead to a greater concentration of economic activity in knowledge intensive sectors in which plant economies of scale, relative to transport costs, are important, but less concentration in sectors which are more dependent on natural resource endowments for their competitiveness." A corollary to this hypothesis is that the FDI/trade ratio among the high income and more industrialized countries of the EC (or between them and wealthier external investors, e.g. US, Japan and Switzerland) is likely to be higher than that between these countries and the medium income and/or less industrialized countries (Markusen and Venables 1995, p 26).

Hypothesis 3

The third hypothesis is that, depending on both country and sector specific factors, the IMP will have an ambivalent effect on the *ownership* of production in the EC. Both the trade and FDI literature suggest that perhaps the most critical component explaining the presence of FDI between and among industrialized countries is the juxtaposition between firm level economies of scale and scope, e.g. such as those that arise from the spreading of various headquarter activities and research and development; plant level economies of scale; the costs of co-ordinating cross-border activities and spatially related costs. MNEs are likely to dominate those sectors where the first and last ingredients are significant, relative to intra-firm co-ordination costs and plant-level scale economies (Markusen 1995; Caves 1996).

If it could be shown that those sectors which are the most sensitive to the effects of the IMP, were more FDI intensive than the non-sensitive sectors, *and* that integration enhances the kind of ownership advantages specific to MNEs, then it may be reasonably hypothesized that the IMP will lead to an increased share of the foreign ownership of activities in the EC in those sectors.

Hypothesis 4

This hypothesis naturally follows on from Hypothesis 3. Since, as the European Commission has suggested, some sectors are likely to be affected more by the IMP than others, it follows that its consequences for trade and FDI will, at least to some extent, be sector specific. Moreover, both the extant literature and empirical data on FDI clearly demonstrate that MNEs tend to concentrate in sectors which demonstrate one or more of the following characteristics: (i) a high level of R&D relative to sales; (ii) supply intermediate products that are either technically advanced and complex, or offer opportunities for scale economies in their production; (iii) supply end products which are highly differentiated and income-elastic in demand; (iv) are trade and/or FDI supporting; and (v) where the cross-border intra-firm co-ordinating costs of MNE activities are low, relative to the cross-border transport of the goods and services being produced by their foreign affiliates (Hirsch 1976).

As it happens, most of the sensitive goods and services sectors identified by the European Commission possess one or other of these attributes. Therefore, it is reasonable to hypothesize that FDI in these sectors, or in countries in which these sectors tend to concentrate, will be more affected by EC 1992 than the less sensitive sectors and countries in which the FDI is less well concentrated.

Some stylized facts

Before proceeding to analyze the evidence for and against these hypotheses, let us first briefly outline the main trends in intra- and extra-FDI in the EC since 1985, and its distribution between member states. The experience of Mark 1 integration (the completion of which took longer to accomplish than is intended for Mark 2 integration[16]), and our knowledge about FDI trends prior to the prescribed date for market unification (viz. 1 January 1993[17]), suggests that the first five to eight years after the start of the implementation of economic integration are (for most sectors at least) the most critical.

(a) The geography of FDI

Table 9.1 gives details of the changing share of the EC as a host region to foreign direct investors between 1980 and 1995. It shows that in 1980, the stock of FDI directed to the EC[18] was 36.7 percent of that of all recipient economies, and 47.4 percent of that of developed economies. Over the five years immediately *prior to* the announcement of the IMP, these shares *declined* to 29.4 percent and 40.0 percent respectively. However, by the end of five years after its announcement, the EC's shares had *risen* to 40.0 percent of all economies and 49.8 percent of all developed economies. Thereafter, the EC's share of FDI directed to all developed economies stabilized, and by 1996 it was 48.3 percent (a slight *decrease* over 1993 of 51.3 percent). At the same time, because of the increasing attractiveness of developing economies, and particularly China to foreign investors, the EC's share of the worldwide FDI stock in that year was even less than 1980, 33.5 percent cf. 36.7 percent (UNCTAD 1998).

Table 9.1 Changing share of inward foreign direct investment stock by host region and economy, 1980–1996 (percentages)

Host Region/Economy	1980	1985	1990	1993	1996
Developed economies	**77.5**	**73.5**	**80.3**	**75.2**	**69.2**
Western Europe	**41.4**	**33.3**	**44.4**	**42.5**	**37.9**
European Community (12)	**36.7**	**29.3**	**40.0**	**38.6**	**34.9¹**
Core countries	32.8	25.7	34.2	31.5	27.9
Non-core countries	3.9	3.6	5.8	7.1	7.0
Other Western Europe	**4.7**	**4.0**	**4.4**	**3.9**	**3.0**
North America	**28.6**	**34.3**	**29.7**	**26.5**	**24.7**
Canada	11.3	8.9	6.6	5.1	4.2
United States	17.3	25.4	23.1	21.4	20.5
Other developed economies	**7.5**	**5.9**	**6.2**	**6.2**	**6.6**
Australia and New Zealand	3.4	3.7	4.9	4.8	4.9
Japan	0.7	0.7	0.6	0.8	1.0
South Africa	3.4	1.5	0.7	0.6	0.4
Israel	–	–	–	–	0.3
Developing economies	**22.5**	**26.5**	**19.6**	**24.1**	**29.2**
Africa	4.3	3.7	2.4	2.4	2.0
Latin America & the Caribbean	10.0	10.0	6.8	8.1	10.5
Asia	7.9	12.6	10.2	13.4	16.5
Other developing economies	0.3	0.2	0.2	0.2	0.2
Central and Eastern Europe	**0.0**	**0.0**	**0.1**	**0.7**	**1.5**
Total inward stock	**100.0**	**100.0**	**100.0**	**100.0**	**100.0**
Total inward stock value (in millions of US dollars)	480,611	727,902	1,709,299	2,079,538	2,732,649

Source: UNCTAD (1998). All figures obtained directly from official sources by UNCTAD have been converted into US dollars at the average exchange rate for the year in question.

Notes

1 Excludes Austria, Finland and Sweden which joined the European Union (previously called the European Community) in 1995.

Whatever else these data show, they reveal a substantial increase in the activity of foreign investors in the EC in the latter part of the 1980s. Normalizing for differences in the growth of GNP between the EC and the rest of the world does not affect this conclusion.[19] However, what *is* of interest (and we shall explore this in more detail later in the chapter) is that at least part of this increase in inbound FDI may have been at the expense of the capital formation of indigenous firms. For example, while gross fixed capital formation (GFCF) in the EC hovered around one-fifth of gross domestic product between 1981 and 1995, the contribution of FDI inflows to that capital formation rose from 2.6 percent in the 1981–1985 period to 5.9 percent in the 1986–1990 period.[20] Between 1991

Table 9.2 The geographical distribution of changes in the inward foreign direct investment stock within the EC, end of year 1980–1985 to 1991–1996[1]

	1980–1985 %	1985–1990 %	1990–1995 %
(1) Core countries			
Belgium and Luxembourg	4.1	5.9	21.6
France	28.6	11.3	20.6
Germany	0.8	15.8	8.0
Italy	26.8	8.3	5.1
Netherlands	15.4	10.4	13.5
UK	2.7	32.8	10.0
Total	**78.4**	**84.5**	**78.8**
(2) Non-core countries			
Denmark	−1.5	1.2	4.2
Greece	10.1	1.2	1.9
Ireland	2.4	0.1	2.6
Portugal	0.6	0.8	0.5
Spain	10.1	12.2	11.9
Total	**21.7**	**15.5**	**21.2**
All EC countries	**100.0**	**100.0**	**100.0**

Source: As for Table 9.1.

Notes
1 Excluding Austria, Finland and Sweden, which joined the European Union (previously the European Community) in 1995.

and 1993 it ranged from 5.5 percent to 5.7 percent, but by 1995 it had risen to 7.2 percent (UNCTAD 1998).[21]

Table 9.2 gives some details on changes in the distribution of the FDI stock[22] within the EC between 1980 and 1995. We have chosen to divide such countries into two groups, viz. the six core countries of the EC, which are also the high income countries, and the non-core or largely medium income countries.[23] Table 9.2 shows that, between 1980 and 1985, the core countries accounted for 78.4 percent of the increase in FDI stock. In the following five years (1986–1990), this ratio increased marginally to 84.5 percent; but, in the following five years (1991–1996), mainly due to a fall in the dollar value of UK inbound FDI stocks, it fell back again to 78.8 percent. Even allowing for the country-specific differences in the compilation of data, they do not point to any increases to the *overall* geographical concentration of FDI in the EC, but this point will be further investigated later in the chapter.

We now turn to consider similarities and differences between the extra- and intra-EC FDI in the EC over the past decade or so.

Table 9.3 presents data on the distribution of inbound FDI in the EC by the leading source regions and countries since the mid-1980s; and Table 9.4 looks at the significance of the EC as a host region from the

Table 9.3 Source of FDI flows and FDI stocks in European Community, 1984–1987 to 1990–1993

	Flows – % of total[1]			*Stocks – % of total*[2]		
	1984–1987	*1988–1990*	*1991–1993*	*1985*	*1990*	*1993*
1. North America	**21.7**	**13.8**	**18.7**	**34.6**	**32.2**	**29.7**
of which US	19.6	12.6	15.7	33.4	30.3	28.0
2. Western Europe	**58.5**	**68.3**	**69.2**	**53.3**	**55.4**	**57.4**
of which EC	45.0	52.9	59.4	40.4	39.2	43.5
3. Other OECD	**7.3**	**10.2**	**5.7**	**3.0**	**7.6**	**7.3**
of which Japan	5.3	7.3	2.8	2.7	4.7	4.6
4. Other countries	**12.5**	**7.7**	**6.4**	**9.1**	**4.8**	**5.6**
Total:	100.0	100.0	100.0	100.0	100.0	100.0
Total amount in US$ million:	72,325	214,025	180,145	173,832	498,561	586,012

Source: OECD (1995).

Notes
1 Annual average
2 Included countries: France, Germany, Italy, Netherlands and UK.

perspective of the three largest source countries or regions. The main conclusion to be drawn from Table 9.3 is that the EC countries[24] have attracted a rising share of FDI since the mid-1980s; although part of the reason for this was the sharp retrenchment of MNE activity in the US in the late 1980s and early 1990s.[25] Within the EC, the *stock* of FDI directed to the core countries decreased slightly from around 90 percent in 1995 to nearer 85 percent in 1993.

By contrast, Table 9.4 shows that the intra-EC share of FDI by EC countries (excluding Ireland and Greece) more than doubled between the mid-1980s and the early 1990s. These data immediately suggest that EC specific factors – such as the IMP – may have had a considerably greater impact on intra-EC FDI than on extra-EC FDI, a conclusion quite the opposite from the one we drew about the effects of Mark 1 economic integration.

Throughout the late 1980s and early 1990s, a somewhat higher proportion of intra-EC FDI was attracted to the non-core countries than in the case of Japanese and US FDI; while, over the period as a whole, there is some suggestion of a decentralization of intra-EC FDI, particularly to Southern Europe.[26] However, *within* the core countries, a noticeable difference between extra- and intra-EC FDI is the considerably lower attraction of the UK as an investment outlet in the former than in the latter, case.[27] The closer linguistic, cultural, legal and institutional ties

Table 9.4 Japanese, US and EC foreign direct investment by regions and countries, 1985–1993 (percent of world total)

Host region/economy	Japan (annual average)			United States (annual average)			European Community (annual average)		
	1985–1987	1988–1998	1991–1993	1985–1987	1988–1990†	1991–1993	1985–1987	1988–1990	1991–1993
Developed economies	**68.2**	**77.3**	**71.3**	**64.3**	**68.7**	**61.7**	**88.1**	**89.3**	**82.0**
European Community (12)	**17.0**	**20.9**	**20.3**	**38.8**	**44.6**	**44.2**	**30.6**	**50.8**	**57.7**
Core countries	**15.9**	**20.1**	**18.8**	**33.5**	**38.9**	**40.1**	**26.4**	**42.9**	**45.1**
Belgium and Luxembourg	5.0	1.4	1.0	1.2	3.0	2.9	2.7	8.3	8.6
France	0.8	1.7	1.6	4.0	5.7	4.7	3.7	6.8	6.7
Germany	1.2	1.6	2.4	3.2	2.9	8.9	1.4	6.4	8.8
Italy	0.2	0.4	0.7	1.9	4.4	3.2	2.4	3.0	3.6
Netherlands	3.1	5.7	5.0	9.9	3.1	0.7	8.1	9.4	9.7
UK	5.7	9.4	8.2	13.4	19.8	19.7	8.2	9.1	7.7
Non-core countries	**1.0**	**0.8**	**1.5**	**5.3**	**5.7**	**4.1**	**4.2**	**7.8**	**12.5**
Denmark	0.0	0.0	0.0	-0.7	0.2	0.3	0.1	0.3	0.5
Ireland	0.3	0.1	0.6	3.6	3.0	2.8	0.7	1.8	4.0
Southern periphery*	0.7	0.7	0.9	2.4	2.5	1.0	3.4	5.7	8.0
Other Western Europe†	**0.7**	**1.3**	**1.1**	**5.5**	**6.7**	**7.8**	**2.8**	**4.0**	**5.4**
United States	**44.8**	**47.0**	**41.9**	**0.0**	**0.0**	**0.0**	**48.1**	**27.9**	**15.9**
Canada	**1.5**	**1.8**	**1.9**	**14.6**	**9.8**	**4.8**	**3.2**	**2.7**	**0.9**
Japan	**0.0**	**0.0**	**0.0**	**3.1**	**2.9**	**1.8**	**0.6**	**0.9**	**-0.1**
Australia and New Zealand	**4.2**	**6.3**	**6.2**	**2.4**	**4.8**	**3.3**	**2.8**	**2.9**	**2.2**
Developing economies	**31.8**	**22.7**	**28.3**	**35.8**	**31.3**	**37.0**	**11.8**	**10.5**	**15.3**
Africa	1.1	1.1	1.4	-0.1	-2.0	0.7	0.7	1.1	1.1
Latin America	17.5	8.8	8.2	33.0	26.4	23.1	5.3	4.9	3.8
Middle East	0.2	0.2	0.9	0.4	-0.3	1.7	0.7	0.6	0.6
Asia	12.8	12.2	17.1	3.6	6.9	11.1	2.3	1.8	3.5
Other developing economies‡	**0.2**	**0.4**	**0.7**	**-1.1**	**0.4**	**0.4**	**2.9**	**2.2**	**6.3**
Central and Eastern Europe	**0.0**	**0.1**	**0.4**	**0.0**	**0.0**	**1.3**	**0.1**	**0.2**	**2.6**
Total	**100.0**	**100.0**	**100.0**	**100.0**	**100.0**	**100.0**	**100.0**	**100.0**	**100.0**
World total (million US$)	**67,497**	**170,922**	**111,212**	**59,405**	**79,771**	**124,910**	**125,876**	**268,431**	**268,352**

Source: Japanese Ministry of Finance, US Department of Commerce (various issues), OECD (1995).

Notes

* Greece, Spain, Portugal

† Austria, Finland, Norway, Sweden, Switzerland

‡ Includes Malta and Cyprus and other countries not reporting separately

between the UK and the US, relative to that of the other core countries of the EC and the US, might have something to do with this.

To what extent does FDI tend to cluster in particular regions or countries; and how far has such clustering, e.g. to take advantage of agglomerative economies, increased in recent years? Table 9.5 compares the FDI intensity ratios[28] of EC countries in selected host regions in the late 1980s or early 1990s, compared with the respective ratios in the early 1980s. Looking, first, at intra-EC FDI intensities, Table 9.5 reveals that, in all countries except the UK, these intensities were greater than 1.00 in the latter period, although, again, apart from the UK, they were even more pronounced for the "other" Western Europe region. Second, in the five EC countries for which we have data, the intra-EC intensity ratios increased in the 1980s. Third, the FDI intensity ratios of EC countries in non-European countries were generally less than 1.00 in 1990 (an exception is the above average UK/US ratio); and that, except in the case of FDI in Japan, these ratios generally fell in the previous decade. Fourth, the FDI intensity ratios of both the US and Japan in the EC rose in the 1980s, in spite of the attractions of other parts of the world (notably East Asia) for US investors and the US for Japanese investors.

(b) The sectoral distribution of FDI

Data on the changing sectoral distribution of extra- and intra-EC FDI are only available for a few countries. Perhaps the best statistics are those compiled by the US Department of Commerce. Unfortunately, such data are only published for selected years.[29] In Table 9.6, we set out the increases in the sales of US affiliates in Europe[30] between 1982 and 1989 (which embrace the years before and immediately after the announcement of the IMP), and between 1989 and 1993. The sectors are classified into three groups according to their likely sensitivity (as perceived by the European Commission) to the IMP.[31] We also present similar data for the rest of the world (ROW). The difference between the Europe and the ROW indices might be interpreted as reflecting, in part at least, the "European" (including the IMP) effect.

The data clearly reveal two things. First, the sales of US affiliates in the highly and moderately sensitive sectors rose distinctly faster than those in other sectors between 1982 and 1989 but only marginally so between 1989 and 1993.[32] Second, the average rate of growth in sales for all sectors – but particularly for some of the most sensitive sectors between 1982 and 1989 in Europe, have consistently outstripped that of the ROW.

Other data published by Eurostat (1994) demonstrate an increasing concentration of FDI by both EC and non-EC investors in the tertiary sector, and particularly in finance, banking and insurance, telecommunications and business services.[33] How much this is due to the IMP *per se*, and

Table 9.5 FDI intensity ratios of selected foreign investing countries by host region, early 1980s–1992

Investor country	Year	European Community	Other Western Europe	North America	United States	Canada	Japan	Rest of the world
European Community								
Belgium and	1980	1.65	2.18	−0.14	−0.31	0.09	0.29	1.26
Luxembourg	1988	n.a.	n.a.	n.a.	n.a.	n.a.	n.a	n.a.
Denmark	1982	1.31	3.68	0.86	0.86	n.a.	0.01	0.62
	1991	1.42	5.45	0.38	0.36	0.45	0.77	0.40
France	1982	1.00	1.88	1.15	1.99	−0.21	0.11	0.79
	1991	1.37	1.63	0.62	0.72	0.30	0.16	0.49
Germany	1980	1.02	2.44	0.84	1.21	0.25	0.17	0.84
	1992	1.19	2.60	0.79	0.91	0.27	0.84	0.38
Italy	1980	n.a.	n.a.	n.a.	n.a.	n.a.	n.a	n.a.
	1992	1.52	2.84	0.31	0.37	0.12	0.41	0.59
Netherlands	1984	0.89	1.65	1.19	1.44	0.43	0.15	0.44
	1992	1.03	2.27	0.99	n.a.	n.a.	0.48	0.52
United	1981	0.50	0.52	1.09	1.43	0.55	0.09	1.25
Kingdom	1992	0.58	0.80	1.32	1.52	0.65	0.61	0.89
Portugal	1985	1.23	0.04	0.49	0.65	0.01	–	1.27
	1988	n.a.	n.a.	n.a.	n.a.	n.a.	n.a	n.a.
Spain	1984	n.a.	n.a.	n.a.	n.a.	n.a.	n.a	n.a.
	1989	1.39	1.02	0.31	0.39	0.06	0.18	1.13
Other countries								
United States	1980	0.60	1.05	0.47	–	1.14	0.26	0.63
	1990	0.73	1.34	0.41	–	1.80	1.74	0.73
Canada	1980	0.45	0.45	2.24	3.63	–	0.06	0.66
	1990	0.45	0.38	1.91	2.44	–	0.40	0.62
Japan	1980	0.30	0.26	0.98	1.44	0.24	–	2.13
	1990	0.38	0.24	1.26	1.54	0.24	–	1.28

Ratios are derived from data on stock of foreign direct investment using formula set out in note 28, p. 311.

Source: Based on UN (1993a) and a variety of national statistical sources.

how much to the deregulation and liberalization of service-related markets in general, it is difficult to say. But, it is, perhaps, worth noting that the sectoral composition of intra-EC foreign direct investment flows, and that of non-EC countries in the EC between 1984 and 1992 is broadly similar.

This conclusion is supported by a study by Agarwal, Hiemenz and Nunnenkamp (1995), which shows that the industrial composition of post-1985 French, German, Dutch and UK FDI in the EC has been very similar to that in other industrialized countries. Their work also reveals that only very modest changes have occurred in the sectoral composition of intra- and extra-EC FDI by these same countries between the mid-1980s and the early 1990s;[34] while there is no real evidence that the growth of

Table 9.6 Growth of sales by US affiliates in Europe and the rest of the world by sectors, 1982–1993

Sector	1982–1989 (1982 = 100)			1989–1993 (1989 = 100)			1982–1993 (1982 = 100)		
	All countries	Europe	Rest of world	All countries	Europe	Rest of world	All countries	Europe	Rest of world
High impact									
Beverages	173.9	162.2	183.3	170.1	204.3	147.2	295.8	331.4	269.9
Drugs	182.0	214.8	141.3	167.3	168.6	164.7	304.5	362.2	232.7
Office/Computing	324.3	296.4	400.2	116.1	101.7	145.0	376.6	301.5	581.4
Radio, TV communications	80.5	98.2	84.7	132.4	96.9	143.2	106.6	95.2	121.3
Electronic components	229.5	203.5	244.6	147.5	154.9	143.9	338.5	315.2	352.2
Instruments	195.6	181.2	247.6	125.3	125.1	125.6	245.1	226.7	311.1
Finance, except banking	247.8	555.8	164.6	159.5	206.2	98.8	372.7	1,146.1	162.6
Insurance	182.4	183.0	182.1	143.7	138.8	153.0	262.1	254.0	278.6
Total high impact	**219.9**	**255.0**	**187.4**	**138.2**	**145.3**	**131.8**	**289.6**	**370.5**	**247.0**
Moderate impact									
Other food products	164.5	218.0	112.8	154.1	155.1	152.4	253.5	338.1	175.0
Other chemical products	145.6	193.6	100.4	115.1	114.3	116.4	167.6	221.3	114.8
Other machinery	127.9	124.2	132.3	92.5	99.8	78.6	118.3	124.0	104.0
Household appliances	321.1	311.5	328.8	119.0	151.5	94.4	382.1	472.0	310.4
Transportation equipment	200.0	218.8	185.1	115.2	186.5	114.2	230.3	253.4	211.4
Textile products and apparel	148.9	140.6	158.7	142.4	160.6	123.8	212.1	225.8	196.5
Rubber products	144.5	237.8	101.9	110.4	102.5	118.8	159.5	243.7	121.1
Glass products	187.0	180.0	200.2	95.4	115.7	61.6	178.4	208.2	123.3
Wholesale trade	179.8	174.5	192.4	120.7	112.4	138.4	217.0	196.1	266.3
Business services	158.1	152.9	171.4	194.4	201.5	178.2	307.4	308.1	305.4
Total moderate impact	**177.2**	**185.6**	**165.5**	**120.7**	**119.0**	**123.4**	**213.9**	**220.9**	**204.2**
Total low impact	**161.9**	**168.0**	**155.8**	**122.8**	**135.1**	**112.7**	**198.8**	**227.0**	**175.6**
All industries (less petroleum)	**181.1**	**193.0**	**167.3**	**126.0**	**125.5**	**126.7**	**228.3**	**242.2**	**212.0**

Source: US Department of Commerce Benchmark Surveys (various) since 1989.

extra-EC FDI in the sectors in which intra-EC trade has expanded the most rapidly has been at the expense of extra-EC FDI in other developed countries.[35] The only exception may be in some service sectors – notably in finance, insurance, telecommunications and data processing services, where the gains from IMP have been higher simply because the earlier barriers to intra-EC trade or investment were so high.

(c) The share of FDI in EC capital formation

While much of our previous discussion has been concerned with the *locational* competitiveness of the EC, and that of its member states, it is possible that part of any increase in FDI (or sales by foreign firms) might represent an increased *share* of the total investment (or sales) of all EC located firms. Such an increase in the foreign ownership of production might occur either as a result of the improved competitiveness of established foreign affiliates, or through foreign firms acquiring or merging with domestic firms in individual European countries.[36] As an earlier section has shown, the received literature would regard such M&As as a means of sustaining or increasing the ownership (O) advantages of the acquiring firms. However, while in some cases the location of the acquired company may be relevant, in others it may have no significance at all.

Table 9.7 reveals that the share of foreign direct inflows to GFCF in the world economy increased in the second half of the 1980s, but that this increase was mainly confined to the EC and North America. By contrast, in the 1990s, the rise in the foreign share of GFCF was most marked in the case of developing economies and in others in Western Europe; and particularly so in the case of Sweden, which, in 1995, along with Finland and Austria, joined the EU. The increased participation of foreign owned firms in the EC (which is confirmed by other data[37]) is entirely consistent with our knowledge about M&As. Both intra-EC and M&As, and cross-border acquisitions of EC firms by non-EC purchasers'[38] corporations, increased more than ten-fold between 1985–1986 and 1989–1990, before dropping back in the early 1990s to nearer their 1986–1987 levels, since when they have increased again isolating the affects of the IMP (De Long, Smith and Walter 1996).

Isolating the effects of the IMP

So much for some stylized facts about recent FDI into the EC, which lend some support to the four hypotheses set out earlier in this chapter. We now turn to examine more rigorously the empirical evidence for these hypotheses, and also some related work of other scholars on the effect of IMP on extra- and intra-EC FDI and trade. In doing so, we are faced with a difficult – indeed, almost an intractable problem – viz. how to isolate the specific impact of the IMP from the other variables which might influence

Table 9.7 The ratio of foreign direct investment inflows to gross fixed domestic capital formation, 1981–1995 (percent)

Host region/economy	1981–1985 (Annual average)	1986–1991 (Annual average)	1991	1992	1993	1995
All economies	**2.3**	**3.6**	**3.5**	**3.3**	**4.4**	**5.6**
Developed economies	**2.2**	**3.5**	**3.3**	**3.0**	**3.0**	**3.9**
Western Europe	**2.6**	**5.6**	**5.4**	**5.3**	**6.1**	**7.2**
European Community (12)	**2.7**	**5.7**	**5.7**	**5.5**	**6.0**	**7.0**
Belgium and Luxembourg	7.6	17.5	22.8	25.2	26.1	20.4
Denmark	0.4	3.8	7.3	4.6	8.4	15.3
France	2.0	4.5	5.9	8.2	9.0	8.6
Germany	1.2	1.1	1.2	0.6	0.5	2.6
Greece	6.0	5.9	8.7	5.5	5.2	4.8
Ireland	4.0	5.9	1.3	17.0	15.3	14.2
Italy	1.1	2.0	1.0	1.7	2.6	2.6
Netherlands	6.1	12.8	10.7	12.2	14.2	14.8
Portugal	3.0	9.9	13.7	8.3	7.9	2.7
Spain	5.3	9.6	10.0	10.5	8.6	5.4
United Kingdom	17.6	13.6	9.5	9.8	11.0	13.1
Other Western Europe	**1.7**	**4.3**	**4.0**	**2.5**	**3.9**	**6.2**
North America	**2.8**	**6.3**	**2.9**	**2.7**	**8.4**	**14.1**
Canada	1.0	5.8	2.4	2.4	5.1	11.0
United States	2.9	6.5	3.0	5.0	8.8	5.8
Other developed economies	**0.7**	**0.9**	**0.7**	**0.9**	**0.5**	**1.2**
Developing economies	**3.3**	**3.4**	**4.0**	**4.2**	**6.1**	**7.4**
Africa	**2.3**	**3.9**	**4.2**	**5.2**	**6.1**	**7.9**
Latin America and the Caribbean	**4.1**	**5.3**	**5.2**	**7.6**	**6.4**	**9.8**
Asia	**3.1**	**2.8**	**3.4**	**3.2**	**6.0**	**6.6**
Central and Eastern Europe	neg.	**0.1**	**0.4**	**1.1**	**7.4**	**10.2**

Source: UNCTAD (1995, 1996 and 1998).

the level and pattern of extra- and intra-FDI in the EC? For, even if all the data were available (which they are not), the answer would be conditional on: (a) the kind of FDI being discussed; (b) particular country and industry specific factors; (c) how one measures the IMP effect; and (d) what assumptions one makes about what would have happened in the absence of the IMP, viz. the *anti-monde* or *alternative* position.

Basically, there are two main ways of proceeding. One is to construct a model in which an IMP variable is added to the usual determinants of FDI hypothesized by received FDI, and/or trade theory; and then attempt to estimate the significance of that variable. In principle, such an exercise could be conducted for extra- and intra-EC FDI, and for different kinds of FDI. In practice, the data on FDI only allow us to travel this path to a limited extent. We shall, however, review the research which has recently been conducted on this issue.

The second approach is more deductive and predictive, and seeks to test a number of specific hypotheses about the likely effects of economic integration on FDI. The particular hypotheses we shall examine in this chapter were set out in our earlier chapter.

In practice, the two approaches are quite similar, and use almost identical statistical procedures. They also confront the same analytical and measurement problems. Both, for example, need to construct a quantifiable proxy for what is essentially a non-quantifiable phenomenon, viz. the removal of non-tariff barriers to intra-EC trade. Both, too, in the design and specification of their chosen models face the difficulty that many of the other variables hypothesized to influence FDI are, themselves, likely to be affected by the IMP. Introducing leads and lags may help resolve this latter problem, but only to a limited extent.

Since, up to now, most attempts to explain recent movements in FDI into the EC have followed the first approach, we will give most of our attention to these.

Incorporating IMP into traditional FDI models

We are aware of only two attempts to do this, viz. Clegg (1995) and Pain and Lansbury (1996), although other models have identified the significance of non-IMP variables influencing FDI in the EC (or Western Europe[39]). In such cases, it *could* be argued that the value of the residual (i.e. unexplained) variables might be taken as a proxy for the IMP,[40] or, at least, a reflection of its importance, *apart* from its effects on the value of the other variables. An alternative procedure would be to estimate the impact of the IMP on the non-IMP variables and then to credit the IMP with that impact in any explanation of FDI. Thus, for example, if it could be shown that, over the five-year period 1987–1992, the IMP had raised GNP by 6 percent (the most optimistic forecast of the Cecchini report (Cecchini *et al.* 1988); then, using the estimates of Julius (1990) and the UNCTAD (1993a), of the elasticities of FDI with respect to changes in the GNP – viz. between 3.5 percent and 4.5 percent – one could then infer that between 21 percent and 27 percent of any increase in FDI over those years was due to the IMP.

Of the more recently published research which has sought to evaluate the determinants of FDI in the EC, those of UNCTAD (1993a), Buigues and Jacquemin (1994), Srinivasan and Mody (1998), Clegg (1995) and Pain and Lansbury (1996) are worthy of special attention. We will now briefly summarize the results of their work in the following paragraphs.[41]

UNCTAD (1993)

The UNCTAD study regressed the annual flows (at times "t") of FDI (both intra- and extra-EC) into the EC and other developed countries, over the period 1972–1988, against five explanatory variables, viz. the level of GNP in year t-1, the change in GNP between t-1 and t, the ratio of *domestic* investment to GNP in year t-1, the exchange rate at year t (defined as the ratio of the domestic currency to the US dollar) and the squared deviation of the exchange rate from its mean over the period 1972–1988. The authors found that, apart from the exchange rate variable, which was insignificant, the remaining four factors explained about 90 percent of the fluctuations in FDI in *both* the EC and other developed countries; and that the coefficients of the explanatory variables always had the correct size. Of these variables, GNP was consistently found to be the most significant, with its coefficient being much larger for the EC than for the other developed countries. The share of domestic investment in GNP was also positively and significantly associated with FDI for both the EC and other developed countries. The variance in the exchange rate was seen to have had a significant negative effect on FDI inflows.

The UNCTAD study also estimated the elasticity of the response of FDI to changes in the value of the independent variables. It found that an increase in both the level of GNP and the ratio of domestic investment to GNP in the EC in one year coincided with an increase in the inflow of FDI of 4 percent in the following year; while, a 1 percent change in the variance of the exchange rate would have a relatively small negative (but statistically significant) impact on FDI inflows of $37 million.

Unfortunately, the data in the UNCTAD study do not go up beyond 1988; nor do the authors split their analysis into a pre- and post-IMP timeframe. But, some estimates for the period 1989–1995, made from a variety of sources, including the IMF and World Bank – and which implicitly take account of the IMP – predicted that the annual rate of growth of FDI flows in the EC would outpace that of other developed nations, except Japan.[42] Primarily, this was because the projected growth of GNP and the ratio of domestic investment to GNP was higher in the EC[43] than in other regions of the world. Although the UNCTAD study did not specifically incorporate an IMP variable into their model, the results do suggest that the *indirect* approach to evaluating its significance, viz. by its effects on GNP, domestic investment and the exchange rate, might offer a promising line for further research.

Srinivasan, K. and Mody, A. (1998)

This study was confined to US and Japanese FDI for the period 1977 to 1992. It embraced 35 countries, including 10 EC countries. One of its main purposes was to evaluate the significance of four rather different groups of factors which the literature has suggested influence FDI. These are:

a   *Classical factors* – which the authors proxied by host country market size, and labor and capital costs.
b   *Agglomeration factors* – proxied by the previous level of FDI and the quality of supportive infrastructure to FDI.
c   *Trade restricting factors* – proxied (in reverse) by the degree of openness of an economy; and a dummy for the IMP variable.
d   *Risk factors* – proxied by information provided by various corporate data banks on country risk assessment

The authors compiled a number of multi-regression equations, using mainly log linear estimates of the FDI function for all developed countries, and for the EC separately.[44] They found that, for each group of countries, both the size of market and cost of labor were significant explanatory variables – but not the cost of capital in the case of the EC. Agglomeration factors, measured in this instance by the production of electricity *per capita,* and the number of telephone lines *per capita,* were significantly related to FDI in the case of the EC, but not for developed countries as a whole.[45] As might be expected, and in contrast to the situation in developing countries, country risk was of only trivial importance, but openness (or negative trade restrictions) was positively and significantly signed in both groups. Eliminating country risk, these three groups of factors explained about 70 percent of the variation in FDI in the EC (and rather less in the case of FDI in all developed countries).

In some additional (unpublished) calculations undertaken by the authors, Srinivasan and Mody found that, when they split their data into three time periods, viz. 1977–1981, 1982–1986 and 1987–1992, there was no evidence that the formation of the IM significantly improved the EC's share of either US or Japanese FDI. Indeed, the case of Japanese FDI, assuming last Asia to be the benchmark group of countries, the share of FDI directed to the EC fell in the period 1987–1992.

Clegg, J. (1995)

In a long-range longitudinal study, Clegg attempted to model the determinants of US FDI in the original six member countries of the EC between 1951 (seven years before the European Common Market (ECM) came into effect) and 1990. The unique characteristics of his model were: first, an attempt to incorporate both real and financial variables into three multiple regression equations (one embracing the whole and one each for two sub-periods, 1951–1972 and 1973–1990); and second, in the latter subperiod, the introduction of a dummy variable for the IMP.[46]

Clegg found that of the 10 or 11 explanatory variables included in his equations, market size (proxied by GNP or GDP deflated to constant prices) market growth, a trade discrimination variable, the exchange rate (of the dollar against the six EC currencies) and relative interest rates were all significantly and correctly signed for one or other of the sub-periods, and for the 40-year period as a whole. However, contrary to expectations, for longer, market size was shown to be negatively associated with FDI – and significantly so – although, for the first two decades, the two variables were positively correlated. Clegg suggested the reasons for this was that, whereas in the 1950s and early 1960s, most US FDI was defensive and was directed to the larger local markets in Europe, in the later years, particularly after the UK joined the EC, it was more of an efficiency or strategic asset-seeking kind, and geared to exploiting the EC market as a whole.[47]

Clegg's insertion of a dummy variable for the IMP (set to unity for the period 1987–1990) gave inconclusive results. For the period 1951–1990, the variable was positively but insignificantly associated with FDI; but for the sub-period 1973–1990, it was negatively associated. Part of the reason for the apparent conflict in these findings may be that the significance of the other variables in the equation (e.g. market size) quite dramatically changed in the 1980s. At the same time, as Clegg himself recognized, the use of an *aggregate* dummy for the IMP inevitably fails to capture the industry-specific effects of the program.

Buigues, P. and Jacquemin, A. (1994)

One of the distinctive features of this study was its attempt both to evaluate the relationship between extra-EC FDI in the EC and exports to the EC, and to estimate the significance of trade barriers as a determinant of FDI. Taking the share of global FDI directed to seven or nine manufacturing sectors in the EC by US and Japanese MNEs as the dependent variable, the authors regressed its value against that of four independent variables, viz. the share of total US and Japanese exports directed to the EC, intra-EC non-tariff barriers, the sectoral growth in demand in the EC divided by the growth in demand in the US and Japan, and the Community's sectoral specialization, which they defined as the EC's exports for sectors in the total EC exports of manufactured goods divided by the same index for all OECD countries.[48]

The relevant linear regression produced results which were generally supportive of expectations. In particular, extra-EC FDI and trade were shown seen to be significantly complementary to each other (see Hypothesis 1, above). Second, while non-tariff barriers to trade were a significant determinant of Japanese FDI, they played only a minor role in influencing US FDI.[49] For US sectoral demand growth and EC sectoral specialization, the results were different for US and Japanese investors. In the Japanese case, both variables were shown to have a significant positive association with FDI, while, for the US, only the sectoral specialization variables were significantly related. Although the authors did not include an agglomeration variable in their analysis, they found that both US and Japanese firms tended to strengthen their share of FDI and exports in those sectors in which they already had a comparative advantage in 1980, while they contracted their share of FDI and exports in the sectors in which they had an initial comparative disadvantage.

Pain and Lansbury (1996)[50]

Since, as we have seen, the effects of the IMP are unlikely to be evenly distributed between industries, it is only by incorporating sector-specific variables that one can properly evaluate the impact of the IMP. Moreover, apart from our own estimates presented later in this chapter, the Pain and Lansbury study is the only one we know which has made a formal attempt to incorporate *discriminate* dummy variables to proxy the IMP.

The Pain and Lansbury study is unique in another respect, in that it examined the impact of the IMP on the *outward* intra-EC FDI[51] of two of the core EC countries, viz. the UK and Germany.[52] In doing so, it used received FDI theory to test three hypotheses. These are:

1   That intra-EC FDI by UK and German firms has risen more rapidly than it would have done in the absence of the IMP.
2   That intra-EC by UK and German firms has risen either more rapidly than that outside the EC or at the expense of such investment.
3   That the IMP has had a more marked effect on the growth of FDI by UK and German firms in the less trade intensive sectors, notably financial services, since, in the past, non-tariff barriers have constrained both FDI and trade in these sectors relative to that in the more trade intensive sectors.

The econometric model devised by Pain and Lansbury consisted of both location and internalization specific explanatory variables.[53] Of the former, they included the size of the sectoral output in the host country, relative factor costs, currency variability, the extent of trade barriers and the corporate financial conditions in the home country.[54] Of the latter, they used data on the US registered patents of UK and German firms as proxy for their preferences for FDI, rather than cross-border licensing; the idea being that firms would be more likely to internalize the markets for their technology and organizational expertise in high value-added sectors than in low value-added sectors.[55] Estimates of the non-tariff barriers – ranging along an ordinal scale of 1 to 3 – as they were perceived to effect particular sectors – were obtained from Buigues, Ilzkovitz and Lebrun (1990) and Sapir (1993).

The sample period taken for the dependent and explanatory variables apart from the IMP was 1981–1992 in the UK case and 1980–1992 in the German case. For each country, the authors first calculated a (log linear) multi-regression equation *excluding* the IMP variable. In each case, the results were similar and broadly consistent with those of other studies. Host country output was shown to be positively and significantly correlated with UK and German FDI in the EC, although the (sectoral) output elasticities (1.54 and 0.84) were considerably lower than that recorded for GNP by the UNCTAD study (4.34).

Both the UK and German equations recorded a positive, but insignificant, relationship between relative unit labor costs and FDI. This finding is consistent with the notion that high labor costs may reflect the availability and productivity of high-skill labor, and be associated with agglomeration economies, rather than with low (real) labor productivity. Both the corporate gearing ratios and the proxy variable used to capture the currency variability were correctly signed, but insignificant. Taking a three-year cumulative measure of patents registered by the two groups of firms in the US, they found that in equations the coefficients were correctly signed and significant. Overall, Pain and Lansbury estimated that the coefficient between the dependent and the five explanatory variables was very high at 0.972, although, almost certainly, there was some auto correlation between the explanatory variables.

The authors then produced two equations embodying the IMP indicator ordinally ranked according to perceived sensitivity (3 = high, 1 = low). This variable was shown to be positively and significantly related to FDI in the case of both the UK and Germany, i.e. it led directly to an increased level of FDI in the EC; although the coefficient was somewhat higher for the UK. The effect of the inclusion of this variable was to reduce the elasticities on output (in the UK case) and patents (in the UK and German cases), which confirms an earlier point made in this chapter that, in the absence of a specific IMP variable, some of its affects are captured by other variables.

The next part of the Pain and Lansbury exercise was to estimate the difference made to the *value* of FDI in the EC as a result of the IMP. The authors calculated that, by the end of 1992, the IMP may have raised the constant price stock of UK FDI by $15 billion (or 31 percent of the capital stake at that date) and the stock of German FDI by $5 billion (or 6 percent of the aggregate stock level). In both instances, the prime gainers were shown to be the financial and other service sectors and the electronics sector (which includes telecommunications equipment). For the UK, major gains were also recorded in the distribution and food, drink and tobacco sectors, in both of which the UK has a comparative advantage.

Because of the differences in the industrial structure of individual EC countries, the impact of the IMP on UK and German intra-EC FDI investment is likely to be country specific – at least to some extent. Thus, according to Pain and Lansbury, the primary beneficiary of the IMP, in so far as it has affected German outward FDI, has been in the UK, in which it is estimated that the German stake in 1992 was $4.3 billion, or a third higher than it might otherwise have been. Other gainers appear to be Italy, the Netherlands and Portugal; but France and Belgium are both shown to have lost German investment as a result of the IMP, mainly, it would seem, because of the size of German chemicals and distribution investment there. Overall, the study offers little support for the proposition that the IMP has led to a more pronounced intra-EC concentration of economic activity.

Formulating specific hypotheses about the efficiency of the IMP

So much for an examination of a selection of studies which have sought to add an IMP dimension to the explanation of extra- or intra-FDI in the EC; or which help shed light on that dimension if its impact on other explanatory variables could be assessed. The following paragraphs return to consider more specifically the hypotheses set out earlier in this chapter, and to examine first how far the studies so far described throw light on these, and second to present some new findings of our own.

Hypothesis 1, above. While the Barrell and Pain study showed that Japanese FDI in the EC was significantly and positively related to non-tariff barriers, the Buigues and Jacquemin and Clegg studies supported the proposition that the IMP is leading to an increase in extra-EC FDI, as the US and Japan seek to be "insiders" in a market favoring the production of firms located in that market.[56] At the same time, research by Agarwal, Hiemenz and Nunnenkamp (1995) and Pain and Lansbury (1996) would appear to refute the hypothesis that intra-EC FDI will fall as a result of deeper economic integration. On the relationship between FDI and trade, the Buigues and Jacquemin research confirmed that US and Japanese exports to the EC were likely to be complementary to, rather than substitute for, US and Japanese FDI in the EC. Another study conducted by ourselves (to be considered later in the chapter) shows a positive relationship exists between these variables and intra-EC transactions, although, consistent with trade theory, the ratio between exports and FDI flows is higher in intra-, than in extra-, EC transactions.

Other evidence on the relationship between intra- and extra trade and FDI is more casual, although none the less instructive. Data on both extra- and intra-FDI in the EC suggest that the growth in downstream services (notably wholesale trade and business services) is closely correlated with exports from the investing country. For example, the gross product (= value added) of EC based wholesale trading affiliates of US firms rose by 102.9 percent between 1982 and 1989, and by 9.6 percent in the following three years; while over the same time periods, the exports of the US MNEs shipped to their European affiliates rose by 73.7 percent and 28.2 percent.

Over the period 1982 and 1989, the rank correlation coefficient between changes in the stock of US assets in EC wholesaling affiliates and US exports to EC countries about which data are available was +0.53, but for that of 1989–1993 it was −0.08.[57]

How far do the above conclusions hold for intra-EC trade and FDI, and to what extent are they country and industry specific? Certainly, as shown by both Eurostat and national data, there appears to be a significantly positive correlation between the recent growth in intra-EC FDI in trade related activities and exports from the investing countries, although the former has tended to outpace the latter.[58] Since, in their more general model, Pain and Lansbury calculated that the IMP program raised intra-EC UK and German FDI in distribution by 27 percent and 2 percent of the 1992 stock of FDI, so it may be concluded that, in part at least, the rise in intra-EC trade is also the result of the IMP.[59]

What next of the interface between trade and FDI in particular industrial sectors? In their analysis of the changing share of US and Japanese FDI in, and exports to, the EC for the period 1984–1990, by two digit manufacturing sectors, Buigues and Jacquemin (1994) found a Pearson coefficient of +0.10 for the former and +0.64 for the latter. (The respective coefficients which related the share of exports and of FDI for 1990 were +0.75 and +0.28.) However, a more detailed industrial breakdown between changes in the sales of US affiliates in Europe and exports shipped by parent companies to their European affiliates between 1982 and 1989 reveals less impressive correlation coefficients of +0.15 in the case of 22 sensitive sectors and a +0.08 in the case of 12 "non-sensitive sectors."

Details on the relationship between the sectoral distribution of *intra*-EC FDI and trade are hardly better! We have drawn on two sources of information. The first is that contained in a study by Davies and Lyons (1996), which examined changes in intra- and extra-EC FDI penetration ratios and the export shares of German, French and Spanish industries, between 1987 and 1992.[60] The authors showed there was little systematic relationship between the level of foreign ownership, or changes in that ownership, and the level and change in either intra- or extra-EC trade. While, for example, trade and FDI appeared to closely parallel each other in computers, this was not so in the aerospace and the more traditional sectors, while in the Spanish telecommunications sectors and German electrical machinery sectors, a *decrease* in foreign ownership was associated with an increase in the significance of both intra- and extra-EC trade flows.

The second source of data is that of intra-EC FDI and intra-EC trade, published by Eurostat (or related agencies) for the years 1984 to 1992; these data are only available for some two digit industrial groups. In Table 9.8 we set out a comparison between the changing share of intra-EC FDI flows and intra-EC trade; and, in Table 9.9, the changing trade/FDI ratios over this period.

Table 9.8 Comparisons between share of intra-EC FDI and trade by broad industrial sector, 1984–1992 (percent)

	1984–1986 FDI	1984–1986 Trade	1987–1989 FDI	1987–1989 Trade	1990–1992 FDI	1990–1992 Trade
More technology intensive	**73.0**	**59.9**	**47.0**	**61.3**	**50.6**	**62.1**
Chemicals	30.8	18.4	28.4	16.6	9.9	15.9
Non-electrical machinery	15.7	10.6	3.2	11.4	10.1	11.1
Electrical and electronic equipment	18.4	14.8	13.3	15.4	15.3	15.6
Transport equipment	8.1	16.1	2.1	18.0	15.3	19.5
Less technology intensive	**26.9**	**40.1**	**43.0**	**38.7**	**49.5**	**37.9**
Primary and processed food products	9.6	12.5	22.7	11.3	27.2	10.8
Metal and metal products	0.7	3.6	6.4	3.8	3.5	4.1
Other industries	16.5	23.9	23.9	23.7	18.8	23.1
All industries	**100.0**	**100.0**	**100.0**	**100.0**	**100.0**	**100.0**
ECUs (billion)	**1.33**	**319.9**	**6.67**	**424.2**	**9.02**	**547.2**

Table 9.9 Intra-EC trade/FDI ratios, 1984–1992

	1984–1986	1987–1989	1990–1992
More technology intensive	**196.4**	**82.9**	**74.4**
Chemicals	142.7	37.1	97.2
Non-electrical machinery	160.8	325.5	66.5
Electrical and electronic equipment	192.9	73.8	61.9
Transport equipment	478.1	540.3	77.5
Less technology intensive	**355.6**	**46.4**	**46.6**
Primary and processed food products	312.2	31.5	24.1
Metal and metal products	1,047.2	37.7	69.7
Other industries	346.5	62.9	74.6
All industries	**239.5**	**63.5**	**60.7**

Source: Eurostat (1994).

Note
Annual average, Intra-EC FDI is defined as inward investment flows into all Member States of the EC from other Member States of the EC; and intra-EC trade as value of exports between members of the Community.

Three particularly interesting features emerge from these tables. The first is the increasing share of intra-EC FDI flows directed to the less technology intensive sectors particularly in the 1980s; this is in marked contrast to the industrial pattern of US and Japanese direct investment in the EC. However – and second – as shown by the changing share of trade flows, it would seem that the intra-EC exports of EC countries is also becoming less technology intensive. Since the more technology intensive sectors are also those which tend to be more integrated across national boundaries, these data suggest that, even by the early 1990s, the European MNEs had still not fully geared their European operations to meet the needs of the internal market. Third, as revealed by Table 9.9, the trade/FDI ratios have fallen substantially over the last decade, although there is no distinct sectoral pattern which emerges.

Hypothesis 2, above. We set out some of the changes in the geographical distribution of both extra- and intra-FDI in the EC over the past decade or so. Overall, the share of all FDI by the major EC countries directed to the EC increased in almost all manufacturing and service sectors between the mid-1980s and mid-1990s. However, there seems little to suggest that there has been any general increase in the geographical concentration or agglomeration of FDI *within* the EC, except in a few technology or information intensive sectors thought likely to be the most responsive to the IMP program. For example, the UK, which already had a revealed comparative FDI advantage in financial services has continued to maintain that advantage. In the pharmaceutical sector, there has been further concentration of both intra- and extra-EC FDI in the UK and France. The six core countries accounted for more than four-fifths of the EC related cross-border M&A transactions between 1989 and 1994 (UNCTAD 1998). However, if anything, the data – fragmentary as they are – suggest that there has been a modest decrease in concentration of FDI in the electronic components, office and computing machines, industrial instruments and business services in the four most populated EC countries.

Outside the knowledge-intensive sectors, we observe that, while the core EC countries have continued to attract the bulk of new FDI and cross-border M&A activity, in auto components and in auto assembling, Spain has become a major new production outlet and has attracted both Japanese auto companies and joint ventures of EC and US MNEs. In chemicals, too, there has been some geographical restructuring of new FDI, particularly from Germany and the UK towards the Netherlands and Spain. At the same time, all the major EC chemical MNEs have increased their share of production both elsewhere in the EC (and, outside the EC, in the US) since the IMP program was first announced. This pattern of localization and globalization going hand and hand is also repeated in the textile and clothing industry; but, in spite of the increased Europeanization of this sector, imports from outside the EC continued to rise at the expense of the output of indigenous firms (Agarwal, Hiemenz and Nunnenkamp 1995).

A related hypothesis to the one stated at the beginning of this section is that the lowering or removal of non-tariff barriers will reduce the growth of *extra*-EC FDI in those sectors in which *intra*-EC FDI expands the most rapidly. But, according to Agarwal, Hiemenz and Nunnenkamp (1995), this has not happened. By considering up to nine sectors for each of four countries, viz. France, Germany, the Netherlands and the UK, the authors secured bivariate correlation coefficients between changes in the intra- and extra-FDI between 1985 and 1992, which were generally positive, rather than negative as might be predicted. This, in the words of the authors, suggests that the "globalization strategies of the major EC investors were largely independent of integration in Europe" (Agarwal, Hiemenz and Nunnenkamp 1995, p. 12).

Hypothesis 3, above. Earlier in this chapter we showed that the share of FDI inflows to the GFCF of all EC countries, except Ireland, increased markedly in the five years immediately following the announcement of the IMP, since when it has fluctuated between 5.3 percent and 7.2 percent. It may be further noted that, although the share of inbound FDI flows to GFCF varies between member states (in 1995 it varied from 2.6 percent in Germany and Italy to 20.4 percent in Belgium), the same or similar rate of increase between the first and second half of the 1980s was experienced by most countries.

When the foreign participation ratio of the EC is compared with that of other developed countries, including the rest of Europe, it can be seen that, in the early 1990s, there was some relative retrenchment of FDI in North America, although, in 1994, the ratios for both Canada and the US were nearer their level of the late 1980s. The buoyancy of the foreign participation ratio in the EC in the 1990s is entirely consistent with the increased share of intra-EC cross-border M&As in all cross-border M&As.

Although we only have piecemeal evidence about the *changing* share of the foreign ownership of particular sectors in EC countries, we do know that, during the 1980s, the share of foreign enterprises in the manufacturing production of five EC countries, viz. France, Germany, Ireland, Italy and the UK, increased in all cases except for Germany where it remained the same. We also know the sectors in which MNEs or their affiliates tend to concentrate, viz. computers, motor vehicles, pharmaceuticals, electronic equipment and industrial instruments (OECD 1993, Dunning 1993a). If one, then, examines the industrial composition of the sales of US affiliates in the EC manufacturing in 1993, one sees that between 70 percent and 75 percent were in one or the other sensitive sectors identified by the Commission; and that this percentage has hardly changed since 1982.[61] This percentage compares with a figure between 50 percent and 55 percent of the value added in all manufacturing by *both* indigenous and foreign owned firms in the Community (Buigues, Ilzkovitz and Lebrun 1990). Since the pattern of FDI by the other major European countries in the EC is broadly similar to that of the US, it may be reasonably concluded that, relative to locally owned firms, the affiliates of foreign MNEs are more concentrated in IMP sensitive sectors; and, excepting for medical instruments, that their share of the output of the *most* sensitive sectors has increased – at least marginally – since the early or mid-1980s.[62]

To some extent, then, these data are further corroboration that, since the mid-1980s, quite a substantial part of FDI in both North America and Europe has been undertaken as part of a deliberate strategy of MNEs designed to maintain or advance their global competitive positions. In so far, too, as economic integration increases inter-firm rivalry, and reduces the transaction costs of engaging in cross-border M&As, it may lead to a change in the ownership of firms, without there being any change in the location of production or trading patterns.

Again, such fragmentary evidence as we have points to M&As being concentrated in the sectors which have been most affected by the IMP. Using data on M&As involving US and European companies[63] between 1985 and 1991 and classified by 19 industrial sectors, it can be shown that 69 percent of the value of the transactions, in which US firms were the buyers and 75 percent of those in which European firms were the buyers, were in the sensitive sectors. For this chapter, we conducted an additional econometric exercise which attempted to test the proposition that changes in the sectoral distribution of US FDI in the leading EC countries would be related to the sensitivity of the sectors to the IMP program. The proposition here, derived from the trade and FDI literature, is that the FDI directed to the EC, both absolutely and relative to trade, will be positively correlated to the removal of the trade barriers as US firms seek to become "insiders" in a more liberalized EC market.

In testing this hypothesis, we compared (by use of pooled data for two time periods, viz. 1982 to 1989 and 1989 to 1993), the change in the sales of US affiliates in Europe, in 31 industrial sectors between 1982 and 1993 to five explanatory variables, viz. (1) the sales of established US affiliates in 1982 and 1989 (this we took to be a proxy for agglomeration economies and a "familiarity" index for new investors),[64] (2) changes in market size of the EC, (3) changes in the value added per person employed in the EC (as a measure of labor productivity), (4) changes in exports of US MNEs to their European affiliates, and (5) a dummy variable for the IMP, which we relate to the perceived sensitivity of the sectors on a scale of 1 (little sensitivity) to 3 (high sensitivity).[65]

We calculated two equations: one with and one without an IMP variable. The results of the former are set out in Table 9.10. Only the market size variable was statistically significant at the 5 percent level for a one-tailed test. The perceived impact of the IMP was shown to be negatively (although not significantly) related to the sectoral increases in the sales of US subsidiaries.

Inadequate sectoral statistics preclude us from conducting such a detailed exercise for intra-EC FDI. The best we can do is to use the Eurostat data on the sectoral composition of intra-EC FDI flows for the period 1985 to 1992, and see how far these are related to the kind of variables identified in the earlier exercise. However, we did not, in this instance, calculate an agglomeration variable, partly because there are no data on

Table 9.10 The determinants of changes in sales of US industrial affiliates in Europe classified by industrial sector, 1982–1993

	Δ Sales[a]
Constant	.5317 (.7407)
Actual sales[b]	−.0171 (1.0563)
Change in market size[c]	.6500* (.3694)
Change in productivity[d]	.4444 (.7065)
Change in exports[e]	−.0298 (.0688)
Dummy[f]	−.1175 (.1360)
Adjusted R^2	.1020
F Statistic	1.976

Source: US Department of Commerce 1985, 1992 and 1995, Eurostat 1994, Buiges, Ilzkovitz and Lebrun 1990.

Notes
a Change in sales of US affiliates in Europe 1982–1983 and 1989–1993. These are treated as pooled data.
b Actual sales of US affiliates in Europe 1982, 1989.
c Change in EC market size 1982–1989 and 1989–1993.
d Change in EC labor productivity 1982–1989 and 1989–1993.
e Change in exports of US MNEs to Europe 1982–1989 and 1989–1993.
f Dummy variable on a scale of 1 to 3 to reflect perceived sensitivity of the sector to IMP.
* Significance level 5% (one-tailed test).

the stock of intra-EC FDI in the early 1980s; and partly because the sectoral breakdown is too broad to calculate a meaningful index. Also, in place of variable (4) in the previous exercise, we computed an index of intra-EC trade published by DEBA (vd). However, because Eurostat FDI data are only available for seven industrial sectors – and there are no sectoral breakdowns by countries – we have divided the period into six three-year intervals[66] to obtain an acceptable number of observations. All FDI data are then expressed as a ratio of the three-year average flow to the average FDI flow for 1984 and 1985. For the first three explanatory variables, viz. change in market size, labor productivity and intra-EC trade, we adopt a similar procedure. However, instead of introducing a dummy variable for the IMP of 1–3, we ranked each of the seven sectors according to their perceived sensitivity of that to the removal of non-tariff barriers (1 = high and 7 = low).[67]

We again formulated two regression equations; one with and one without the IMP variable. The results of the former are set out in Table 9.11. Although these should be treated with even greater caution than the previous exercise, they suggest that the negative effect of IMP on defensive market seeking FDI was outweighed by its positive effect on other forms of FDI – including strategic asset seeking FDI; productivity was also significant at the 1 percent level and correctly signed.

Hypothesis 3, above. Previous sections of this chapter have, in fact,

Table 9.11 The determinants of changes in intra-EC FDI flows

	Δ *Intra-EC FDI*[a]
Constant	−28.4742 (8.9720)
Change in market size[b]	−2.0322 (19.5751)
Change in productivity[c]	36.0070* (9.4544)
Change in intra-EC trade[d]	−.3782 (14.8770)
Dummy[e]	1.3865* (.2225)
Adjusted R^2	.6521
F Statistic	15.244

Source: US Department of Commerce 1985, 1992 and 1995, Eurostat 1994, Buiges, Ilzkovitz and Lebrun 1990.

Notes
a Intra-EC FDI flows, expressed as 3-year moving averages from 1985 to 1992, as a percentage of an average of the base years 1984 and 1985.
b Change in EC market size by industrial sector; 3-year moving averages (apparent consumption).
c Change in EC labor productivity by industrial sector; 3-year moving averages.
d Change in intra-EC trade by industrial sector; 3-year moving averages.
e Dummy variable on a scale of 1 to 7 to reflect perceived sensitivity of the sector to IMP.
* Significance level 1%.

touched upon this hypothesis indirectly in as much as we have shown that many of the effects of the IMP have been sector specific. Moreover, we have indicated the types of sectors in which the foreignness or multinationality of enterprises is perceived to confer a competitive advantage. However, it is worth recalling that the main indigenous competitors to foreign firms investing in the EC are significant MNEs in their own right. Moreover, for the most part, the MNEs for Europe are from the same industrial sectors in which inbound FDI is concentrated.[68]

To test hypothesis 4, above, we decided to sidestep the issue of the distinctive characteristics of MNEs – and, indeed, that of the intra-firm co-ordination and transaction costs – by estimating the revealed employment advantage (REA) of foreign, in this case the US, affiliates in the EC. This we did by calculating the share of *total* EC employment in the EC accounted for by US affiliates in each of some 30 industrial sectors in 1993 and then dividing that share by the share of all EC industrial employment accounted for by all US affiliates. A ratio above 1 would indicate US firms had a comparative REA in that sector; and a ratio below 1 that they had a comparative disadvantage.

The REA is the first of the explanatory variables we relate to the dependent variable, which, again, is the increase in the sales of US affiliates in Europe between 1982 and 1993. The other independent variables are export/local sales (FDI) ratios of US MNEs, which we use as a proxy for the preference of US firms to satisfy their European markets from a

Table 9.12 Some determinants of change in sales of US affiliates in the EC classified by industrial sector

	Δ *Sales*[a]
Constant	.9814** (.3258)
REA[b]	.7227* (.2776)
Log export/FDI intensity[c]	−.3891** (.1389)
DUM[d]	−.0309 (.1182)
Adjusted R^2	.2827
F Statistic	7.174

Source: US Department of Commerce 1985, 1992 and 1995, Eurostat 1994, Buiges, Ilzkovitz and Lebrun 1990.

Notes

a Change in the sales of US affiliates in Europe, 1989/1982 and 1993/1989. These are treated as pooled data.

b Revealed Employment Advantage (REA) of US affiliates in Europe (EU). The first step was to calculate year values for each of the years 1982, 1989 and 1993. The numerator here is the ratio of the percentage of employment in US affiliates of all employment in the EC for each industrial sector, and the denominator is the percentage of the employment in US affiliates of all employment in the EC for all industrial sectors. The second step was to use these values to calculate changes in the REA ratio between 1982 and 1989, 1989 and 1993.

c Export/FDI intensity is the ratio of the growth of exports of US MNEs to their European affiliates (1989/1982 to 1993/1989), the growth of sales of the EC affiliates of US firms (1989/1982 and 1993/1989).

d Dummy variables (on a scale of 1 to 3) perceived sensitivity of the sector to the IMP.

* Significance level 5%.

** Significance level 1%.

US cf. a European location, and a dummy variable (on a scale of 1 to 3) which measures the perceived sensitivity of the sector to the IMP.

The results, which are also set out in Table 9.12, explain almost 30 percent of the sales growth of US affiliates. Both the REA and export/local sales ratios are significant at the 5 percent level; however, the IMP variable adds little explanatory value. The REA variable is positively related and the export/FDI ratio is negatively related to the increase in the sales of US subsidiaries in Europe.

Conclusions

The preparation of this chapter has been like doing a difficult jigsaw puzzle with many pieces missing! Only very faintly and imperfectly is one able to see the full picture.

We have used most of the statistical evidence at our disposal to examine changes in the extent and pattern of extra- and intra-FDI in the EC (or Western Europe) since the early 1980s. That part of the jigsaw is reasonably clear. FDI in the EC has risen faster than in most other parts of the world (save for Japanese FDI in parts of East Asia); but there is little reason to suppose that this has been at the expense of non-EC FDI.

Within the EC, there have been some discernible changes, both in industrial structure and in the geography of economic activity. Of the former, the relative growth of FDI in knowledge-intensive activities is, perhaps, the most significant trend – although this is by no means confined to Europe. Of the latter, the access of Greece, Portugal and Spain – and particularly Spain – has led to a modest decentralization of other than the most technology and information intensive activities from the six core EC countries.

Our analysis also confirms that the growth of intra-EC and Japanese FDI has outpaced that of the US over the last decade or more. However, whereas the proportion of goods exported from US subsidiaries in the EC has remained about the same since 1982, other forms of intra-EC trade – including that of European MNEs, have risen quite rapidly.

When trying to isolate the significance of the possible explanation for these events, one is faced with the most challenging conceptual and data problems; and our conclusions must be extremely tentative. We would, however, make five observations:

1   While regionalization and globalization are distinct spatial concepts, it is difficult to perceive how globalization could have had the consequences it has in Europe if the IMP program (or something like it) had not come about. This is particularly the case in sectors which are the most internationalized; although, it is worth recalling that even the most globally oriented MNEs tend to practice regional, rather than global R&D and production strategies (UNCTAD 1993b).

2   Almost all the studies examined in this chapter point to the fact that the main dynamic impact of the IMP on FDI flows has been through its effects on other variables affecting FDI – and noticeably marketsize, income levels, the structure of economic activity and agglomeration economies. *Inter alia*, this makes it very difficult – and indeed, of questionable value – to consider IMP (or a proxy for same) as an independent variable, except perhaps, in the years immediately following 1985, when FDI was influenced more by the expectations of the program's outcome. But, even considering the IMP as an independent variable, the few studies – including some new ones presented in this chapter – all generally agree that it has stimulated both extra- and intra-EC FDI, but the former more than the latter – but not as significantly so as have other variables.

3   It seems clear that the effects of IMP are sector specific, and there is some evidence that, as hypothesized by trade and FDI theory, extra-EC FDI has increased more in sensitive than in non-sensitive sectors since the early 1980s – and equally important – more in these sectors than elsewhere in the developed world. The Pain and Lansbury study also reveals that, within the IMP, both UK and German FDI in either EC countries would have been less – and particularly so in some of the more sensitive sectors, e.g. finance and insurance.

4   This chapter has examined the validity of several propositions which emerge from trade and FDI theory. First, it has shown that there is only limited evidence that the geographical concentration of economic activity has increased, even in the sectors which benefit from the substantial plant economies of scale. At the same time, the fact that higher value, e.g. innovatory activities have remained so highly embedded in the core countries, while the markets for the products has increased substantially, is testimony to the continuing drawing power of the economies of agglomeration in these sectors. Again, consistent with the predictions of neo-classical trade theory, the IMP may well have helped disperse resource based and/or lower value activities; and, in part, this is documented by the changing structure of intra-EC FDI and trade.

Second, we have found that there is a complementarity between FDI and trade in most of (but not all) industrial sectors, and that the IMP has done nothing to lessen this complementarity. However, this relationship is less strong for intra-EC than for extra-EC FDI. Third, as predicted by FDI theory, the most significant growth in the *share* of sales of foreign affiliates has occurred in those sectors and countries in which the competitive advantages of the these – relative to their indigenous rivals – firms are the most marked. Such fragmentary evidence as we have gives no support to the proposition that non-MNEs have improved their competitive positions *vis-à-vis* MNEs; though, in some sensitive sectors, EC based MNEs have improved their competitive position *vis-à-vis* US and Japanese MNEs; and it is highly likely the IMP has contributed towards this improvement.

5   A substantial proportion of the extra- and intra-EC FDI in the EC since the mid-1980s has taken the form of M&As; and part of the rationale for this has been to acquire strategic assets to advance the regional and/or global competitiveness of the acquiring firm. Although such M&As are essentially a global phenomenon (Walter 1993), those involving EC firms as sellers have undoubtedly been facilitated by the IMP. The effect of these M&As on the intra-EC location (cf. the ownership) of economic activity is ambiguous; but, in the majority of cases, there has been some restructuring of activity of the acquired firm; and this, as well as the distinctive sourcing and exporting policies of the acquiring firms may well effect both intra- and extra-EC trade.

Our final observation is that, while for some sectors and for some foreign investors, the dynamic effects of the IMP program have already largely materialized, for others – and especially for the service sectors and for Japanese (and possibly some European) investors – these consequences have yet to work themselves out. Hopefully, the next few years will help us fit some new pieces into the jigsaw portraying the effects of the IMP; although these will become increasingly difficult to isolate from the consequences of European monetary integration – mark 3 – in the ever deepening integration of Europe.

NOTES

1 Now called the European Union (EU). However, as most of the analysis contained in this chapter predates the formation of the European Union, we shall use the expression European Community (EC) throughout.
2 For a review of these studies, see UN (1993a).
3 Particularly in the Irish case, where intra- and extra-EC inward investment increased dramatically in the decade after Ireland joined the EC in 1973.
4 A good example is provided by Spain and Portugal. In the five years after their accession to the EC, the average annual increase in the stock of extra- and intra-EC FDI into Portugal was 56.7 percent and into Spain 128.3 percent. In the period 1990–1996, the corresponding increases were 5.7 percent 10.2 percent (UNCTAD 1998). Moreover, a serious deficiency of multi-variate studies is that they rarely consider the second-order affects of FDI on the other variables – notably market size and GNP per head – which are usually included in the regression equations.
5 The year prior to the announcement of the Internal Market Program (IMP).
6 Estimates by scholars vary. Yannopoulos (1992) calculated that, for the period 1980–1984, extra-EC FDI *flows* were two-thirds of all inbound FDI; this compared with an estimate made by Molle and Morsink (1991) for the years 1975–1983 of 75 percent; and that by Pelkmans of the percentage of extra-FDI stocks for 1978 of total FDI in the EC of 57 percent (Pelkmans 1984).
7 Defined both in terms of their GNP per head, and the proximity of their industrial and commercial heartlands to Central Western Europe, viz. Belgium, Luxembourg, France, Germany, Italy, Netherlands and United Kingdom. We accept, of course, that *parts* of industrial France, the UK and Italy are as far removed from the Ruhr Valley as is Southern Denmark!
8 The ratio is a kind of revealed comparative advantage of the EC in attracting FDI from other EC countries. In 1980 the ratio for German/EC FDI was 1.06; for France 1.00; for Belgium/Luxembourg 1.65; for Denmark 1.31; for the Netherlands 0.89; and for the UK 0.50. The below average figures for the Netherlands and the UK reflected the above average share of North American FDI attracted to these countries. By contrast, the US/EC intensity ratio was 0.60 and the Japanese/US ratio was 0.30.
9 Obviously there were exceptions to this rule. Philips of Eindhoven is one example of an EC MNE which totally restructured its European activities in the first 20 years of the ECM.
10 The most noticeable increase was, perhaps, recorded by the UK where the share of its outward stock directed to the EC rose from 7 percent in 1960 to 15 percent in 1971 and 21 percent in 1985.
11 The transaction costs of tariff barriers primarily represent an addition to the transport costs of exporting or importing goods and services. Those of non-tariff barriers represent a whole range of cost-enhancing measures which affect not only the plant-specific costs for production of goods and services, but firm-specific costs of transacting and co-ordinating the various extra-plant activities, including the procurement of inputs and the marketing and distribution of outputs. It is only very recently that economists have paid serious attention to

the effects of economic integration on these latter costs – and on how integration may help upgrade the competitive advantages of multi-product firms whose activities spread across national boundaries.

12 The theory of international production attempts to explain the extent and pattern of the foreign owned value activities of firms (i.e. production financed by FDI). Like trade, the unit of account is the output of firms and countries, as distinct to FDI, which is an input measure. At the same time, FDI is often taken to be a proxy for foreign production.

13 As, for example, determined by most articles in a special edition of the *Oxford Review of Economic Policy* (Vol. 14, No. 2) 1998 on Trade and Location. Exceptions include the work of trade theorists, such as Helpman and Krugman (1985), Markusen (1995) and Markusen and Venables (1998).

14 For a survey of the current state of FDI theory, see Dunning (1993a) and Caves (1996). For a recent examination of the impact of MNEs on the geography of international production, see Chapter 7 of this volume and Kozul Wright and Rowthorn 1998)

15 This it may do for two reasons. First, the IMP is likely to improve the efficiency of "insider" relative to "outsider" firms (this, after all, is one of its main intentions). Second, it will encourage the restructuring of activities by foreign firms in so much as the unified market enables a more efficient disposition of resources.

16 Although the Common Market came into being on 1 January 1958, it was not until the late 1960s that a tariff-free zone in the EC was finally accomplished.

17 Although between 1985 and 31 December 1992, the majority of directives designed to remove non-tariff barriers had already been put into effect.

18 Throughout, we consider the 12 countries. These include Spain, Portugal and Greece which joined the EC in the early 1980s, but exclude Austria, Finland and Sweden, which acceded to the EU in 1995.

19 There are, of course, other normalizing factors which one should consider, e.g. changes in exchange rates. Most data in this chapter are expressed in US dollars and there have been some noticeable fluctuations in the value of that currency relative to European countries over the past 15 years – and particularly in the £/$ rate.

20 Of course, for individual sectors of the EC, the share of FDI was considerably higher. For further details see UN (1993b).

21 Before dipping again in 1996 to 5.9 percent.

22 Broadly equivalent to flows, except that changes in stock are more likely to incorporate reinvested profits than the flow data.

23 For the purposes of this exercise, we have included Denmark in the non-core countries.

24 Greece joined the 9 EC countries in 1981 and Portugal and Spain in 1985.

25 For further details, see the various annual surveys on foreign direct investment in the US, published in the Survey of Current Business (US Department of Commerce).

26 These two countries alone increased their share of intra-EC FDI from 3.3 percent in 1985–1987 to 8.6 percent in 1992–1993.

27 Particularly – and rather surprisingly – in the financial services sector. While, for example, in the period 1989–1994, 56.9 percent of all extra EC mergers and acquisitions (M&As) involved UK target firms, the corresponding UK proportion for intra-EC M&As was 15.4 percent.

28 Defined as the ratio of the share of a recipient (host) country (or region) (b) of the total FDI from another (= home) country (or region) (a) to the share of the former country (or region) of the total FDI from all countries, excluding

that of the investor country. Expressed algebraically, qab = Iab/Ia*/[I* b/I*-I*a], where qab = intensity of a's investment in b, Iab = investment by a (home country) in b (host country) and * = summation of FDI across all countries (world). See Petri (1994).

29 In 1990, the European Commission identified 40 industrial (e.g. goods-producing) sectors which, prior to the announcement of the IMP, were subject to high or moderate non-tariff barriers. To this list may be added some service sectors, notably finance, insurance, business services and wholesale trade in the service sector. See Buiges, Ilzkovitz and Lebrun (1990), and Sapir (1993).

30 Namely the years of the benchmark surveys of US foreign direct investment (1977, 1982 and 1989) and for each year from 1991 onwards.

31 Unfortunately, there are no recent separate data for the EC itself, but, since the sales of FDI in the EC in 1992 were 90 percent of those in all Western Europe, these data serve as a good proxy for those of the EC.

32 One exception is the business services sector. Particularly impressive was an increase in sales of computer and data processing services of US affiliates in Europe of 399.6 percent between 1989 and 1993.

33 Which includes business services.

34 The authors note some exceptions to the rule, e.g. German FDI in all developing countries and in Asia, and UK FDI in Asia.

35 Contrary to the investment diversion hypothesis, the authors found that the correlation coefficients (again for France, Germany, Netherlands and the UK) between trade and investment were shown to be positive and significant.

36 Notably where agglomerative economies are present, e.g. in some high technology sectors.

37 When expressed as a proportion of the GNP of EC countries, the stock of inbound FDI increased from 4.8 percent in 1980 to 10.6 percent in 1990 and 12.2 percent in 1993, and to 15.2 percent in 1997 (UNCTAD 2000).

38 Mainly US. According to Walter (1993), the value of cross-border M&As involving EC firms (but excluding extra-EC M&As, where EC were the buyers) rose from $11,526 million in 1985 to $139,033 million in 1989–1990.

39 Often taken as a proxy for EC when separate data on the EC are not available.

40 And, of course, of other determinants not identified by the other variables.

41 For a more detailed specification and formal results of these models, see Dunning 1997a and b.

42 In fact, the growth of the FDI stock into the EC between 1990 and 1995 was almost exactly the same as that into other developed countries (excepting Japan), viz. 37.7 percent compared with 37.9 percent (UNCTAD (1998)).

43 A prediction which seems unlikely to be borne out by the facts!

44 For US FDI only. The study also included an analysis of FDI in developing countries, but we are not concerned with these results here.

45 A study on Swedish FDI, covering the period 1975–1990, confirmed the significance of agglomerative effects, particularly in high technology sectors, but finds that market size and the availability of skilled labor are generally more important locational determinants (Braunerhjelm and Svensson 1995).

46 A dummy variable of 1 was included for each year from 1986 onwards and 0 for 1985 and previous years.

47 The size of which was, itself, increasing as a result of more intra-EC trade and FDI. This idea is confirmed in a study by Yanawaki (1993) on the intra-EC distribution of employment in 236 Japanese manufacturing subsidiaries in 1988. Yanawaki found that the most significant explanatory variables were relative labor costs, market size and the quality of indigenous technological capacity.

His regression analysis supports the predictions of trade theory that inbound FDI will be attracted by the advantaged factor endowments of host countries.

48 As set out by Buigues, Ilzkovitz and Lebrun (1990).

49 This is also the conclusion of Barrell and Pain (1993), in a study of trade barriers (proxied by anti-dumping measures) to Japanese FDI in Europe.

50 The following paragraphs set out some of the results of a study by the authors, commissioned by the Economists Advisory Group (EAG). Full results appear in EAG (1998). For a more general analysis of the interaction between FDI, technological change and economic growth in Europe, see Barrell and Pain (1997).

51 Apart from that in Ireland.

52 These two countries accounted for 45 percent of the outward FDI stock of EC countries in 1994.

53 As identified in the FDI literature. See Dunning (1993a).

54 These were predicated to affect the availability of finance for foreign investment.

55 Perhaps an even more telling statistic might have been the share of US registered patents by firms of particular countries attributable to research undertaken by their foreign affiliates. See, for example, Cantwell and Hodson (1991).

56 Swedenborg and Agmon and Hirsch came to a similar conclusion in respect of Swedish and Israeli FDI in the EC (Swedenborg 1990; Agmon and Hirsch 1995).

57 Viz. share of total US exports directed to EC growth of demand in EC divided by growth of demand in the US/European market and non-tariff barriers.

58 Between 1984–1986 and 1990–1992 intra-EC FDI in manufacturing industry rose by 239.4 percent, and inter-EC exports of manufactured goods by 70–9 percent (Eurostat 1994).

59 Presumably it would be possible to test this hypothesis directly by replacing the FDI related dependent variable by a trade related variable.

60 For the pharmaceuticals, computers, electrical machinery, telecommunications, aerospace, medical instruments, boilers and containers, shipbuilding and rail stock sectors.

61 These and other data are derived from the periodic benchmark surveys of US foreign direct investment published by the US Department of Commerce. More exact estimates are not possible due to differences in the industrial classification used by the Department of Commerce and the European Commission.

62 In their estimates of the changing foreign ownership ratios of nine sensitive sectors in three countries, viz. France, Germany and Spain (27 observations), Davies and Lyons (1996) found that in 18 of these the ratio had increased or remained the same.

63 As derived by the Securities Data Corporation Merger and Corporate Transactions Data base.

64 See also a discussion on the relationship between information costs and FDI; see Mariotti and Piscitello (1995).

65 Again, as derived from the European Commission.

66 These are (i) 1985, 1986, 1987, (ii) 1986, 1987, 1988, (iii) 1987, 1988, 1989, (iv) 1988, 1989, 1990, (v) 1989, 1990, 1991, (vi) 1990, 1991, 1992.

67 We did this by expressing employment in the three-digit sensitive sectors – as identified by the Commission as a proportion of the employment in the seven two-digit sectors, and ranked these latter sectors by the size of the percentages we obtained.

68 In other words, the EC is involved in a good deal of intra-industry FDI (as well as intra-industry trade).

REFERENCES

Agarwal, J. P., Hiemenz, U. and Nunnenkamp, P. (1995), *European integration: a threat to foreign investment in developing countries*, Kiel Institut für Weltwirtschaft an der Universitat Kiel, Discussion Paper No. 246.

Agmon, T. and Hirsch, S. (1995), "Outsiders and insiders: competitive responses to the internal market," *Journal of International Business Studies 26* (2), pp. 1–18.

Barrell, R. and Pain, N. (1993), *Trade Restraints and Japanese Direct Investment Flows*, London: NIESR (mimeo).

Barrell, R. and Pain, N. (1997), "Foreign direct investment, technological change and economic growth within Europe," *Economic Journal 107*, pp. 1170–97.

Braunerhjelm, P. and Svensson, R. (1995), *Host Country Characteristics and Agglomeration in Foreign Direct Investment*, Stockholm: Industrial Institute for EC and Social Research (mimeo), October.

Buigues, P. and Jacquemin, A. (1994), "Foreign investment and exports to the European Community," in Mason, M. and Encarnation, D. (eds), *Does Ownership Matter?*, Oxford: Clarendon Press.

Buigues, P., Ilzkovitz, F. and Lebrun, J. (1990), "The impact of the internal market by industrial sector; the challenge of member states," *European Economy*, Special Edition, pp. 1–114.

Cantwell, J. and Hodson, C. (1991), "Global R&D and UK competitiveness," in Casson, M. C. (ed.), *Global Research Strategy and International Competitiveness*, Oxford: Basil Blackwell, pp. 133–82.

Caves, R. (1996), *Multinational Firms and Economic Analysis*, Cambridge: Cambridge University Press.

Cecchini, P., Catinat, M. and Jacquemin, A. (1988), *The European Challenge 1992. The Benefits of a Single Market*, Aldershot, Hants: Wildwood House.

Clegg, J. (1995), "The determinants of United States foreign direct investment in the European Community: a critical appraisal," Bath: University of Bath (mimeo).

Davies, S. and Lyons, B. (1996), *Industrial Organization in the EC*, Oxford: Oxford University Press.

DeLong, G., Smith, R. C. and Walter, I. (1996), *Global Merger and Acquisition Tables 1995*, New York: Salomon Center (mimeo).

DEBA (vd) (Data for European Business Analysis), Various statistics on EC trade, production and employment issues, Brussels: European Commission.

Dunning, J. H. (1993a), *Multinational Enterprises and the Global Economy*, Wokingham, England and Reading, Mass.: Addison Wesley.

Dunning, J. H. (1993b), *The Globalization of Business*, London and New York: Routledge.

Dunning, J. H. (1997a and b), "The European internal market program and inbound foreign direct investment," *Journal of Common Market Studies 35* (1 and 2), pp. 1–30 and pp. 189–224.

Dunning, J. H. (1998), "Globalization and the new geography of foreign direct investment," *Oxford Development Studies 26* (1), pp. 47–69.

EAG (1998), "The single market review sub-series IV," *Impact on Trade and Investment, Vol. 1, Foreign Direct Investment,* Brussels: The European Commission.

Eurostat (1994), EU Direct Investment 1984–1992, Luxembourg: The European Commission.

Helpman, E. and Krugman, P. R. (1985), *Market Structure and Foreign Trade,* Cambridge, MA: MIT Press.

Hirsch, S. (1976), "An international trade and investment theory of the firm," *Oxford Economic Papers 28,* pp. 258–70.

Julius, Dee Anne (1990), *Global Companies and Public Policy,* London: Royal Institute of International Affairs.

Kozul-Wright, R. and Rowthorn, R. (1998), "Spoilt for choice? Multinational corporations and the geography of international production," *Oxford Review of Economic Policy 14,* pp. 274–92.

Krugman, P. (1990), *Rethinking International Trade,* Cambridge, MA: The MIT Press.

Mariotti, S. and Piscitello, L. (1995), "Information costs and location of FDIs within the host country: empirical evidence from Italy," *Journal of International Business Studies 26* (4), pp. 815–41.

Markusen, J. R. (1995), "The boundaries of multinational enterprises and the theory of international trade," *Journal of Economic Perspectives 9* (2), pp. 169–89.

Markusen, J. R. and Venables, A. (1998), "Multinational firms and the new trade Theory," *Journal of International Economics 46,* pp. 183–203.

Molle, W. T. M. and Morsink, R. L. A. (1991), "Intra-European direct investment," in Bürgenmeier, B. and Mucchielli, J. L. (eds), *Multinationals and Europe 1992,* London: Routledge.

OECD (1993), *The Contribution of FDI to the Productivity of OECD Nations,* Paris: OECD.

Pain, N. and Lansbury, M. (1996), "The impact of the internal market on the evolution of European direct investment," London: NIESR (mimeo).

Pelkmans, J. (1984), *Market Integration in the European Community,* The Hague: Martinus Nijhoff.

Petri, P. A. (1994), "The regional clustering of foreign direct investment and trade," *Transnational Corporations 3* (3), pp. 1–24.

Sapir, A. (1993), "Sectoral dimension in market services and European integration," *European Economy 3,* pp. 23–40.

Srinivasan, K. and Mody, A. (1998), "Japanese and US firms as foreign investors. Do they march to the same tune?", *Canadian Journal of Economics 31* (4), pp. 778–97.

Swedenborg, B. (1990), "The EC and the locational choice of Swedish multinational companies," Stockholm: *Industrial Institute for Economic Social Research,* Working Paper No. 284.

UN (1993a), *From the Common Market to EC,* New York: UN Transnational Corporations and Management Division, Department of Economic and Social Development.

UN (1993b), *World Investment Directory, 1992. Vol. III Developed Countries,* New York: UN Transnational Corporations and Management Division, Department of Economic and Social Development.

UNCTAD (1993a), *Explaining and Forecasting Regional Flows of Foreign Direct Investment,* New York: UN.

UNCTAD (1993b), *World Investment Report 1993, Transnational Corporations and Integrated International Production*, New York and Geneva: UN.

UNCTAD (1994), *World Investment Report 1994: Transnational Corporations, Employment and the Workplace*, New York and Geneva: UN.

UNCTAD (1998), *World Investment Report 1998: Trends and Determinants*, New York and Geneva: UN.

UNCTAD (2000), *World Investment Report 2000: Cross Border Mergers and Acquisitions and Development*, New York and Geneva: UN.

US Department of Commerce (vd) *US Direct Investment Abroad*, Washington DC: US Government Printing Office.

Walter, I. (1993), "The role of mergers and acquisitions on foreign direct investment," in Oxelheim, L. (ed.), *The Global Race for Foreign Direct Investment*, Berlin and New York: Springer-Verlag.

Yamawaki, H. (1993), "Location decisions of Japanese multinational firms in European Manufacturing industries," in Hughes, K. (ed.), *European Competitiveness*, Cambridge: Cambridge University Press, pp. 11–28.

Yannopoulos, G. N. (1992), "Multinational corporations and the single European market," in Cantwell, J. C. (ed.), *Multinational Investment in Modern Europe: Strategic Interaction in the Integrated Community*, Aldershot, Hants and Brookfield, Vermont: Edward Elgar.

10 Re-energizing the transatlantic connection

Introduction

How are the economic relationships between Europe and North America being affected by the globalization of firms and markets? In attempting to answer this question, this chapter sets it within a historical perspective. It does so because the level and pattern of contemporary transatlantic trade, investment and technology flows are not only the outcome of recent economic forces, but are a reflection of the social and religious values of the European and American people, their institutions and their forms of economic governance, which were initially crafted more than three centuries ago, and which only now are being challenged by the advent of the global village.

For the most part, the institutional and social architecture of the nations bordering the North Atlantic are very similar, which is not surprising, as each stems from a common idealogical tradition. However, it is also the case that the spirit and course of democratic capitalism in North America – and particularly in the US – has followed a rather different trajectory to that in most Western European nations – we would argue this is due not so much to any disagreement about the virtues of a market economy *per se*, but rather about the means by which these virtues can best be promoted and preserved. More specifically, this chapter suggests that the somewhat ambivalent relationship which still exists between European and American civic society and interest groups lies in the different emphasis each places on the respective roles of individualism (in the form of persons and firms), communitarism (in the form of government and non-profit organizations), in the value forming and systemic decision-taking processes underpinning economic activity. It further asserts that world events of the closing years of the twentieth century are not only leading to much deeper transatlantic connections, but to a re-evaluation of the tenets of individualism and communitarism, so that each may blend into a new set of organizing principles, which elsewhere (Dunning 1997) we have referred to as alliance capitalism – or to coin a new word – "alliancism."

Alliancism, like individualism, focuses on the individual person's families, and commercial institutions as the main initiators and beneficiaries of economic activity, but also suggests that in the pursuit of self-interest, private economic agents need to co-operate with each other. Like communitarism, alliancism recognizes the worth of collective goals, systemic cohesion and social institutions. It further accepts the critical task of government in economic activities; but regards that task as less to regulate or participate in the creation and deployment of indigenous resources and capabilities, and more to set goals, help build institutions, and facilitate the workings of an efficient market system. It also acknowledges the increasing role of the not-for-profit sector in many capitalist countries as a provider of social capital and as a promoter of civil society (Rifkin 1995).

With these thoughts in mind, this chapter first offers a thumbnail sketch of the history of transatlantic economic relationships (TAERs), before turning to consider how these are being affected by contributory events; and also the response of the business community and of national and/or regional governments – and particularly that of the European Union (EU) and the US – to these effects.

The history of TAERs

The hallmark of the transatlantic economic connection for the first two and a half centuries, following the European settlement of North America was that of asymmetrical economic interdependence; although, after the American Revolution, the ideologies, political systems and institutions supporting this interdependence began to diverge. Most commercial intercourse took the form of arm's length trade in goods and assets; and of the westward migration of people and enterprises. In the US, the organization of everyday life evolved from an elemental subsistence economy in the North, and that of a more internationally oriented plantation economy in the South, to that of a predominantly free market industrial economy of the mid-nineteenth century, built on the principles enunciated in the Declaration of Independence, and those espoused by Thomas Jefferson, John Locke and Adam Smith.

From the very beginning of the new American republic, there was a bottom-up attitude to the functions and power of government, which was quite different from the top-down philosophy of Colbert and much of European Mercantilism (Lodge and Vogel 1987). Although for most of the nineteenth century, both Federal and State governments played a major entrepreneurial, and sometimes protective, role in shaping American economic development (Kozul-Wright 1995), the importance placed on the liberty of the individual and of interest groups, rather than on collective responsibility and social equality, was considerably greater than that then evolving in Western Europe (Novak 1982). There, in most countries, after a brief embracement of *laissez-faire* principles, the earlier spirit of communitarism returned – this time in the guise of the socialism of

Marx, Engels and F. D. Maurice. Due possibly to the greater social unrest and political upheaval following the industrial revolution in Europe, relative to that in North America, issues of equality and brotherhood were given at least as much attention as those of liberty; and, in the leading Continental European countries, that of the State's role in curbing or redressing the less desirable consequences of free markets.

Yet, such ideological issues probably had little affect on the economic links then being forged between the North Atlantic economies. This, we believe, was due to the fact that, for much of the nineteenth century, these links were less determined by the cultural mindsets and domestic economic strategies of the participating nations; and more by the discipline of the internationally accepted gold standard. In such conditions, assets, goods and people moved freely across the Atlantic ocean; and, by the First World War, closer trade and investment ties had been established between the major European nations and the US than between those countries and the rest of the world. At the same time, by the late nineteenth century, not only had the US economy overtaken that of the major European economies, but it was rapidly becoming less dependent on them for its prosperity. In spite of concerns expressed, in some US quarters, about the increasing domination by European investors of several US industries (Wilkins 1989), by 1914, the combined value of trade and the inward and outward foreign direct investment (FDI) stock of the US, expressed as a proportion of its GNP, was only 15 percent, compared with around 50 percent in the case of the leading European nations (Lewis 1938).

The late nineteenth and early twentieth century were also a time of quantum leaps in technological and organizational styles, which presented new challenges to both US and European democratic capitalism. The emergence of managerial hierarchies coincided – indeed may have been fostered by – the enormous private wealth of such US family dynasties as the Rockefellers, Astors, Vanderbilts and Pierpoint Morgans. At the same time, the spirit of voluntarism was very much alive, as demonstrated by the burgeoning of a host of privately sponsored philanthropic and fraternal associations at that time (Fukuyama 1995). But few now doubt that the ideology of individualism not only reached its zenith in these years; but, it also helped fashion the mass production system – better known as Fordism – which the US later exported to the rest of the world. By contrast, in Europe – particularly continental Europe – markets were more fragmented, family businesses were less scale intensive and less professionally managed; and governments were increasingly taking communitarian postures towards markets, and becoming more predatory in their actions.

While the First World War helped promote closer social affinities between the transatlantic allies, the inter-war years saw a retrenchment of Euro-American trade and investment, as, on both sides of the Atlantic, the attention of governments and markets was given over to internal economic problems. It was in the 1930s that the individualistic philosophy of the American founding fathers was most put to the test; and particularly so through the "new deal" of Franklin Roosevelt, which, along with the earlier abandonment of the gold standard, brought some aspects of European communitarism to the US. At the same time, on both continents and in transatlantic commercial transactions, there was little sign of alliance capitalism; indeed, if anything, there was a strengthening of competitive and adversarial relationships between interest groups, e.g. management and labor, suppliers and customers, firms and national governments. In such conditions, not only was there little transatlantic greenfield foreign investment; but there were very few Euro-American mergers and acquisitions (M&As) or strategic alliances, designed either to exploit, or to augment, the competitive advantages of the acquiring or partner firms.

In the years following the Second World War, the US shared its growing hegemony with an economically ravaged Western Europe, mainly through government sponsored schemes, e.g. the Marshall Plan, and the FDI by US multinational enterprises (MNEs). Indeed, by the mid-1960s, so much of European industry had fallen into US hands that several writers, such as Jacques Servan-Schreiber (1968), were predicting that Europe would soon become a technological satellite of the US. These forebodings were premature. Less than 20 years later, European firms were investing as much in the US as the US was in Europe; while by the mid-1990s, West–East flows of goods, services and assets across the North Atlantic had become almost perfectly balanced by East–West flows (UNCTAD 1996). Aggregate Euro-US trade and the sales of US affiliates in Europe and European affiliates in the US, in 1994, totalled over $1.5 trillion – 50 percent higher than their transpacific equivalent. In that same year, not only was one-half of the total US FDI stock and three-fifths of Canadian FDI stock outside North America directed to the European Union; but over two-thirds of the inbound FDI into the US and Canada originated from the European Union (UNCTAD 1996).

In 1998, the US was the largest non-European foreign investor in all EU countries, while Europe was the largest foreign investor in 41 US states and the second largest in the remaining nine states. Europe is also the leading, or second leading, export market for 42 states – and outside the US – for Canada as well. Moreover, much of the transatlantic FDI is high-quality investment. In 1992, for example, the US subsidiaries of European firms accounted for nearly two-thirds of the research and development (R&D) expenditures of all foreign firms in the US; while three-fifths of the foreign R&D expenditures of US MNEs was undertaken in their European affiliates (Dunning and Narula 1995). In that same year, royalties and fees paid by US corporations to European firms and vice versa accounted for two-thirds of the global royalties and fees paid or received by US corporations.

While these data all point to a growing deepening of TAERs, they neither confirm nor deny the proposition that these links are becoming more co-operative and less adversarial; or, that they are more in keeping with alliance, than with hierarchical, capitalism; or, that they are symptomatic of a convergence or harmonization in the political and social architecture supporting democratic capitalism in Europe and North America. To give force to this proposition, this chapter now turns to consider some of the more significant events now occurring in the world economy.

Recent economic events and TAERs

Most residents in the North Atlantic Community live in a closely knit globalizing economy, the prosperity of which is being increasingly driven by advances in human creativity, and made possible by the liberalization of cross-border markets and fast falling transport and communication costs. Chapter 1 has shown that information, knowledge and skills embodied in human and physical capital in the late 1990s, is what land was to the early European settlers in North America, and what the ownership of the means of production – and particularly that of machine power – was to our ancestors in the last century. Together with the emergence of new economies, today's globalizing environment is challenging some of our cherished notions about both the organization of economic activity, and the moral and political foundations of democratic capitalism. Again, as Chapter 1 has demonstrated, such an ideological reconfiguration is seen, first, in a new interpretation of the role of markets and non-market institutions (especially governments and voluntary associations) in the creation and deployment of human and physical capital; and second, as a response to the paradox that, while some of these assets – especially all kinds of information – have become more mobile over geographical space, others, notably most kinds of knowledge-supportive infrastructure and social capital have not only become less mobile, but have become more embedded in agglomerative clusters of economic and social activities.

Due primarily to the kinds of economic motors now driving globalization, this is demanding changes to the established international division of labor. Originally this division – including that between North America and Europe – was based on the spatial distribution of natural assets and on relatively free arm's length trade. Over the last century, it has been increasingly determined by the distribution of created assets; while, in the high technology and scale-related commercial sectors, trade is increasingly taking place within firms rather than between firms. Today, the specialization of economic and social tasks and the pattern of cross-border transactions are determined not just by the location specific resource endowments and institutions of countries and the core competencies of firms, but by the way in which these are combined with each other, and with the assets, competencies and institutions of other countries and firms, through a network of formal and informal alliances. Let us explain what we mean.

Globalization is causing corporations to question a purely individualistic approach towards their production and marketing systems for two reasons. First, more intensive competition resulting from the liberalization of markets, reduced cross-border transport costs and the emergence of new producers from third world countries is compelling them to search for new ways to reduce their production and transaction costs, to upgrade the quality of their existing products and innovate new ones, and to seek out new markets. Frequently, to achieve these goals speedily and effectively, producers have had not only to streamline the range of their own value-added activities, but to engage in on-going collaborative arrangements with other producers – including those supplying the products previously manufactured within their own organizations.

Such alliancism is being further stimulated by the nature of contemporary technological advances. First, many of the new technologies are generic and multi-purpose in their uses. Telecommunication and computer aided design and manufacturing equipment are no less applicable to the food processing and business consultancy industries as they are to the biotechnology and semi-conductor sectors. Second, many kinds of economic activity require the inputs of a variety of technological inputs; genetic engineering and the exploration of space are two cases in point. Such activities prompt collaboration both between the various suppliers of the technologies and between them and user firms. Third, in today's innovatory global environment, not only is the upgrading of technological capacity a competitive necessity for most firms; it is becoming increasingly expensive as existing technologies become obsolete more quickly. To spread the costs, or speed up the rate, of innovation, to share its risks and to capture new markets, firms are engaging in asset acquiring investments or alliances, both along and between value chains. Fourth, the success of the use of the core competencies of firms is increasingly resting on their being able to gain access to a wide range of enabling competencies, which are sometimes supplied by non-market institutions. This is leading both to a spatial clustering of complementary activities, and an increased pressure on the public sector and various non-profit interest groups to provide the social capital necessary to support an efficient market economy.

The idea of "co-operating to compete," and that alliancism should be regarded as complementary to individualism, and to a strong civil sector (Rifkin 1995) no less applies to intra-firm as to inter-firm relationships. The individualistic or adversarial relationships between managers and workers, and the lack of co-operation between different departments within the same firm, is not just less tolerable in today's environment; it is totally counter-productive. Labor under Fordism was primarily treated as a passive factor input like a raw material or a machine. In today's age of flexible production, it is better to be regarded as an active partner in the productive process and a potential source of creative ideas and programs. Outside the marketplace, the roles of the individual, and of small groups of individuals, are also under scrutiny; as the principle of subsidiarity in government and the contribution of non-profit organizations to social well-being are being increasingly recognized. Today, too, it is inconceivable to think of a billion dollar R&D program for a new aircraft, or drug, or generation of computers, being conducted without the close and active co-operation between the manufacturer of the product, its main suppliers and its leading industrial customers. Each association is a facet of alliancism.

Perhaps these observations are not particularly controversial; and certainly when one examines the evolving pattern of the Euro-American connection over the past decade or so, the evidence, scant as it is, points to a major thrust – which is perhaps more pronounced than in any other part of the world – towards asset acquiring FDI and inter-firm alliance formation. Let us give just one example. Walter Kuemmerle of Harvard University, in a recent paper (Kuemmerle 1999), has examined both the geographical distribution of the R&D activities of some 32 of the leading MNEs in the pharmaceutical and electronics industries over the period 1980–1995; and, the extent to which the R&D directors of the participating firms perceived that the main purpose of their foreign based laboratories was to exploit or augment their home-based assets. Kuemmerle not only found that 80 percent of the innovatory activity of these MNEs was located in the US, Canada and the EC, but a significant, and increasing, proportion of this activity was undertaken outside their home countries, and was designed to add to, rather than utilize, their existing technological capabilities.

If the interaction between alliancism and individualism is fairly evident at a corporate level – and to some extent too in the non-profit sector (see Chapter 1) – it is much less so at either a corporate-government or an inter-government level. Yet, it is here where, if the North American and European economies are to sustain, let alone improve, their competitive positions in today's globalizing economy, there needs to be some convergence in the ideologies and institutions underpinning their approach to economic management – and particularly micro-economic management. Or, putting it rather differently, more attention needs to be given to reducing transatlantic "system friction" (Ostry 1990).

The present author is not optimistic that this will be accomplished in the near future, at least not as far as EU–US relations are concerned. This is for two reasons. The first is the current friction between the US and Europe on a variety of trade related issues.[1] The second is that, in spite of the growing internationalization of several sectors of the US economy over the last two decades, and the blurring of the economic policies of the left and right of politics on both sides of the Atlantic, by far the greater amount of US economic activity remains firmly wedded to the satisfaction of domestic needs, and is supportive of the ideology of individualism. Only if and when the interests of the US citizens and interest groups are better identified with those of the global economy, is individualism likely to be modified by alliancism; and are domestic policies towards foreign competition and dispute settlement with foreign interests likely to become less adversarial or contractual (Chang and Rowthorn 1995). In Europe there is much less evidence of such dualist philosophy; as most nations are highly dependent on foreign markets for their prosperity. But, even here, it is becoming increasingly clear that despite the statements by the European Parliament and the European Commission about issues such as the social charter, that the communitarism of the past needs remodelling if the Union is to combat the competitive challenges from both East Asian and North American firms.

New forms of transatlantic-economic co-operations

How might cross-border co-operation between the European and North American governments be advanced and what form might it take? How far, indeed, is such co-operation necessary or desirable to extract the benefits of inter-firm alliancism? To what extent might such alliancism be a trailblazer for a transatlantic free trade area (TAFTA)? How formal should it be? How might it differ from existing intra-European and intra-North American regional integration schemes, or from the multilateral agreements now being drawn up by such organizations as the WTO and the OECD?

These are all questions yet to be resolved, but to conclude this chapter we would like to very briefly describe one initiative in alliance capitalism which is designed first, to promote a more co-ordinated approach by the EU and the US governments to reducing or eliminating non-tariff barriers in transatlantic trade and investment; and second, to energize the reform of the social and institutional frameworks underpinning these, and related domestic markets.

The experiment is the Transatlantic Business Dialogue (TABD), which is an unprecedented form of government-business partnership, specifically aimed at encouraging the US and EU governments to work together to enable their companies to better take advantage of the new realities of the global market place. TABD has been variously called an experiment in entrepreneurial diplomacy and "a quadrilateral negotiating forum." It is a business level dialogue, yet it is intended to influence the participating governments in their policy formation. It was first launched at a meeting sponsored by the EC Committee of the American Chamber of Commerce in December 1994 by the late US Secretary of Commerce – Ron Brown. A year later, at Seville in Spain, a group of CEOs from the leading US and European MNEs got together to discuss practical ways in which obstacles to transatlantic trade and investment might be removed or reduced. More precisely, the goal of the TABD is to encourage the political leaders to analyze the competitive situation on both sides of the Atlantic to ensure that laws and regulations converge wherever possible to allow market forces to accelerate economic growth and job creation and improve international competitiveness (Jackson 1996, p. 22).

Shortly after the conference in Spain, there was a Summit meeting between US President Bill Clinton and European President Jacques Santer at which many of the 70 specific recommendations, which emerged from Seville, were incorporated into a new transatlantic agenda, and into a strategic US–EU action plan agreed upon by both governments. These recommendations included the increased transparency of and co-operation on, environmental standards and regulatory policies; the adoption of a common approach to the strengthening of the multilateral trading and investment regimes, and to the future work of the WTO; the mutual recognition of conformity assessment procedures; the extension of US–EU customs co-operation and procurement procedures; the establishment of common eligibility standards to govern access to European and US R&D programs; the development of a global information infrastructure and the removal of all market access barriers for information technology; the initiation of a transatlantic labor dialogue, and the setting up of a task force on EC–US employment related issues; and a commitment to better harmonize the tax treatment of foreign earned income to encourage more transatlantic investment.

By November 1996 – a year after the Seville Conference – some progress had been made on a variety of these issues, and in particular the successful conclusions on a EU/US Customs Co-operation and Mutual Assistance Agreement, and the launching of a Transatlantic Small Business Initiative. Sector-specific initiatives include the conclusion, or near conclusion, of Euro–US Mutual Recognition Agreements in the information technology, medical devices and pharmaceutical industries. Less satisfactory progress has been made on harmonization of standards and technical regulations.

As yet, the TABD cannot be regarded as more than a small – albeit an important – step towards reconciling the different cultural mind sets of the US and European governments towards global democratic capitalism: nor, indeed, is it its main purpose to do so. But, most certainly, in so far as the consequences of this unique and pragmatic model of intergovernmental transatlantic negotiations – which, incidentally, go well beyond trade and investment issues – spill over into other – including domestic – domains of economic activity, they will help transform at least some of the individualistic values of the US and the communitarian tendencies of the EU into the kind of alliancism I am arguing for, without destroying the virtues of either.

Already, international corporations are well aware of the benefits of cross-border alliance formation in their efforts to improve their global competitive positions. So, indeed, are several non-profit clubs or organizations interested in promoting a variety of social objectives.[2] As yet, however, for obvious reasons, governments have been reluctant to do so. However, we believe that the content and consequences of globalization will eventually force them to co-operate. Indeed, we would argue, it is not so much a question of whether governments will work together with each other; but, how, how much and what form such co-operation will take. While we are not suggesting that alliance capitalism will, or indeed should, lead to a complete homogenization of the ideological philosophies and institutional super-structures underpinning different national economies, we do think that the successful embrace of globalization will demand some movement in this direction. In this respect, because of their innate political and cultural empathies, North Atlantic rim countries – and Canada and the UK in particular[3] – offer an excellent experimental ground both for tackling the challenges and opportunities of alliance capitalism, and for fashioning a new social architecture in a focused and co-ordinated way.

NOTES

1   Particularly in respect of agricultural products. These and other inter-regional disputes are detailed in Brewer and Young (1999) and Rugman (2000).
2   For an account of the role of internationally oriented clubs in a globalizing economy see Eden and Hampson (1990) and Lawrence Bressard and Ito (1996).
3   Canada, because its cultural and political autonomy is more communitarian than in the US; and the UK because its economic philosophy is more individualistic than that of the rest of Europe.

REFERENCES

Brewer, T. L. and Young, S. (1999), *Locational Determinants of Multinational Firms. The Effects of Firms' Strategic Choices of the WTO Trade-Investment Regime.* Paper presented at Seventh Sorbonne International Conference on Multinational Firms; Strategies, Paris, 1999, pp. 17–18.
Chang, H.-J. and Rowthorn, R. (eds) (1995), *The Role of the State in Economic Change*, Oxford: The Clarendon Press.
Cowles, M. G. (1996), "The Collective Action of Transatlantic Business: The Transatlantic Business Dialogue," Charlotte, North Carolina: University of North Carolina, mimeo.
Dunning, J. H. (ed.) (1993), *The Globalization of Business*, London and New York: Routledge.
Dunning, J. H. (1994), *Globalization, Economic Restructuring and Development*, Geneva: UNCTAD, The 6th Prebisch Lecture.

Dunning, J. H. (1997), *Alliance Capitalism and Global Business*, London and New York: Routledge.

Dunning, J. H. and Narula, R. (1995), "The R&D activities of foreign firms in the US," *International Studies of Management and Organization 25*, Nos 1–2, Spring-Summer, pp. 39–75.

Eden, L. and Hampson, F. O. (1990), *Clubs are Trumps; Towards a Taxonomy of International Regimes*, Ottawa: Carleton University Center for International Trade and Investment Policy Studies, Working Paper 90–102.

European-American Chamber of Commerce (1996), *The United States and Europe: Jobs, Trade and Investment*, Washington: European-American Chamber of Commerce.

Jackson, S. (1996), "The TABD: an entrepreneurial force behind the new transatlantic agenda," *ECSA Review IX* (3), Fall, pp. 21–23.

Kozul-Wright, R. (1995), "The myth of Anglo-Saxon capitalism: reconstructing the history of the American State," in Chang, H.-J. and Rowthorn, R. (eds), *The Role of the State in Economic Change*, Oxford: The Clarendon Press, pp. 81–113.

Kuemmerle, W. (1999), "The drivers of foreign direct investment into research and development," *Journal of International Business Studies 30* (1), pp. 1–24.

Lawrence, R. Z., Bressard, A. and Ito, T. (1996), *A Vision for the World Economy*, Washington: Brookings Institution.

Lewis, C. (1938), *America's Stake in International Investment*, Washington, D.C.: Brookings Institution.

Lodge, G. C. and Vogel, E. (1987), *Ideology and National Competitiveness*, Boston, MA.: Harvard Business School Press.

Novak, M. (1982), *The Spirit of Democratic Capitalism*, New York: Simon and Schuster.

Ostry, S. (1990), *Governments and Corporations in a Shrinking World: Trade and Innovation Policies in the United States, Europe and Japan*, New York and London: Council on Foreign Relations.

Rifkin, J. (1995), *The End of Work*, New York: G. P. Putnam's Sons.

Rugman, A. (2000), "Multinational enterprises and the end of global strategy," in Dunning, J. H. and Mucchielli, J. L. (eds), *Multinational Firms' Strategies and the New Global Competition*, Reading: Harwood Academic Publishers (forthcoming).

Servan-Schreiber, J. J. (1968), *The American Challenge*, London: Hamish Hamilton

Svedberg, P. (1981), "Colonial enforcement of foreign direct investment," *Manchester School of Economic & Social Studies 49*, pp. 21–38.

UNCTAD (1996), *World Investment Report 1996:* Investment, Trade and International Policy Arrangements, New York and Geneva: UN.

Wallace, C. D. and Kline, J. M. (1991), *EC 1992 and Changing Global Investment Patterns: Implications for the US–EC Relationship*, Washington Center for Strategic and International Studies, Significant Issues Series, Vol. XIV, No. 2.

Wilkins, M. (1989), *The History of Foreign Investment In the United States Before 1914*, Cambridge, Mass.: Harvard University Press.

Part IV

National governments and global capitalism

11 Globalism

The challenge for national economic regimes

Introduction

The role of government, as an organizing force in a global market economy, is coming under increasing scrutiny. Yet, in spite of a widespread eagerness to contain or reduce the extent of governmental intervention in the management of domestic resource allocation, it remains a fact that the countries which have recorded the most impressive economic performances over the past three decades are those whose governments have exerted a strong and positive influence over all aspects of commercial affairs.[1]

This chapter addresses just one, but an increasingly important, aspect of this enigma, viz. the implications of the globalization of business activity for the economic sovereignty of individual nation states. In particular, it considers the implications of the globalization of business activity for the organization and management of location bound human and physical assets. Its main thesis is that the pace and direction of technological, political and institutional change, especially as it has affected the extent and character of international transactions, is demanding a systemic recasting of the traditional role of national governments as custodians of the economic welfare of the citizens within their jurisdiction.

Central to this thesis is the premise that, as a result of the dramatic growth in the cross-border linkages forged by multinational enterprises (MNEs), the latitude for autonomous and purely domestic oriented actions on the part of the governments of nation states – that is to say actions which only affect the constituents of those states and not those of others – is being severely curtailed. Increasingly, too, national authorities – particularly those of the advanced industrial countries – are competing with each other for a share of the world's supply of technological and organizational capacity, and for the global economic rents of international production. Given this scenario, both the economic sovereignty of governments and the efficacy of their policy instruments for affecting domestic wealth-creating activities are being called into question.[2]

This chapter will be divided into three parts. The first part will briefly outline the main features of the global economy now emerging, and the reasons why globalization is likely to continue for the foreseeable future. The second part discusses the implications of globalization – and, in particular, the cross-border activities of MNEs – for governments, and for the organization of economic activity for which they are responsible. The third part of the chapter is more normative in that it speculates a little about what some of the responses of national governments should be to globalization. Although, clearly, these responses will vary between countries according, for example, to their size, industrial structures, institutional regimes, cultures and stages of development, we believe there are some general implications for the behavior of all governments; and it is to these, rather than the more country specific consequences of globalization, which this chapter addresses.

The main features of economic globalization

As Chapter 1 has shown, while scholars and business practitioners continue to debate the meaning of the terms "global business" and the "global economy," there is less disagreement about globalization as a process towards the widening of the extent and form of cross-border transactions; and of the deepening of the economic interdependence between the actions of globalizing entities – be they private or public institutions or governments – located in one country and those of related or independent entities located in other countries.

The shallowest form of globalization – if that is not a misnomer for the term – is where an economic entity in one country engages in arm's length trade in a single product with another economic entity in one other country. The deepest form of globalization – and it is here we can most easily distinguish globalization from other forms of internationalization – is where an economic entity transacts with a large number of other economic entities throughout the world; where it does so across a network of value-added chains;[3] where these exchanges are highly co-ordinated to serve the worldwide interests of the globalizing entity; and where they consist of a myriad of different kinds or forms of transactions.

In practice, few firms – or for that matter countries – engage in either the shallowest or deepest forms of globalization. However, it is possible to identify a number of firms or countries which are towards the bottom or top of the globalization spectrum. More to the point of our present thesis, however, is the almost universal trend towards the deeper internationalization of economic activity. The structure of the world economy is, indeed, very different today than it was even a generation ago.[4] In particular, three features may be emphasized. First, the significance (and scope) of all kinds of cross-border transactions has greatly increased. For example, as a proportion of world gross national product (GNP), such transactions have more than doubled since 1970.[5] Second, the value of the foreign production of firms, i.e. production financed by foreign direct investment (FDI), and that arising from cross-border strategic alliances – both of which are deeper forms of internationalization than that of arm's length trade – now considerably exceeds that of trade.[6] And third, there are a variety of signs that the organization of international transactions, particularly among the largest MNEs, has become both more systemic and geographically integrated (UNCTAD 1993, 1999).

It is, of course, true that the pace and pattern of globalization has been very uneven among firms, sectors and countries. Indeed, since many of the features of globalization just described are principally applicable to members of the triad nations, some scholars (Morrison, Ricks and Roth 1991; UNCTAD; Rugman 2000) have argued that the term regionalization better describes the current stage of development. This may well be the case; certainly, intra-regional transactions of all kinds in Europe, America and Asia have risen faster than inter-regional transactions. It is also true that certain parts of the world, notably sub-Saharan Africa, have been relatively unaffected by globalization.

Finally, since globalization has been largely driven by events in the industrialized nations, it is understandable that – up to now, at any rate – its greatest impact should have been felt in these countries. But, like ripples in a pond, regionalization tends to spread, initially to the immediate hinterland of the developed countries, but then further as this hinterland generates its own momentum of growth. Neither should one overlook the surge of autonomous development within certain parts of the developing world – particularly in East Asia and parts of Latin America. Indeed, international transactions involving developing countries have risen faster in the last decade than those internal to the triad countries (UNCTAD 1999). The critical issue – to which we shall return later in this chapter – is whether regionalization will develop into a form of regionalism (a kind of extended nationalism, with all that this implies) or is a step – a phase – in the globalization process.

Explaining globalization

As Richard Lipsey (1997) and others have shown, the movement towards globalization is essentially technology driven.[7] Admittedly, the tremendous growth in all forms of international transactions over the last two or more decades could not have taken place without the introduction of new organizational structures within and between firms; or the widespread restitution of the market system by many national economies;[8] or, indeed, without the removal of many obstacles to intra-regional or international trade. But, these events, together with the dramatic reduction in the time and costers of traversing space, have, themselves, been accelerated by techno-electronic innovations, notably the advent of the Internet and their impact on the competitive pressures on corporations to seek out new markets and conclude cross-border coalitions with other firms.

However, perhaps the most critical distinction between the globalizing economy of the turn of the millennium and the international economy of the last century rests in the nature of income generating assets. In 1900, the international division of labor was primarily based on the spatial distribution of natural resources, such as the fruits of the earth and untrained or semi-trained human capital. Today, the capabilities of a country to produce wealth rests increasingly on the extent to which it can create new resources or assets – such as information, technological capacity, management techniques and organizational competence. Particularly, in the triad nations, where there is slow population growth, it is the upgrading of the quality of human and physical assets and the more efficient use of existing assets – both natural and created – which is the critical determinant of economic progress.

Consider, for a moment, some of the implications of the growing importance of created, relative to natural, assets in the wealth producing process. First, by definition, created assets have to be produced. Unlike natural resources, they are not God-given; they are man-made and, in the case of many created assets (e.g. a University, an airport and the knowledge embodied in a new drug), they are very costly – both in terms of human and physical capital – to produce.

Second, because of their intangibility, many created assets are locationally mobile – although the degree of their mobility may rest on the quality and cost of other, or complementary, assets, e.g. transport and communication facilities. Most kinds of knowledge, information, professional skills, entrepreneurial talents and organizational principles acknowledge few national borders, even though there may be considerable costs incurred in transferring or diffusing these assets between different cultures (Kogut and Parkinson 1993). The "quicksilver" character of both financial and real assets is in marked contrast to the spatial fixity of many natural assets – a fact which helped shape the Ricardian and neo-classical theories of trade.

Third, created assets tend to be firm specific, i.e. proprietary to the firms producing them. In consequence, the market for created assets is likely to be much more imperfect than that for natural assets. Often created assets are the result of successful innovations; but, for every successful innovation, there are many more which are unsuccessful. To encourage firms to bear the risks and uncertainties inherent in innovatory activities, and to prevent the free-riding by competitors of successful innovations which cost little to reproduce, society – or, more specifically, government on behalf of society – has introduced various devices, e.g. the patent system, either to counteract such market failures or to reduce their net social costs.

Fourth, the markets for created assets tend to become more imperfect as and when they cross national boundaries. This is because the territorial expansion of firms into different political, institutional and cultural regimes is likely to raise the transaction costs of using such markets. Examples include the monitoring of quality control, the protection of proprietary rights, and the reduction of information asymmetries. Indeed, the desire to lower cross-border transaction costs and to exploit the cross-border economies of internal governance is one of the main reasons for the recent rapid growth of MNE activity which has, itself, helped sustain, or advance, globalization.

Fifth, the conditions under which created assets are produced and marketed are often strongly influenced by national governments – and much more so than in the case of natural assets. Sometimes, this is because governments – be they federal or state, central or local – are the main providers of the assets; primary and secondary educational services, roads and airports are examples. Sometimes it reflects the quality of the legal and commercial infrastructure they help provide; sometimes it is a direct result of the economic strategies and policies they pursue; and sometimes it is because of the general business climate and entrepreneurial ethos they foster. Several writers, notably Wallis and North (1986) and North (1993), have shown that, over the last century, government influenced production and transaction costs and benefits have become a more important component of the total costs of economic activity; and particularly so in those of knowledge intensive manufacturing and service sectors, which are the fastest growth points in the contemporary world economy.

The net result of all these characteristics of created assets – which, to repeat, though primarily a consequence of technological change, are also affected by the way in which economic agents respond to them – is that the determinants of the international division of labor and of the optimum distribution of a nation's resources and assets are more affected by the behavior of hierarchies – and especially multinational hierarchies – and that of national governments, than that of unregulated market forces.

The globalizing economy, then, is, first and foremost, an expression of a new international division of labor. This new division of labor is based increasingly on the way in which countries and firms are able to engineer the production of new income generating assets, and to combine these with location bound natural resources – the quantity and quality of which, itself, is influenced by the policies and strategies of governments.[9] It also comprises a network of imperfect intermediate product markets which is frequently under the common governance of multi-activity enterprises. The key wealth-creating actor in this scenario is the MNE, which is also the main determining institution of the spatial distribution of created assets. By internalizing the market for the intermediate products it wishes to acquire or use, and co-ordinating its markets throughout the world, it brings about a different pattern of resource allocation than by that which would have been dictated by purely external transactions.

Multinationals and national governments

The relationship between international companies and national governments has always been an uneasy, if not a schizophrenic, one. This is primarily because, while MNEs normally aim to maximize the economic rent on their global activities, governments are more concerned with maximizing the value-added created by MNEs, and particularly that part which is retained within their national boundaries. Moreover, because of their wider locational options, MNEs are frequently perceived to possess more bargaining power than national governments. Frequently, in the past, MNEs have been targeted for criticism by host countries for attempting to extract an unacceptably large share of the value added they – the MNEs – have helped create; or for not engaging in the kind of economic activity which is perceived to be in the best long-term interests of the country. Similarly, home countries have been anxious lest MNEs should export jobs, worsen the balance of payments or, by transferring technology to foreign competitors, inhibit the upgrading of their own resources and capabilities.

At the same time, both host and home governments well recognize the benefits which MNE activity may confer. To host countries, MNEs bring new technologies, management skills, access to markets and organizational capabilities. They may inject new entrepreneurial cultures, competitive stimuli and working procedures. By their procurement practices and marketing and distribution techniques, they may help elevate the capabilities of their suppliers and raise the productivity of their industrial customers. To home countries, MNEs may not only earn valuable investment income and open up new markets, but they are the principal means of tapping into and monitoring the competitive advantages of foreign firms and countries.[10]

The last 100 years is a story of the ambivalent and shifting attitudes of governments (particularly host governments) towards the perceived costs and benefits of MNE activity. In retrospect, a kind of Kondratieff long-wave cycle seems to have been at work. Inbound investment has been particularly welcomed at times of strong market oriented economic growth, and when the need for the innovating and competitiveness enhancing qualities of FDI has been especially marked. Such was the case in the late nineteenth and early twentieth century, the 1960s and for most of the past two decades.

By contrast, it has been less enthusiastically acclaimed when the perceived need for its unique qualities has been less pressing, and where host governments have been pursuing market distorting or self-reliant economic policies; or where there has been a particular sensitivity to the strategic or cultural impact of MNE activity. The inter-war years and the 1970s saw one or other of these attitudes holding strong and, there is some suggestion that in the early 2000s, some of the earlier concerns are reasserting themselves,[11] reflected, for example in the less than cordial response by some US interest groups. Similarly, but we shall not do more than mention these, there have been periods, dating back at least to the first part of the nineteenth century, when the attitude of governments towards outbound MNE activity has been very restrictive.[12]

For the most part, however, the reactions of governments in the 1990s to MNE activity fall into the first category. According to a study published by UNCTAD in 1999 (UNCTAD 1999), of 895 changes in the investment regimes of countries between 1991 and 1998, 843, or 94.2 percent, were favorable to FDI. Korea is the latest example of a country which has completely liberalized its policies towards inbound FDI since the economic crisis of the late 1990s (UNCTAD 1999).

Of the several reasons for the change in governmental attitudes toward MNE activity since the 1970s, two deserve especial mention. The first is the reconfiguration of economic growth and structural unemployment in countries of the world, which, coupled with the implementation of new labor and materials saving technologies and the increased mobility of intangible assets, has added to the pressure on countries to seek the ingredients of competitiveness and growth from wherever they can. The second factor is the opening up and development of new territories – especially in East Asia and Central and Eastern Europe – which has meant that the locational options open to MNEs have widened. These options have occurred at a time when global competitive pressures have compelled enterprises – especially MNEs – to be more adventurous in seeking out the most cost efficient locations for their value-added activities, and to form an increasing number and variety of cross-border alliances.

At the same time, there has been some reprioritization of the objectives of governments. From an emphasis on socially enhancing domestic goals in the 1960s and 1970s, the lenses of governments have been refocused towards identifying and deploying every means by which global competitiveness of their firms and their location bound resources may be enhanced; although the renewed quest for cultural autonomy and the growing resurgence of ethnic fruitions and tribalistic sentiments within nation states (possibly a reaction to the trend towards the harmonization of economic values) may well demand much more attention by governments in the next two decades or more.[13]

In so doing and in recognizing the innate mobility of many created assets, national authorities have begun to accept that, to best achi-
social objectives, they have to offer at least as
opportunities for the production and marketing
do their main competitors; and to ensure that
economic and organizational policies are such th
foreign firms are induced to invest in upgrading th
ties best suited to the dynamic comparative advantag
resources and capabilities.

Most certainly, one of the mistakes many national governments made in the 1970s and early 1980s was to try to force MNEs and their affiliates to accept the mould of established economic policies, and to exact penalties from those who did not. Often, the imposition of further market distorting programs not only did more harm than good, but soured the relations between MNEs and governments. Today it is recognized that in a world which is technologically *force majeure*, becoming economically interdependent and, for the most part, driven by international capitalism, the pursuance of domestic policies which are out of line with those of one's major competitors, is an unaffordable luxury. But – and this is a point worth stressing – although, in the 1980s, the inappropriateness of some government strategies was becoming sharply exposed by the activities of MNEs, such activities were not the primary cause. MNEs do, indeed, respond to the imperatives of the globalizing marketplace. But, although they are the main agents of change, they do not alone, determine the consequences and shape of that change. This responsibility is shared by the macro-economic and organizational systems devised and implemented by governments, and by international economic regimes, e.g. WTO, the World Bank and the IMF. In considering, then, the shift currently taking place in national government policies towards MNEs, it is necessary to look beyond the determinants and outcome of the latter's activities – and toward the implications of the globalizing economy *per se*.

The changing role of national governments

We have suggested that globalization – and its main enabling vehicle – the telematics revolution – is dramatically encapsulating space, and by so doing, is linking national economies in a way undreamed of by our forefathers. In addition, since economic growth is increasingly dependent on the enhancement and disposition of created, rather than natural assets, it follows that there is much more inter-country competition for the former and their products than for the latter and their products.

At the time of David Ricardo, i.e. the early years of the nineteenth century, it was possible to draw a clear dividing line between the foreign and domestic economic policies of national governments. As regards the former, the debate largely centered about the merits of protectionism in those cases where foreign competition was perceived to be damaging – or potentially damaging.

Not surprisingly, the stance taken by countries rested on their relative pecking orders in the development stakes; and also the lobbying power of firms from those sectors most likely to be adversely affected by trade liberalization. But, in general, the "near" free traders – like the UK – asserted each country should efficiently produce those goods and services required resources in which they possessed a comparative advantexchange those for others requiring resources in which they were comparatively disadvantaged. The preferred organizational route for achieving this goal was the unfettered market, with national administrations only intervening when the market was thought to operate inefficiently or unfairly, or where the barriers to entry into socially beneficial economic activities were too high for private investors to bear.

However, with one major exception, resources and capabilities were assumed to be location bound within national borders. Since, too, domestic firms could not "escape" from unwelcome fiscal, macro-economic and micro-management policies – nor foreign firms be tempted to take advantage of more favorable policies – the only constraint on the behavior of governments was that of the demands of foreign countries and the supply capabilities of foreign producers via trade; and even here the connection was an indirect one. The one exception was that of finance capital – the one created asset that was able to flow freely across national boundaries. Hence, the argument later put forward by economists such as Robert Mundell (1957) that trade in capital and goods were largely substitutable for each other. In such a scenario, national governments could pursue domestic economic and social policies largely independent of each other without fear that these policies would provoke undesirable reactions by other governments. And, in point of fact, for much of recent economic history, such policies have differed greatly both between countries, and in the same country at different periods of time.

In the globalizing world of the early 2000s, the options open to national administrations are much more constrained. Primarily because of the easy movement of the critical wealth-creating assets, and the fact that there is more intensive competition among nation states to produce similar goods and services than once there was, the domestic economic strategies of national governments are more closely intertwined than once they were. This is because of the widening choice of the owners of the mobile assets as to the location of their production and usage. Thus, in pursuance of legitimate domestic objectives, if the government of one country imposes too high a corporation tax, firms – be they domestic or foreign – may decide to relocate their value-added activities in another country where taxes are lower; or, in considering where to site their new plants, firms may choose that country with the least burdensome environmental constraints, or whose government pursues the most favorable industrial policy, or which offers the most advanced telecommunication facilities or the most attractive tax breaks for R&D activities. Indeed, as several studies ably summarized in UNCTAD (1996) have shown, anything and everything a government does which affects the competitiveness of those firms which have some latitude in their cross-border locational choices must come under scrutiny. In such cases, the boundaries of domestic economic jurisdiction becomes blurred. And, because of this, one of the critical assumptions underlying the behavior of any government – viz. its autonomy in the framing and implementation of its economic strategy – is no longer valid. The mould is broken; it needs to be recast.

The last 20 or more years have seen a growing recognition by the leading industrial nations of the need for some co-ordination in their macro-economic policies to avoid counter-productive domestic monetary and fiscal policies, and to cushion the adverse affect of shocks to an increasingly volatile international financial system. Though the Group of Seven has had some success in this area – and, indeed, it may be argued that the decisions of this informal group of leaders has exerted more influence on the domestic macro-economic policies of the triad nations than the actions of more formal supra-national regimes, e.g. EEC, World Bank, etc. – the recent fragility of European currencies vividly demonstrates some of the difficulties of maintaining a unified exchange mechanism, where the member countries vary in economic well-being or are faced with different economic and social needs. When the crunch comes, national interests always seem to triumph over regional or international interests.

More recently, attempts to widen the terms of reference of the WTO, notably to embrace issues relating to FDI, labor standards and intellectual property rights are perhaps, the most explicit acknowledgement – at least by some governments – that their domestic economic programs can and do affect the playing field of international transactions; and that market distorting micro-management policies may be as damaging to the level and direction of world trade as any tariff or non-tariff barriers.[14] Once again, as in many other issues – notably the initiation of EC 1992 – MNEs, through such institutions as the European Round Table UNICE (Union of Industrial and Employers Confederation) (and the Transatlantic Business Dialogue (TABD))[15] have played a critical role. More than most other economic agents, they – the MNEs – understand the implications of the gamut of legislation and policies – designed by governments to advance their own political and economic goals – not just on their own competitive position in international markets, but on how, in turn, these measures may induce a reaction from other governments.

The idea that governments, like corporations – on behalf of their constituents – compete with each other for resources and markets, and that, like corporations, they may behave as oligopolists in their rent seeking activities, is one which has, so far, gained only limited intellectual support. This is particularly so among neo-classical economists who believe that firms are the sole wealth creators in society; and that the role of government is simply (sic) to provide the legal and commercial backdrop to the market allocative mechanism, which alone and unaided, should provide the signals as to what should be produced, how it should be produced, who should produce it and where it should be produced. The idea of a UK, US or Ireland Ltd. smacks too much of corporatism, and of the kind of economic interventionism which, in the past, has proved to be less effective than the imperfect markets which it sought to replace. In particular – so it is argued – the experiences of mainland China and Central and Eastern Europe, over much of the previous century, have shown that there is an unacceptable face of government just as there is an unacceptable face of the market place.

Yet, there can be no escaping the fact that in our complex and interdependent global village, markets do not always operate costlessly,[16] neither can one deny that in social democracies, the government of the day is accountable to the electorate for its conduct of the economy, just as it is responsible for defence, law and order, the environment and public administration, and for the welfare of the less able and most disadvantaged members of society. Indeed, there is a parallel between the task of the elected authority to protect its citizens against military conquest or unacceptable political intervention and that of the sustenance of its economic security.[17] In conditions of economic isolation, this latter task is a minimal one. In the textbook world of a simple division of labor, perfect markets, immobile resources and complementary trade and production, there is little need for governments to intervene with the decisions of producers and consumers. But this is not the global economic scenario at the turn of the millennium. Countries and firms are intricately linked with each other. Resources are mobile. Governments do compete with each other. The division of labor is making for more, rather than less, interdependence of economic activities and more, rather than less, asset specificity. And markets do not always perform in the way that neoclassical economists like to think they should.

The literature on the rationale of government intervention to overcome or mitigate the inability of markets to fully optimize economic welfare is substantial and growing. It is also quite recent, although many of the justifications for government intervention date back to the time of A. C. Pigou and beyond. Economists today argue that there are three main reasons why governments may wish to intervene in markets.[18] The first – and one which will not be addressed in any detail in this chapter – is to achieve goals other than the efficient use of resources – notably to advance social, political or cultural mores – which the market system, is not (and never was), set up to achieve. This form of intervention by government is only relevant in the present context in so far as the money spent on the attainment of social goals may be at the cost of maintaining or upgrading a country's competitiveness in international markets, and, hence, the resources available to support social objectives in a future period of time. In other words, the competitiveness of US, British, German or Irish firms relative to their foreign competitors in period 1 will – in part at least – determine how much the US, British, German or Irish governments can afford to spend on social welfare in period 2.

The right, or optimum, balance of allocating a country's resources and capabilities between wealth creating and other welfare-enhancing activities cannot be decided on economic grounds alone; moreover it is likely to be highly country specific. However, in comparing the economic performances of nations over the last 20 to 30 years, several studies, have pointed to the very different emphasis to the creation and the distribution of wealth and social capital by the US and UK governments, compared with that given by the Japanese and German governments.[19] We will write no more on this issue, save to observe that the growing imperative of countries to be competitive in world markets – to maintain, let alone advance the living standards of their constituents – is requiring an increasing proportion of their resources to be directed to competitive enhancing activities; and it is this realization which is compelling some administrations to reappraise some of their spending programs and the means of financing them.

The second, and least controversial, reason why governments intervene in markets is because they perceive that the terms and conditions of exchange are being distorted by the conduct of one or more of the participants in the market – or of foreign governments. Such structural market impurities essentially result from the monopolistic, or monopsonistic behavior, on the part of producers, labor unions or consumers, although sometimes the desire to eradicate these distortions gets confused with the debate of whether some markets, e.g. those for education, housing, rail transport and health should perform a social as well as an economic function. *Inter alia,* this ambivalence of objectives explains why state run sectors are often uncompetitive. Here the concept of the social market economy becomes relevant, although in recent years, this concept has been widened to embrace societal goals which seek to balance the benefits of economic liberty with those of personal and social responsibility (Novak 1998).

National governments possess a plethora of instruments to deal with structural market failures – most of which are directed to making markets more contestable, and to inhibiting one group of participants from exploiting such economic power as they may have at the expense of other groups. Anti-trust policies represent the kernel of such instruments. Insofar as the globalization of economic activity intensifies competition between firms, the intervention of governments may be less necessary. But, more relevant is the fact that technological and organizational advances are shifting the main locus of inter-firm rivalry from being intranational to being international.

At the same time, market structures are becoming more complex as firms both compete and collaborate with each other. The growth of cross-border acquisitions and mergers (A&Ms) and strategic business alliances has been one of the most dramatic phenomenon of the last decade (UNCTAD 2000). Such alliances as the design and production of a supersonic aircraft, or a new generation of computers, are usually intended to accomplish a very specific purpose and, while some observers are concerned lest they are an excuse for monopolistic behavior, the general consensus is that many help protect or advance the global competitive positions of the participating firms.

Several European governments are currently encouraging transatlantic alliances between small to medium-size firms. However, the point we wish to underline is that one government's attitude – *vis-à-vis* that of another government competing for the same resources – towards the increased oligopolistic structure of trans-national production and the conclusion of cross-border A&Ms and alliances, may decisively affect both the incentive and capabilities of its domestically based firms to service foreign markets, and the locational options open to foreign based MNEs (or increase their investments) in that country. The mould of competition policy which is suitable to a closed economy may need to be recast in a global economy. At the same time, to discourage governments from using their competition policies to achieve goals other than those consistent with efficient markets, some kind of supra-national surveillance may be necessary where other governments are promoting economic strategies which are structurally distorting. We shall return to this point a little later.

Let us now turn to the third justification for governments to intervene in the way markets allocate resources; and one which globalization is forcing a major reassessment of the whole ethos of their macro-organizational strategies. This is to overcome, or to counteract, endemic or pervasive market failure. There are two kinds of such failure. The first reflects the costs required to create and sustain an efficient market. Economists refer to these costs as transaction costs; but, *de facto*, they include all expenditures which have to be incurred to ensure that the buyers and sellers in the market have the knowledge and incentives to behave as they would in a situation of perfect competition.

The second kind of endemic market failure arises from the fact that contrary to the assumptions of neo-classical economic theory, individual markets – be they product, labor or financial markets – are not always self-contained, independent entities, but are complementary to, and interdependent of, each other. The main implication of this interdependence is that a particular transaction may affect, for good or bad, the welfare of individuals or institutions other than those involved in that transaction. These are the so-called externalities of markets. Sometimes in their evaluation of the efficiency of markets, analysts distinguish between private costs and benefits (i.e. those incurred or enjoyed by the transacting parties to an exchange) and social costs and benefits, viz. those enjoyed by the wider community. To give just one example; it has been calculated (by some economists)[20] that the average social returns to research and development exceed those appropriated by the investing firms by 50 percent–100 percent.

The literature provides countless examples of situations in which endemic market failure is likely to flourish. Broadly speaking, these fall into two main groups. The first relate to characteristics of the goods or services being transacted; and the second to the conditions under which they are exchanged. Of the former, products whose production requires assets with a high level of specificity (or start-up) to variable costs of production (i.e. capital or technology intensive products); products the demand for which or supply of which is inelastic, uncertain or unstable; products, the supply of which is subject to substantial economies of scale or whose value rests on strict quality control; products which are more valuable if they are used jointly with other products; and products the output or use of which generates substantial external economies or costs (e.g. environmentally sensitive products).

As to market specific transaction costs, these are frequently the outcome of imperfections in interpersonal relationships, information asymmetries, moral hazard and inappropriate macro-organizational policies. They include country related political and economic uncertainties; the inadequacy of the legal or regulatory system with respect, e.g. to contract enforcement and protection of property rights; exchange risks; unacceptable or misunderstood business practices; undemanding consumer attitudes towards product improvement and quality; abrasive work and worker-management relationships; and the failure of government to adequately acknowledge or cope with endemic market failure.

It may not have escaped the reader's notice that the products which possess the characteristics just identified – or, to put it another way, when produced and sold through the market, incur substantial relational and transaction costs – are the output of created assets. They are also products which are currently predominantly supplied by large firms – though, due to the advent of electronic markets and the opportunities offered by strategic alliances, are likely to be increasingly provided by small to medium-size corporations; and the conditions of their production are markedly influenced by the actions of national governments. They are products the supply of which tends to increase proportionately as a country moves along its development path. They are also trade and FDI intensive; while the markets for them vary in their degree of imperfection according to the location of the participants involved. Finally, they are the products at the forefront of globalization, which, to be produced efficiently, often require the use of complementary assets.

Some of the responses to market failure – both by the market participants and by extra market institutions have been set out in previous chapters. Here, we would simply reiterate three of the more important. The first is for firms to internalize intermediate product markets by the vertical integration of value chains or the horizontal diversification of products or processes. Such action may either lower or increase economic welfare, depending on whether it is prompted by the desire of the internalizing firms to raise economic efficiency or to advance monopoly power. An example of the former kind of exit strategy is where a hierarchy internalizes a market to lower its transaction costs or to exploit the economies of scale or scope. This is likely to be welfare raising, especially where the firm is faced with competition in the less idiosyncratic factor or intermediate goods markets, and in the final goods or services markets. On the other hand, a hostile takeover could be prompted by the desire of the acquiring firm to eliminate a competitor and engage in market distorting practices.

The second response to market failure is for the participants in the market – sometimes assisted by non-participants – to try to reduce that failure. For example, quality variation and an inability of sub-contractors to adhere to delivery dates might be reduced by a closer and more productive working relationship between the buying firms and their suppliers; while, by reducing macro-economic uncertainties and removing market inhibiting governmental practices, e.g. discriminatory purchasing procedures, transaction costs might be lowered. These are all examples of "voice" strategies to market failure emphasized by Hirschman (1970) in his writings.

The third solution is for governments or some other extra-market institutions (e.g. groups of firms) to counteract the intrinsic deficiencies of the market by offering producers and consumers inducements to behave as if a perfect market existed. Examples include the provision of tax concessions and subsidies to increase the private benefits of R&D and training to the level of their social benefits; improving information about the export opportunities for small firms; setting up investment guarantee schemes to protect outbound MNEs against political risks; making certain that patent legislation and procedures properly reflect the needs of innovators; assisting the market in its provision of risk capital – especially for projects which are likely to generate social benefits and are long-term in their gestation – and ensuring, directly or indirectly, that the transaction or "hassle" costs of doing business – e.g. industrial disputes, inadequate transport and communication facilities and time-consuming bureaucratic controls, are kept to the minimum.

While it is possible to cite many other examples of endemic market shortcomings, most reduce to the presence of X inefficiency of one kind or another. There is, however, another aspect of market failure which economists are apt to neglect, mainly because they tend to assume human beings behave in a consistent and rational manner and are only interested in the pursuance of wealth. But – one might question – is this a realistic interpretation of why individuals and institutions engage in market transactions? Organizational theorists question this, and talk about the bounded rationality and opportunistic behavior of producers and consumers; and about the *homo psychologicus* of cognitive psychology as compared with the *homo economicus* of economics.[21]

We consider extending this idea of psychological man to the mentality or culture of wealth creating activities by countries and corporations. Even the most cursory glance at the ways in which (say) the Arab countries and the Germans conduct day to day business; or the attitudes of the Japanese and Nigerians to inter-firm relationships and contractual obligations; or the ethos of work and leisure of the Taiwanese and Greeks; or the perceived personal and social morality of workers, business managers and governments of the Koreans, Chileans and Russians – or the cross-border operational and organizational strategies of Nissan and Toyota or Motorola and Texas Instruments – reveals wide differences in the culture or ideology of wealth creating behavior. As Chapters 1 and 2 have shown, the globalizing economy is unearthing a new importance to concepts such as trust, forbearance and reciprocity; and of informal, rather than formal, organizational forms in affecting national competitiveness, and, hence, the disposition of resources and capabilities.

The extent to which the culture of wealth creating behavior is an intrinsic characteristic of a country or corporation or can be shaped by exposure to other cultures, by decree or economic pressure, or by a reorientation of personal or business values, is debatable. So indeed, is the question of which, if any, moral virtues can be considered absolute or universal (Fukuyama 1999). At the same time, there can be little doubt that the forces of globalization are compelling firms and governments to review their respective roles in influencing mental attitudes towards wealth creating activities. Whether we like it or not, the trade-offs between these and other activities, such as leisure pursuits, are changing; and, whether we like it or not, to a large extent, they are being set by countries which value competitiveness the highest. The grasshopper's attitude to life is fine as long as the grasshoppers do not aspire to the living standards of the ant. The trouble is that most of us want to retain our lifestyles of work and leisure, but also enjoy all the material benefits of our economically more successful neighbors.

Here, again, I believe governments have a critical role to play, both as information providers to their constituents about the real costs of not being competitive in an open world economy; and in helping to create a culture or psychology of economic behavior which encourages, rather than discourages, competitiveness. Much more contentious is the extent to which some culturally related business or work practices are perceived to be the "unacceptable face of competitiveness"; or, how far the promotion of the twin goals of wealth creation and social justice are mutually consistent? Why should British, or American, or Dutch textile workers be expected to have their wages or working conditions reduced to the level nearer their counterparts in Bangladesh or Sri Lanka – or lose their jobs? Although the question of harmonizing cross-country cultures of work, wealth creating activities and social needs is not yet on the political agenda of countries, it is not far below the surface, and is likely to become an increasing talking point as globalization impels governments to reappraise their attitudes on this issue.

Of course, the culture of economic behavior does not start or end with the work ethic. A no less – and perhaps, a more important consideration – and one which is in line with the principle of comparative dynamic advantage – is for a country threatened by low labor cost competitiveness to upgrade or restructure its resource usage and efficiency. Governments again can play a decisive part not just by providing the right kind of market enabling incentives and structural adjustment assistance (Ozawa 1987), but by encouraging – and be seen to be encouraging – an ethos of entrepreneurship and innovation; a readiness by enterprises to anticipate and take advantage of technical and economic change; and an appreciation by workers of the need for job restructuring and retraining.

If what has been written is familiar to most economists and business scholars, we do not think it is generally acknowledged. And this, primarily, is because the average Westerner's perception of the appropriate tasks of government is 50 to 100 years out of date. Part of the reason is, most certainly, a cultural or ideological one – compare, for example, a Christian with an Islamic or Confucian viewpoint of such issues as personal initiative, authority and collective responsibility; but, part is because Western governments have not seen the need for, or have had the political will to, recast the mould of their economic responsibilities. Some recent contributions by scholars have urged governments to reappraise their policies[22] – but these are not helped by analysts who continue to preach a minimal role for governments, or encourage a "them" and "us" attitude between private firms and the public sector; with the former being perceived as the wealth creators and the latter as the profligate spenders of that created wealth.

The core economic task of government as an enabler or facilitator of wealth creation is not yet appealing to most people. The reality – as opposed to the idea – of a partnership between government, firms and individuals in enhancing competitiveness is only now starting to take root in Europe and North America. The suggestion that the globalized economy demands a fundamental rethink of the "how," "why" and "wherefore" of the organization of government, as it does of firms is still not generally supported. For the most part, political scientists and economists either assert that governments should not involve themselves at all in macro-organizational affairs, or that they should play a direct and activist interventionist role in shaping or manipulating markets to better meet perceived social and economic needs.

Yet, *de facto*, the rhetoric of government ministers is often far removed from the practice. To take one example; in her time as Prime Minister, Mrs Thatcher constantly applauded the virtues of the free market. Yet, a reading of her record suggests that she was one of the most interventionist of Prime Ministers – if one uses the word interventionist to include any and every action taken by a government which might affect the competitiveness of the resources under its jurisdiction. But somehow, either out of ignorance, lethargy, or for some reason best known to themselves, right wing politicians seem reluctant to acknowledge that such actions as tax hikes, environmental regulations, a new educational curricula, attitudes towards monopolies, investment in roads, energy policies, regional development, health care programs, industrial relations legislation and the finance of universities – all affect competitiveness just as much as direct intervention (mainly via industrial policy) in the allocation and use of resources. And certainly, there seems little appreciation of how these policies interact with each other; hence, there is no holistic or systemic approach to them.

We would not want to press our critique of Western governments too far. In several countries – noticeably the UK and the US – there is a growing recognition that the globalizing economy is compelling an upscaling of industrial competitiveness on the political agenda, and a reappraisal of traditional macro-organizational strategies. Issues such as training, the funding of R&D, information and advice for small businesses, competition policy, attitudes towards inward investment, new road and rail links and so on are being increasingly viewed and evaluated in terms of their perceived impact on competitiveness. But, for the most part, most of the action so far taken by Western governments has been *ad hoc*, unco-ordinated and fragmentary; and as an "add-on" to existing policies, rather than part of a systemic remoulding of the organizational structure of decision taking so that it may best embrace the challenges and opportunities of a globalizing economy.

To some extent, the problem is educating the decision takers in government. Here, the fault partly lies with the academic community. We have just not got over the message that there is a fundamental difference between the kind of government action necessary to help overcome endemic market failure and to facilitate the upgrading of resources and capabilities, and that which seeks to replace or modify the behavior of firms in the belief that central planning can do a better job in advancing economic and social welfare than can markets. We have not got over the message that, to optimize their efficiency and response to market signals, firms require the availability of created assets and a wealth creating ethos which only governments can provide. We have not got over the message that increasingly what governments do and how they do it, is much more important than how much government involvement should there be!

To some extent, too, the problem is one of re-forming opinions and attitudes towards the role of governments. We need a new vocabulary to promote the image of government as a public good rather than as a necessary evil. We need a "perestroika" of government. We need to recognize that, just as "Fordism" is an outdated method of organizing work, so the kind of government interventionism appropriate to a "Fordist" environment is outdated. And, just like the emerging managerial structure of twenty-first century firms, we need governments to be lean, flexible and anticipatory of change. The new paradigm of government should eschew such negative or emotive sounding words as "command," "inter-vention," "regulation," and replace them by words such as "empower," "steer," "co-operative," "co-ordination" and "systemic." Moreover, not only must governments recognize the need for a much more integrated and holistic system of organizing their responsibilities, which demands a "spider's web" rather than a "hub and spoke" relationship between the various decision taking departments and the core of government, viz. the cabinet of the Prime Minister or President (Dunning 1992); but, for all those affected by governments, and particularly the ordinary tax payers, to take a more positive view of the benefits which only the former can produce.

It is not the purpose of this chapter to suggest how the organization of governments should change to accommodate the kind of remoulding we have articulated. But, this issue is now very much being considered in the literature. For example, Douglas Hague (Hague 1993) has identified four ways in which institutions – be they public or private – can re-engineer themselves, viz. by coercion, contagion, coaching and learning. While the latter three are usually more acceptable agents of change than the first; in practice, as demonstrated by the East Asian crisis of the late 1990s, such change usually has to wait until some kind of crisis coerces action.

At the same time we would not wish to imply that actions taken by national governments to overcome or reduce market failure are costless, or that such actions are necessarily the most cost effective way of achieving that objective.[23]

More generally, it is possible to identify the kind of situations which favor government intervention of one kind or another. Table 11.1, which is derived and adapted from Robert Wade's evaluation of the role played by national administrations in fostering the economic development of Japan, Taiwan and Korea (Wade 1988) sets out some of these situations, and the ways in which they may help reduce the transaction costs of governance.

While the data in Table 11.1 are fairly self-explanatory, and provide a set of guidelines for governmental intervention, they have not yet been subject to rigorous scrutiny by scholars. The globalizing economy may well enhance the need for such a scrutiny, as it increases the costs of misin-formed or inappropriate government action.

Multilateral action

We cannot end this chapter without at least the briefest of mentions of the implications of globalization for the existing supra-national regimes of governance; although some of the relevant issues have been dealt with in Chapter 1. If our thesis that governments are increasingly competing with each other for resources and markets to maintain or increase their living standards is correct; and, if *de facto*, such competition tends to be oligopo-listic, then, there is a real danger that the strategic rent seeking measures

Table 11.1 Some examples of situations in which governments might successfully contain their own organizational costs

Intervention or form of government intervention	*Consequences for the reduction of government related transaction costs*
• The enhancement of national competitiveness by market facilitating measures; and publicly promoting this objective	• Reduces effectiveness of rent seeking special interest groups
• The containment of interventionist policies to activities severely hampered by market failures	• Increases work effort of public agents
	• Makes policy trade-offs easier to identify and solve
• A holistic approach to the co-ordination of complementary policies and institutional mechanisms	• Clarifies policy makers' task and reduces problem of bounded rationality
	• Reduces likelihood of sub-optimization
• An ethos of consensus and co-operation between private and public policy makers, e.g. with respect to mutually beneficial goals and the means by which goals can best be achieved	• Captures economies of scope in governance and increases intra-organizational information flows and learning
• The recruitment of the most talented and well-motivated individuals for public sector employment, e.g. by offering competitive working conditions and encouraging initiative and entrepreneurship	• Reduces transaction costs of interaction between representatives of private and public sector
	• Increases knowledge of public decision takers
	• Reduces chance of uninformed or biased media coverage in forcing governments into ill-advised or hasty decisions
• The insulation of the policy making process from the strongest (and most undesirable) pressure groups	• Likely to inhibit the pursuance of sub-optimal goals and to reduce bounded rationality and opportunism and use of inefficient production technologies
• The presence of a national ethos or mentality of the need to be competitive and create wealth. Partly, this embraces a "commutarian" culture and partly one which encourages personal initiative, entrepreneurship, scientific specialization and competition	• Reduces the effectiveness of rent seeking by special interest groups, and relieves the policy making process from the pressure of day to day politics
	• Favors co-ordination of strategies and policies of public and private organizations and reduces the sub-optimization problem in the public sector
• The absence of strong sectoral interest groups, e.g. farmers and left-wing labor groups, which might press for interventionist measures by governments other than those which are market facilitating	• Reduces possibility of ideological conflicts and undue emphasis being placed on the redistribution of incomes as a (short-term) social good

Sources: Wade (1988), Stiglitz (1989), Grestchmann (1991), Hämäläinen (1994).

taken by individual governments might lead to a situation not unlike the "beggar my neighbor" restrictive trade policies of the inter-war years. For the last 40 years, GATT – and latterly the WTO – has helped set the rules of the game for trade. But, today the playing field of international competition is structured very differently. As we have argued in this chapter, it embraces many policy instruments of governments, which as much affect the capabilities of nations trade and compete with each other, just as much as the conditions underlying trade per se.

And, it is in pursuance of industrial, technology, taxation and competition strategies to advance national interests where the level of the playing fields is currently the most uneven. Again, *inter alia*, because of their unique business cultures, different countries have different interpretations of the fairness or otherwise of government interventions; hence – to give just one example – the strategic initiative talks between Japan and the US have been designed to try to reconcile some of the differences between the two nations in their interpretations of the legitimacy of government enabling measures.

The next decade is likely to see much written about the remoulding of international institutions such as WTO, the World Bank, IMF and the UN so that they can better cope with the problems of globalization – including those occasioned by the dictates of MNEs – which cannot easily be tackled or solved at a national, or even a regional, level. Several scholars, notably Joseph Stiglitz (1998), have argued the need for a new paradigm of economic growth and development to replace that of the Washington consensus of the late 1980s.[24] Again, the role of national governments in championing their own causes will be a critical one. But, just as we have argued in this chapter, the kinds of restructuring of the organization of markets and firms demanded by globalization is impelling national governments to redesign their world of governance; so, too, the functions and authority of international institutions may need to be reconsidered if globalization is to offer the fullest possible benefits – which a free exchange of people, goods and services demands.

NOTES

1 The concept of strong and positive government does not necessarily imply there should be substantial government intervention in economic affairs. For example, an IMF study of East Asia's experience suggests there is little evidence to suggest that even "selective" interventionism is correlated with superior growth performance. Instead, high domestic savings and investment rates, an emphasis on the upgrading of human capital, flexible labor markets and an unrestricted access to foreign resources, capabilities and markets are among the shared factors in the success of the Asian economies (Ostry 1993). However, it is our contention that, by their macro-economic and organizational strategies, governments may play a critical role in influencing the value of these, and other, competitive enhancing variables.

2 Teece (1992) has pleaded for a re-evaluation of the role of the *corporation* in the light of the global economy; our analysis argues for a similar reconceptualization of the role of government; see also Dunning (1997).
3 There are various other expressions which, like globalization, are difficult to define precisely. Interdependence and integration are two of these.
4 Some writers, indeed, Drucker (1989), trace the evolution of the globalization of economic activity back to the thirteenth century.
5 In the US, for example, the percentage of GDP accounted for by trade rose from 7 percent to 12 percent between 1970 and 1996, while that accounted for by the stock of inward and outward direct investment increased from 4.2 percent to 9.4 percent. (See Appendix Table 2 of Chapter 1.)
6 Latest figures published by UNCTAD (1999) suggest that in 1998, the sales of the foreign affiliates of MNEs amounted to $11.4 trillion compared with that of trade of goods and non-factor services of $6.7 trillion.
7 We use the world technology to embrace all forms of assets which make for the more efficient development of resources and capabilities.
8 McKenzie and Lee (1991), for example, argue that the fall of Communism in Central and Eastern Europe was triggered by economic, rather than political, forces and, in particular, by the former's impact on increasing inter-firm competition and reducing cross-border psychic distance between the countries of the world. See also Chapter 1 of this volume.
9 Chapters 3 and 4 of this volume explore these and related issues in more detail.
10 The role of MNEs in upgrading the competitive advantages of both home and host countries is described by several writers in a special edition of *Management International Review*, edited by Alan Rugman and published in Spring 1993. See also the annual World Investment Reports of UNCTAD, especially UNCTAD (1995 and 1999).
11 As documented for example in Vernon (1998).
12 These are more fully described in Dunning (1993a).
13 For example, John Naisbitt, has argued that, in the next 20 years or so, the number of sovereign states will dramatically increase from around 200 to upwards of 500 (Naisbitt (1994)).
14 At the same time, as explained in Chapter 1, other governments and several non-governmental organizations, are generally opposed to the enlargement of the WTO's agenda – at least in so far as that agenda is (or is perceived to be) dominated by the interests of developed nations and by those of the larger MNEs.
15 For further details, see Chapter 10 of this volume.
16 This was recognized by Emile Durkheim in 1893, when he stated that increasing internationalization and division of labor in a society – the hallmarks of economic progress – leads to the "accumulation of government tasks" (Durkheim 1964, pp. 219–26).
17 Indeed, in the past, many wars have been fought to preserve or advance such security.
18 The literature on this subject is extensive. Much of it is summarized in Dunning (1997). See also Ostry (1990), Stopford and Strange (1991) and Prakash and Hart (1999). For an analysis of the changing balance between the role of governments, hierarchies and markets as economic development proceeds, see Stiglitz (1989), Dunning (1993b), Hämäläinen (1994), and Porter (1998).
19 See particularly the annual *World Competitive Yearbook* issued by IMD, Lausanne, Switzerland; and the writings of Francis Fukuyama, e.g. Fukuyama 1995 and 1999.

20 See especially Aaron and Schultze (1992).

21 As, for example, explored by Williamson (1992).

22 See especially those identified by various authors in Dunning (1997).

23 Among the possible failures of direct government intervention to successfully overcome the deficiencies of the market, one might mention the rent seeking activities of powerful pressure groups; the magnification of market failures (e.g. with respect to the supply of environmental or social products) by the news media or other politically motivated interests; the inability of governments to attract the best talents (due *inter alia* to ineffective incentive systems); the lack of commercial expertise and bounded rationality of public decision takers; the pursuance of non-economic (especially ideological) goals by politicians; the inadequacy of market related performance indicators which may lead to the establishment of sub-optimal standards (e.g. with respect to budgets, investment and control of information flows); the high time discount (or short-termism) of political decision takers; the lack of market pressures to minimize X inefficiency, especially in the case of public monopolies; uncertainties and ambiguities inherent in the provision of goods and services, which are in the domain of governments, e.g. defense equipment, educational and health services; and the lack of a co-ordinated system of governance (cf. with that in case of private hierarchies); and the difficulty of adjusting policies and institutional structures to quickly meet the needs of technological and economic change. For a more detailed examination of these and other factors which might lead to excessive or inappropriate governmental intervention or the sub-optimal provision of public goods and services, see for example Wolf (1988), Grestchmann (1991), Stiglitz (1989), Hämäläinen (1994), and Dunning (1997).

24 For a recent summary of some of the issues involved in promoting the appropriate supra-national governance as a public good in its own right see Levy (1999). For an earlier exposition of the changing role of governments in a global economy see Ostry (1990), Preston and Windsor (1992) and Graham (1992).

REFERENCES

Aaron, H. J. and Schultze, C. L. (eds) (1992), *Setting Domestic Priorities: What Can Government Do?*, Washington: The Brookings Institution.

Audretsch, D. B. (1989), *The Market and the State*, New York and London: Harvester Wheatsheaf.

Bergsten, C. F. and Graham, E. M. (1992), "Needed: New rules for foreign direct investment," *International Trade Journal VII*, pp. 15–44.

Colclough, C. and Manor, J. (eds) (1991), *States or Markets*, Oxford: Clarendon Press.

Cowles, M. G. (1993), "The rise of the European multinational," *International Economic Insights IV*, July/August, pp. 15–18.

Drucker, P. (1989), *The New Realities*, Washington: Library of Congress.

Dunning, J. H. (1988), *Multinationals, Technology and Competitiveness*, London: Allen and Unwin.

Dunning, J. H. (1992), "The global economy, domestic governance, strategies and transnational corporations: interactions and policy recommendations," *Transnational Corporations 1*, December, pp. 7–45.

Dunning, J. H. (1993a), *Multinational Enterprises and the Global Economy*, Wokingham, England and Reading, MA: Addison Wesley.

Dunning, J. H. (1993b), *The Globalization of Business*, London and New York: Routledge.

Dunning, J. H. (ed.) (1997), *Governments, Globalization and International Business*,
Oxford: Oxford University Press.

Durkheim, E. (1964), *The Division of Labor in Society*, New York: The Free Press
(reprinted from original monograph in 1893).

Fukuyama, F. (1995), *Trust: The Social Virtues and the Creation of Prosperity*, New York:
The Free Press.

Fukuyama, F. (1999), *The Great Disruption*, London: Profile Books.

Guisinger, S. E. and associates (1985), *Investment Incentives and Performance Requirements*, New York: Praeger.

Grestchmann, K. (1991), "Analyzing the public sector: The received view in economics and its shortcomings," in Kaufman, Franz-Xaver (ed.), *The Public Sector:
Challenge for Coordination and Learning*, Berlin: Water de Gruyter.

Hague, D. C. (1993), *Transforming the Dinosaurs*, London: Demos.

Hämäläinen, T. J. (1994), "The evolving role of government in economic organization," Newark: Rutgers University (mimeo).

Hirschman, A. (1970), *Exit, Voice and Loyalty*, Cambridge, MA: Harvard University
Press.

Kogut, B. and Parkinson, D. (1993), "The diffusion of American organizing principles to Europe," in Kogut, B. (ed.), *Country Competitiveness, Technology and the
Organization of Work*, pp. 179–202, Oxford: Oxford University.

Krueger, A. O. (1990), "Economists' changing perceptions of government,"
Weltwirtschaftliches Archiv 126, pp. 417–31.

Lipsey, R. G. (1987), "Globalization and national government policies; an economist's view." in Dunning, J. H. (ed.), *Governments, Globalization and International
Business*, pp. 73–113, Oxford: Oxford University Press.

Lodge, G. C. and Vogel, E. F. (1987), *Ideology and National Competitiveness: An Analysis of Nine Countries*, Boston: Harvard Business School Press.

Management International Review, Spring 1993. Special edition on Michael
Porter's *Diamond of Competitive Advantage*, edited by Alan Rugman, 33, No. 2.

McKenzie, R. B. and Lee, D. R. (1991), *Quicksilver Capital*, New York: The Free Press.

Morrison, A. J., Ricks, D. A. and Roth, K. (1991), "Globalization versus regionalization: which way for the multinational?," *Organizational Dynamics 19* (3) Winter,
pp. 17–29.

Mundell, R. (1957), "International trade and factor mobility," *American Economic
Review 47*, pp. 321–35.

North, D. (1993), *Institutions, Transaction Costs and Productivity in the Long Run*,
Paper presented to Eighth World Productivity Congress, Stockholm, May.

Novak, M. (1998), *Is there a Third Way?* London Institute of Economic Affairs,
Health and Welfare Unit Choice in Welfare, No. 46.

Ostry, S. (1990), *Governments and Corporations in a Shrinking World: Trade and
Innovation Policies in the United States, Europe and Japan*, New York and London:
Council on Foreign Relations

Ostry, J. (1993), *Selective Government Interventions and Economic Growth: A Survey of the
Asian Experience and its Applicability to New Zealand*, Washington: IMF (Paper on
Policy Analysis and Assessment).

Ozawa, T. (1987), "Can the market alone manage structural upgrading? A challenge posed by economic interdependence," in Dunning, J. H. and Usui, M. (eds), *Structural Change, Economic Interdependence and World Development*, Vol. 4, pp. 45–62, London and Basingstoke: Macmillan.

Porter, M. (1998), "The microeconomic foundations of economic development in World Economic Forum," *Global Competitiveness Report 1998*, Geneva World Economic Forum.

Preston, L. E. and Windsor, D. (1992), *The Rules of the Game in the Global Economy*, Boston and London: Kluwer.

Rugman, A. (2000), "Multinational enterprises and the end of global strategy," in Dunning, J. H. and Mucchielli J. L. (eds), *Multinational Firms' Strategies and the New Global Competition*, Reading (UK): Harwood Academic Publishers (forthcoming).

Scott, B. R. and Lodge, G. R. (eds) (1985), *US Competitiveness in the World Economy*, Boston: Harvard Business School Press.

Stiglitz, J. (1989), *The Economic Role of the State*, Oxford: Basil Blackwell.

Stiglitz, J. (1998), *Towards a New Paradigm of Development*, Geneva. The 9th Prebisch Lecture, UNCTAD.

Stopford, J. and Strange, S. (1991), *Rival States, Rival Firms*, Cambridge: C.U.P.

Teece, D. J. (1986), "Transaction cost economics and the multinational enterprise," *Journal of Economic Behavior and Organization 1*, pp. 21–45.

Teece, D. J. (1992), "Competition, cooperation and innovation," *Journal of Economic Behavior and Organization 7*, pp. 1–25.

UNCTC (1991), *Government Policies and Foreign Direct Investment*, New York: UN sales No. E91 II A 20.

UNCTAD (1991), *World Investment Report 1991 The Triad in Foreign Direct Investment*, New York and Geneva: UN.

UNCTAD (1993), *World Investment Report 1993: Transnational Corporations and Integrated International Production*, New York: UN.

UNCTAD (1995), *World Investment Report 1995 Transnational Corporations and Competitiveness.* New York and Geneva: UN.

UNCTAD (1996), *Incentives and Foreign Direct Investment*, New York and Geneva: UN.

UNCTAD (1999), *World Investment Report 1999: Foreign Direct Investment and the Challenge of Development*, New York and Geneva: UN.

UNCTAD (2000), *World Investment Report 2000: Cross Border Mergers and Acquisitions and Development*, New York and Geneva: UN.

Wade, R. (1988), "The role of government in overcoming market failure in Taiwan Republic of Korea and Japan," in Hughes, H. (ed.), *Achieving Industrialization in East Asia*, Cambridge: Cambridge University Press.

Wallis, J. J. and North, D. C. (1986), "Measuring the transaction sector in the American economy; 1870–1970," in Engerman, S. L. and Gallman, R. E. (eds), *Long-term Factors in American Economic Growth*, Chicago: University of Chicago Press.

Wilkins, M. (1989), *Foreign Investment In The United States*, Cambridge, Mass: Harvard University Press

Williamson, O. E. (1992), "The evolving science of organization," Berkeley: University of California, Business and Public Policy Working Paper 53.

Wolf, C. J. (1988), *Markets or Governments*, Cambridge, Mass: MIT Press.

Index

FDI *see* foreign direct investment
features, global capitalism 13–15
Fiat 241
firm-specific factors, geographical issues 231–43
fiscal incentives
  governments 29, 124, 204, 339–40, 345–8
  NPOs 26
follow-my-leader theories 86, 91, 94
food industry 240
Ford 241
foreign direct investment (FDI)
  Asia 251–76
  eclectic paradigm 82–117, 128–9, 148–70, 221–50
  economic issues 185–220, 277–316
  European Internal Market Program 277–316
  European Union 259, 260–9, 277–316
  firm-specific factors 231–43
  FPIs 141–81
  historical background 1–4, 14–16, 116–44, 159–70, 185–91, 221–50, 277–91, 336–40
  incentives 26, 29, 121–4, 339–40, 345–8
  Internal Market Program 277–316
  internationalization sub-paradigm 99–106
  locational issues 93–9, 116–40, 185–220
  new geography 221–50
  political changes 225–43
  product cycle theory 86, 90, 94–6
  reasons 99–106
  sectoral factors 239–43
  statistics 14, 16, 41–2, 120, 162–75, 189–91, 222–316
  types 84, 121–2, 150
  UK/US capital flows 159–65, 189–91
foreign exchange
  European fragilities 340
  locational issues 93–4, 97, 133, 259
  statistics 16
foreign portfolio investments (FPIs) 3
  eclectic paradigm 148–70
  emerging countries 165–70, 256–9
  FDI 141–81
  general paradigm 141–81
  major actors 154–7
  returns 157–8

  statistics 14, 16, 162–75, 189–91, 253, 256–9
  UK/US capital flows 159–65
FPIs *see* foreign portfolio investments
France 222–4, 231–4, 285–309
future scenarios 18–20, 351

GATT *see* General Agreement on Tariffs and Trade
GDP *see* gross domestic product
General Agreement on Tariffs and Trade (GATT) 351
General Motors 241
geographical issues
  see also locational issues
  clusters 193–200, 203–5, 229
  concepts 93–9, 116–40, 189–95
  eclectic paradigm 82–117, 128–9, 148–70
  firm-specific factors 231–43
  management considerations 206–7
  new geography 221–50
  regional perspectives 31–4, 197–200, 201–5
  sectoral factors 239–43
Germany 6, 14, 190, 224, 233–4, 285–309, 342, 345–6
global capitalism, background 1–47, 185–93
global village concept 61–3
globalization
  background 1–47, 61–3, 118, 185–93, 332–5
  definitions 13, 252
  new geography 221–50
globally integrated MNEs 197–200
globaphobia 11
GNP *see* gross national product
governance issues 12, 16, 18–40, 201–5, 227, 341
  see also institutional frameworks
  diamond diagram 19–34
  forms 19–20, 349–51
  regional perspectives 201–5
governments 2–3, 12, 18–19, 23–9, 35–8, 201–5, 331–55
  see also policies; public sectors
  actions-recommended 28–9, 40, 134, 171–2
  anti-competitive firms 87–8, 131, 341–2, 348
  background 7–8, 16, 26–9, 35–8, 65–6, 201–5, 331–55

125–33, 151, 189–91, 225–6, 256,
277–316
restrictive trade policies 351
political changes 225–43
Porter, M. 87, 92, 97, 98, 134, 206–7
portfolio investments 2, 3, 84, 94
general paradigm 141–81
statistics 3, 14, 16, 162–75, 189–91
Portugal 132, 198, 203, 285–309
Prahalad, C. K. 101
pre-industrial capitalism 50, 52–3, 56,
60, 67
private costs/benefits 343–5
private sectors 2–3, 7–8, 12–13, 40, 141
product cycle theory 86, 90, 94–6, 252
production methods 236–8
profit maximization issues 191–3
public sectors 2–3, 7–8, 12–13, 40, 141,
204
see also governments

quality failures 345

R&D *see* research and development
Reagan, R. 225
reforms, markets 63–6
regional perspectives 31–4, 197–200,
201–5
regional supra-national entities 31–4
regionalization, globalization 255, 333
regionally integrated MNEs 197–200
regulations 12, 19, 25–6, 27–9, 36, 265,
325, 337–51
see also rules
Asia 265–6
supra-national entities 33–4, 351
relationship issues 192
see also alliances
cooperation virtues 34–8, 60–1, 70–1,
340, 349
European Internal Market Program
277–316
historical background 52
interdependencies 191–3, 256–9,
332, 338, 343–4
moral issues 68–71
transatlantic economic relationships
317–27, 340
religious issues 4, 48–79
religious leaders, forum suggestion 69,
71
Renault 241

research and development (R&D) 65,
122–3, 187, 189, 191–2, 197, 252–3
centres of academic excellence
199–200, 204
changes 227–8
clusters 203–4
participation restrictions 205, 325
returns 343–5
siting decisions 207
resource issues 1, 13–15, 20, 84–5,
87–93, 101–4, 121–7, 150
responsibilities 34–8, 49, 53–4, 70–1,
338
restrictive trade policies 351
returns
FPIs 157–8
research and development 343–5
rhetoric, governments 347–8
Rhone Poulenc 239–42
Ricardo, D. 338
Rio Earth Summit, 1994 24
risk diversification theories 90, 94, 97,
151, 154–8
RJR Nabisco 239–42
Roosevelt, F. 320
Royal Dutch Shell 239–42
rules 12, 19, 27–9, 36–7
see also regulations
NGOs 25–6
supra-national entities 33–4, 351
Russia 6, 38–9, 84, 346
statistics 2

Sacks, J. 68–9
sanctions 23, 36–7
Santer, J. 325
Sara Lee 239–42
sectoral factors, geographical issues
239–43
SEMATECH 205
Servan-Schreiber, J. 320
service industries, statistics 118, 187,
237–8
Siemens 241
Singapore 190, 222–4, 259, 260–73
Smadja, C. 11, 29, 34
Smith, A. 53–4, 60, 67, 191
social costs/benefits 343–5
social issues 4, 7–8, 12–13, 14–18, 49,
172, 341–2
asset-augmentation benefits 205
Christian responses 4, 48–79
historical background 52–7